MILLER'S
Collectables
PRICE GUIDE

MILLER'S
Collectables
PRICE GUIDE

General Editor
Madeleine Marsh

2000–2001
(Volume XII)

MILLER'S COLLECTABLES PRICE GUIDE 2000–2001

Created and designed by
Miller's
The Cellars, High Street
Tenterden, Kent, TN30 6BN
Tel: 01580 766411
Fax: 01580 766100

General Editor: Madeleine Marsh
Editorial & Production Co-ordinator: Jo Wood
Editorial Assistants: Carol Gillings, Lalage Johnstone
Production Assistants: Elaine Burrell, Gillian Charles, Léonie Sidgwick
Advertising Executive: Elizabeth Smith
Advertising Assistants: Jill Jackson, Melinda Williams
Designers: Kari Reeves, Philip Hannath
Advertisement Designer: Simon Cook
Indexer: Hilary Bird
Additional Photographers: Ian Booth, Magnus Dennis, Dennis O'Reilly, Robin Saker
North American Consultants: Marilynn and Sheila Brass

First published in Great Britain in 2000
by Miller's, a division of Mitchell Beazley,
imprints of Octopus Publishing Group Ltd,
2–4 Heron Quays, London E14 4JB

© 2000 Octopus Publishing Group Ltd

A CIP catalogue record for this book is
available from the British Library

This 2001 edition published by Chancellor Press,
an imprint of Bounty Books, a division of
Octopus Publishing Group Ltd.,
2-4 Heron Quays, London, E14 4JP

ISBN 0 7537 0499 4

Illustrations and film output by CK Litho, Whitstable, Kent
Colour origination by Pica Colour Separation Overseas Pte Ltd, Singapore
Printed and bound by Rotolito Lombarda, Italy

Miller's is a registered trademark of
Octopus Publishing Group Ltd

How To Use This Book

I t is our aim to make this guide easy to use. In order to find a particular item, turn to the contents list on page 7 to find the main heading, for example, Jewellery. Having located your area of interest, you will see that larger sections have been sub-divided by subject or maker. If you are looking for a particular factory, maker, or object, consult the index, which starts on page 486.

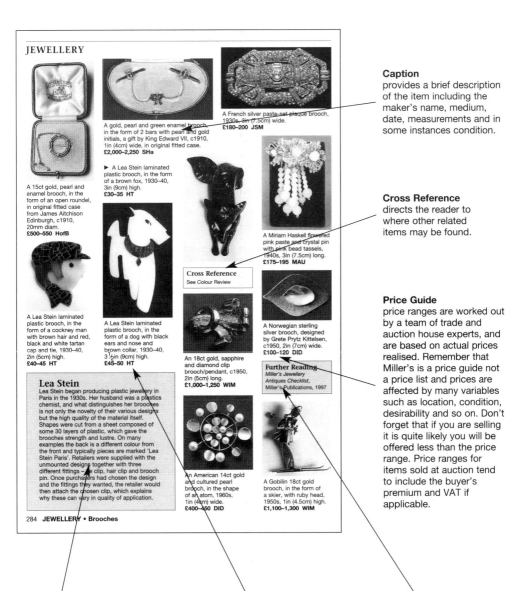

JEWELLERY

A gold, pearl and green enamel brooch, in the form of 2 bars with pearl and gold initials, a gift by King Edward VII, c1910, 1in (4cm) wide, in original fitted case.
£2,000–2,250 SHa

A French silver paste-set plaque brooch, 1930s, 3in (7.5cm) wide.
£180–200 JSM

A 15ct gold, pearl and enamel brooch, in the form of an open roundel, in original fitted case from James Aitchison Edinburgh, c1910, 20mm diam.
£500–550 HofB

▶ A Lea Stein laminated plastic brooch, in the form of a brown fox, 1930–40, 3in (9cm) high.
£30–35 HT

A Miriam Haskell flowered pink paste and crystal pin with pink bead tassels, 1940s, 3in (7.5cm) long.
£175–195 MAU

Cross Reference
See Colour Review

A Lea Stein laminated plastic brooch, in the form of a cockney man with brown hair and red, black and white tartan cap and tie, 1930–40, 2in (5cm) high.
£40–45 HT

A Lea Stein laminated plastic brooch, in the form of a dog with black ears and nose and brown collar, 1930–40, 3¹⁄₂in (9cm) high.
£45–50 HT

An 18ct gold, sapphire and diamond clip brooch/pendant, c1950, 2in (5cm) long.
£1,000–1,250 WIM

A Norwegian sterling silver brooch, designed by Grete Prytz Kittelsen, c1950, 2in (7cm) wide.
£100–120 DID

Further Reading
Miller's Jewellery Antiques Checklist, Miller's Publications, 1997

Lea Stein
Lea Stein began producing plastic jewellery in Paris in the 1930s. Her husband was a plastics chemist, and what distinguishes her brooches is not only the novelty of their various designs but the high quality of the material itself. Shapes were cut from a sheet composed of some 30 layers of plastic, which gave the brooches strength and lustre. On many examples the back is a different colour from the front and typically pieces are marked 'Lea Stein Paris'. Retailers were supplied with the unmounted designs together with three different fittings – e clip, hair clip and brooch pin. Once purchasers had chosen the design and the fittings they wanted, the retailer would then attach the chosen clip, which explains why these can vary in quality of application.

An American 14ct gold and cultured pearl brooch, in the shape of an atom, 1960s, 1in (4cm) wide.
£400–450 DID

A Gobilin 18ct gold brooch, in the form of a skier, with ruby head, 1950s, 1in (4.5cm) high.
£1,100–1,300 WIM

284 **JEWELLERY** • Brooches

Caption
provides a brief description of the item including the maker's name, medium, date, measurements and in some instances condition.

Cross Reference
directs the reader to where other related items may be found.

Price Guide
price ranges are worked out by a team of trade and auction house experts, and are based on actual prices realised. Remember that Miller's is a price guide not a price list and prices are affected by many variables such as location, condition, desirability and so on. Don't forget that if you are selling it is quite likely you will be offered less than the price range. Price ranges for items sold at auction tend to include the buyer's premium and VAT if applicable.

Information Box
covers relevant collecting information on factories, makers, care, restoration, fakes and alterations.

Source Code
refers to the 'Key to Illustrations' on page 476 that details where the item was photographed.

Further Reading
directs the reader towards additional sources of information.

Acknowledgements

We would like to acknowledge the great assistance given by our consultants who are listed below. We would also like to extend our thanks to all the auction houses, their press offices, dealers and collectors who have assisted us in the production of this book.

ALAN BLAKEMAN
BBR Elsecar Heritage Centre
Wath Road
Elsecar, Barnsley
Yorks S74 8AF
(Advertising, Packaging, Bottles, Breweriana)

DAVID HUXTABLE
S03/05 Alfies Antique Market
13–25 Church Street
London NW8 8DT
(Advertising Tins)

BEN BOULTER
Phillips
1 Old King Street
Bath BA1 2JT
(Whisky)

ANTIQUE AMUSEMENT CO
Mill Lane
Swaffham
Bulbeck
Cambridge CB5 0NF
(Amusement & Slot Machines)

PETER LEATH
Isle of Wight
(Kathie Winkle Ceramics)

KEITH MARTIN
St Clere Carlton Ware
PO Box 161
Sevenoaks
Kent TN15 6GA
(Carlton Ware)

MALCOLM PHILLIPS
Comic Book Postal Auctions
40–42 Osnaburgh Street
London NW1 3ND
(Comics)

MARTIN BURTON
York
(Yo-yos)

ANDREW HILTON
Special Auction Services
The Coach House
Midgham Park
Reading
Berks RG7 5UG
(Commemorative Ware)

ELIZABETH LEE
c/o Fashion Doll Collectors' Club of Great Britain
PO Box 228
Brentford
Middlesex TW8 0UU
(Barbie Dolls)

KEN LAWSON
Specialized Postcard Auctions
25 Gloucester Street
Cirencester GL7 2DJ
(Postcards)

JIM BULLOCK
Romsey Medal Centre
5 Bell Street
Romsey
Hants SO51 8GY
(Military Medals)

RICHARD BARCLAY
Barclay Samson Ltd
65 Finlay Street
London SW6 6HF
(Posters)

DR D. DOWSON
Old Tackle Box
PO Box 55
Cranbrook
Kent TN17 3ZU
(Fishing Tackle)

GAVIN PAYNE
The Old Granary
Battlebridge Antique Centre
Nr Wickford
Essex SS11 7RF
(Telephones)

Contents

Introduction

It is often said that Britain has more antiques and collectables per capita than any other nation in the world. The reasons for this are partly historical – a great tradition of industrial manufacture and individual craftsmanship, the wealth and breadth of the British Empire causing objects to be imported from across the globe, and the fact that the country has not been successfully invaded since 1066, giving houses and their contents a greater chance of survival. But it is not just a question of our national past, but also our national character. As we at Miller's know, the British are a nation of passionate collectors, and the new edition of *Miller's Collectables Price Guide* celebrates collectables in all their infinite and surprising variety.

The items we feature span the centuries, ranging from Greek and Roman antiquities to Beanie Babies, one of the last great collecting crazes of the millennium. The urge to collect often begins in childhood, and many adult collectors return to the toys of their youth. This year we explore the story of Action Man, the butch doll for boys, and Barbie, the first teenage fashion doll for girls. Since 1959 over one billion Barbie dolls and friends have been sold – if placed head-to-toe they would circle the earth more than seven times. But which ones can now be worth hundreds of pounds? Read Miller's to find out. We look at the history of the jigsaw puzzle, invented by a London map-maker in 1760 as a learning tool for children, and spin the tale of the yo-yo, which first came to Britain in the late 18th century.

For those with more adult tastes, we throw open the Art Deco cocktail cabinet to admire the glamourous drinking ephemera from the 1920s and '30s, and we also look at the value of whisky collectables. Alcohol has inspired many of the objects in this guide, from corkscrews to drinking glasses, and gambling is represented with a magnificent display of amusement machines. Ceramics are a perennial favourite. This year's edition shows pottery and porcelain from across the centuries and around the world, and includes features on Beswick, Carlton Ware, Goss and Crested China, Wade and Kathie Winkle. Glass is another popular theme, from vintage perfume bottles to Victorian cranberry glass to the dayglow vessels of the 1960s. As interest in modern design continues to grow, we devote special sections to the 1950s and to 1960s and '70s collectables; dig out your platforms, turn on your lava lamp or your fibreoptic light, and tune into swinging style. In our rock and pop section we explore the value of records from vinyl to picture discs to CDs; check out vintage guitars and synthesisers, and look at Beatles collectables – always number one in the collectors' chart.

New sections in this year's *Miller's Collectables Price Guide* include religious artefacts and wedding memorabilia, we look at WWI trench art, medals and militaria, and include a feature on WWII remembering rationing and the Utility Scheme.

During wartime, people were encouraged to 'make do and mend' and not waste anything. Ironically, what makes many objects in this guide so collectable is the fact that they were designed to be disposable, making surviving examples rare and sought-after. A case in point is children's comics, and this year we illustrate a *Dandy No. 1* (1937), one of only a handful of copies known to exist, originally sold for 2d and now worth an astonishing £4,900–5,200 ($8,000–8,500). Another ephemeral example is posters, which can fetch huge sums because they were all too often just thrown away.

One of the questions we are most often asked at Miller's is what will be the collectables of the future, we rely very much on suggestions from you the reader. Please write to us to tell us about your collections, objects you think might become collectable, and subjects you would like to see covered in future editions. It is our close contact with dealers, collectors and enthusiasts in every possible subject that makes *Miller's Collectables Price Guide* the best selling manual in its field, and a book that truly encapsulates the fun and excitement of collecting.

Thank you for sharing your collecting passions with us and, as ever, happy hunting!

Advertising & Packaging

An H. J. Heinz catalogue of Picklers and Preservers, containing 46 full-page chromolithograph illustrations, all tied into a soft leather cover with gold-tooled Heinz trade-mark on the front, 1895, 10½ x 7½in (26.5 x 19cm).
£1,100–1,300 DN

This Heinz catalogue was among the contents of a deceased estate sent for auction at Dreweatt Neate in Berkshire. 'It was a complete surprise and a lovely find,' explains auctioneer Dick Heywood. 'It was a very rare volume, in good condition, and each page had a beautiful chromolithograph illustration of a Heinz product, factory or one of the firm's railway wagons.' Assessing each plate to be worth about £20, the auction house valued the whole catalogue at £200–300. This unusual item attracted serious interest from dealers and private collectors, and sold for over 3 times its estimate.

A Quaker Oats enamel advertising sign, c1910, 34 x 24in (86.5 x 61cm).
£150–200 JUN

A Balloon Yeast plate, 1920s, 12in (30.5cm) wide.
£70–80 SMI

A Spratt's enamel advertising sign, 1930s, 12 x 24in (30.5 x 61cm).
£60–75 JUN

A Bosch plaster advertising figure, c1928, 66in (167.5cm) high.
£800–900 JUN

A Leeds Provincial Building Society mortgage prospectus, 1930s, 8 x 5in (20.5 x 12.5cm).
£6–8 MRW

◄ A Jester Towel Soap box, with original contents, 1930s, 6¼in (16cm) wide.
£14–16 HUX

A selection of cigarette packets, 1930–40s, 2¼in (5.5cm) high.
£2–3 each MRW

An Allwoods and Atkins & Turton advertising tin coffee measuring spoon, 1940s, 4in (10cm) long.
£6–8 MRW

A Fowlers Treacle recipe booklet, 1930–40s, 7¼ x 4¾in (18.5 x 12cm).
£1–2 RAD

A Bisto recipe booklet, 1930–40s, 6¼ x 5in (16 x 12.5cm).
£1–2 RAD

Bisto, launched in 1910 by Cerebos, was inspired by the demands of company wives for a product that could create perfect, lump-free gravy. The name combined the initials of the famous slogan 'Browns, Seasons, Thickens-In-One'. Equally celebrated were the famous sniffing Bisto Kids, who were created by illustrator Will Owen in 1919, and they went on to become an advertising legend.

▶ A container of Pulvo bathroom and household cleaner, 1950s, 9in (23cm) high.
£10–12 HUX

An Oxo recipe booklet, entitled *Cooking the Oxo Way*, 1930–40s, 7 x 5½in (18 x 14cm).
£4–5 RAD

A Photo-Union Film-Strip of the Royal Wedding of Princess Elizabeth and Prince Phillip, 1947, 2¼in (5.5cm) high.
£6–7 Law

A Luvil stain remover box, with contents, 1960s, 7 x 4in (18 x 10cm).
£6–8 MRW

A box of Texleen cleaner for nylon products, complete with contents, 1960, 7in (18cm) wide.
£8–10 MRW

A box of Cusson's Damask Rose soap and bath cubes, with matching talc, box 5in (12.5cm) wide.
£18–20 HUX

Cross Reference
See Colour Review

A Dubarry Bewitch bath set, 1960s, 10¼in (26.5cm) wide.
£10–12 HUX

A Chivers advertising alarm clock, 1970–80s, 7in (18cm) high.
£4–5 Law

A pack of Heinz Noodle Doodles playing cards, 1980s, 3¾in (9.5cm) high.
£1–2 CMF

A Coke plastic fridge magnet, 1980s, 3in (7.5cm) high.
£2–3 COB

BADGES

A Wright's Biscuits Mischief Club badge, 1950s, 1¼in (3cm) diam.
£3–4 SVB

A Regent badge, 1950s, 1¼in (3cm) diam.
£3–4 SVB

A Rose Hip Collectors Club 1955 badge, 1in (2.5cm) diam.
£2–4 SVB

Two McDonald's badges, 1970s, 2in (5cm) diam.
20–25p each TRE

A London Zoo badge, 1960s, 2in (5cm) diam.
20–25p TRE

BROOKE BOND

Two Brooke Bond coffee mugs, possibly trade offers, 1970s, 3½in (9cm) high.
£8–10 each FMu

A set of 4 PG Tips egg cups, 1970s, 3in (7.5cm) high.
£75–100 TOY

▶ A Brooke Bond PG Tips personalized story book package offer, c1985, 7in (18cm) high.
£10–15 FMu

Two blue and white Corgi Toys Surtees T. S. 9. F/1 model racing cars, advertising Brooke Bond Oxo, early 1970s, 7½in (19cm) long.
£30–35 each FMu

Several different colours and styles were produced.

DISPLAY CARDS

A W. D. & H. O. Wills's Star
cigarettes shop display, c1900,
9in (23cm) wide.
£120–150 MRW

A W. D. & H. O Wills's Gold Flake
cigarettes shop display, c1900,
10in (25.5cm) wide.
£65–75 MRW

A Pedigree cardboard cut-out sign,
1950s, 26in (66cm) high.
£85–100 JUN

TINS

Biscuit tins were very much a British speciality. The market was pioneered by Huntley & Palmers (est. 1822). Situated opposite the Crown Hotel in Reading, a major stop on the London to Bath coach route, the bakery supplied hungry travellers with hand-made biscuits, and soon orders began to pour in from across the Empire. Initially, the firm used plain tins with paper labels. However, these were easily torn off, so the company sought a more permanent way to advertise its name, and new printing technology provided the answer. In 1868, Huntley & Palmers produced the first transfer-printed biscuit tin, and in 1879 it was granted a licence to print directly on to tins using offset lithography. Other manufacturers soon followed Huntley & Palmers' lead, and packaging, as well as contents, became a major selling point

for biscuits and many other products, especially in the all-important Christmas market, which generated the finest and most elaborate designs.

Shaped or novelty tins tend to command the highest prices today. Also look out for commemorative pieces (for example, those celebrating royal events) and any examples with fine decoration. While many containers blatantly advertise their products, novelty tins were often marked by the manufacturer on the base or inside the lid rather than on the outside, so as not to detract from the overall design. Condition is all-important to value. Tins should not be dented or rusted, and remember to examine the hinges and interior. Finally, keep tins out of direct sunlight and away from damp, steamy places, such as kitchens and bathrooms.

A Hurry Up cigarette tin, with original contents,
1890–1900, 2½in (6.5cm) high.
£350–400 MRW

A Rowntree chocolate tin, c1905, 6in (15cm) wide.
£55–65 HUX

A Rowntree sweet tin, in the shape of a rugby ball, c1900, 3in (7.5cm) long.
£70–80 MRW

A sponge tin for golfers, c1910, 2½in (6.5cm) wide.
£15–20 HUX

A Golden Pyramid 78rpm gramophone needle dispenser tin, c1910, 3in (7.5cm) high.
£20–25 MRW

A Huntley & Palmers biscuit tin, in the form of a display cabinet, c1911, 7in (18cm) high.
£300–350 HUX

A Bird Seed tin, 1920–30s, 4¾in (12cm) high.
£3–5 Law

A Cénou biscuit tin, 1920–30s, 9¾in (25cm) high.
£15–20 BTB

A Crawfords money bank biscuit tin, The Lucy Attwell "Kiddibics", 1930s, 7in (18cm) high.
£100–120 WWY

A cake tin, decorated with the Royal family group, c1937, 7in (18cm) diam.
£25–30 MRW

◀ A Dainty Dinah toffee tin, by George W. Horner & Co, c1930, 7in (18cm) wide.
£12–15 MRW

Two Belgian biscuit tins, decorated with Snow White and the Seven Dwarfs, 1938, 12¾in (32.5cm) wide.
£100–120 each HUX

An Ostermilk No. 2 tin, 1940, 5½in (14cm) high.
£5–7 UTP

A Harry Vincent Blue Bird toffee tin, late 1940s, 6in (15cm) wide.
£6–8 MRW

An Oxo tin, 1960s, 5½in (14cm) wide.
£4–5 WEE

◀ A Wills's Whiffs cigarette tin, 1950–60s, 5in (12.5cm) wide.
£5–10 PPe

A tin string box, with weighted bottom, advertising Camp coffee, 1940–50s, 7in (18cm) high.
£20–25 MED

A Nipits throat pastilles tin, c1960, 3in (7.5cm) wide.
£3–5 MRW

ROBERTSON'S GOLLIES

A Robertson's Golly teapot, 1970, 8½in (21.5cm) high.
£180–200 MED

A Robertson's Golly toast rack, with a Golly on a motorbike, 1980–90s, 6in (15cm) wide.
£25–30 MED

A set of Robertson's ceramic Dinkies, in original box, 1980–90s, 12in (30.5cm) wide.
£120–140 MED

Aeronautica

The Aeroplane magazine,
43 copies, 1915–16,
12½ x 8½in (32 x 21.5cm).
£50–60 LF

Items relating to the R34,
comprising RAF Permanent
Pass, RNAS East Fortune, named
to 'J. H. Guile of H.M.A. R34'
and dated '10.10.19', a letter
written by the airship's captain,
Major G. Herbert Scott, headed
'Airship Station East Fortune 7th
Oct 1919', 6 photographs and a
postcard of a Zeppelin over London.
£325–375 S(S)

**The R34, captained by Major
Scott, completed the first
transatlantic return crossing by
airship, 2–6 July 1919. Leaving
East Fortune, she took just over
108 hours to reach Mineola,
Long Island. The return trip
lasted some 75 hours, 9–13 July.**

A group of personal effects relating
to 2nd Lt. H. P. Greenhill, RFC,
RAF, WWI period, including a
matchbox holder, a monogrammed
brass lighter, RAF cloth wings,
buttons and insignia, an ashtray
inset with enamelled RAF
sweetheart's brooch, a bank book,
photographs, and a watercolour
of a dog-fight, initialled 'HPG'
and dated '27.10.19', 14¼ x 10½in
(36 x 26.5cm), in original frame.
£400–450 S(S)

A selection of Alcock and Brown
material, including a section of
fabric from the transatlantic
Vickers Vimy, a piece of paper
signed and inscribed in pencil by
the aviators, in Marconigram
envelope, and a photograph, 1919.
£1,000–1,200 S(S)

A Cobham gilt and enamel flying
brooch, 1920–30s, 1in (1.5cm) long.
£45–55 BCA

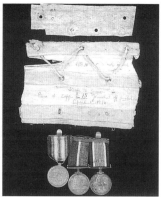

A piece of fabric from German
Naval Zeppelin L15, 7½ x 5½in
(19 x 14cm), and a piece of metal,
7 x 2in (18 x 5cm), British War
Medal 1914–20, Mercantile Marine
Medal 1914–18, Victory Medal
1914–18, each named to
'G. Pellatt', mounted, in leather case.
£350–400 S(S)

**Commanded by Joachim
Breithaupt, L15 raided London
on the night of 31st March 1916
but crash-landed in an area of
the North Sea known as Knock
Deep. George Pellatt was on
board one of the several British
gunboats sent to the scene.
Breithaupt and all but one of his
18-man crew were taken prisoner.**

A Zeppelin ribbon, in ivory-coloured
silk with gold border and lettering,
1920–30s, 33 x 7in (84 x 18cm).
£300–350 S(S)

A silver-coloured flying brooch,
dated '1939-1944', 1¼in (3cm) long.
£55–65 BCA

Amusement & Slot Machines

A Victorian cast-iron double-headed Mutoscope, 'What The Butler Saw' 56in (142cm) high.
£1,700–2,000 CAm

A rosewood musical cigar vending machine, 1880, 10in (25.5cm) high.
£5,000–6,000 CAm

A floor-standing roulette wheel, by Mills Dewey, 1898, 67in (170cm) high.
£3,000–3,500 CAm

◄ An Allwin-style ball game, 1914, 31¼in (79cm) high.
£600–650 BB

An improved penny-operated Pickwick machine, by Triumph Auto Co, dispenses tokens on winning, 1914, 41¼in (105cm) high.
£1,000–1,200 BB

Mutoscopes provided simulated moving pictures. After inserting a coin, the viewer would turn the handle causing a reel of minutely-differing photographs to flip over, creating the appearance of movement. Mildly titillating subjects were a favourite with the paying public, and occasionally brought arcade owners into conflict with the authorities.

A Caille Mascot cast-aluminium grip tester, with the slogan 'If you can ring the bell then you are as strong as a bull', 1910, 18in (45.5cm) high.
£500–600 CAm

A Pickwick wall machine, 1914, 35½in (90cm) high.
£800–900 SAF

A penny-operated catcher-type skill game, 1914, 26in (66cm) high.
£700–800 BB

A Princess Doraldina fortune-teller machine, 1920s, 85in (216cm) high.
£2,200–2,500 CAm

◀ A German 'Clown' wall machine, c1915, 26in (66cm) high.
£900–1,100 AMc

Le Francais amusement machine, by Boux & Co, Paris, 1914, 26in (66cm) high.
£1,000–1,200 HAK

The Brooklands Racer, cast-iron, penny-operated, chrome handle, restored, 1920s, 36in (91.5cm) high.
£1,500–2,000 CARS

Up to 3 players spin different coloured racing cars, stopping them in sequence, and the winner takes the jackpot.

◀ High Stakes, by Groetchen, dispenses a gum ball, restored, 1930s, 12in (30.5cm) high.
£250–300 AMc

◀ Gipsy Fortune Teller, coin-operated with spinning arrow and chrome-plated Art Deco front, 1930s, 24in (61cm) high.
£200–250 AMc

◀ A Polk figure one-armed bandit, by Mills, 1940s, 72in (183cm) high.
£1,800–2,000 CAm

In the 1940s, Frank Polk created a series of slot machines in the form of life-sized characters from American history and the Wild West, including cowboys, Native Americans and Civil War soldiers. Today these are known as Polk figures. Mills Novelty Company was one of the best-known and longest established names in the business. In 1910, 5 years after the invention of the first three-wheel slot machine, Mills copyrighted the famous fruit symbols that gave the slot machine its other name: the fruit machine.

The Hat Trick wall machine, by Ruffler & Walker, restored, c1955, 32in (81.5cm) high.
£375–450 AMc

A Bryan's 3 ball Forks wall machine, in a streamlined case, 1950s, 28in (71cm) high.
£350–400 CAm

A Bryan's Payramid wall machine, 1950, 33in (84cm) high.
£450–500 CAm

Cross Reference
See Colour Review

▶ A Fill-Em-Up wall machine, by Ruffler & Walker, 1954, 32in (81.5cm) high.
£350–400 AMc

A German Arizona wall-mounted one-armed bandit, 1960, 28in (71cm) high.
£100–120 AMc

◀ A Double Your Money Allwin machine, by Oliver Whales, requires restoration, 1950s, 32in (81.5cm) high.
£225–275 AMc

A Mills Blue-Bell one-armed bandit-fruit machine, c1950, 26in (66cm) high.
£250–300 CARS

◀ A Win-a-Chew Allwin machine, by Oliver Whales, original condition, 1954, 32in (81.5cm) high.
£325–375 AMc

Antiquities

A Danish Neolithic boat-shaped axe, intact, 2nd millennium BC, 4in (10cm) long.
£250–300 HEL

A West Asian bronze eagle from a helmet finial, intact, 1st millennium BC, 3in (7.5cm) wide.
£350–400 HEL

A Roman bronze-mounted iron key, 3in (7.5cm) long.
£45–55 BAC

◄ A Luristan bronze lance-head, 2000–1500 BC, 17in (43cm) long.
£175–225 AOH

A medieval spearhead, 11in (28cm) long.
£65–75 BAC

A bronze padlock, from Essex, complete, 13th–14th century AD, 1¼in (3cm) long.
£35–40 ANG

GLASS

A Roman blue glass bead,
1in (25mm) diam.
£14–16 BAC

A Roman glass bowl, 1st century AD,
3in (7.5cm) diam.
£400–450 PARS

◄ A Roman glass flask, 3rd–4th
century AD, 4in (10cm) high.
£85–95 BAC

► A Roman blown glass dimpled
vase, eastern Mediterranean,
3rd–4th century AD,
3¼in (8.5cm) high.
£220–250 PARS

A Roman iridescent glass platter,
from Jordan, 2nd–3rd century AD,
8in (20.5cm) diam.
£450–500 AOH

JEWELLERY

A Bronze Age decorated bangle,
circa 1200 BC, 5in (12.5cm) diam.
£40–50 BAC

A Celtic-style bronze horse
brooch, complete with hinge
and catchplate, pin missing,
from Roumania (Roman Dacia),
2nd century AD, 1½in (3.5cm) long.
£85–95 ANG

A bronze eagle, finely
modelled with feather decoration,
with leather mount, found
in Norfolk, 2nd century AD,
1in (25mm) long.
£85–95 ANG

A Hellenistic bronze bangle, with
beast terminals, Near East, circa
300–30 BC, 4in (10cm) diam.
£110–130 BAC

A tinned-bronze brooch, in the
form of a Celtic hunting dog,
with detailed body markings,
complete with hinge and pin
catch, pin missing, 1st century AD,
1½in (4cm) long.
£125–145 ANG

A bronze and niello rabbit brooch, complete with hinge lugs and catchplate, pin missing, from Norfolk, 2nd century AD, 1in (2.5cm) long.
£85–95 ANG

A Celtic-style horse brooch, complete with pin, hinge and catchplate from Pannonia, 1st century AD, 1½in (4cm) long.
£90–100 ANG

Roman Pannonia was in the region of Hungary.

An enamelled lozenge brooch, complete with spring and catchplate, pin missing, 2nd century AD, 1½in (3.5cm) long.
£65–75 ANG

A boar brooch, complete with pin, spring and catchplate, from Northern France, 1st century AD, 1¼in (3cm) long.
£160–180 ANG

A Roman hollow gold ring, with a garnet engraved with a stylized bird, 3rd–4th century AD.
£600–700 HEL

A Roman glass necklace, mixed with garnet and agate, 1st–3rd century AD, 20in (51cm) long.
£250–280 PARS

A brooch with cruciform headplate, arched bow, triangular terminal with punched annulet down either side, pin missing, from Norfolk, 6th century AD, 2¼in (6cm) long.
£85–95 ANG

▶ A gilded badge, found in London, 16th century, 1in (25mm) long.
£80–90 BAC

◀ A bronze token, depicting Thomas à Becket's head, late 14th century, 1¼in (3cm) high.
£175–200 GRa

This token was found in the River Thames.

A Roman gold earring or pendant, decorated with wirework, glass inlay and a cabochon garnet, 4th century AD, ¾in (19mm) wide.
£250–300 HEL

A bronze token, in the form of Thomas à Becket's sword sheath, late 14th century, 2in (5cm) high.
£55–65 GRa

Pilgrim badges & relics

The medieval period saw the flourishing of the Christian pilgrimage in which the faithful would journey to a holy place as an act of devotion, penance or to gain supernatural help. The pilgrim would begin his expedition with a blessing from the local priest. Recognizable by his cockle hat, staff and sandalled feet, he would stay at religious hostels en route, and on reaching the saint's shrine he would then buy a hat badge. Often made of pewter and shaped in the form of saints and their symbols, these badges were not just souvenirs but were also considered powerful amulets. The major centre of pilgrimage in Britain was Canterbury, site of the martyrdom of Thomas à Becket (1118–70). As Chancellor of England and Archbishop of Canterbury, Becket's career was marked by a prolonged quarrel with Henry II, as the British King sought to increase his authority over the church. The dispute culminated in one of the most celebrated murders of all time. 'Who shall rid me of this turbulent priest?' demanded the King. Four Barons took him at his word, and the Archbishop was cut down in Canterbury Cathedral. The news of his murder shocked Christendom. Thomas à Becket was canonized in 1173, and hundreds of miracles were soon reported at his tomb, which was visited by pilgrims from across the Christian world.

A Spanish bronze pilgrim's badge, complete with hinge and catchplate, excavated in Santiago, 15th century, 2in (5cm) high.
£250–275 GRa

◄ A pilgrim's whistle, 16th century, 2in (5cm) high.
£65–75 GRa

Like hat badges, whistles were bought at shrines as souvenirs of a pilgrimage.

POTTERY

Two ancient Egyptian (Old Kingdom) alabaster vessels, circa 3000 BC, largest 5in (12.5cm) diam.
£130–150 BAC

A late Bronze Age Cypriot painted jug, 1200–1000 BC, 4½in (11.5cm) high.
£130–160 HEL

A Magna Graecia Apulian Red Figure ware pelike, restored, 4th century BC, 8in (20.5cm) high.
£350–400 BAC

◄ A Palestinian terracotta dipper cup, 3200–2500 BC, 4in (10cm) diam.
£30–40 BAC

Pottery vessels

A pelike is a Greek amphora with a pear-shaped body, for storing oil and water.
A lekythos is a slender, loop-handled jug for oil, perfume or ointment, often used as funeral offerings.
A guttus is an oil flask, used for filling oil lamps.

A Greek Black Figure
lekythos, base missing,
6th century BC,
6in (15cm) high.
£350–400 HEL

Three oil lamps, all intact, 1st–4th century AD,
largest 4in (10cm) long.
£30–60 each HEL

A late medieval glazed bowl, on tripod feet,
6in (15cm) diam.
£140–160 AOH

▶ A Roman vessel, 2nd century AD,
5½in (14cm) high.
£400–450 INC

A Roman jug, Middle East, 1st–2nd
century AD, 5¼in (13.5cm) high.
£50–60 IW

SCULPTURES & FIGURES

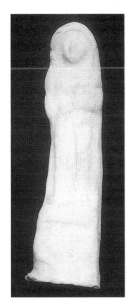

A Phoenician hollow
terracotta figurine of Thanit,
intact, 6th century BC,
7in (18cm) high.
£130–150 HEL

A silver figurine of Venus
standing arranging her
coiffure, found in the
Balkans, 1st–2nd century AD,
1¾in (4.5cm) high.
£600–650 ANG

A clay nativity figure,
16th century,
3in (7.5cm) high.
£45–50 BAC

A Romano-Egyptian
terracotta figure of the god
Bes, repaired on crown,
circa 1st century AD,
5½in (14cm) high.
£150–200 HEL

**The Egyptian god Bes
was the god of marriage
and childbearing who also
presided over women's
toilet. He was considered
a protector against
poisonous and dangerous
animals and also
safeguarded the dead.**

Architectural Salvage

A stone sink, 1850–1900,
29½in (75cm) wide.
£60–70 BYG

A pair of Victorian metal stable
dividers, 1880s, 108in (274.5cm) wide.
£700–800 A&H

Three circular stone water troughs,
c1800, largest 22in (56cm) diam.
£160–200 each A&H

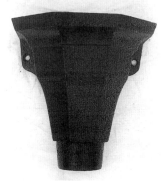

A Victorian cast-iron rainwater
hopper, c1890, 9½in (24cm) high.
£30–40 BYG

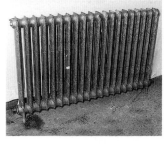

A Victorian cast-iron rainwater
hopper, c1890, 11in (27.5cm) wide.
£20–30 BYG

► A cast-
iron radiator,
c1900, 60in
(152.5cm) wide.
£350–400 A&H

A Victorian cast-
iron newel post,
with Spanish
mahogany hand-
rail, c1890,
41in (104cm) high.
£250–300 A&H

A Victorian
pitch pine
newel post,
c1890, 45in
(114.5cm) high.
£85–100 A&H

A Victorian oak
newel post,
c1890, 55in
(139.5cm) high.
£120–150 A&H

A Victorian terracotta
chimney pot, c1890,
26in (66cm) high.
£70–85 NET

A pair of cast-iron pub
table legs, 19thC,
27in (68.5cm) high.
£95–110 NET

A set of 4 cast-iron legs, c1900, 27in (68.5cm) high.
£80–100 A&H

A selection of stone steps, 1920s, 48in (122cm) long.
£10 per ft A&H

Canadian maple strip flooring, 1930s, 2¼in (5.5cm) wide.
£15–25 per sq yd A&H

A cast-iron clock face, c1900, 26in (66cm) diam.
£150–175 A&H

A cast-iron Mexican hat pig trough, 1920s, 35in (89cm) diam.
£80–100 A&H

A salt-glazed pig trough, c1910, 38in (96.5cm).wide.
£125–150 A&H

A pair of stained-glass window panels, 1920s, 21in (53cm) high.
£40–50 OOLA

A pair of iron gates, c1950, 50in (127cm) wide.
£70–85 AL

BATHROOM FITTINGS

A pair of Victorian solid nickel long-reach bath taps, with ornate indices, restored, c1900, 6in (15cm) high.
£180–220 ACT

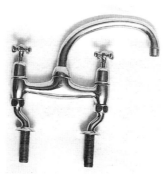

A brass kitchen mixer tap, 1900–20s, 8in (20.5cm) high.
£120–145 WRe

A Victorian enamelled oval pedestal basin, with taps and waste plunger, on fluted tapering pedestal and base, c1900, 33in (84cm) wide.
£200–240 E

A roll-edge basin, by Doulton & Co, 1905, 25in (63.5cm) wide.
£380–420 ACT

A French roll-top bath, on paw feet, early 20thC, 67in (170cm) wide.
£800–1,000 POSH

A roll-edge lavatory pan, inscribed 'The Flood', c1910.
£520–570 ACT

An Art Deco lavatory pan, by Gresham, 1920s.
£180–220 ACT

◄ A pair of nickel-plated basin taps, restored, 1920s, 5in (12.5cm) high.
£85–95 ACT

A French Art Deco bidet, complete with taps and pop-up waste, c1920.
£340–380 ACT

◄ A brass bath rack, originally chrome, adjusts to bath width, 1920s, 28in (71cm) wide.
£75–85 LIB

A pair of brass kitchen taps, 1930s.
£125–155 ACT

An Art Deco washbasin, by Desmond Norman, with decorative overflow, 1930s, 22in (56cm) wide.
£280–320 ACT

A French ceramic combined toothbrush, soap and glass holder, 1930s, 9in (23cm) wide.
£85–95 ACT

► A polished copper low-level WC cistern, 1930–50s, 17in (43cm) wide.
£340–380 ACT

A French ceramic soap dish and toothbrush holder, 1930s, 5in (12.5cm) wide.
£40–45 ACT

An adjustable chromed bath rack, 1960, 26in (66cm) wide.
£18–20 UTP

A chromed bath rack, 1960, 30in (76cm) wide.
£20–25 UTP

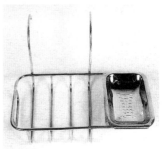

A brass bath soap rack, 1930–50s, 8in (20.5cm) wide.
£25–30 PJa

BOOT SCRAPERS

A Victorian cast-iron boot scraper, 1860, 14in (35.5cm) wide.
£60–70 Rac

A Victorian cast-iron boot scraper, designed for wall-mounting, c1900, 11in (27.5cm) wide.
£40–45 BYG

A Victorian cast-iron boot scraper, c1900, 13½in (34.5cm) wide.
£40–45 BYG

Boot scrapers

Cast-iron boot scrapers were popular in the Victorian and Edwardian periods. They range from simple grid-shaped models to more elaborate moulded designs, often with a tray for catching the mud. Prices reflect level of decoration. Rust can be removed with a wire brush, although care must be taken if the surface is badly pitted.

A Victorian cast-iron boot scraper, with open grid, c1900, 13in (33cm) square.
£40–45 BYG

◄ A Victorian cast-iron rococo boot scraper, c1900, 13in (33cm) wide.
£40–45 BYG

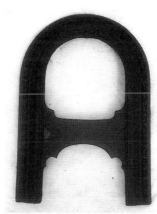

DOOR FURNITURE

An elm door, with horizontal boarded construction, 17thC, 77in (195.5cm) high.
£210–230 RAW

A Georgian riveted door latch, 4in (10cm) wide.
£60–75 A&H

A Victorian cast-iron door stop, in the form of a shoe last, c1900, 6½in (16.5cm) high.
£10–12 BYG

A Victorian four-panelled pine door, with stripped finish, c1900, 80in (200.5cm) high.
£45–60 RAW

A rim lock and keep, by Hobbs, Hart & Co Ltd, 1895, 6in (15cm) wide.
£30–35 HEM

A pair of Art Nouveau-style brass pull handles, c1900, 13in (33cm) high.
£60–75 A&H

▶ A pair of brass pull handles, c1900, 13in (33cm) high.
£50–60 A&H

A pair of French brass furniture handles, 1920.
£40–50 RUL

A copper bell push, c1918, 3½in (9cm) wide.
£25–30 HEM

A pair of brass door handles, with keyholes, 1920–30, 7in (18cm) high.
£50–60 RUL

STOVES & RANGES

A Victorian cast-iron, enamel and chrome cooking range, by Fred Verity & Son, c1890, 57in (145cm) wide.
£800–1,000 A&H

A French cast-iron stove, by Godin, 1950s, 30in (76cm) high.
£400–450 A&H

An enamelled cast-iron stove, 19thC, 36in (91.5cm) high.
£280–325 NET

▶ A French enamelled cast-iron stove, enamel damaged, 1920s, 21in (53.5cm) wide.
£250–300 A&H

A French enamelled cast-iron stove, with glass-panelled door, 1930, 38in (96.5cm) high.
£250–300 A&H

TILES

A terracotta handmade fluted valley or hip tile, 18thC, 12in (30.5cm) wide.
£1–2 BYG

An ornamental terracotta end ridge tile, c1800, 12in (30.5cm) long.
£60–70 BYG

An ornamental clay ridge tile, 1880–1900, 11½in (29cm) wide.
£12–15 BYG

A terracotta castellated ridge tile, 1880–1920, 12in (30.5cm) wide.
£12–15 BYG

A Victorian terracotta path edging tile, c1900, 9in (23cm) wide.
£3–4 BYG

A Victorian terracotta path edging tile, c1900, 6in (15cm) wide.
£3–4 BYG

Art Deco

An orange glass bowl, by Louis Majorelle and Daum, with wirework metal mount, etched marks 'L. Majorelle' and 'Daum Nancy', c1925, 12¼in (31cm) diam.
£550–650 P(Ba)

A pair of white onyx and lapis lazuli urns, with applied handles, inlaid and banded with lapis lazuli, 1930s, 12½in (32cm) high.
£1,600–1,800 Bri

A pair of French silver candle holders, by Puiforcat, with rose-pink quartz liners, c1930, 6¼in (16cm) high.
£4,000–5,000 SFL

A pair of ceiling light fittings, with frosted glass panels decorated with a stylized fish pattern, 1930s, 15¾in (40cm) high.
£250–300 P(Ba)

A chrome and marble-topped console table, 1930s, 38in (96.5cm) high.
£380–425 NET

A wood and copper light stand and table, 1930s, 70in (178cm) high.
£250–280 NET

CERAMICS

A Hollinshead & Kirkham, Tunstall, fluted plate, decorated with Plums pattern, c1920, 10in (25.5cm) diam.
£140–160 AOT

A Hollinshead & Kirkham, Tunstall, fluted plate, decorated in cobalt blue with Pheasant pattern, c1920, 10in (25.5cm) diam.
£160–180 AOT

A Wilkinson's vase, decorated with tube-lined flowers on a blue ground, c1930, 11½in (29cm) high.
£200–220 AOT

A Wadeheath Flaxman charger, decorated with Trees and House pattern with orange and blue flowers, c1930, 12in (30.5cm) diam.
£75–90 AOT

◄ A Gray's Pottery dish, painted with pink flowers and green leaves, 1930, 9½in (24cm) wide.
£60–70 CSA

A Grimwades Byzantaware enamelled blue and orange plate, c1930, 10in (25.5cm) diam.
£40–50 AOT

A Bavarian bone china cup and saucer, decorated with blue and orange flowers, 1930s, saucer 5½in (14cm) diam.
£7–8 Law

A Royal Cauldon tube-lined green and yellow charger, designed by Edith Gater, c1938, 11½in (29cm) diam.
£125–150 AOT

A noted designer of the period, Edith Gater worked for Samson Hancock & Sons and Cauldon Potteries.

◄ An Empire ware hand-painted jam pot and cover, decorated with blue and orange flowers on a yellow ground, 1933, 3½in (9cm) high.
£40–50 BKK

A Soho Pottery Solian Ware white-glazed biscuit barrel, with original cane handle, 1930s, 6¼in (16cm) high.
£35–40 DEC

An Arthur Wood lustre vase, decorated with red and yellow flowers on a cream and brown ground, 1930s, 16in (40.5cm) high.
£120–140 BEV

FACE MASKS

Face masks were popular in the 1920s and 1930s. Inspired by African art – an important influence during the Art Deco period – they were modelled on famous film stars and fashionable young women, and were produced by many different companies. One of the most famous names in the field was Goldscheider (1885–1953). The Viennese company produced several mask designs of sculptural female faces, Art Deco in style and highlighted with strong colours, typically iron-red. Other firms known for wall masks include Lenci in Italy and Royal Dux in Czechoslovakia, while in the UK they were made by potteries such as Clarice Cliff, Beswick and Cope.

Formed from terracotta, masks are prone to chipping, and condition is important when it comes to value.

A Beswick wall mask, depicting a woman's head, with blue and green flowers, 1930s, 12in (30.5cm) high.
£250–300 BEV

A Bosse wall mask, depicting a woman wearing a green hat, 1930s, 9in (23cm) high.
£400–450 HEW

Cross Reference
See Colour Review

A Colclough & Co wall mask, depicting a woman with red hair and green earrings and collar, signed 'C. Cope', 1934, 7in (18cm) high.
£65–75 BEV

A Goldscheider pottery wall mask, depicting the face of an Oriental woman with coiled green hair, 1930s, 11in (28cm) high.
£300–350 GAK

STATUETTES & DECORATIVE FIGURES

A gilt hollow-cast spelter figure of a female holding a fan, on a black marble base, regilded, 1920–30s, 10½in (26.5cm) high.
£200–250 CARS

A gilt hollow-cast spelter figure of a female dancer, on a white marble base, left hand damaged, 1920s, 14¾in (37.5cm) high.
£160–200 CARS

A gilt-bronze figure of a female dancer, by Lorenzl, on a waisted square onyx plinth, signed in the bronze 'Lorenzl', 1930s, 9in (23cm) high.
£350–400 AH

A silvered-spelter figure of a female dancer holding a tambourine, on a square marble base, 19in (48.5cm) high.
£250–300 BTB

Art Nouveau

A brass writing set, surmounted by a model of an owl, chips to glass inkwells, 1890s, 10in (25.5cm) wide.
£90–100 STK

A pair of shelf or WC cistern brackets, c1900, 10in (25.5cm) wide.
£25–30 BYG

A Liberty & Co Tudric pewter bowl, attributed to Oliver Baker, with 4 legs terminating in pad feet, stamped '067', 1903–33, 12½in (32cm) diam.
£180–220 P(Ba)

A German Jugendstil metal casket, with domed hinged lid, decorated with fields of cast stylized flowers, 2 ring handles, 1900, 10in (25.5cm) long.
£160–200 P(Ba)

A Hukin & Heath plated candelabra, with 6 sconces on curved arms on a central column with openwork ball knop, mounted on circular foot with hammered finish, stamped with maker's mark, 1880–1900, 14¾in (37.5cm) high.
£100–120 P(Ba)

A brass ceiling light, with 3 bulb holders, c1900, 17in (43cm) diam.
£450–500 RUL

A pewter brooch, with a Ruskin Pottery domed variegated blue insert, 1920s, 1¼in (3cm) diam.
£12–15 AnSh

A cast-iron sink and stand, c1900, 29in (73.5cm) high.
£125–150 A&H

A Liberty & Co pewter tankard, c1900, 5in (12.5cm) high.
£350–400 SHa

A Kayserzinn twin-handled pewter vase, decorated with twin panels depicting a seated fox looking up at a grapevine, stamped 'Kayserzinn 4497', c1910, 11½in (29cm) high.
£180–220 P(Ba)

TILES

A brown-glazed
tile, 1900–15,
6in (15cm) square.
£16–20 BAS

Cross Reference
See Ceramics

A black ceramic tile,
decorated with cream and
blue tube-lined flowers,
c1900, 6in (15cm) high.
£24–28 HIG

A Delft tile, by Thooft
& Labouchère, decorated
with a peacock and green
leaves on a yellow ground,
c1910, 13in (33cm) high.
£170–200 OO

▶ A vertical panel of
5 tiles, decorated with
brown tube-lined pattern
on a cream ground,
1890s, 30in (76cm) high.
£25–30 GIN

WMF

Wmf stands for the Wurtembergische Metallwarenfabrik. Established in Göppingen in 1880, this metal foundry was the most successful German manufacturer of Art Nouveau-style Continental pewter – an electroplated metal alloy that was more akin to Britannia metal than British pewter.

WMF items were flamboyant in style, very commercial and decorative rather than practical. Typically, they were embellished with sinuous foliage and female figures with flowing hair and trailing drapery. Wares made before 1914 are marked with a stork within a lozenge shape; later wares simply bear the initials 'WMF'.

An inkwell in the form of a female
figure seated by a pool, c1906,
9in (23cm) wide.
£500–550 AOH

A pair of vases, each with
original glass liner, c1906,
6in (15cm) high.
£450–500 AOH

A Secessionist silver-plated metal
and glass table centrepiece, with
boat-shaped stand decorated
with classical scenes, glass liner,
stamped marks, inscribed in
Swedish 'Julius Rohlen on his 50th
Birthday, 27–10–1923', 1920–23,
18¼in (46.5cm) wide.
£220–260 P(Ba)

Arts & Crafts

A wardrobe, with decorative panels and door mirror, late 19thC, 87in (221cm) high.
£300–350 NET

An oak safe cabinet, attributed to Richard Bridgens, decorated with fretwork and fitted with brass furniture, c1860, 24in (61cm) high.
£375–425 NET

A Liberty & Co oak easel, pierced with stylized trees, c1895, 66in (167.5cm) high.
£700–850 MoS

A stencilled work table, standing on 3 legs, the top decorated with flowers, c1900–10, 19in (48.5cm) diam.
£275–325 NET

A Liberty mahogany magazine rack, c1900, 39in (99cm) high.
£450–550 ANO

An oak and elm swivel desk chair, c1900, 32in (81.5cm) high.
£270–300 COLL

◄ A Keswick School of Industrial Art copper vase, c1900, 7in (18cm) high.
£100–125 ANO

A W. A. S. Benson copper and brass kettle, c1900, 8in (20.5cm) high.
£165–185 RUSK

A pair of silver napkin rings, inlaid with agate in thistle pattern, by G. C. Rait & Sons, in original case, c1900, 2¼in (5.5cm) diam.
£250–300 BWA

A Birmingham Guild of Handicrafts silver and copper biscuit box, designed by Arthur Stanisford Dixon, 1904, 5in (12.5cm) high.
£750–900 MoS

A Liberty & Co Tenbury wall mirror, with pewter-covered frame, c1905, 25in (63.5cm) wide.
£600–700 MoS

A Birmingham Guild of Handicrafts brass and copper vase, designed by Arthur Stanisford Dixon, c1905, 6in (15cm) high.
£350–400 MoS

An anodized metal coal scuttle, decorated with Ruskin Pottery embellishments and wrought-iron handles, c1900, 20in (51cm) high.
£280–350 MRW

▶ A W. A. S. Benson Rhodium plated tray, decorated with intertwining roses, impressed marks, c1910, 19in (48.5cm) diam.
£650–750 RUSK

POTTERY

A Martin Brothers brown stoneware vase, c1877, 1¾in (4.5cm) high.
£250–300 DSG

A Lauder Pottery jardinière, decorated in blue, brown and cream, with sgraffito fish and aquatic foliage, signed 'Lauder Barum', 1880–1900, 15⅜in (40cm) diam.
£300–350 P(Ba)

A Martin Brothers stoneware jug, decorated with brown and cream sgraffito leaf pattern, incised 'R. W. Martin 1875', 6¼in (16cm) high.
£180–220 P(Ba)

▶ A Moore Brothers vase, in the form of a turquoise peacock perched on a tree stump, on a mound base, some restoration, impressed mark, c1880, 13¼in (33.5cm) high.
£400–450 DN

A Mettlach half-litre stein, with pewter lid, decorated in blue, yellow, orange and green, No. 2091, 1890–1900, 8¼in (21cm) high.
£450–475 PGA

An Elton ware orange and brown vase, by Clevedon Pottery, 1890, 8¼in (21cm) high.
£100–120 OD

A Rookwood serving bowl, in brown, naturalistically decorated with yellow flowers, 1891, 10in (25.5cm) diam.
£650–800 YAN

A pair of Lauder Pottery green candlesticks, each decorated with a bird and on a hexagonal base, 1880–1900, 14¼in (36cm) high.
£200–250 P(Ba)

A Burmantofts faïence stick-stand, decorated with diamond pattern in turquoise-blue, c1900, 24¼in (61.5cm) high.
£300–400 DSG

> **Cross Reference**
> See Colour Review

A Lauder Pottery vase, decorated with sgraffito birds and foliage on a yellow ground, 1880–1900, 10½in (26.5cm) high.
£200–250 P(Ba)

A Baron Pottery vase, with sgraffito decoration and painted slip-glaze in green, brown and blue, 1900, 11¼in (28.5cm) high.
£130–160 COHU

◄ A John Pearson plate, decorated with townscape and hills in blue, red, brown and grey, c1900, 10in (25.5cm) diam.
£350–400 NCA

An Elton ware vase, decorated with gilt crackleware glaze, c1902, 7½in (19cm) high.
£400–450 P(Ba)

A Pilkington vase, shape No. 2104, decorated with blue curdle and feathered glaze, c1906, 6in (15cm) high.
£200–225 PGA

Asian Works of Art

A Chinese bronze belt hook, Han Dynasty, 3in (7.5cm) long.
£70–80 BAC

A Chinese bronze belt hook, decorated with flowers, Song Dynasty, 9in (23cm) long.
£40–50 BAC

A Chinese bronze hairpin, Tang Dynasty, 5in (12.5cm) long.
£25–30 BAC

Chinese Dynasties

There are eight principal Chinese dynasties:

Shang	c1600 BC	–	c1050 BC
Zhou	c1050 BC	–	c221 BC
Han	206 BC	–	AD 220
Tang	AD 618	–	AD 917
Song	AD 960	–	1279
Yuan	1279	–	1368
Ming	1368	–	1644
Qing	1644	–	1916

A Chinese wooden devotion figure, Longqing period, 1567–72, 10in (25.5cm) high.
£120–140 BAC

A Chinese gilt-bronze Bodhisattva, seated with long flowing robes and wearing a crown, traces of original colour, 17thC, 9¾in (25cm) high.
£500–600 Bea(E)

A Chinese wooden water bucket, 19thC, 14in (35.5cm) diam.
£200–230 HGh

A Japanese *shakudo tsuba*, decorated with horses in gold and silver, early 19thC, 3in (7.5cm) wide.
£350–400 GRa

Encouraged by the samurai culture, sword-making was a highly revered art form in Japan, with an almost religious significance. Each element of the sword was carefully crafted. The *tsuba* was the sword guard. The blade passed through the main aperture, while the openings on each side held a small dagger (*kozuka*) and a skewer (*kogai*). *Tsubas* were often very decorative, being embellished with precious metals and coloured inlay.

A Chinese elm wine or water barrel, 19thC, 12in (30.5cm) diam.
£250–300 SOO

Miller's is a price GUIDE not a price LIST

▶ A pair of Chinese silk sleeve panels, decorated with flowers, scrolls, books and birds in Peking stitch, 19thC, 20in (51cm) high, mounted and framed.
£300–350 PBr

A four-case lacquer *inro*, decorated in *hiramakie* and *takamakie*, minor chipping, 19thC, 3½in (9cm) high.
£700–800 JaG

A two-case silver *inro*, decorated with flowers, 19thC, 2in (5cm) diam.
£300–365 JaG

▶ A four-case gold lacquer *inro*, decorated in *hiramakie* and *takamakie* with Chinese lion on rear, *nashiji* interior, slight damage on one corner and flaking, 19thC, 3in (7.5cm) high.
£700–800 JaG

A five-case *inro*, decorated with black and gold lacquer, slight damage on upper corners, 19thC, 3in (7.5cm) high.
£900–1,000 JaG

Makie (meaning literally 'sprinkled picture') was a technique by which metallic particles were combined with wet lacquer. In *hiramakie* the gold is flush with the surrounding lacquer, in *takamakie* it is applied to a raised design.

A wooden *netsuke*, depicting the poetess Onono Komadi, 18thC, 1½in (4cm) high.
£230–260 JaG

A wooden *netsuke* depicting a man with a jug before him, c1800, 1½in (4cm) high.
£450–500 HUR

A wooden *netsuke*, depicting a *karashishi* seated on a pierced low table, 19thC, 2in (5cm) high.
£300–340 JaG

An ivory *netsuke*, depicting a dog with puppy, late 19thC, 1½in (4cm) high.
£300–340 JaG

An ivory *netsuke*, depicting a reveller, 19thC, 1½in (4cm) high.
£320–360 JaG

A resin *netsuke*, depicting an elephant, made for the tourist market, 1950s, 1½in (4cm) long.
£70–80 AnS

BASKETS

A Chinese wicker hanging fruit basket, 19thC, 13in (33cm) diam.
£85–95 SOO

A Chinese cane basket with lid, from Guangxi province, late 19thC, 15in (38cm) diam.
£100–120 GHC

A Japanese or Chinese split-cane vase, c1930, 33in (83.5cm) high.
£85–95 NET

◄ A pair of southern Chinese wedding baskets, 1930s, 36in (91.5cm) high.
£500–600 K

► A Vietnamese Brau Tribe basket, with woven head-strap, early 20thC, 17in (43cm) high.
£65–80 K

CERAMICS

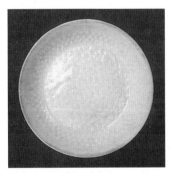

A Chinese blue and white bowl, Ming Dynasty, 16thC, 6in (15cm) diam.
£550–650 GeW

A Chinese painted pottery jar, Neolithic period, circa 2000 BC, 12in (30.5cm) high.
£350–400 BAC

A Chinese Ding ware dish, moulded with fish and water lilies, Song Dynasty, AD 960–1279, 5¼in (13.5cm) diam.
£375–425 HUR

Further Reading

Miller's Chinese & Japanese Antiques Buyer's Guide, Miller's Publications, 1999

► A Chinese Imari teapot and cover, with overglaze decoration, c1750, 9in (23cm) high.
£400–450 RBA

A Chinese blue and white basin, decorated with 9 scholars or Immortals in a garden landscape, Kangxi period, 8½in (21.5cm) diam.
£400–450 Bon(C)

A Chinese blue and white basin, decorated with a mountainous river landscape, Kangxi period, 9¼in (23.5cm) diam.
£350–400 Bon(C)

A Chinese blue and white bowl, with moulded under-glaze decoration and later Dutch polychrome floral pattern, Kangxi period, c1720, 6in (15cm) diam.
£375–450 GeW

A Chinese blue and white saucer dish, decorated in early Ming style with a tied bunch of lotus, Qing Dynasty, 11in (28cm) diam.
£300–400 Bon(C)

A Chinese *famille rose* guglet, decorated with ladies at leisure, enamels rubbed, 18thC, 10in (25.5cm) high.
£50–60 Bon(C)

A Chinese teabowl and saucer, decorated with pine trees in underglaze blue, from the Nanking cargo, c1750, saucer 4½in (11.5cm) diam.
£170–190 RBA

A Chinese Imari washbasin, with iron-red, blue and gold pattern, early 18thC, 10½in (26.5cm) diam.
£600–750 GeW

A Chinese glazed figure of a seated dignitary, from the *Diana* cargo, c1816, 3¾in (9.5cm) high.
£60–75 RBA

A Chinese Peony Rock bowl, decorated in blue enamels, from the Nanking cargo, c1750, 6½in (16.5cm) diam.
£175–200 RBA

◄ A saucer-shaped dish, decorated with blue flowers, Qianlong period, c1790, 9in (23cm) diam.
£130–150 GeW

A Chinese tea cup and saucer, decorated with Daisy Terrace pattern, from the Nanking cargo, c1750, saucer 5in (12.5cm) diam.
£70–85 RBA

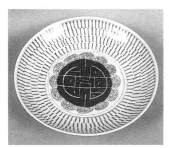

A Chinese Provincial ware longevity dish, decorated in blue and white, from the *Diana* cargo, c1816, 11in (28cm) diam.
£200–250 RBA

A pair of Japanese vases, decorated with dragons, signed 'Fukagawa', Meiji period, 1868–1911, 10in (25.5cm) high.
£350–400 MCN

A Chinese blue and white teabowl and saucer, decorated with Diving Birds pattern, from the *Diana* cargo, c1816, saucer 6¼in (16cm) diam.
£275–300 RBA

A pair of earthenware cachepots, printed in colours and decorated with coats-of-arms, c1890, 17in (43cm) wide.
£1,300–1,500 MLL

These cachepots were made in the Far East for the French market.

A Japanese dish, decorated with the Imari pattern, signed 'Fukagawa', Meiji period, 1868–1911, 10¼in (26cm) diam.
£250–300 MCN

A Japanese Sumidagawa sake pot, c1900, 6in (15cm) diam.
£135–155 JaG

◄ A Japanese Kutani cup and saucer, c1900, saucer 5½in (14cm) diam.
£8–10 MCN

NORITAKE

A Noritake Japanese-style red and green vase, c1910, 3in (7.5cm) high.
£50–60 DgC

A Noritake dressing table part set, decorated with pink roses and blue border, c1910, tray 13in (33cm) wide.
£75–85 DgC

► A Noritake coffee can and saucer, decorated in gold on cream, 1915, saucer 4½in (11.5cm) diam.
£25–30 DgC

A pair of Noritake vases, each decorated in iron-red and green, c1911, 4½in (11.5cm) high.
£40–50 DgC

A Noritake bowl, decorated with a desert scene depicting a camel and rider and palm trees, 5½in (14cm) diam.
£20–25 EAS

◄ A Noritake jug and bowl, decorated in gilt on a cream ground, with black rims, 1920, bowl 5in (12.5cm) diam.
£40–50 DgC

A Noritake coffee set, comprising 6 cups, 6 saucers, pot, milk jug and sugar bowl, decorated with roses, 1920, pot 6¾in (17cm) high.
£200–250 DgC

A Noritake cup and saucer, decorated with green and black, 1930s, saucer 5in (12.5cm) diam.
£30–35 UNI

► A Noritake six-sided bowl, Japanese mark, 1920–30, 3in (7.5cm) diam.
£5–6 EAS

PRINTS

A Japanese *oban* triptych woodcut print, depicting Tosen-Kyo (a game of throwing a fan) played by the court ladies, by Chikanobu, from the *Noble Ladies of the Tokugawa Period*, published by Hasengawa, 1898, 14 x 28½in (35.5 x 72.5cm).
£300–330 JaG

A Japanese woodcut print, depicting the courtesan Kicho of the Owariya, with the view of Tsukuda jima from Zensei Azuma Fukei, by Sencho, c1830, 14½ x 10in (37 x 25.5cm).
£400–450 JaG

◄ An Utagawa School *oban* triptych, depicting women at work, some damage, Meiji period, 12 x 25in (30.5 x 63cm).
£50–60 Bon(C)

A Chinese poster, depicting Chairman Mao visiting the iron-foundry workers, 1975, 30¼ x 20¾in (77 x 52.5cm).
£120–140 Wai

LOCATE THE SOURCE

The source of each illustration in Miller's can be found by checking the code letters below each caption with the Key to Illustrations, pages 476–484.

Automobilia

A glass decanter, by Stevens & Williams, in the form of a tyre, with a silver stopper in the form of a wheel, Birmingham 1908, 10½in (26.5cm) high.
£1,200–1,500 ALiN

This decanter may have been made for a director at the Dunlop tyre factory.

A KPM car badge, early 20thC, 3¼in (8.5cm) wide.
£125–135 WAB

An Italian 18ct gold Porsche keyring, marked, 1970s, 6in (15cm) long.
£240–270 BND

◀ The 100 Greatest Cars silver miniature collection, by John Pinches Ltd, 1980s, in presentation case, 10in (25.5cm) wide.
£180–200 PC

A tapestry depicting a Ferrari F40 and a 166MM Barchetta, together with Enzo Ferrari and his signature, by Keith Collins, c1985, 94½ x 157½in (240 x 400cm).
£2,700–3,000 BKS

A mural celebrating the 1938 Grand Prix of Germany, acrylic on board, by Tony Upson, framed, 48 x 96in (122 x 244cm).
£1,200–1,400 BKS

MASCOTS

◀ A Cat on Moon mascot, by Etienne Mercier, c1920, 5in (12.5cm) high.
£450–550 BKS

▶ A grey satin glass motorist's head mascot, by Red Ashay, mounted on a wooden base, c1925, 5in (12.5cm) high.
£1,600–1,800 BKS

A French nickel advertising mascot, in the form of an elephant, signed 'Franjou', 1920s, 5in (12.5cm) high.
£170–200 BKS

A French 'Le Tank' mascot, in the form of a nude riding a snail, by Brunswick, marked 'MLG 67', on a mid-vintage radiator cap, c1925, 6in (15cm) high.
£1,800–2,000 BKS

An Art Deco horse mascot, by Casimir Brau, signed 'C. Brau', 1925, 6in (15cm) long.
£1,500–1,700 BKS

▶ A French glass owl mascot, retailed by Mestre & Blatge of Paris, with original enamel eyes and mounting, c1930, 2½in (6.5cm) high.
£1,400–1,600 BKS

◀ A chrome Pontiac Chieftain mascot, 1950–53, 19in (48.5cm) long.
£35–40 WAB

PICNIC SETS

A Finnigan's four-person picnic set, with a brass-edged lid, fitted with gilt-edged plates, food boxes, ceramic cups and saucers, preserve jars, Thermos flask, milk bottle, biscuit jar and metal condiment bottles, 1903, 30in (76cm) wide.
£1,400–1,600 BKS

▶ A Brexton six-person picnic set, with tan case, 1960s, 23in (58.5cm) wide.
£125–150 PPH

A Coracle four-person wicker picnic set, by G. W. Scott & Sons, with 2 sandwich boxes, 2 wicker drinks bottles, glasses, butter jar and cutlery, 1930s, 20in (51cm) wide.
£500–600 BKS

Books

CHILDREN'S BOOKS

Lucie Atwell's Read Me A Story Pop-up Book, published by Dean, 1977, 7 x 9in (18 x 23cm).
£8–10 J&J

The books in this section are arranged alphabetically, by author, illustrator or publisher. The annuals are arranged alphabetically by title.

Tatterjack, published by Blackie, 1940s, 13 x 10in (33 x 25.5cm).
£50–60 MRW

Enid Blyton, *Be Brave Little Noddy!*, first edition, with dust cover, 1955, 7½in (19cm) high.
£25–30 WWY

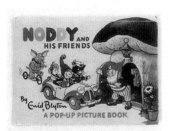

Enid Blyton, *Noddy And His Friends*, with pop-up pictures, 1960s, 6 x 9in (15 x 23cm).
£5–6 HarC

Enid Blyton, *Noddy's Broken Chimney Pot*, with pop-up pictures, published by Purnell, 1969, 6 x 9in (15 x 23cm).
£5–6 HarC

Bookano Stories, No. 1, with pop-up pictures, published by Strand Publications, c1936, 8½ x 6¾in (21.5 x 17cm).
£75–90 AHa

Walter Crane, *Flora's Feast, a Masque of Flowers*, published by Cassell and Co, 1899, 10 x 8in (25.5 x 20.5cm).
£80–100 MRW

Lewis Carroll, *Alice's Adventures in Wonderland* and *Through the Looking Glass*, illustrated by John Tenniel, first editions, published by Macmillan & Co, London, 1866 and 1872, 7½ x 5¼in (19 x 13.5cm).
£3,000–3,500 PHa

▶ Walt Disney, *Father Noah's Ark*, from Disney's *Silly Symphony*, 1934, 9 x 7in (23 x 18cm).
£40–50 MRW

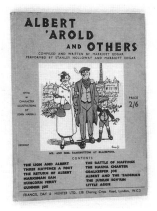

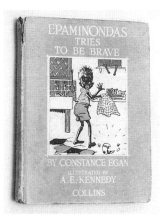

Marriott Edgar, *Albert, 'Arold and Others*, published by Francis, Day & Hunter, c1920, 10 x 8in (25.5 x 20.5cm).
£40–50 MRW

Constance Egan, *Epaminondas Tries to be Brave*, illustrated by A. E. Kennedy, published by Collins, 1947, 7 x 6in (18 x 15cm).
£18–20 J&J

Magdalen Eldon, *Highland Bumble*, published by Collins, 1952, 10 x 7in (25.5 x 18cm).
£14–16 J&J

Stanley Holloway (1890–1982) was a much-loved British character actor and singer. A concert-party entertainer, he became famous when he introduced comic monologues into his act in 1927. Although Holloway was London-born and middle-class, these humorous narratives were delivered in a flat, unemotional, Lancastrian accent. The stories of *Albert and the Lion* and *'Arold at the Battle of Hastings* became huge successes, both in the theatre and on record. Holloway went on to star in many plays and films, most notably playing Alfred Doolittle in the stage and cinema versions of *My Fair Lady*. This volume contains his best-known monologues, written by Marriott Edgar and illustrated by John Hassall, the well-known poster designer, advertising artist and book illustrator.

Giles cartoon book, 1958, 7¾ x 10in (19.5 x 25.5cm).
£10–12 RAC

Eleanor Farjeon, *Kaleidoscope*, illustrated by Edward Ardizzone, published by Oxford University Press, London, 1963, 9 x 6in (23 x 15cm).
£16–20 DAC

Pop-Up Pictures of The Circus, illustrated by G. Higham, published by Juvenile Productions Ltd, London, 1950s, 8 x 10in (20.5 x 25.5cm).
£25–30 MRW

George MacDonald, *At the Back of the North Wind*, illustrated by Arthur Hughes, published by Strahan & Co, London, 1881, 7 x 5in (18 x 12.5cm).
£35–40 DAC

A. A. Milne, *Winnie-The-Pooh*, illustrated by Ernest Howard Shepard, No. 133 of a limited edition of 350, on handmade paper, in two-tone blue cloth binding, signed by the author and illustrator, 1926, 7 x 5in (18 x 12.5cm).
£1,250–1,500 MCA

A. A. Milne, *When We Were Very Young*, seventh edition, in red leather binding with gold embossed cover, c1932, 7 x 5in (18 x 12.5cm).
£120–150 WWY

T. J. S. Rowland and L. G. Smith, *Moving Things for Lively Youngsters*, 1937, 10 x 8in (25.5 x 20.5cm).
£12–15 MRW

Further Reading

Miller's Collecting Books, Miller's Publications, 1995

▶ Anna Sewell, *Black Beauty*, published by The Reward Classics Rylee Ltd, 1950, 7½ x 5in, (19 x 12.5cm).
£450–550 JAC

Anna Sewell (1820–78) only wrote one book, *Black Beauty*, which was published the year before her death.

Kay Nielsen, *East of the Sun and West of the Moon*, first edition, with 25 colour and black & white illustrations, published by Hodder & Stoughton, 1914, 11½ x 9in (29 x 23cm).
£800–1,000 PHa

Kay Rasmus Nielsen was born in Copenhagen in 1886, the son of the Director of the Royal Danish Theatre. He trained as an artist in Paris, then moved to London, producing illustrations for publishers Hodder & Stoughton. Influenced by Aubrey Beardsley and the art of the Orient and Middle East, Nielsen drew in pen and ink, adding brilliant water-colour washes. In 1926, Nielsen emigrated to America. He was employed on Disney's film *Fantasia* and, living in Hollywood, worked as an actor, set designer and muralist until his death in obscurity in 1957. Today, his work is sought after, and this is one of his most important books.

Jean Parsons, *Fiery Gets his Wish*, published by Hutchinson's, 1949, 9in (23cm) square.
£35–40 MRW

Christina G. Rossetti, *Sing-Song, a Nursery-Rhyme Book*, illustrated by Arthur Hughes, first edition, 1872, 8 x 6in (20.5 x 15cm).
£50–60 DAC

The Big Book of Fun, edited by Herbert Strang, published by Oxford University Press, 1931, 9 x 7in (23 x 18cm).
£8–10 J&J

ANNUALS

Bubble and Squeak Annual, 1952, 10 x 8in (25.5 x 20.5cm).
£5–6 HarC

The Book of Blue Peter and *The Third Book of Blue Peter*, 1965 & 1967, 10 x 8in (25.5 x 20.5cm).
£5–12 each HarC

Buffalo Bill Wild West Annual, 1955, 10 x 8in (25.5 x 20.5cm).
£5–6 HarC

Eagle Annual, published by Fleetway, 1985, 10 x 8in (25.5 x 20.5cm).
£2–3 HarC

J. Horrabin, *Japhet & Happy's Annual*, published by News Chronicle Publications, London, 1938, 10 x 8in (25.5 x 20.5cm).
£20–25 J&J

The Girl Guides' Annual, 1960, 11 x 8in (28 x 20.5cm).
£2–3 HarC

Judy for Girls annual, 1975, 11 x 8in (28 x 20.5cm).
£5–6 HarC

Lion Annual, published by Fleetway, 1983, 10 x 8in (25.5 x 20.5cm).
£2–3 HarC

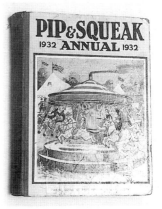

Pip & Squeak Annual, 1932, 10 x 8in (25.5 x 20.5cm).
£12–15 J&J

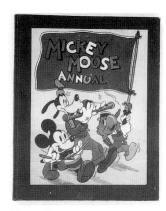

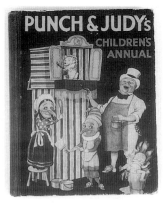

Mickey Mouse Annual, 1947,
10 x 8in (25.5 x 20.5cm).
£12–15 HarC

Punch & Judy's Children's Annual,
c1950, 10 x 8in (25.5 x 20.5cm).
£25–30 MRW

*More Adventures of Rupert,
The Daily Express Annual*, 1947,
10 x 8in (25.5 x 20.5cm).
£50–60 HarC

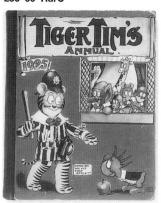

Sooty's Storyland, published
by Purnell & Sons, 1967,
11 x 7in (28 x 18cm).
£4–5 J&J

Sparkler Annual, with cover
illustration by Wilson, 1939,
11 x 8in (28 x 20.5cm).
£25–30 MRW

Tiger Tim's Annual, 1925,
11 x 8in (28 x 20.5cm).
£15–18 HarC

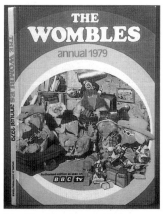

Tuck's Annual, with pop-up
pictures, 1920s, 10 x 6in
(20.5 x 15cm).
£65–80 MRW

Valiant Annual, published by
Fleetway, 1978, 10 x 8in
(25.5 x 20.5cm).
£2–3 HarC

The Wombles Annual, BBC
TV authorized edition, 1979,
10¾ x 8in (27.5 x 20.5cm).
£3–4 CMF

LONDON

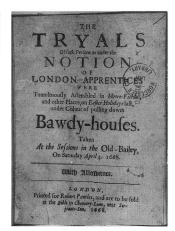

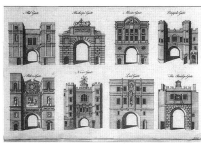

W. Maitlands, *History of London, Volume I*, printed for T. Osborne, J. Shipton & J. Hodges, 1756, 11 x 17½in (28 x 44.5cm).
£1,300–1,500 AHa

An Exact Abridgement of the Records in The Tower of London, collected by Sir Robert Cotton, raised bands and gilt on spine, small hole in title page, tear to preface page extending slightly into text, 1657, 13½ x 9in (34.5 x 23cm).
£180–220 AHa

The Tryals of Such Persons as under the Notion of London Apprentices were Tumultuously Assembled in Moore-Fields, and other Places, on Easter Holidays last, under Colour of pulling down Bawdy-houses, 1668, 7 x 5¼in (18 x 13.5cm).
£280–350 AHa

Thomas Faulkner, *History of Chelsea*, published by the author, 1810, 9¾ x 6in (25 x 15cm).
£120–150 AHa

This section is devoted to books on the subject of London and is arranged chronologically.

◀ Reverend Daniel Lysons, *The Environs of London*, large paper copy with many illustrations, 6 volumes, 1796, 11¾ x 9½in (30 x 24cm).
£2,000–2,350 PHa

John Woods, *The History of London*, with 64 engraved plates, light browning, 1850, 10¾ x 8¼in (27 x 21cm).
£350–400 PHa

On the River Police, first edition, 19thC,
8¾ x 5¾in (22 x 14.5cm).
£150–180 AHa

Mayhew, *The Great Exhibition of 1851*,
illustrated by George Cruikshank,
published by David Bogue, 1851,
19¾ x 13¾in (50 x 35cm).
£180–220 AHa

Great Metropolis, edited by
William Gray Fearnside and
Thomas Harrel, with 50 steel
engraved plates, published by
Thomas Holmes, London, spine
split at hinges, slight marginal
foxing to a few plates, 1851,
9¾ x 6in (25 x 15cm).
£120–150 AHa

▶ W. G. Fearnside,
*Eighty Picturesque Views
on the Thames and
Medway*, published by
Tumbleson & Co, 8°,
foxing to some plates,
slight rubbing, 19thC.
£350–400 AHa

*Reynolds' New Distance
Map of London and Visitors
Guide*, with fold-out street
map and illustrations, some
tears and repairs, 1860,
6 x 3¾in (15 x 9.5cm).
£50–60 AHa

Henry Mayhew, *London Labour & the London Poor*,
4 volumes, with 97 wood-engraved plates, purple
cloth binding with gilt title, spines faded, published
by Charles Griffin and Co, London, 1865.
£750–850 PHa

**Henry Mayhew's *London Labour & the London Poor*
is one of the most famous examples of Victorian
pioneering journalism. Mayhew (1812–87) plumbed
the depths of London's poverty, interviewing the
street-sweepers, sewer-dwellers, mud-larks and
rag-sellers, to discover how the silent underclass
scratched a living. His series of articles for the
Morning Chronicle were combined in *London Labour
& the London Poor*, first published in two volumes
in 1851, then in an expanded four-volume edition
in 1864 and 1865, when characters including
prostitutes, thieves and beggars were added to
the interviewees. A work of supreme importance in
the social history of London and Victorian England,
Mayhew's ground-breaking study influenced many of
his contemporaries, most notably Charles Dickens,
who used its findings as background for his novels.**

Robert Pollack, *The Course of Time*, with Tower of
London fore-edge painting, published by William
Blackwood & Son, Edinburgh, 1860, 6½ x 6¼in
(16.5 x 16cm).
£140–170 AHa

Holland House, 2 volumes, with extra illustrations,
published by Macmillan, 1874, 12 x 9½in (30.5 x 24cm).
£650–800 AHa

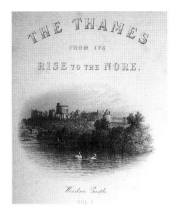

The Thames, 2 volumes, published by J. S. Virtue & Co, London, c1880, 12 x 10in (30.5 x 25.5cm).
£245–275 PHa

Doré's London, published by Harpers, New York, 1890, 13 x 11in (33 x 28cm).
£200–250 AHa

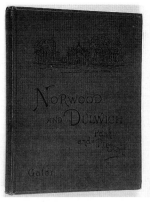

Allen M. Galer, *Norwood and Dulwich Past and Present*, with 17 plates and 2 maps, light rubbing on spine, 1890, 9¼ x 7½in (23.5 x 19cm).
£75–90 AHa

◀ J. H. Leigh Hunt, *The Old Court Suburb: Memorials of Kensington Regal, Critical, & Anecdotal by the late J. H. Leigh Hunt Esq.*, with 108 plates, one of 150 copies, signed by the artists, published by Freemantle & Co, London, 1902, 9 x 7in (23 x 18cm).
£150–180 AHa

W. J. Loftie, *The Inns of Court and Chancery*, illustrated by Herbert Railton, published by Seeley & Co Ltd, 1893, 14 x 10¼ (35.5 x 26cm).
£75–90 AHa

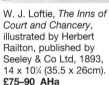

Familiar London Painted by Rose Barton, published by A. & C. Black, 1904, 9 x 6¾in (23 x 17cm).
£120–135 PHa

▶ H. W. Dickinson, *Water Supply of Greater London*, printed for the Newcomen Society, Leamington Spa, signed limited edition, 1954, 10¼ x 8in (26 x 20.5cm).
£35–40 AHa

Canon Benham, *Old London Churches*, illustrated by Arthur Garratt, pencil marks to end papers and last page, published by Hodder & Stoughton, London, 1908, 11½ x 9in (29 x 23cm).
£75–90 AHa

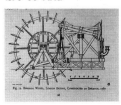

Bottles

A pre-Columbian storage bottle, decorated with a face, circa 800 AD, 4¼in (11cm) high.
£100–120 OD

▶ A green glass poison bottle, embossed 'Poison', 'H. Gilbertson & Sons' and 'Regd 30th Octr–1861', slight chip, 6¼in (16cm) high.
£750–850 BBR

This bottle is the only recorded 6oz example of its type.

◀ A dark olive-green glass bottle, with applied collar lip and base pontil, impressed seal embossed '1772, M. Scanlan Esq, Ballynaha', 9½in (24cm) high.
£550–650 BBR

This bottle is very desirable, in that it bears a date, the name of its owner, and place of production.

A dark olive-green bottle, with white enamel flecks, impressed Alloa-type seal embossed 'S.W, 1792', 11½in (29cm) high.
£3,000–3,500 BBR

Pre-1800 dated seals of the type shown on this bottle are extremely rare.

A pottery bottle and stand, decorated with enamelled flowers on a pale blue ground, 1850–60, 10½in (26.5cm) high.
£60–70 OD

A blue glass castor oil bottle, 1900–10, 4¾in (12cm) high.
£10–12 OD

▶ Three one-pint milk bottles, each advertising Cadbury's Drinking Chocolate, 1986–87.
£1–2 each JMC

Boxes

A William III document box, with original studded leather covering and later swan-neck brass handle, original lock and key, c1700, 14in (35.5cm) wide.
£300–350 OTT

A George III inlaid fruitwood table box, c1790, 14in (35.5cm) wide.
£300–350 MB

▶ An oval ivory patch box, decorated with enamel, gold and seed pearls, 1780, 3¾in (9.5cm) wide.
£400–450 CHAP

Cross Reference
See Colour Review

A George III mahogany decanter box, with boxwood edging, c1790, 9in (23cm) wide.
£450–500 OTT

A George III kingwood trinket box, with spring drawers, 1790, 9in (23cm) wide.
£350–400 TMi

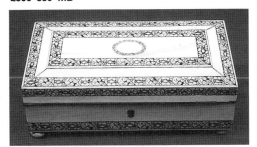

A Vizagapatam ivory casket, decorated with stylized flowers and foliage, India, early 19thC, 8in (20.5cm) wide.
£350–400 TMi

◀ A Regency mahogany and rosewood writing slope, on a stand, with secret drawers, 1820, 19in (48.5cm) wide.
£500–600 MB

A rosewood cigar box, with brass inlay and cedar lining, 1820, 12in (30.5cm) wide.
£335–375 MB

A William IV rosewood writing slope, with pewter and mother-of-pearl inlay, c1830, 16in (40.5cm) wide.
£400–450 OTT

A William IV tortoiseshell tea caddy, with ball feet, c1830, 8in (20.5cm) wide.
£1,000–1,200 TMi

A walnut tobacco box, with mother-of-pearl inlay, c1880, 4in (10cm) wide.
£70–80 MB

A Victorian burr-yew workbox, c1890, 9in (23cm) wide.
£160–200 SPU

◀ An elm box, late 19thC, 12½in (32cm) wide.
£180–200 GHC

A Victorian olivewood table box, with brass mounts, c1890, 8in (20.5cm) wide.
£160–200 OTT

CARD CASES

A metal card case, inlaid with mother-of-pearl and abalone, 1840, 3in (7.5cm) wide.
£125–140 MB

A silver card case, inlaid with tortoiseshell, mother-of-pearl and ivory, 1850–60, 3in (7.5cm) wide.
£375–420 THOM

A metal card case, inlaid with mother-of-pearl, 1840, 3in (7.5cm) wide.
£115–130 MB

A mother-of-pearl card case, 1850, 3in (7.5cm) wide.
£50–60 MB

▶ A card case, inlaid with mother-of-pearl, 1880, 4in (10cm) high.
£65–80 MRW

SNUFF BOXES

◄ A leather snuff box, with silver plaque engraved 'Wm Gardner', 1760, 3in (7.5cm) wide.
£160–200 MB

► A silver snuff box, decorated with mother-of-pearl, engraved 'IW', 18thC, 3in (7.5cm) wide.
£200–225 MB

◄ An oval tortoiseshell snuff box, with blonde tortoiseshell lining, 1780, 4in (10cm) wide.
£850–950 CHAP

A pressed-horn table snuff box, 1780, 3in (7.5cm) diam.
£270–300 MB

A turned rosewood snuff box, with gold mounts, 1790, 2in (5cm) diam.
£125–150 MB

► A Scottish horn snuff mull, c1800, 2½in (6.5cm) wide.
£225–260 CoHA

◄ A horn snuff box, with silver inlay, 1800, 12in (30.5cm) wide.
£60–75 MB

A silver-gilt snuff box, by
A. J. Strachan, London, 1807,
3in (7.5cm) wide.
£450–500 CHAP

A burr-birch snuff box, 1820,
3in (7.5cm) wide.
£120–150 MB

A wooden snuff box, with concave
lid, 1830, 4in (10cm) wide.
£80–100 MB

A Scottish oval horn snuff box,
decorated with silver thistles,
1850, 3in (7.5cm) wide.
£80–100 MB

A Victorian silver snuff box,
decorated with an engraved
Oriental scene, 4in (10cm) wide.
£160–175 MB

A mahogany ape-head snuff box,
1820, 2in (5cm) wide.
£850–950 CHAP

A burr-mulberry snuff box, with
mother-of-pearl inlay, 1820,
5in (12.5cm) wide.
£70–80 MB

A papier mâché snuff box,
with pewter inlay, 1840,
2½in (6.5cm) wide.
£40–50 MB

A Scottish horn snuff mull, the
silver lid inset with crystal, 1852,
3¾in (9.5cm) wide.
£550–650 CHAP

> **Cross Reference**
> See Colour Review

▶ A Mauchline ware snuff box,
decorated with a view of Mont
St Michel, 1880, 2½in (6.5cm) diam.
£40–45 VB

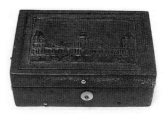

A French music and snuff box,
1820, 4in (10cm) wide.
£210–240 MB

A tortoiseshell snuff box, with gold
inlay, 1830, 3in (7.5cm) wide.
£70–80 MB

A tortoiseshell snuff box, with
silver and mother-of-pearl inlay,
depicting a horse and rider, 1840,
2¾in (7cm) wide.
£450–500 CHAP

An oval papier mâché snuff box,
decorated with flowers and
butterflies, 1880, 3in (7.5cm) wide.
£35–40 MB

Breweriana

A salt-glazed flask, the front embossed with two drinkers seated at a table, the reverse impressed 'G. Peacey, Lord Nelson, 145 Whitechapel Road', 19thC, 5½in (14cm) high.
£150–170 BBR

A Buckley pottery brewing jar, mid-19thC, 21½in (54.5cm) high.
£90–110 IW

A salt-glazed Reform flask, one side embossed with a portrait of Queen Victoria, the other with Prince Albert, minor chip to base, 1840, 8¼in (21cm) high.
£675–750 BBR

A stoneware spirit flask, in the form of the young Queen Victoria, the oval base titled in relief 'Victoria', repaired, 1840, 14in (35.5cm) high.
£300–350 DN

A Ramsden's beer mat, 1950s, 3½in (9cm) wide.
£1–2 PC

A Carlton Ware Martell water jug, in the form of a monocled man holding a glass, 1950s, 9in (23cm) high.
£155–175 HarC

A miniature bottle of Guinness, in a wooden tankard, 1960s, 5in (12.5cm) high.
£8–10 Law

A Beswick Worthington E water jug, in the form of the letter 'E' and 2 rugby players, 1970s, 8in (20.5cm) high.
£165–185 HarC

WHISKY

The word 'whisky' (spelt without an 'e' in Scotland and Canada, and with an 'e' in Ireland and the USA) derives from the Celtic *usequebaugh*, meaning 'water of life'. The earliest written account of whisky-making is found in Scottish records dating from 1494, and the first centres of manufacture were Scotland and Ireland. Initially, it was a cottage industry, but the late 18th and 19th centuries saw the development of commercial production. In Ireland, John Jameson opened his distillery in 1780, while in Scotland, John Haig set up in business in 1824, followed by William Teacher in 1830 and John Dewar in 1846. American production began in the 18th century, bourbon – made from corn grain rather than barley – gaining its name from Bourbon County, Kentucky, where it was first distilled. The industry for Canadian whisky, which was made from rye, emerged during the 19th century.

Vintage whiskies can be extremely valuable. 'An 1899 Glenlivet was recently offered with an estimate of £1,500–2,000, and rarities do fetch four-figure sums,' says Ben Bolter from Phillips' Auction House in Bath. 'It's a drink with a truly international appeal and an equally global collectors' market.' But what makes a whisky collectable as opposed to simply drinkable? 'Serious collectors often look for early whiskies, and prefer the more obscure distilleries,' he notes. Ideally, packaging should be complete and the bottle must be unopened. 'With whisky, a stopper, as opposed to a screw top, is a good indicator of age,' advises Bolter, 'and another tip is to look out for the inscription "By appointment to the King", which means the bottle must pre-date Elizabeth II.' Single malts tend to be worth more than mixes or blends, and decanters more desirable than bottles. While serial-numbered, limited-edition pieces are sought-after, Bolter warns against assuming that every commemorative bottle or decanter must be a good investment. 'Whisky manufacturers will celebrate anything and everything, and some items are produced in vast numbers.'

Over the years, the volume of liquid will shrink, even in an unopened container but, according to Bolton, the taste of the whisky itself only improves with age. Although the whiskies that pass through his hands might cost hundreds, perhaps even thousands, of pounds, most purchasers, he notes, buy to drink.

A mallet-shaped whisky jug, commemorating Queen Victoria's Jubilee, by Thom & Cameron, Glasgow, sepia transfer-printed with 'The Cream of Highland Whiskies', 'My Queen' and 'Jubilee Blend', impressed mark 'Port Dundas Glasgow', c1897, 7¾in (19.5cm) high.
£200–250 BBR

A salt-glazed whisky jug, transfer-printed with 'Thorne's Whisky', some restoration to lip, impressed Royal Doulton circle mark, lion and crown, 1890–1910, 7¾in (19.5cm) high.
£180–220 BBR

A glass whisky tumbler, with acid-etched decoration of a fist holding a cross and 'Long John's Dew of Ben Nevis', c1900, 4in (10cm) high.
£20–25 HUX

A glass whisky tumbler, with acid-etched decoration of Lord Kitchener, figures and animals, inscribed 'Robertson Sanderson & Co, Celebrated Mountain Dew, Leith', c1900, 4in (10cm) high.
£20–25 HUX

A stemmed whisky glass, acid-etched with 'Arrowsmith's Glenlivet' on one side, a female head wearing a hat on the reverse, c1900, 5in (12.5cm) high.
£20–25 HUX

A Dunville's ashtray and match striker, Foley Faïence mark, c1900, 4in (10cm) diam.
£45–55 HUX

A double whisky container, impressed to both sections 'Dewars Scotch Whisky', circle mark, lion and crown, 1900–20, 6in (15cm) high.
£170–200 BBR

◄ A whisky jug, red transfer-printed with 'Cruiskeen Lawn, Mitchell's Old Irish Whisky, Belfast', impressed mark to base, 1920–30, 6¾in (17cm) high.
£180–200 BBR

A bone measure, embossed 'John Hopkins & Co Ltd, "Old Mull" Scotch Whisky', c1920, 3in (7.5cm) long.
£12–14 HUX

A bottle of White Horse whisky, with driven cork and embossed lead capsule, 1915, 11½in (29cm) high.
£250–300 P(B)

► A miniature twin-handled whisky jug, black transfer-printed with 'The Greybeard, Heather Dew, Blended Scotch Whisky', 1930–40, 3in (7.5cm) high.
£90–110 BBR

A White Horse whisky bottle, empty, c1940, 7½in (19cm) high.
£8–10 HUX

A Macallan-Glenlivet Highland Single Malt Liqueur Whisky crystal decanter, with contents and presentation case, 1937, 1¼in (3cm) high.
£300–350 P(B)

A White Horse Scotch Whisky ceramic advertising display model, in the form of a horse, 1950s, 9in (23cm) wide.
£20–25 HarC

A Burleigh Ware Abbot's Choice Scotch Whisky ashtray, 1950s, 5½in (14cm) wide.
£10–12 HUX

A Robbie Burns Whisky composition advertising figure, 1950s, 12in (30.5cm) high.
£110–130 DBr

A Teacher's Scotch Whisky composition advertising figure, 1950s, 11in (28cm) high.
£120–130 DBr

A Long John Scotch Whisky composition advertising figure, 1950s, 10in (25.5cm) high.
£120–130 DBr

An export Claymore Scotch Whisky bottle, with British Customs Certificate 13.6.58, imported by Renglet & Bonnakens, Brussels, empty, 1950s, 9¾in (25cm) high.
£12–15 HUX

A Black & White Scotch Whisky ashtray, designed by James Green's Nephew Ltd, 1950s, 5in (12.5cm) wide,
£15–20 HUX

A Crawford's Old Scotch Whisky water jug, 1960s, 8in (20.5cm) wide.
£30–35 HarC

► A Famous Grouse Finest Scotch Whisky water jug, 1970s, 4in (10cm) high.
£12–15 HarC

A Glenmorangie Single Highland Malt water jug, 1970s, 5in (12.5cm) high.
£15–18 HarC

A Czechoslovakian enamel sign, advertising soda water, c1910, 12½ x 10in (32 x 25.5cm).
£100–120 HUX

A Foursome Mixture tobacco tin, depicting a golfing scene, 1920s, 3 x 4in (7.5 x 10cm).
£120–140 HUX

A Hornby Trains shop display card, c1930, 10 x 12in (25.5 x 30.5cm).
£220–260 RAR

A Cussons Apple Blossom soap bar, in original box, 1950s, 3 x 2in (7.5 x 5cm).
£2–3 MRW

A tin money box, depicting a guardsman, c1910, 6½in (16.5cm) high.
£100–120 HUX

An Atkinson's Black Tulip complexion powder box, complete with contents, c1930, 3in (7.5cm) diam.
£8–10 MRW

A Mazda painted wood advertising figure, c1940, 15in (38cm) high.
£40–50 WP

A Rowntree & Co tin, commemorating the coronation of King George V and Queen Mary, 1911, 4½ x 6½in (11.5 x 16.5cm).
£25–35 WAB

A biscuit tin, in the form of a French Autorail Brun streamlined electric train, 1930s, 19in (48.5cm) long.
£250–300 HUX

A Rudge bicycle advertising poster, 1950s, 13 x 29in (33 x 74cm).
£30–40 JUN

An Inta plastic advertising lipstick, c1990, 20in (51cm) high.
£25–30 ET

A Columbus cast-iron gum ball dispensing machine, 1920s, 18in (46cm) high.
£150–200 AMc

A Reel "21" gum ball dispenser, in the form of an early gaming machine, restored, 1930s, 12in (30.5cm) high.
£225–275 AMc

A pinball machine, with coloured Bakelite bumpers, c1940, 40in (101.5cm) long.
£100–150 AMc

A Watling Rol-A-Top one-armed bandit, Castle Front or Checkerboard design, restored, 1947, 26in (66cm) high.
£1,800–2,000 AMc

This was the last machine made by Watling.

A Mills Black Beauty Polk figure one-armed bandit, in the form of a Native American, 1940s, 72in (183cm) high.
£1,500–2,000 CAm

An Oliver Whales 'Players Please' cigarette vending machine, restored, 1949, 32in (81.5cm) high
£375–450 AMc

An Oliver Whales 'Penny Points' spinball machine, restored, 1950s, 32in (81.5cm) high.
£375–425 AMc

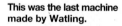

Miller's is a price GUIDE not a price LIST

◄ An Oliver Whales 'Jet Play' spinball machine, restored, 1950s, 32in (81.5cm) high.
£450–500 AMc

A Bryans 'Elevenses' spinball machine, 1955, 25in (63.5cm) high.
£325–375 AMc

A Double Nudger fruit machine, 1970s, 61in (155cm) high.
£250–300 BYG

A glass vase, internally-decorated in mottled orange, in an ornate cast-iron mount, 1920–25, 12½in (32cm) high.
£100–120 P(Ba)

A Barbola oval mirror, decorated with flowers and leaves, 1920s, 31in (79cm) high.
£40–50 SUS

An Art Deco stained-glass panel, framed in brass, 23in (58.5cm) wide.
£260–300 RUL

A set of 6 Bakelite napkin rings, 2 each in mottled red, green and brown, c1930, 2in (5cm) diam, in original box.
£30–35 DEC

A Goldscheider figure of a young girl, wearing a patterned red dress, c1939, 10in (25.5cm) high.
£400–450 HEW

◄ A cold-painted bronze figure of a female golfer, on a circular marble base, 1920s, 8in (20.5cm) high.
£150–200 WaR

A pair of brass wall lamps, c1920, 8in (20.5cm) high.
£170–200 RUL

A Briand patinated spelter figure of a girl with a hoop, c1920, 9½in (24cm) high.
£250–300 BTB

A Goldscheider terracotta bust, depicting a nude female with turquoise curled hair and clasping a blue flower, printed and impressed factory marks, 1930s, 14½in (37cm) high.
£300–350 P(Ba)

A pair of Kelety gilt-bronze and ivory female figures, on an onyx base, c1920, 9¾in (25cm) high.
£2,600–3,000 ART

A Royal Dux figure of a nude female, kneeling on a circular base, 1935, 12½in (32cm) high.
£300–350 BTB

A Canning vase, marked 'Flame', 1930s, 4½in (11.5cm) high.
£25–35 OD

A Belgian Art Deco jug, decorated in orange and green, 1930s, 8in (20.5cm) high.
£25–30 OD

A Royal Falcon ware hand-painted charger, signed 'C. Trent', 1930s, 10½in (27cm) diam.
£150–180 BEV

A Czechoslovakian pottery hand-painted wall plaque, depicting a galleon, c1929, 13in (33cm) high.
£50–60 BKK

A Losol ware footed dish, by Keeling & Co, c1930, 10in (25.5cm) wide.
£80–90 AOT

A Shorter ware jug, decorated in pink with wave pattern, 1930s, 6in (15cm) high.
£25–30 OD

A Czechoslovakian wall mask, 1930s, 8in (20.5cm) high.
£160–180 HEW

A Cope wall mask, c1930, 12in (30.5cm) wide.
£120–150 BEV

A Tuscan ware centre-piece, with a figure bearing a shell and surrounded by flowers, 1920–30, 6½in (16.5cm) high.
£100–125 BEV

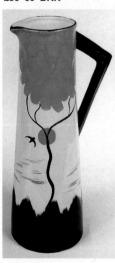

A Kensington Ware hand-painted jug, 1930s, 12¾in (32.5cm) high.
£75–115 BEV

◀ A Goldscheider wall mask, 1930s, 11¼in (28.5cm) high.
£700–780 BEV

A Royal Dux wall mask, 1930s, 8in (20.5cm) high.
£400–450 HEW

A copper and brass crumb tray, decorated with stylized flowers, c1910, 12in (30.5cm) long.
£80–120 ASA

A silver spoon, the bowl decorated with an enamelled scene of Marienbad, c1896, 5in (13cm) long.
£100–150 ALiN

A copper tray, depicting a female head emerging from water and surrounded by fish, bullrushes and starfish, some damage, c1910, 8in (20.5cm) wide.
£80–100 ASA

A WMF dish, decorated with a female figure with trailing hair, design No. 232, c1906, 11in (28cm) wide.
£500–600 AOH

A Weduwe Brantjes, Purmerend ceramic vase, decorated with lappets and stylized flowers, c1900, 8¼in (21cm) high.
£500–600 OO

A ceramic vase, decorated with a girl and flowers, c1910, 14¼in (36cm) high.
£100–120 SER

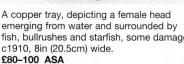

An Amphora pottery vase, each roundel centred with a different cabochon, 1910–15, 8¼in (21cm) high.
£300–350 P(Ba)

A Liberty & Co ceramic vase, c1900, 12in (30.5cm) high.
£350–380 SUC

◀ A dust-pressed tile, decorated with a moulded pattern in a single glaze, c1900, 6in (15cm) square.
£10–15 GR

▶ A tube-lined tile, c1900, 6in (15cm) square.
£25–30 HIG

A German pottery vase, with enamelled flowers in green, yellow and gilt, and 2 gilt drop handles, factory mark 'Royal Bonn', painter's signature 'B. Gusgen', 1880–1910, 19¼in (49cm) high.
£220–260 P(Ba)

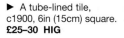

A Clutha glass *solifleur*, designed by Christopher Dresser for Liberty & Co, c1890, 7in (18cm) high.
£100–110 NCA

A pair of Arts & Crafts hammered wall sconces, with repoussé decoration of roses on thorny stems, 17in (43cm) high.
£300–340 RUSK

A copper casket, decorated with an enamelled landscape scene, c1905, 5in (13cm) wide.
£300–350 MoS

A Keswick School of Industrial Arts flared brass vase, c1900, 7½in (19cm) high.
£100–120 MoS

A Newlyn copper tea caddy, by Henry Dyer, with repoussé decoration of nautical scenes, marked 'Longships' and 'H. Dyer', c1920, 6in (15cm) high.
£450–500 MoS

An Amphora pottery vase, with 7 irregular handles resembling stalactites, 1880–1910, 16¾in (42.5cm) high.
£360–420 P(Ba)

A Baron pottery vase, with sgraffito decoration of fish amid aquatic foliage, an applied lizard to the neck, incised 'Baron Barnstaple', 1893–1920, 14in (35.5cm) high.
£280–320 P(Ba)

A Bretby *trompe l'oeil* nut dish, impressed mark, c1890, 9in (23cm) diam.
£100–115 OD

An Elton Ware jug, in the form of a Peruvian pouring vessel, decorated in gilt on a green crackle ware ground, c1902, 6¾in (17cm) high.
£350–400 P(Ba)

► A Fulham Pottery vase, incised with leaves in blue, red and green on a brown ground, heightened with beads in white slip glaze, marked 'Fulham', 1880–1900, 10¼in (26cm) high.
£140–160 P(Ba)

A Linthorpe Pottery vase, designed by Christopher Dresser, with geometric and foliate banding, 1879–89, 10¼in (26cm) high.
£230–260 P(Ba)

A pair of Lauder pottery vases, incised with fish swimming amid aquatic foliage, each vase with 3 loop handles, 1880–1900, 9¾in (25cm) high.
£180–220 P(Ba)

◀ A Bernard Moore flambé vase, marked 'Bernard Moore', 1850–1935, 9½in (24cm) high.
£180–220 P(Ba)

▶ A Bernard Moore bowl, decorated by R. R. Tomlinson, c1910, 7½in (19cm) diam.
£500–600 DSG

A Pilkington's vase, decorated with turquoise curdle-glaze effect, 1910–12, 5½in (14cm) high.
£175–200 PGA

A Watcombe Pottery jug, c1900, 7¼in (18.5cm) high.
£75–90 DSG

A Japanese woodcut print, by Kuniyoshi, depicting Sumino Juheiji Tsugufusa, from *Stories of the True Loyalty of the Faithful Samurai*, published by Ebirin, restored, 1847, 14¾ x 10¼in (36 x 26cm).
£135–155 JaG

A Japanese woodcut print, by Kuniyoshi, depicting Mitono Kotaro fighting three ruffians, from *The Sixty-nine Post Stations of the Kiso Kaido Road*, published by Minatoya, 1852, 14 x 9½in (35.5 x 24cm).
£145–165 JaG

A Japanese woodcut print, depicting a young woman washing her hair, Kunishisa's view of Imagawa bashi above, by Toyokuni III, from *Famous Places of Edo and a Hundred Beautiful Women*, published by Marukyu, 1858, 14¾ x 10¼in (36 x 26cm).
£300–330 JaG

A Japanese gold lacquer five-case *inro*, decorated in *hiramakie*, *takamakie* and inlaid with stained ivory, some inlay restored, 19thC, 3½in (9cm) long.
£600–675 JaG

A Japanese cloisonné vase, 19thC, 6in (15cm) high.
£180–200 ELI

A Japanese four-case *inro*, decorated in *hiramakie*, some pieces missing, 19thC, 3½in (9cm) long.
£600–685 JaG

A Japanese tsuba, decorated with masks, early 19thC, 2¾in (7cm) wide.
£450–500 GRa

Three leather hat boxes, from central China, late 19thC, largest 20in (51cm) high.
£250–300 K

◄ A roundel of Chinese appliqué in Peking knot stitch, late 19thC, 9½in (24cm) diam, mounted and framed.
£100–130 PBr

A blue and white soup plate, from the Nanking cargo, underglaze-decorated with Willow Terrace pattern, c1750, 9in (23cm) diam.
£350–380 RBA

A Provincial Ware blue and white porcelain dish, from the *Diana* cargo, decorated in Starburst pattern, c1816, 11in (28cm) diam.
£175–200 RBA

A Chinese blue and white porcelain jar and cover, decorated with the design of Double Happiness, Tonzhi period, Qing Dynasty, 1862–74, 9½in (24cm) high.
£250–300 GHC

A Japanese Noritake tray, decorated with flowers in blue panels, 1920, 5½in (14cm) wide.
£25–30 DSC

◀ An Islamic bottle, probably Moroccan, 1890, 10in (25.5cm) high.
£30–40 IW

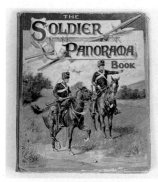

Ernest Nister, *The Soldier Panorama Book*, with pop-up pictures, published by E. P. Dutton & Co, New York, 1890–1900, 10 x 12in (25.5 x 30.5cm).
£80–100 MRW

Baa Baa Black Sheep, illustrated by E. Caldwell, c1890, 4 x 5in (10 x 12.5cm).
£10–15 MRW

Mother Goose, cloth book published by Dean's Rag Books, USA, 1905, 8 x 7in (20.5 x 18cm).
£60–70 J&J

Millie Brown, *Tom, Dick and Harry*, illustrated by Jaques Browne, published by John F. Shaw & Co, c1920, 8 x 10in (20.5 x 25.5cm).
£15–20 MRW

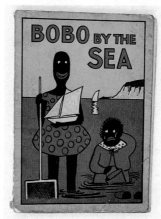

BoBo by the Sea, 1924, 8 x 11in (20.5 x 28cm).
£30–40 MRW

Daily Express Adventure Book, 1934, 10 x 11in (25.5 x 28cm).
£10–12 J&J

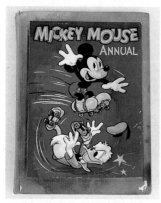

Mickey Mouse Annual, published by Disney, 1949, 8 x 10in (20.5 x 25.5cm).
£40–60 MRW

Songs of our Grandfathers, Re-set in Guinness Time, Dublin, 1936, 9 x 6in (23 x 15cm).
£50–60 MRW

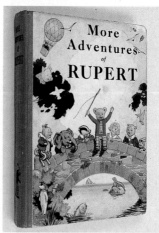

More Adventures of Rupert annual, published by the *Daily Express*, 1937, 10 x 8in (25.5 x 20.5cm).
£200–225 HarC

Enid Blyton, *Noddy Goes To Toyland*, illustrated by Beek, first edition, 1949, 7½ x 6in (19 x 15cm) high.
£10–15 WWY

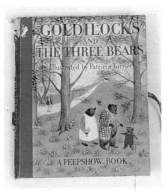

Goldilocks and the Three Bears, a peepshow book, illustrated by Patricia Turner, c1950, 6 x 7in (15 x 18cm).
£80–100 MRW

The Adventures of Tuffy, with pop-up pictures, published by Robert Edwards, c1950, 5 x 8in (12.5 x 20.5cm).
£20–30 MRW

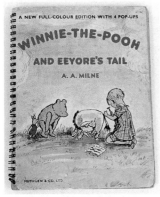

A. A. Milne, *Winnie-the-Pooh and Eeyore's Tail*, with pop-up pictures, published by Methuen & Co, 1950s, 4½in x 7in (11.5 x 18cm).
£30–40 MRW

The Beano Book, 1955, 11 x 8in (28 x 20.5cm).
£35–40 HarC

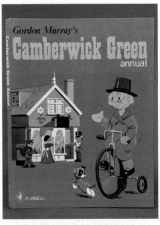

Gordon Murray's *Camberwick Green Annual*, published by Purnell, 1969, 11 x 9in (28 x 23cm).
£4–5 CMF

Top Pop Stars, 1970, 11in (28cm) high.
£4–5 MARK

The Magic Roundabout Goodnight Stories Book, published by Dean, 1972, 9 x 10in (23 x 25.5cm).
£12–14 CMF

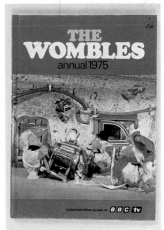

The Wombles Annual 1975, BBC TV authorized edition, 11 x 8in (28 x 20.5cm).
£2–3 HarC

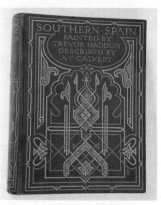

Hoods Poems, with fore-edge painting depicting the Thames at Westminster, published by Edward Moxon, London, 1857, 6½ x 4¼in (16.5 x 11cm).
£120–150 AHa

Pierce Egan, *Life in London*, with 36 hand-coloured plates by I. R. & G. Cruikshank, published by Sherwood, Neely & Sons, and 3 folding pages of piano music, some foxing and marking, 1821, 9½ x 6in (24 x 15cm).
£200–250 AHa

Walter Thurnbury, *Old and New London Illustrated*, 10¼ x 7½in (26 x 19cm).
£70–100 AHa

Philip Norman, *London, Vanished and Vanishing*, with 75 illustrations by the author, published by A. & C. Black, first edition, 1905, 9 x 6¾in (23 x 17cm).
£180–210 PHa

Southern Spain, a book of paintings by Trevor Haddon, described by A. F. Calvert, published by A. & C. Black, first edition, 1908, 9 x 6¾in (23 x 17cm).
£250–275 PHa

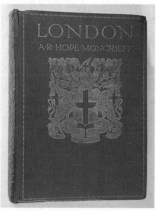

A. R. Hope Moncrieff, *London*, published by A. & C. Black, 1910, 9¾ x 7¼in (25 x 18.5cm).
£65–75 PHa

Mima Nixon, *Royal Palaces & Gardens*, with 60 colour plates and an introductory essay by Dion Clayton Calthrop, published by A. & C. Black, first edition, London, 1916, 8 x 6½in (20.5 x 15cm).
£50–60 PHa

Norman Mailer, *Marilyn*, first edition, 1973, 11 x 10in (28 x 25.5cm).
£45–50 HarC

Robert F. Slatzer, *The Life and Curious Death of Marilyn Monroe*, 1974, 9 x 7in (23 x 18cm).
£12–15 HarC

A William IV tortoiseshell tea
caddy, 7in (18cm) wide.
£700–800 TMi

A tortoiseshell tea caddy, inlaid
with mother-of-pearl flowers
and leaves, on turned ivory feet,
19thC, 7½in (19cm) wide.
£1,000–1,200 DDM

A porcupine and ebony lap desk,
19thC, 15in (38cm) wide.
£500–600 TMi

A Napoleonic prisoner-of-war straw-
work box, in the form of a book,
early 19thC, 8in (20.5cm) wide.
£100–120 TMi

An abalone, mother-of-pearl and
tortoiseshell card case, 1840,
4in (10cm) wide.
£100–110 MB

A Victorian figured-ash toilet box,
1860–80, 12in (30.5cm) wide.
£850–1,000 TMi

An Imperial Russian lacquer box, by
Vichnaichov, 1885, 6in (15cm) wide.
£450–550 SHa

◀ A Continental papier mâché
box, painted with a cavalry officer
on a rearing charger, 19thC,
3½in (9cm) wide.
£220–250 RTO

A papier mâché snuff box, with
hand-painted decoration, 1820,
3½in (9cm) diam.
£100–125 MB

An ivory box, decorated with paper
flowers, 1840, 2in (5cm) diam.
£240–280 CHAP

A Mauchline ware sycamore
watch box, decorated with a view
depicting Herstmonceux Castle,
1880, 4in (10cm) wide.
£40–50 MB

A Murat Jewellery cardboard gift
box, 1950s, 2½in (6.5cm) wide.
£12–15 PC

A salt-glazed gin bottle, 19thC, 11in (28cm) high.
£10–12 IW

A Buckley banded cider bottle, rim restored, c1900, 13in (33cm) high.
£120–140 IW

A Cork Distilleries Co advertising sign, c1905, 12 x 16in (30.5 x 40.5cm).
£60–70 HUX

▶ A Royal Victoria Pottery ashtray, advertising McNish's Special Scotch, c1930, 6in (15cm) wide.
£30–35 HUX

A French St Raphael Quinquina advertising fan, c1900, 15in (38cm) high.
£25–30 HUX

A Bulmer's Woodpecker Cider show-card, 1920–30, 18 x 13in (45.5 x 33cm).
£40–50 MRW

A bottle of John Power & Son Irish Whiskey, 1950s, 12in (30.5cm) high.
£40–50 HUX

A French Richarpailloud Cognac advertising fan, 1920s, 12in (30.5cm) wide.
£12–15 HUX

A French Bénédictine advertising fan, 1920s, 12in (30.5cm) wide.
£12–15 HUX

A Mortlach Highland Malt Scotch Whisky presentation bottle, containing single malt whisky distilled in 1936, with presentation case, 8in (20.5cm) high.
£170–200 P(B)

An engraved glass decanter of Martell Cordon Argent Cognac, with stopper, pre-1949, 7in (17.5cm) high.
£220–250 P(B)

A Guinness tin tray, 1950s,
12½in (32cm) diam.
£40–50 HUX

A Guinness piggy bank, in the form
of a barrel with a pig's face, 1950s,
12in (30.5cm) long.
£100–120 HUX

An Old Smuggler Scotch Whisky
advertising figure, 1950s,
12in (30.5cm) high.
£120–140 HUX

A plastic Babycham Bambi figure,
with 6 Babycham glasses, 1960s,
figure 7½in (19cm) high.
£25–35 MED

A Johnnie Walker advertising
figure, 1950s, 14½in (37cm) high.
£50–60 HUX

A Queen Anne Scotch Whisky tin tray,
c1960, 13½ x 10½in (34.5 x 26.5cm).
£12–14 HUX

A collection of 6 character jugs, Dewar's 'Mr Micawber',
Jim Beam 'Old Mr Turveydrop', Jim Beam 'Town
Crier of Eatanswill', Pickwick Deluxe 'Mr Micawber',
Pickwick John Bull and Jim Beam 'Mr Pickwick &
Sam Weller', 1990s, each 4½in (11.5cm) high, boxed.
£180–220 P(B)

A Glen Moray
Scotch Whisky
tin, 1990s,
11¾in (30cm) high.
£2–3 OD

◄ A set of 3 Wade Royal
Salute 21-year-old Scotch
Whisky miniatures, c1977,
box 9in (23cm) wide.
£25–30 P(B)

A Royal Wedding Ale bottle, 1981,
and a Whitbread Silver Jubilee Ale
bottle, 1977, largest 9in (23cm) high.
£18–20 P(B)

Two Austro-Hungarian buttons, one gilt-metal set with garnets and turquoise, the other silver, 18thC, 1½in (4cm) diam.
£40–60 each TB

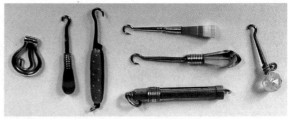

A selection of miniature glove buttonhooks, with silver, agate and enamelled handles, largest 2½in (6.5cm) long.
£15–35 each VB

A transfer-printed porcelain button depicting children skating, mid-19thC, 1¾in (4.5cm) diam.
£100–120 TB

A French enamel button, painted with a portrait of a woman, set in a painted brass border with glass stones, c1880, 1½in (4cm) diam.
£100–120 TB

A Victorian 'jewelled' stamped brass button, with glass centre, c1880, 1¾in (4.5cm) diam.
£30–40 TB

A Japanese Satsuma pottery button, hand-painted and with gold detail, c1890, 1¾in (4.5cm) diam.
£60–80 TB

A French enamelled brass button, c1880, 1¼in (3cm) diam.
£90–110 TB

A silver and enamel button, with Art Nouveau decoration, c1905, 1in (2.5cm) diam.
£25–30 TB

◄ A set of 6 enamelled brass buttons, each depicting a cyclist, ½in (12mm) diam, boxed.
£150–200 BCA

Three Bakelite buttons, each depicting fruit, c1930, largest 1½in (4cm) long.
£15–25 each TB

Six hand-painted moulded glass buttons, 1950s, ½in (12mm) diam.
£8–10 BQ

Two coloured opaque glass buttons, with Art Nouveau floral designs, c1900, ¾in (20mm) wide.
£5–6 each TB

Buttons

A blue and white jasper ware button, with gilded copper mount, probably by Josiah Wedgwood, late 18thC, 1½in (3.5cm) diam.
£250–300 TB

A set of 6 pewter buttons, by A. M. & Cie, Paris, decorated with crossed cannons, mid-19thC, ¾in (19mm) diam.
£16–20 SLL

An ivory button, decorated under glass with a finely-painted miniature of an Indian monument, with a silver border, 1880–90, 1½in (4cm) wide.
£180–220 TB

Prior to the advent of photography, buttons of this type were produced as souvenirs for 19th-century travellers.

A set of 5 mercury gilt buttons, for a gentleman's coat, engraved on reverse 'extra rich triple standard', c1830, 1in (2.5cm) diam.
£165–185 BQ

A porcelain button, decorated with a portrait of a girl, mounted on brass with a paste border, late 19thC, 1¼in (3cm) diam.
£130–160 TB

An Italian micro-mosaic button, depicting a dog, with glass inlay, set in a gilt cup, c1880, ¾in (19mm) diam.
£50–55 TB

A pigmented shell button, engraved with a horse and rider, early 19thC, 2¼in (5.5cm) diam.
£150–180 TB

An ivory button, decorated under glass with the portrait of a woman, mounted on brass with a paste border, mid-19thC, 1in (2.5cm) diam.
£100–125 TB

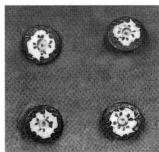

A set of 12 French enamel buttons, decorated with roses, c1880, ¼in (5mm) diam.
£60–70 SLL

◀ A hand-painted porcelain button, in the style of Dresden china, late 19thC, 1¼in (3cm) diam.
£18–20 TB

Victorian picture buttons

Buttons with pictorial designs have been made in many periods, but those known by collectors as 'picture buttons' came into vogue in the second half of the 19th century and usually are metal with stamped designs. The many subjects include animals, children, buildings and landscapes, insects, fruit, flowers, birds, people, theatre, opera and mythology. Many of the images are derived from contemporary illustrations, trade cards and a wide range of literary works, including children's stories and fairy tales.

A stamped brass button, decorated with a whippet's head, with a border of faceted steels, c1870–80, 1½in (4cm) diam.
£80–100 TB

A stamped brass button, decorated with a bird bearing an olive branch, mounted on a velvet background, c1880–90, 1½in (4cm) diam.
£12–15 TB

A Victorian heart-shaped sterling silver button, depicting cherubs lighting a fire, c1890, 1½in (4cm) wide.
£40–45 TB

A stamped metal button, depicting swans entwined with foliage, 1890s, 1½in (4cm) diam.
£6–8 SLL

Three stamped brass and celluloid buttons, of various colours, c1880–90, largest 1¼in (3cm) diam.
£12–14 each TB

Two shell buttons, one decorated with flowers, the other with a faceted metal border, 1890, 1in (2.5cm) diam.
£25–30 EBB

Three Alaskan walrus ivory toggles, with etched and pigmented decoration, c1880–90, largest 1½in (4cm) long.
£28–32 each TB

A stamped brass button, decorated with the image of Canio from the opera *I Pagliacco* by Leoncavallo, c1890–1900, 1½in (4cm) diam.
£25–30 TB

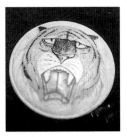

A Japanese ivory button, decorated with the head of a tiger, c1900, 1in (2.5cm) diam.
£40–50 EBB

A Victorian pierced, silver plated metal button, with an Art Nouveau border, c1895–1900, 1½in (4cm) diam.
£25–30 TB

A silver-plated brass button, by A. Bargas, depicting Mona Lisa, signed 'AB', c1900–10, 1¼in (3cm) diam.
£24–28 TB

A porcelain button, decorated with a sailing boat, inscribed 'England, Coalport', early 20thC, 1¾in (4.5cm) diam.
£70–80 TB

A Czechoslovakian painted glass button, in the form of a woman wearing a wide brimmed hat, c1930–35, 1¾in (4.5cm) wide.
£12–15 TB

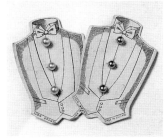

A brass cup button, decorated with a lithograph of a black cat, c1930, 1in (2.5cm) diam.
£20–25 TB

Two sets of Lion Brand shirt buttons, one gold-coloured, the other mother-of-pearl, c1920–30, mounted on original cards.
£20–24 per set DHA

◀ Two Navajo stamped silver buttons, one with a scalloped border, the other set with matrix turquoise, c1910–30, largest 1½in (4cm) diam.
£40–45 each TB

A pair of turned wood buttons, 1920s, 1¾in (4.5cm) diam.
£6–7 BQ

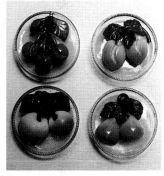

A set of 4 celluloid buttons, designed by Marion Weeber, decorated with fruit applied to a clear plastic background, c1940, 1¼in (3cm) diam.
£12–15 each TB

Two gold-plated buttons, depicting the Trylon and Perisphere at the 1939 World's Fair, on original salesman's sample card, c1939–40, largest 1in (2.5cm) diam.
£5–12 each TB

A Zia hand-painted pottery button, depicting a road-runner, c1940, 1½in (4cm) diam.
£28–32 TB

A moulded plastic button, in the form of a high-fidelity record, c1950, 1in (2.5cm) diam.
£2–3 TB

Cameras

An Agfa Karat camera, with f3.5 Solinar lens, c1938, 4½in (11.5cm) wide.
£25–30 VCL

An Asahi Pentax Spotmatic camera, with an SMC Takumar f2 55mm lens, c1964, 5½in (14cm) wide.
£80–90 VCL

A Canon FTb QL camera, with an f1.4 50mm lens, c1970.
£35–40 VCL

◄ An Erac Mercury I Bakelite Supercamera, in original box with instructions, c1920–30, 4in (10cm) long.
£80–100 BLH

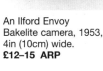

A Goerz stereo detective camera, in original leather case, c1890, 6in (15cm) wide.
£1,600–2,000 TOM

An Ilford Envoy Bakelite camera, 1953, 4in (10cm) wide.
£12–15 ARP

A Mamiya C3 twin-lens reflex camera, 1963.
£60–70 VCL

A Le Coultre Compass miniature 35mm camera, with f3.5 lens, 1938, 2¾in (7cm) high.
£600–700 VCL

► A Nikon FA camera body, c1983, 6in (15cm) wide.
£160–200 VCL

An Olympus 35RC camera, with f2.8 lens, c1972, 4¼in (11cm) wide.
£50–60 VCL

A Praktisix II camera, with Zeiss Jena S f2.8 180mm lens, c1957–62, 6½in (16.5cm) wide.
£400–450 CaH

A Pentax ME Super camera, with an SMC f1.7 50mm lens, c1980, 5¼in (13.5cm) wide.
£80–100 VCL

A Shew & Co Feather Weight mahogany and aluminium field camera, with Dallmayer telephoto lens, complete with dark slides in original case, c1880, case 11in (28cm) wide.
£500–600 TOM

A Voigtländer Vito CL camera, with Color-Skopar f2.8 50mm lens, c1962, 5in (12.5cm) wide.
£50–60 CaH

A Zeiss Ikon 35 camera, with Schneider-Kreuznach Xenar f2.8 45mm lens, 1951, 4¾in (12cm) wide.
£35–40 VCL

An Instanto mahogany and brass tailboard camera, by E. & T. Underwood, Birmingham, complete with dark slides in case, c1890, case 15in (38cm) wide.
£120–150 TOM

▶ A Zeiss Contessa camera, c1954, 6in (15cm) wide.
£40–50 VCL

Ceramics

ANIMALS

A Meissen model of a scruffy dog sitting on top of its kennel, base marked with crossed swords, minor restoration to ears and chain, c1740, 4¼in (11cm) high.
£900–1,000 WW

A creamware model of a cow and milkmaid, the cow mottled in brown on a green-washed rectangular base, c1780, 5¾in (14.5cm) high.
£400–450 CGC

A bisque jar, in the form of a flesh-coloured seated Bonzo, removable head and open mouth for use as a string holder, probably German, 1920s, 5½in (14cm) high.
£150–180 Bon(C)

A Royal Doulton model of a terrier, 1935, 3in (7.5cm) high.
£40–50 PAC

A porcelain whistle, in the form of a dog's head, c1820, 2in (5cm) long.
£140–160 HUM

A ceramic fish, by Fontinelle, c1930s.
£100–120 BTB

A pair of porcelain spill vases, in the form of Mickey and Minnie Mouse, decorated in coloured enamels, marked 'Genuine Walt Disney Copyright, Foreign, Reg. No. 789572' and '789573', 1930s, 4½in (11.5cm) high.
£280–320 F&C

◄ A Royal Doulton model of a yawning dog, 1945, 4in (10cm) high.
£50–60 PAC

A model of a grebe, by Faust Lang, with under-glaze decoration, restored, 1939, 9¾in (25cm) high.
£700–800 PAC

A Russian pottery model of a standard poodle, c1940s, 6in (15cm) high.
£40–50 MRW

► Two ceramic cartoon cats and a mouse, all with movable heads, 1950s.
£7–8 each MRW

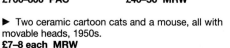

A set of 4 Royal Doulton models of spaniels, each holding a pheasant in its mouth, 1950, largest 6in (15cm) high.
£175–195 PAC

A Szeiler model of a donkey, 1980s, 6in (15cm) high.
£35–40 HarC

A McCoy cookie jar, in the form of a dog, 1962, 10in (25.5cm) high.
£80–90 EKK

A Coalport model of Paddington Bear eating an apple, 1976, 4in (10cm) high.
£40–50 WWY

Two Cat Pottery models of a bull-terrier and puppy, 1990s, largest 15in (38cm) high.
Bull-terrier £80–90   Puppy £25–30 CP

A Royal Doulton model of Mr Toadflax, from *Brambly Hedge* series, No. DBH10, first version, 1984–97, 3¼in (8.5cm) high.
£750–850 PAC

A Border Fine Arts model of Jemima Puddleduck, 1993, 4in (10cm) high.
£50–60 WWY

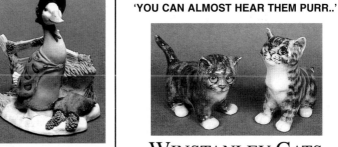

► A Winstanley model of a tabby cat, by Cat Pottery, marked on base '7 I. Winstanley England', 1990s, 13½in (34.5cm) high.
£55–65 CP

BELLEEK

A Belleek pink-tinted Tridacna kettle, restored, First Period, 1863–90, 7½in (19cm) wide.
£380–430 DeA

A Belleek Nautilus creamer, in the form of a shell and coral, 1863–90, 4in (10cm) high.
£350–400 MLa

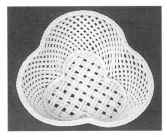

A Belleek flat-rod two-strand bowl, c1955, 5½in (14cm) wide.
£200–250 MLa

A Belleek Shamrock coffee, Third Green Period, 1965–81, pot 7in (18cm) high.
£350–400 RUSK

A Belleek Florence jug, First Period, 1863–90, 5¼in (13.5cm) high.
£750–800 DeA

A Belleek Mask bowl and cover, Third Period, 1926–46, 6½in (16.5cm) wide.
£750–800 DeA

A Belleek butter dish, in the form of a cottage, Second Green Period, 1955–65, 6½in (16.5cm) wide.
£200–250 DeA

A Belleek Violet menu holder, First Period, 1863–90, 5¼in (13.5cm) wide.
£550–600 DeA

A pair of Belleek Celtic candlesticks, in black and gilt, Third Period, 1926–46, 5in (12.5cm) high.
£260–290 MLa

A Belleek Shamrock sugar bowl, Second Green Period, 1955–65, 4in (10cm) diam.
£40–45 MLa

◄ A Belleek paperweight, in the form of a boxer dog on a cushion, Third Green Period, 1965–81, 3½in (9cm) high.
£110–130 MLa

BESWICK

The Beswick family became ceramic manufacturers almost by accident. As Staffordshire coal-mining magnates, in 1840 they purchased a plot of land in Tunstall and built a pot bank, which they leased to local pottery firms on the understanding that they would supply the necessary coal from the family mine. In 1894, James Wright Beswick and his brother, Robert, decided to set up their own ceramics business, and the Beswick pottery was born. Early wares ranged from majolica, through flowerpots, to Staffordshire figures, and the business expanded rapidly.

In 1898, the Beswicks purchased the Gold Street Works in Longton, where the factory remains to this day. At the time, it was described as a 'very modern and fitted-up factory', the Beswicks investing in new kilns and the latest production techniques. Pricing was extremely competitive and production flourished.

During 1911–19, despite the First World War, the company quadrupled its use of clay. The inter-war years saw the development of ornamental and functional tableware designs, such as Lettuce ware, and new ranges of figures, including children, wall masks and Dickens ware. In 1939, modeller Arthur Greddington designed the first of the Beswick horse models, and animals soon became one of the company's most important lines.

After the Second World War, Lucy, wife of managing director Ewart Beswick, suggested the production of Beatrix Potter figures. Designed by Greddington and launched in 1948 with Jemima Puddleduck, the Beatrix Potter models proved very successful, inspiring a host of subsequent figures drawn from children's books and films. Ewart and Lucy had no children and when Ewart retired in 1969, Royal Doulton took over Beswick.

A Beswick jug, designed by Symcox, shape No. 348, decorated with a matt orange glaze with blue splashes, 1934, 8in (20.5cm) high.
£40–45 DEC

A Beswick hand-painted vase, designed by Symcox, shape No. 187, decorated with yellow, orange and brown bands, 1934–40, 8¼in (21cm) high.
£40–50 DEC

Cross Reference
See Art Deco Section

▶ A Beswick wall mask, in the form of a girl's head, 1935, 8in (20.5cm) high.
£290–330 HEW

A Beswick three-piece cottage ware tea set, c1940.
£110–130 AOT

A Beswick wall mask, in the form of a dog's head wearing a blue bow-tie, c1930s, 8in (20.5cm) high.
£45–50 HEW

A Beswick vase, designed by Symcox, decorated in pale blue and lemon, 1939, 8¾in (22cm) high.
£40–50 OD

▶ A Beswick model of a cantering Shire horse, No. 975, decorated in dappled grey, 1950, 8in (20.5cm) high.
£600–700 PAC

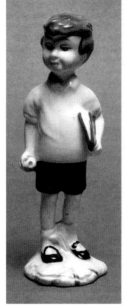

A Beswick model of Rupert the Bear, in red and yellow, entitled 'Snowballing', 2779, 1980s, 4¼in (11cm) high.
£320–360 PAC

A Beswick model of a red fox, 1980s, 3in (7.5cm) high.
£70–80 HarC

A Beswick Beatrix Potter model of Susan, with brown shawl, brown backstamp, discontinued 1989, 4½in (11.5cm) high.
£150–180 MED

A Beswick model of Christopher Robin, in yellow and blue, 1980s, 4¾in (12cm) high.
£120–140 WWY

▶ A Beswick model of a red Friesian calf, made for Collectors Club, 1995, 4in (10cm) wide.
£450–500 PAC

A Beswick Beatrix Potter model of Old Mr Pricklepin, in brown, brown backstamp, discontinued 1989, 2½in (6.5cm) high.
£60–70 MED

A Beswick Beatrix Potter model of Thomasina Tittlemouse, in brown, brown backstamp, discontinued 1989, 3¼in (8.5cm) high.
£70–80 MED

BING & GRØNDAHL

A Bing & Grøndahl dish, moulded with pink flowers and white foliage, 1905, 7in (18cm) diam.
£200–250 FrG

A Bing & Grøndahl model of a tiger and cub, c1915, 11in (28cm) wide.
£300–350 GSW

A Bing & Grøndahl dish, moulded with a hermit crab, in blue and brown 1910, 7½in (19cm) wide.
£130–150 FrG

A Bing & Grøndahl model of a goat, c1948, 6in (15cm) wide.
£90–100 GSW

A Bing & Grøndahl model of a salmon trout, in grey, c1948, 9in (23cm) wide.
£100–125 GSW

A Bing & Grøndahl model of a green budgerigar, c1952, 6in (15cm) wide.
£85–95 GSW

A Bing & Grøndahl figure of a girl with a goose, 1950, 9½in (24cm) high.
£80–90 FrG

A Bing & Grøndahl model of a peacock, c1952, 16in (40.5cm) wide.
£450–500 GSW

A Bing & Grøndahl model of a grey mouse, c1952, 2in (5cm) high.
£55–65 GSW

A Bing & Grøndahl figure of a shepherdess, in blue, c1954, 11in (30cm) high.
£340–380 GSW

A Bing & Grøndahl figure of a girl tennis player, c1960, 8in (20.5cm) high.
£120–140 GSW

A Bing & Grøndahl figure of a girl with a cat, c1952, 7in (18cm) high.
£120–140 GSW

BLUE & WHITE

A Dutch blue and white child's plate, chips to rim, 1760, 6½in (16.5cm) diam.
£70–80 IW

A John & Richard Riley blue and white platter, transfer-printed with Eastern Street Scene pattern, c1815, 21in (53.5cm) wide.
£450–500 GN

A blue and white loving cup, decorated with scenes showing Dick Whittington and his cat, c1820, 12in (30.5cm) high.
£650–750 GN

A blue and white plate, decorated with the Mausoleum of Sultan Purveiz, Near Allahabad pattern, probably by The Herculaneum Pottery of Liverpool, early 19thC, 9¾in (25cm) diam.
£80–90 DDM

A Spode blue and white platter, decorated with Italian Well and Tree pattern, c1815, 18½in (47cm) wide.
£450–550 GN

A Ridgway blue and white transfer-printed plate, from the Angus Seats series, 1820, 9½in (24cm) diam.
£70–80 OD

◄ A Jones blue and white plate, transfer-printed with Landing of William of Orange pattern, from the British History series, c1825, 9in (23cm) diam.
£150–180 GN

A Spode blue and white plate, decorated with Tiber pattern, early 19thC, 9¾in (25cm) diam.
£50–60 DDM

A Minton blue and white platter, decorated with Bamboo and Vase pattern, c1820, 20½in (52cm) wide.
£350–400 GN

A John & Richard Riley blue and white platter, transfer-printed with Europa and the Bull pattern, c1820, 14½in (37cm) wide.
£400–450 GN

A Clews blue and white vase, decorated with Coronation pattern, 1820, 7in (18cm) high.
£350–400 GN

A blue and white platter, decorated with Stirling Castle pattern, from the Antique Scenery series, 1825, 14in (35.5cm) wide.
£300–350 GN

A blue and white mug, decorated with a boy shearing a sheep, possibly with Inverary Castle in the background, c1830, 3½in (9cm) high.
£180–200 SCO

A blue and white platter, decorated with Etruscan and Greek Vase pattern, 1830, 18in (45.5cm) wide.
£350–400 GN

A Minton blue and white invalid feeder, decorated with Moss Rose pattern, 1840, 6in (15cm) wide.
£150–175 GN

A Spode blue and white butter tub, decorated with Filigree pattern, 1825, 4in (10cm) high.
£250–300 GN

A Minton blue and white sponge or pot-pourri pot, decorated with Sheet Floral pattern, 1830, 8in (20.5cm) diam.
£350–400 GN

A Davenport blue and white jug, decorated with flowers, marked, 1840, 7½in (19cm) high.
£220–250 AAN

A blue and white plate, transfer-printed with a floral pattern, 1840, 9¾in (25cm) diam.
£35–40 OD

An N. Neale blue and white plate, decorated with Leighton Buzzard Cross pattern, 1830, 8in (20.5cm) diam.
£100–120 GN

A Read blue and white child's chamber pot, decorated with Boy Musician pattern, 1830, 6in (15cm) diam.
£250–300 GN

A blue and white bourdaloue, decorated with Sicilian pattern, attributed to Pountney & Allies, Bristol Pottery, 1835, 9in (23cm) wide.
£300–350 GN

A Meakin flow-blue jug and basin set, with toothbrush holder, c1890, jug 12in (30.5cm) high.
£260–300 AOT

Blue & White • CERAMICS 93

BRANNAM

A Brannam pottery tyg, in orange, possibly designed by Horace Elliot, early 20thC, 5in (12.5cm) high.
£40–45 IW

A Brannam pottery jug, in the form of a puffin, decorated with a blue glaze, 1900–03, 7¾in (19.5cm) high.
£160–180 P(Ba)

A pair of Brannam pottery vases, each with 3 loop handles, decorated with sgraffito fish, enclosed by cream-coloured slip on a blue ground enhanced with green, dated '1899', 10¼in (26cm) high.
£200–250 P(Ba)

A Brannam pottery vase, in the form of a cormorant, decorated with green, brown and cream feathering on a blue ground, dated '1903', 14½in (37cm) high.
£350–400 P(Ba)

LOCATE THE SOURCE
The source of each illustration in Miller's can be found by checking the code letters below each caption with the Key to Illustrations, pages 476–484.

A Brannam pottery Barum ware earthenware charger, sgraffito-decorated with a bird on a blue ground, c1937, 12in (30.5cm) diam.
£180–200 BKK

BURLEIGH WARE

Burleigh Ware was the trade name given to pottery manufactured by the Staffordshire firm of Burgess & Leigh (established 1851). In the 1930s, the company produced a wide range of novelty ware and domestic items. Jugs with unusually shaped handles and moulded bodies were a popular line. These were modelled in the form of animals, birds and figures. Since all pieces were hand-painted by individual decorators, quality and, therefore, value can vary. Sporting themes are very collectable today, and the golf jug (illustrated on page 148) is a sought-after piece, the more so because of the golfer's checked plus-fours, which make it more desirable than a similar version with the figure in plain trousers.

A Burleigh Ware sandwich set, painted in colours, 1930s, server 12½in (32cm) wide.
£120–150 BEV

A Burleigh Ware basket, decorated in green with blue budgerigars, 1930s, 10in (25.5cm) wide.
£160–200 ERC

A Burleigh Ware egg set, pattern No. 4807, decorated with Meadowland pattern, 1930s, tray 8in (20.5cm) wide.
£80–100 ERC

A Burleigh Ware sauce tureen and stand, decorated with Daffodil pattern, 1930s, 4in (10cm) diam.
£60–70 ERC

◄ A Burleigh Ware Bennett vase, with tube-lined decoration depicting a tree in beige and blue, signed by Harold Bennett, 1930s, 9¼in (23.5cm) high.
£350–400 ERC

A Burleigh Ware hand-painted jug, in the form of a bullfinch, 1930s, 5in (12.5cm) high.
£145–165 BEV

A Burleigh Ware jug, with handle in the form of a squirrel, in yellow, 1931, 8in (20.5cm) high.
£120–150 ERC

The squirrel jug was the first of the series of yellow Burleigh jugs to be modelled.

A Burleigh Ware jug, with handle in the form of a highwayman, in green, 1933, 8in (20.5cm) high.
£350–400 ERC

Four Burleigh Ware Dickens character jugs, modelled as Mr Micawber, Scrooge, Oliver Twist and Nicholas Nickleby, 1940s, 4in (10cm) high.
£50–60 each ERC

A Burleigh Ware vase, decorated with a red and black fern leaf pattern, 1950s, 4¼in (11cm) high.
£25–30 AOS

A Burleigh Ware character jug, modelled as Charles Dickens, 1940s, 6in (15cm) high.
£50–60 BUR

► A Burleigh Ware Nell Gwyn jug, in brown with pink, red, green and yellow, 1950s, 9in (23cm) high.
£160–180 BUR

BURMANTOFTS

A Burmantofts Pottery jug, decorated with a yellow glaze, 1881–83, 10in (25.5cm) high.
£210–240 NCA

> Miller's is a price GUIDE not a price LIST

A Burmantofts Pottery vase, decorated with a red glaze, c1885, 7¾in (19.5cm) high.
£300–330 NCA

A Burmantofts Pottery jardinière, shape No. 1338, impressed with stylized flowerheads on a scale-pattern ground, within scroll and foliate banding under a turquoise glaze, impressed marks, c1900, 14¾in (37.5cm) wide.
£200–250 AH

▶ A Burmantofts Pottery vase, decorated with a red glaze, factory marks, 1881–1904, 5½in (14cm) high.
£75–90 P(Ba)

CANDLE EXTINGUISHERS

A Royal Worcester Kerr & Binns candle extinguisher, in the form of a praying monk, in blush, c1852, 4in (10cm) high.
£575–650 CAW

A Royal Worcester candle extinguisher, in the form of a Japanese woman, in blush pink, c1899, 3in (7.5cm) high.
£340–380 CAW

A Hammersley candle extinguisher, decorated with pink, yellow and mauve flowers, marked, 1970s, 3in (7.5cm) high.
£85–95 TH

A candle extinguisher, in the form of Mr Caudle, in yellow, 1906, 3½in (9cm) high.
£230–260 CAW

◀ Two Royal Worcester candle extinguishers, entitled 'Budge' and 'Toddie', in pink, blue and grey, reproduced from old factory moulds, 1976–86, tallest 4in (10cm) high.
£90–110 each TH

Mr Caudle featured in *Mrs Caudle's Curtain Lectures* by Douglas Jerrold, published by *Punch* magazine in 1846. The luckless Job Caudle had to suffer the lectures of his nagging wife after they had gone to bed and the curtains were drawn, giving rise to the Victorian expression 'Caudle lecture'.

CARLTON WARE

In recent times, Carlton Ware has grown in popularity. At the top end of the market auction prices continue to rise, and in 1999 Christie's sold a 1930s Rainbow Fan vase for £6,500, a world record for a piece of Carlton Ware. The most collectable products are the finely enamelled, gilded lustreware pottery produced during the Art Deco period, which today can fetch three- and four-figure sums.

'For many years, it was very undervalued,' says Keith Martin from Carlton Ware Collectors International, 'but now people are really beginning to recognize the superb quality of this 20th-century art pottery.' Martin has seen membership of the collectors' club rise from 150 to over 1,000 in just five years, and for him the great appeal of Carlton Ware is the sheer variety of works produced by manufacturers Wiltshaw & Robinson (1890–1989). He continues, 'In their 99-year history, they created 8,000 patterns and 600

shapes. It just shows how a small pottery with only between 150 and 250 workers could compete with the big factories, thanks to a good sales team, investment in the latest technology and an imaginative design policy.'

Carlton Ware concentrated on what was known as the 'fancies' market, specializing in decorative and novelty pieces rather than tableware. Although the early enamelled ware is expensive, other lines are still very affordable. Collectors often start off with the floral embossed ware from the 1930s, a favourite with many enthusiasts.

Martin's tips for the future include contemporary-style, space-influenced designs from the 1950s and 1960s, and novelty designs from the 1970s and 1980s, including the Walking Ware and Spitting Image satirical ceramics. 'You've got to buy what you like, and you can't let your wallet rule your heart,' he concludes, 'but I think the values of post-World War II Carlton Ware are set to rise.'

A Carlton Ware vase, decorated with orange flowers on a blush background, 1890–1918, 7½in (19cm) high.
£200–250 BEV

▶ A Carlton Ware vase, decorated with Art Deco-style Egyptian Fan pattern on a blue ground, with gilt rim, c1920, 5½in (14cm) high.
£700–800 AOT

A Carlton Ware vase, decorated with Chinaland pattern, in green, orange, blue and yellow, 1920–25, 12in (30.5cm) high.
£1,000–1,200 BEV

A Carlton Ware boat, decorated with matt and lustre blue, pink and yellow flowers on a dark green ground, with gilt handles and feet, 1920s, 12½in (32cm) high.
£450–500 BEV

A Carlton Ware powder bowl, decorated with green, amber and yellow chinoiserie on a deep blue background, with gilt handle, 1920–30, 6in (15cm) diam.
£160–200 ChA

A Carlton Ware vase, decorated with an exotic bird on a dark blue ground, with gilt rim and base, 1920–30, 6½in (16.5cm) high.
£225–275 BEV

A Carlton Ware Fairyland lustre bowl, decorated with an orange ground, 1920–30, 10½in (26.5cm) diam.
£300–350 BEV

A Carlton Ware dish, decorated with a red squirrel on a green ground, with gilt rim and handles, 1920–30, 5in (12.5cm) diam.
£200–250 BEV

A Carlton Ware ginger jar, decorated with chinoiserie-style flowers and bird of paradise on a deep blush and dark brown ground, 1920–30, 9in (23cm) high.
£225–275 ChA

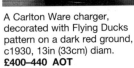

A Carlton Ware bridge set, decorated with playing card patterns, 1930s, largest 5in (12.5cm) wide.
£160–200 BEV

A Carlton Ware charger, decorated with Flying Ducks pattern on a dark red ground, c1930, 13in (33cm) diam.
£400–440 AOT

A Carlton Ware dish, decorated with stylized yellow and mauve flowers on a pale green ground, c1930, 8in (20.5cm) diam.
£140–160 AOT

A Carlton Ware tea set for 2 persons, decorated with Foxglove pattern on a pale green ground, c1940.
£280–320 AOT

A Carlton Ware napkin ring, in the form of a sailor, in blue, 1930s, 4½in (11.5cm) high.
£75–85 ChA

A Carlton Ware jam spoon, butter knife and dish set, decorated with Pink Daisy pattern, in original box, c1940, dish 5in (12.5cm) wide.
£150–170 AOT

Double boxed sets of this type are quite rare.

A Carlton Ware salt and pepper set, 1960s, 5in (12.5cm) high.
£40–45 ZOOM

A Carlton Ware jug, decorated with Grape pattern on a pale cream ground, c1940, 6in (15cm) high.
£210–240 AOT

A Carlton Ware cruet set, in red, 1960s, 6½in (16.5cm) diam.
£50–60 ZOOM

A Carlton Ware tea set for 2 persons, decorated with Primula pattern on a pale green ground, c1940.
£320–360 AOT

A Carlton Ware jam knife and dish set, decorated with Magnolia pattern, in original box, c1960, 4in (10cm) wide.
£70–80 AOT

A Carlton Ware money box, decorated with Noah's Ark pattern in mustard yellow and orange, 1970s, 7in (18cm) wide.
£35–40 AOS

► A Carlton Ware Cockatoo mug, the beak in orange, late 1980s, 3¼in (8.5cm) high.
£12–15 StC

CHINTZ WARE

A Royal Winton teapot, decorated with Welbeck pattern, 1930, 7in (18cm) high.
£550–600 BEV

A Royal Winton cup, saucer and tea plate, decorated with Hazel pattern, c1940, saucer 4½in (11.5cm) diam.
£100–120 AOT

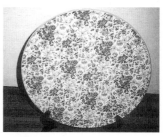

A Barker Bros cake plate, decorated with all-over pink and mauve floral pattern, c1940, 11in (28cm) diam.
£80–90 AOT

A Royal Winton tea set, decorated with Victorian Rose pattern, c1930–40s.
£550–650 RBB

A Royal Winton comport, decorated with Hazel pattern, c1940, 5½in (14cm) diam.
£150–170 AOT

A Royal Winton basket, decorated with all-over multi-coloured floral pattern, 1940s, 8in (20.5cm) diam.
£450–500 BEV

CLARICE CLIFF

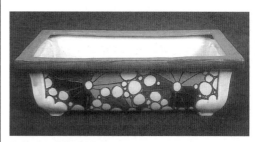

A Clarice Cliff plant trough, decorated with Broth pattern in orange, green and blue, c1930, 11in (28cm) wide.
£850–950 BEV

◀ A Clarice Cliff plate, decorated with Blue Autumn pattern, 1930, 7in (18cm) diam.
£300–330 HEW

A Clarice Cliff Bon Jour shape tea set for 2, banded in green and browns, 1933, teapot 5in (12.5cm) high.
£400–450 HEW

◀ A Clarice Cliff plaque, decorated with moulded floral pattern in yellow, brown, orange and black, 1935, 13in (33cm) diam.
£400–500 HEW

A Clarice Cliff charger, decorated with Coral Firs pattern, 1933, 13in (33cm) diam.
£1,800–2,000 HEW

A Clarice Cliff Tankard shape coffee set, decorated with Blue Chintz pattern, marked 'Fantasque' and 'Bizarre' to base, 1930s.
£2,000–2,200 P(Ba)

A Clarice Cliff basket, decorated with Celtic Harvest pattern of moulded wheatsheaves, fruit and flowers, 1939, 13in (33cm) wide.
£200–250 HEW

◀ A Clarice Cliff Isis jug, decorated with Aurea pattern, 1934, 10in (25.5cm) high.
£600–700 HEW

A Clarice Cliff corn-on-the-cob dish, stamped 'Clarice Cliff, Newport Pottery', late 1930s, 9¾in (25cm) wide.
£25–30 DEC

▶ A Clarice Cliff Newport ewer, decorated with Celtic Harvest pattern of moulded wheatsheaves, green rubber stamp mark, c1939, 10in (25.5cm) high.
£170–200 GAK

CROWN DEVON

Crown Devon was produced by the Stoke-on-Trent firm of S. Fielding & Co (1873–1982). The majority of pieces shown here date from the 1920s and 1930s, when the company became well-known for moulded tableware, novelty designs and decorative items.

Similar in style to Carlton Ware, the designs range from elaborate, hand-gilded and enamelled lustreware – much sought-after by collectors today – to the more affordable moulded earthenware and salad ware that was targeted at the middle market and manufactured in large quantities.

A Crown Devon lustre dish, decorated with gilt and enamel flowers on a cobalt blue ground, c1930, 10in (25.5cm) wide.
£150–180 AOT

A Crown Devon cress dish and plate, decorated with flowers on a pale blush ground, 1930s, 9in (23cm) diam.
£40–50 HEI

A Crown Devon jug, decorated with green and brown stylized leaves, 1930s, 5in (12.5cm) high.
£30–35 OD

A Crown Devon charger, decorated with a hand-painted and gilded galleon on an azure ground, c1930, 12in (30.5cm) diam.
£260–320 AOT

A Crown Devon footed bowl, decorated with horses and trees on a red ground, 1930s, 4½in (11.5cm) high.
£60–70 ChA

A Crown Devon wall plaque, in the form of a Swiss walker, 1930s, 9½in (24cm) high.
£225–275 BEV

A Crown Devon wall plaque, in the form of a Russian girl, 1930s, 10in (25.5cm) high.
£225–275 BEV

A Crown Devon musical cigarette box, in brown, plays *Daddy Wouldn't Buy Me A Bow Wow*, c1935, 9in (23cm) high.
£180–220 AOT

A Crown Devon butter knife and dish, decorated with embossed Fuchsia pattern, in original box, c1940, 4in (10cm) wide.
£50–60 AOT

A Crown Devon money box in white with black line, 1970s, 4in (10cm) wide.
£16–20 BTB

CROWN DUCAL

A Crown Ducal bowl, decorated with Ivory Chintz pattern, c1926, 8in (20.5cm) diam.
£200–240 AOT

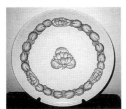

A Crown Ducal charger, tube-lined with pink water lilies, attributed to Charlotte Rhead, c1935, 17in (43cm) diam.
£250–300 AOT

A Crown Ducal vase, decorated with orange flowers, 1930, 16in (40.5cm) high.
£25–30 CSA

A Crown Ducal shouldered vase, decorated with yellow, orange and blue running glazes, 1920–30, 8½in (21.5cm) high.
£50–60 DEC

► A Crown Ducal vase, decorated with blue and pink leaf pattern, signed 'Charlotte Rhead', c1940, 7½in (19cm) high.
£500–600 AOT

A Crown Ducal vase, decorated with Gloria Lustre pattern in the style of Susie Cooper, c1930, 6in (15cm) high.
£100–120 AOT

CUPS, SAUCERS & MUGS

A Worcester mug, transfer-printed in black with the King of Prussia, marked 'R H Worcester' with anchor, c1757, 3½in (8.5cm) high.
£250–300 CGC

A New Hall tea bowl and saucer, decorated with pink flowers and gilded foliage, c1800, saucer 5¼in (13.5cm) diam.
£55–65 SER

◄ A Whitehaven Pottery earthenware loving cup, transfer-printed with green and puce foliate and wheatsheaf decoration, c1820, 4¼in (11cm) high.
£160–180 Mit

◀ A porcelain trio, enamelled in iron-red and blue, c1810, saucer 5¼in (13.5cm) diam.
£110–130 OD

A two-handled mug, transfer-printed and overpainted in enamels with various animals, the interior with three yellow frogs, c1840, 5in (13cm) high.
£160–180 CGC

An Alcock porcelain trio, decorated in gold and green, c1850, saucer 6in (15cm) diam.
£16–20 OD

A Victorian teacup and plate, enamelled in iron-red and blue, 8in (20.5cm) wide.
£40–45 TAC

An earthenware mug, sponge-decorated in brown, pink and green, c1860, 4½in (11.5cm) high.
£90–110 Byl

A Rockingham mug, decorated with baskets of flowers within gilded cartouches on a puce ground, marked, 19thC, 4½in (11.5cm) high.
£100–120 GAK

A Sèvres cup and saucer, with pierced and gilt decoration, c1887, saucer 4¾in (12cm) diam.
£350–400 JE

A Bovey Tracey Pottery mug, banded in blue and black, impressed 'J' at base of handle, c1880, 3½in (9cm) high.
£45–55 IW

The 'J' at the base of the handle of this mug is a feature of the Bovey Tracey Pottery in Devonshire, manufacturers of Prattware, Mocha ware and earthenware.

A Susie Cooper moustache cup and saucer, the cup decorated in black with 2 moustached men and the saucer with shaving implements, 1930s, saucer 6in (15.5cm) diam.
£320–360 P(Ba)

A Devonmoor tankard, by Art Pottery, Newton Abbot, Devon, decorated in mottled green, 1930s, 4¾in (12cm) high.
£16–20 DEC

DENBY

A Denby Orient Ware brown vase, marked, 1925–30, 5in (13cm) high.
£40–50 OD

A Denby brown tobacco jar, in the form of a bale, c1925–30, 5in (13cm) high.
£55–65 KES

A Denby chamber pot, decorated with electric-blue glaze, c1930, 8½in (21cm) diam.
£180–200 KES

▶ A Denby Regent green pastel-coloured lamp base, designed by Gilbert, relief-moulded with wild geese, c1930s, 7in (18cm) high.
£180–200 KES

A Denby jug, designed by Glyn Colledge, decorated in green and grey, 1950s, 12in (30.5cm) high.
£50–60 OD

A Denby Regent cream and blue model of a penguin, designed by Gilbert, early 1930s, 9½in (24cm) high.
£350–400 KES

▶ A Denby red stoneware pipe rest, c1960, 4¼in (11cm) high.
£12–15 KES

A Denby Orient Ware tobacco jar and a pair of candlesticks, decorated in blue and bronze colours, c1930s, candlesticks 6in (15cm) high.
Tobacco jar £145–165 Candlesticks £180–200 KES

A pair of Derby pointer and setter dogs, on green bases, c1800, 5½in (14cm) long.
£2,000–2,500 JO

A Derby figure of a baby lying on a brown rug, marked 'Derby' with crown in red, c1835, 2in (5cm) long.
£335–375 DMa

A Derby group, entitled 'Time clipping the wings of Love', on a multi-coloured base, repaired, patch marks, c1770, 8½in (21.5cm) high.
£450–500 DMa

A Derby figure of Dr Syntax on horseback, decorated with coloured enamels and gilt, marked, late 19thC, 7½in (19cm) high.
£375–425 WW

A Royal Crown Derby blue and gilt ramekin dish and stand, made for Tiffany & Co, New York, c1908, saucer 4¾in (12cm) diam.
£1,100–1,300 JE

A Royal Crown Derby dish, decorated with Olde Avebury pattern, 1930s, 3½in (9cm) wide.
£18–22 PSA

A Royal Crown Derby two-handled vase, decorated with gilt flowers and foliage on a dark blue ground, the domed cover moulded with gilt floral swags and surmounted by a floral knop, early 20thC, 11½in (28.6cm) high.
£600–700 TMA

A Royal Crown Derby iron-red, blue and gilt bowl, pattern No. 1128, 1930s, 5½in (14cm) diam.
£100–120 DKH

Miller's is a price GUIDE not a price LIST

► A Royal Crown Derby 19-piece iron-red, blue and gilt tea service, pattern No. 2451, impressed and printed marks, 1917.
£500–600 DDM

DOULTON

A Doulton Lambeth jug, by Frank Butler, decorated in brown and dark green, c1879, 16½in (42cm) high.
£600–700 JE

A set of Doulton Lambeth egg cups, decorated in brown and dark green, on a stand by Mappin & Webb, c1880, 8in (20.5cm) high.
£800–900 JE

A Doulton Lambeth oil lamp, by Edith Lupton, decorated in brown and dark green, c1882, 12in (30.5cm) high.
£800–900 JE

A Doulton Carrara vase, by Edith Rogers, decorated in rose, green, gold and blue on a white ground, c1882, 8½in (21.5cm) high.
£200–225 DSG

A Doulton jardinière, decorated with impressed brown leaves, 1870–90, 9½in (24cm) diam.
£180–220 P(Ba)

A Doulton Lambeth footed bowl, by Florence & Lucy Barlow, decorated with panels depicting birds surrounded by dark green foliage, 1883, 10in (25.5cm) diam.
£600–700 JE

A Doulton Lambeth stoneware Moonflask, by Florence Barlow, decorated with wrens, c1885, 10¼in (26cm) high.
£800–900 JE

Items in the Doulton section have been arranged in date order.

A Doulton Lambeth jug, by Mark V. Marshall, decorated with a stylized bird in dark brown and dark green, c1888, 5in (12.7cm) high.
£600–700 JE

A Doulton Lambeth biscuit barrel, by Florence Barlow, decorated with dark green birds on a mustard ground, c1888, 8in (20.5cm) high.
£600–700 JE

◄ A Doulton Lambeth faïence vase, decorated on a pale blue ground with children and a lamb, c1885, 10in (25.5cm) high.
£800–900 JE

A Doulton Lambeth group of mice, entitled 'Play Goers', by George Tinworth, c1890, 5in (12.5cm) high.
£1,800–2,200 JE

A Royal Doulton Kingsware whisky flask, entitled 'Bonnie Prince Charlie', decorated in amber, green, blue and brown, early 20thC, 7in (18cm) high.
£90–110 P(B)

Kingsware was made at Doulton between 1898 and 1939. The rich distinctive glaze, devised by Charles Noke, was achieved by using coloured slips for the design, a brown slip for the body and a transparent glaze, which allowed the various tones to shine through. Doulton had a long-established connection with brewers, distillers and publicans, supplying everything from tiled murals to tankards and ashtrays. Kingsware was commonly used to create whisky flasks and these decanters are much sought after today.

A Doulton Burslem vase, by David Dewsberry, decorated with flowers on a green ground, c1895, 10½in (26.5cm) high.
£600–700 JE

A Doulton mug, by Frank Butler, made for the Victorian Era Exhibition, decorated in brown, blue and green, c1897, 4in (10cm) high.
£800–900 JE

◄ A Royal Doulton stoneware baluster vase, decorated with 4 Art Nouveau-style flowers on a mottled blue and grey ground, c1900, 18¼in (46.5cm) high.
£250–300 Bea(E)

A Doulton Lambeth shaped bowl, by Frank Butler, decorated with stylized leaves and flowers on a dark blue ground, c1895, 15in (38cm) wide.
£700–800 JE

◄ A Doulton bowl, by Frank Butler, decorated in brown and green, c1895, 11in (28cm) diam.
£400–500 JE

► Two Royal Doulton Kingsware whisky flasks, decorated in browns, one with the portrait of a Dickensian man, the other with a Highlander, both restored, early 20thC, tallest 9in (23cm) high.
£80–100 P(B)

A Royal Doulton plate, by C. Beresford Hopkins, made for Tiffany & Co, New York, decorated with a woodland scene surrounded by a brown, blue and gilt rim, c1902, 10¼in (26cm) diam.
£800–900 JE

A Royal Doulton plate, by H. Piper, for Tiffany & Co, New York, decorated with pink flowers and a gilt rim, c1902, 9¼in (23.5cm) diam.
£350–400 JE

LOCATE THE SOURCE

The source of each illustration in Miller's can be found by checking the code letters below each caption with the Key to Illustrations, pages 476–484.

A Royal Doulton plate, by David Dewsberry, decorated with purple irises and a gilt rim, signed, c1905, 10in (25.5cm) diam.
£350–400 JE

A Royal Doulton cup and saucer, decorated in dark blue and gilt, gilt handle and rim, c1905, saucer 5¼in (13.5cm) diam.
£450–500 JE

Doulton

Henry Doulton was well aware of the importance of national and international exhibitions for promoting the Doulton name. At the Great Exhibition of 1851, the company's displays were limited to industrial and sanitary products, but at the Paris Exhibition of 1867, Doulton showed his first art pottery. Thereafter, the factory participated in a wide variety of major exhibitions, both in Europe and the USA, producing exhibition pieces of the finest quality and using the shows to launch new lines.

A Royal Doulton vase, by Percy Curnock, decorated with scarlet poppies on a pale pink ground, with a gilt rim, c1910, 8in (20.5cm) high.
£750–800 JE

A Doulton Lambeth tyg, decorated with three applied sporting figures depicting high-jump, shot-put and relay, enclosed by blue and green flowers, with a silver collar, 1900–10, 6in (15cm) high.
£300–350 P(Ba)

> **Cross Reference**
> See Colour Review

▶ A Royal Doulton exhibition vase, by H. Allen, decorated in brown with baby birds and flowers, c1910, 18in (45.5cm) high.
£2,000–2,500 JE

◀ A Doulton Lambeth dish, by Frank Butler, decorated in brown, blue and olive green, 1905, 10in (25.5cm) wide.
£350–400 JE

A Royal Doulton vase, decorated in dark green, dark blue and brown, c1910, 12¼in (31cm) high.
£175–200 DSG

A Doulton vase, decorated in olive green, brown and light blue, 1910, 8¼in (21cm) high.
£130–150 MARK

A Royal Doulton plate, commemorating the coronation of King George V, printed in blue with portrait medallions, the border listing the countries and territories of the Empire, green and blue printed marks, 1911, 10½in (26.5cm) diam.
£120–140 DN

◀ A Doulton hot water bottle, 1920, 9in (23cm) wide.
£30–35 AL

Doulton's success was built on providing sanitary wares, such as sewer pipes, lavatories and kitchen sinks. One of Henry Doulton's many innovations included pioneering in 1844 the first ceramic screw-top hot water bottle, which could be placed in either a flat or upright position, and was recommended for use in motor vehicles and carriages. It cost a shilling or two, and if retailers ordered enough units their name and address were printed on the bottle free of charge. Such inscribed pieces are collectable today.

A Royal Doulton vase, by H. Nixon, decorated in yellow and green with a ploughing scene, c1915, 5½in (14cm) high.
£350–400 JE

A Royal Doulton 22-piece bone china tea service, decorated with Roses pattern in pink and green on a white ground, c1920.
£360–400 AOT

A Royal Doulton plate, decorated with Pansy pattern in yellow, pink and blue, c1920, 11in (28cm) diam.
£120–140 AOT

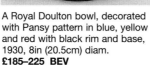

A Royal Doulton figure, depicting a snowman beating a drum, 1987, 5½in (14cm) high.
£120–140 WWY

A Royal Doulton bowl, decorated with Pansy pattern in blue, yellow and red with black rim and base, 1930, 8in (20.5cm) diam.
£185–225 BEV

A Royal Doulton figure, entitled 'Christopher Robin and Pooh', blue and yellow on a green base, discontinued 1997, 5in (13cm) high.
£55–65 GRa

EARTHENWARE, STONEWARE & COUNTRY POTTERY

A slipware bowl, decorated with cream and green flowers on a brown ground, damaged, c1607, 6in (15cm) wide.
£750–850 AOH

A black-glazed earthenware jar, slight damage, early 19thC, 20in (51cm) high.
£90–110 OD

▶ A Derbyshire brown salt-glazed stoneware jug, with greyhound handle, c1835, 6in (15cm) high.
£135–155 IW

A brown salt-glazed stoneware money box, possibly Scottish, early 19thC, 5in (12.5cm) wide.
£1,000–1,200 JHo

A brown-glazed stoneware jug, probably Kishere, Mortlake, c1810, 4¾in (12cm) high.
£100–120 IW

A Derbyshire brown salt-glazed porringer, cracked, c1840, 5in (13cm) high.
£50–60 IW

A Derbyshire brown salt-glazed money box, c1840, 6½in (16.5cm) high.
£70–80 IW

▶ A Derbyshire brown salt-glazed one-gallon flagon, decorated with impressed pattern, 1840, 12½in (32cm) high.
£50–60 OD

A brown salt-glazed coffee pot, probably Eccleshall, Yorkshire, c1846, 9in (23cm) high.
£145–165 IW

A Brampton brown salt-glazed money box, inscribed 'Minnie Cope', 1860, 6in (15cm) high.
£180–200 OD

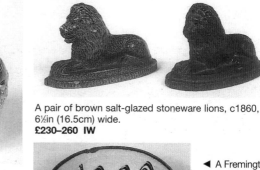

A pair of brown salt-glazed stoneware lions, c1860, 6½in (16.5cm) wide.
£230–260 IW

◄ A Fremington slipware dish, with brown combed pattern on cream, damaged, late 19thC, 10½in (26.5cm) diam.
£100–125 IW

A Verwood Pottery brown earthenware flagon, 1880, 8½in (21.5cm) high
£70–80 OD

A brown earthenware jug, possibly from the West Country or south Wales, inscribed '3' on base, c1890, 8¼in (21cm) high
£35–40 IW

A Verwood Pottery brown jug, slight damage, c1900, 12½in (32cm) high.
£85–95 IW

A black-glazed storage jar, 1900, 5¼in (13.5cm) high.
£16–20 IW

A French slipware jug, with brown sgraffito oak leaves and acorns, lip with old cement repair, dated '1890', 7¼in (18.5cm) high
£85–95 IW

A brown earthenware dog bowl, late 19thC, 2½in (6.5cm) diam.
£40–50 IW

A Verwood Pottery bedpan, early 20thC, 13in (33cm) wide.
£40–45 IW

► A Verwood Pottery brown basket, marked, c1920, 5½in (14cm) wide.
£35–40 IW

► A Ewenny brown pottery tyg, slight damage, inscribed 'Dwfr Da Rhodd Duw' ('Good Water Gift of God') and dated, 1904, 5in (13cm) high.
£120–140 IW

FAIRINGS

A German fairing pin box, in the form of a baby in a basket, late 19thC, 4in (10cm) wide.
£150–175 LeB

A German fairing, entitled 'Twelve months after marriage', late 19thC, 3in (7.5cm) wide.
£120–140 LeB

A German fairing, entitled 'Tug of War', late 19thC, 5in (12.5cm) wide.
£140–160 LeB

A German fairing, entitled 'Which is prettiest?', late 19thC, 3in (7.5cm) wide.
£150–170 LeB

A Victorian fairing, entitled 'To Let', 3in (7.5cm) wide.
£250–280 SAS

A Victorian fairing, entitled 'Three o'clock in the morning', 3in (7.5cm) wide.
£30–35 SAS

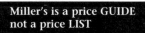

A Victorian fairing, entitled 'Before', 3¼in (8.5cm) wide.
£220–250 SAS

A Victorian fairing, entitled 'Who is coming?', 3½in (9cm) wide.
£160–180 SAS

▶ A German fairing, entitled 'When a man is married his troubles begin', slight damage, c1900–20, 4in (10cm) wide.
£120–140 LeB

A German fairing, entitled 'A Knight of Labor', late 19thC, 3in (7.5cm) wide.
£135–155 LeB

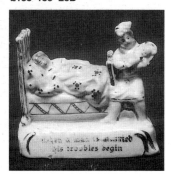

A Brexton plate, printed with Italian Gondola pattern, with realistic colours on a white ground, marked, 1950s, 7in (18cm) diam.
£2–3 Law

A Foley dish, transfer-printed in red, blue and yellow with London Pride pattern, 1950s, 5½in (14cm) wide.
£3–4 Law

A Monaco vase, decorated and applied with blue, yellow and black fish on a pink ground, with pale blue interior, 1950s, 8in (20.5cm) high.
£70–80 MLL

A Grindley trio, decorated with stylized lanterns in red and green, 1950s, plate 7in (18cm) diam.
£16–18 AOS

A Hornsea Pottery flower bowl, with incised decoration in red, 1950s, 13in (33cm) diam.
£35–45 RAT

A J. & G. Meakin studio ware jug, painted with yellow flowers and green leaves, printed mark, 1953–60, 7½in (19cm) high.
£12–14 Law

An Arthur Wood wall vase, decorated with hand and footprints in red and black, 1950s, 8in (20.5cm) diam.
£20–25 DAC

A Pearsons bowl, with incised pattern on a black ground, c1950, 8¼in (21cm) high.
£50–60 DSG

An Alfred Meakin tureen, decorated with a fairground scene in red, yellow and green, 1950s, 8in (20.5cm) diam.
£15–20 RAT

◄ A Pearsons vase, with incised pattern on a powder blue ground, marked 'Pearsons of Chesterfield', c1950, 8¼in (21cm) high.
£50–60 DSG

FIGURES

A French porcelain figure of a boy, painted in soft enamelled colours, some restoration, late 18thC, 8¾in (22cm) high.
£180–220 WW

A creamware figure of a man holding a basket, decorated in Prattware colours of yellow, brown and green, 1790–1800, 5½in (14cm) high.
£230–260 OD

A Copeland Parian bust of Oenone, by Calder Marshall, c1860, 13in (33cm) high.
£500–550 JAK

Oenone, the daughter of a shepherd, lived in the woods and was known to have healing powers. Her lover, Paris, rejected her in favour of Helen of Troy and when he was wounded at the battle of Troy, Oenone at first refused to offer her powers of healing to save his life. She later relented, but it was too late. She was so distraught she took her own life. Her story was told by both Tennyson and William Morris.

A Goebbels cigarette holder and striker in the form of a golfer, with yellow trousers and hat and blue shirt, the base in green, 1930s, 5in (12.5cm) high.
£200–250 BEV

A Royal Dux figure of a nude running with a brown and white dog, 1958, 14in (35.5cm) high.
£200–250 BTB

A pair of Wade Mabel Lucie Attwell figures of Sam and Sarah, with yellow shirts, 1930s, 3¼in (8.5cm) high.
£380–420 PGA

A Crown Staffordshire figure of lady, with a green bodice, her skirt decorated with flowers, 1930s, 7½in (19cm) high.
£150–175 PAC

▶ Two Goldscheider figures of ladies, one wearing green trousers and one with a yellow hat, each marked 'Dakon' and 'Goldscheider Wien Made in Austria', 1930s, largest 12½in (32cm) high.
£450–500 P(Ba)

A figure of a dancer, her grey dress trimmed with black, and wearing black gloves, the base pale pink, 1940s, 12in (30.5cm) high.
£125–150 BTB

GOSS & CRESTED CHINA

With the development of the railway system in the 19th century, and the introduction of bank holidays in 1871, tourism flourished. Everyone wanted to bring back a little memento of their day-trip, and in the 1880s William Henry Goss developed a new kind of porcelain for this growing tourist market – ivory-coloured ceramic miniatures, hand-painted with the crests of British towns and modelled on famous buildings, monuments and objects of local interest.

Fun, affordable and small enough to be carried home in the daintiest handbag, this crested china was an instant success and provided the perfect souvenir. You could only buy a specific coat-of-arms in its town of origin, and when you showed off your model of Blackpool Tower, all the neighbours would know where you'd spent your holidays. A host of other potteries jumped on the heraldic china bandwagon, producing tiny ceramics in every conceivable shape from seaside subject to comic characters, and new-fangled inventions such as the aeroplane and gramophone.

Collecting crested china became a national hobby, popular with everyone from ordinary working folk, enjoying their first paid holidays, to royalty. Princess Alexandra had a huge collection of miniature animals which, much to the irritation of her attendants, had to be carefully wrapped and taken with her on every journey. The crested craze peaked in the Edwardian period when an estimated 90 per cent of British homes had at least one piece. By the 1920s, however, trade was on the decline, coming to an end with the Depression in the 1930s when factories either shut down or switched production. Old-fashioned and unsaleable, crested china collections were shoved in the attic or simply dumped. It was not until the 1960s, when Victoriana became fashionable, that this souvenir pottery was once again hotly collected.

An Arcadian model of field glasses, with Bournemouth crest, 1914–20, 2½in (6.5cm) high.
£18–20 G&CC

A Carlton model of a hat, with Belfast crest, c1915, 2in (5cm) high.
£40–50 MLa

A Carlton dish, with 'Yes! We Have No Bananas' and Windsor crest, 1910–30, 4½in (11.5cm) wide.
£18–20 MGC

A Bagware cup and saucer, with crest commemorating the Golden Jubilee of Queen Victoria, 1887, saucer 5in (12.5cm) diam.
£55–60 MGC

A Corona cheese dish and lid, with Arundel crest, 1910–30, 2¼in (5.5cm) wide.
£6–8 G&CC

A Gemma model of an ankle boot with eyelets, with Cambridge crest, 1910–30, 5in (12.5cm) wide.
£12–15 G&CC

A Goss Wareham Roman bottle, with crest commemorating the coronation of King George V and Queen Mary, 1910, 3in (7.5cm) high.
£20–22 MGC

A Goss Walmer Lodge Roman vase, with badge of The Hampshire Regiment, 1900–30, 2⅕in (6.5cm) high.
£90–100 MGC

A Goss model of The Old Horse Shoe, with 'The Legend' and City of Nottingham crest, 1900–30, 4in (10cm) wide.
£20–25 MGC

A Goss Taper jug, with Southwold Ancient crest, 1900–10, 2¾in (7cm) high.
£18–20 G&CC

▶ A Goss Bagware tea plate, decorated with 6 Allied flags of The Great War and 'To Cook a German', 1914–18, 6in (15cm) diam.
£135–155 MGC

◀ A Goss miniature Melon teapot and lid, with Staines crest, 1910–30, 4½in (11.5cm) high.
£55–60 G&CC

A Grafton model of a Welsh hat, with blue trim and Royal Leamington Spa crest, 1900–33, 2in (5cm) high.
£11–13 G&CC

A Grafton model of a Trench Howitzer, with Weston-super-Mare crest, c1914–18, 3in (7.5cm) wide.
£16–18 MGC

A Grafton model of an alpine gun, with Sheffield crest, c1918, 4in (10cm) wide.
£400–450 CCC

An Arcadian model of a swan, with Cirencester crest, 1910–35, 2½in (6.5cm) wide.
£7–9 G&CC

An Arcadian model of an open-mouthed frog, with Bournemouth crest, c1910, 2¼in (5.5cm) high.
£15–20 MGC

An Arcadian model of Black Cat with Bottle, part of the registered series of 24 humorous black cats, 1920–39, 2¾in (7cm) high.
£70–80 G&CC

From WWI Arcadian became the leading factory producing crested china souvenirs. The Black Cats, manfactured from 1920–39, were a very popular line. Originally retailing for as little as a shilling a piece, now they can fetch tens and even hundreds of pounds for the rarest cats in the series.

A Carlton model of a terrier, with Westcliffe-on-Sea crest and verse, 1910–30, 3in (7.5cm) long.
£22–26 G&CC

A Podmore model of a penguin, with Brighton crest, 1920s, 3½in (9cm) high.
£16–18 MGC

A Savoy model of a whelk shell, with crest, 1910–33, 3in (7.5cm) wide.
£5–7 G&CC

A model of a seated cat with bandaged face, with Windsor crest, 1910–30, 4in (10cm) high.
£30–33 MGC

LOCATE THE SOURCE

The source of each illustration in Miller's can be found by checking the code letters below each caption with the Key to Illustrations, pages 476–484.

A Saxony model of an eagle, with Dover Court crest, c1910, 5in (12.5cm) high.
£80–100 CCC

A model of a seated cat, with Plymouth crest, 1910–30, 3¾in (9.5cm) high.
£16–18 G&CC

An Arcadian model of a Lifeboat Memorial, with Caister-on-Sea crest, c1905, 6in (15cm) high.
£50–55 CCC

A Carlton model of a pit head, with Northleach crest, c1910, 5½in (14cm) high.
£130–160 CCC

A Willow model of Chesterfield church, with crest, c1910, 5in (12.5cm) high.
£45–55 CCC

An Arcadian model of a war memorial, with Loughborough crest, 1920, 6in (15cm) high.
£90–110 CCC

A Strand China model of the Cenotaph, with Westminster crest, 1918–25, 5in (12.5cm) high.
£24–26 G&CC

A Goss model of St Martin's Cross, Iona, 9in (23cm) high.
£220–250 MGC

A Goss model of a lighthouse, with Teignmouth crest, 1912, 4½in (11.5cm) high.
£110–130 CCC

◄ A Goss model of Grinlow Tower, with Buxton crest, 1910–25, 3¾in (9.5cm) high.
£250–300 G&CC

An Arcadian part-coloured model of a couple in bed, with Hastings & St Leonard's crest, c1920, 3in (7.5cm) wide.
£100–110 CCC

A pair of Carlton busts, King Edward VII and Queen Alexandra, each with Teignmouth crest, c1905, 5in (12.5cm) high.
£120–140 CCC

A Carlton model inscribed 'Shrapnel Villa', 'Tommy's Dugout Somewhere in France' and Windsor crest, 1914–18, 3½in (9cm) wide.
£65–75 MGC

An Arcadian figure of a sailor winding a capstan, with Hythe, Hants, crest, c1914, 4in (10cm) high.
£150–175 CCC

A Carlton figure of Xit, with Lewes crest, c1920, 5½in (14cm) high.
£80–100 CCC

An Arcadian figure of a nurse, inscribed 'Soldiers Friend', with Bagshot crest, 1915–20, 5¼in (13.5cm) high.
£70–85 G&CC

A Carlton figure of a drunk sitting by a barrel, with Scarborough crest, c1920, 3½in (9cm) wide.
£85–100 CCC

A Gemma model of a piper, with Bridlington crest, c1920, 5in (12.5cm) high.
£130–150 CCC

A Rita figure of Robert Blake, with Bridgwater crest, c1910, 7in (18cm) high.
£100–130 CCC

A Podmore figure of HRH The Prince of Wales, with Margate crest, c1925, 6in (15cm) high.
£130–150 CCC

◄ A Shelley figure of a Scottish soldier, inscribed 'Scotland For Ever', with Perth crest, c1920s, 4½in (11.5cm) high.
£180–200 CCC

An Arcadian model of a charabanc, 1910, 5in (12.5cm) long.
£45–55 CCC

The term charabanc comes from the French *char à banc*, ie carriage with seats.

An Arcadian model of a battleship, with Swanage crest, 1920s, 5in (12.5cm) long.
£35–40 MGC

A Carlton model of a minesweeper, with Blackpool crest, c1920, 5in (12.5cm) long.
£35–40 MGC

A Carlton model of a coal truck, inscribed 'Black Diamonds', with Morecambe crest, c1920, 4in (10cm) long.
£28–33 MGC

A Carlton model of a British anti-aircraft car, with Blackpool crest, c1918, 5in (12.5cm) long.
£220–240 CCC

A Goss model of a sedan chair, with Boulogne crest, c1900, 3in (7.5cm) wide.
£50–60 CCC

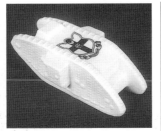

A Goss model of a British tank, with Keynsham crest, c1918, 4in (10cm) wide.
£80–90 MGC

A Continental model of a hot air balloon, with Matlock Bath crest, c1920, 3in (7.5cm) high.
£75–90 CCC

Miller's is a price GUIDE not a price LIST

A Swan model of a zeppelin, on a plinth, with Cambridge crest, 1916, 5in (12.5cm) wide.
£45–50 CCC

GOUDA

A Gouda Zuid-Holland clog, decorated with stylized green floral pattern on a mustard-yellow background, c1900, 7¼in (18.5cm) long.
£150–175 OO

A Gouda clog, decorated with a band of Paysage pattern on a dark brown ground, 1910, 6½in (16.5cm) long.
£150–175 OO

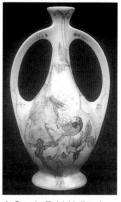

A Gouda Zuid-Holland Rosenburg-style two-handled vase, decorated with a bird of paradise in orange, blue and green, c1905, 11½in (29cm) high.
£300–350 OO

Did You Know?

The Gouda factory in the Netherlands was established in 1898. The pottery specialized in hand-painted earthenware, often with floral or Islamic-influenced patterns, decorated in strong colours with much use of black. Particularly popular in the inter-war years, Gouda pottery was much exported to Britain. Pieces tend to be clearly marked on the base, with hand-painted details of the pattern, date and place of production.

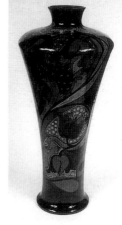

A Gouda Zuid-Holland vase, painted by C. A. J. Hornig, with purple, brown and red flowers amid green leaves, 1920, 19in (48.5c) high.
£1,200–1,400 OO

A Gouda Shinski vase, decorated with blue, brown and cream, 1923, 12in (30.5cm) high.
£200–250 OO

A Gouda Matapan design night-light, decorated in blue, green and mustard on a cream ground, 1910, 10½in (26.5cm) high.
£200–250 OO

A Gouda vase, with extended neck, painted with purple and red flowers amid green leaves, marked 'Gouda Holland', 1900–20, 10in (25.5cm) high.
£150–170 P(Ba)

◄ A Gouda vase, decorated with white amoebic shapes on a mustard ground, signed 'Gouda Arnhem', 1924, 4¼in (11cm) high.
£60–70 OO

A Gouda four-handled candlestick, 1925, 8¼in (21cm) high.
£150–175 OO

A Gouda plate, decorated with blue and brown flowers on a cream background, 1924, 7½in (19cm) diam.
£40–50 OO

A pair of Gouda miniature candlesticks, decorated in brown and cream, 1925, 3¼in (8.5cm) high.
£100–120 OO

A Gouda night-light, decorated in brown with Plato design, 1925, 9½in (24cm) high.
£175–225 OO

This night-light was designed for children. A candle was placed inside and shone through the holes and piercings in the body, making patterns on the ceiling.

A Gouda candlestick, decorated by Johanna Kelder in brown, orange and yellow with Plato design, 1925, 7½in (19cm) high.
£100–125 OO

◄ A Gouda bottle vase with handle, decorated by J. F. Miedema in brown, green, blue and gold with Pico design, 1928, 11in (28cm) high.
£275–325 OO

A Gouda vase, decorated in blue, brown and cream with Gael design, 1930, 7¾in (19.5cm) high.
£180–220 OO

A Gouda vase, decorated with stylized multi-coloured flowers on a brown ground, c1930, 6½in (16.5cm) high.
£40–50 CSA

A Gouda inkwell, decorated with orange flowers in Machaco design, 1931, 3¾in (9.5cm) high.
£75–100 OO

A Gouda clog, decorated in navy, gold and red with Kapo design on a cream background, c1940, 5½in (14cm) long.
£60–75 OO

HANCOCK

A set of Hancock & Sons tureens, ladles and meatplates, decorated in blue and white with gilt rims, c1890.
£170–200 AOT

A Hancock & Sons Corona ware jug, decorated with Grey Day pattern, c1930, 5½in (14cm) diam.
£35–40 CSAC

A pair of Hancock & Sons vases, decorated with Daffodil pattern in yellow, green and blue, signed by F. X. Abrahams, c1930, 9in (23cm) high.
£200–250 AOT

A Hancock & Sons Corona ware plate, decorated with Dragon pattern in blue and green, 1930s, 7in (18cm) diam.
£60–70 PIC

A Hancock & Sons Corona ware Kensington bowl, decorated in blue, pink and green, c1930, 8in (20.5cm) diam.
£100–130 AOT

A Hancock & Sons Ivoryware Butterfly dish, decorated in orange, blue and green, c1937, 5in (13cm) wide.
£18–22 AOT

HUMMELS

A Hummel group, Homeward bound, the girl wearing a green bonnet, 1960s, 5in (12.5cm) high.
£180–220 ATH

A Hummel group, Telling Her Secret, one girl wearing a green skirt, 1957–64, 5½in (14cm) high.
£145–185 ATH

A Hummel figure, Goose Girl, wearing a yellow frock, c1972, 4in (10cm) high.
£90–100 TAC

A Hummel figure, Apple Tree Boy, wearing a green hat and blue jacket, from 1972, 4in (10cm) high.
£70–80 TAC

JUGS

A smear-glazed black basalt jug, 1830, 4in (10cm) high.
£20–25 OD

A Grimwades sepia-printed Old Bill jug, 1917–18, 7in (18cm) high.
£85–95 LeB

Old Bill was a favourite WWI cartoon character, created by illustrator Captain Bruce Bairns-father (1888-1959).

A Lorna Bailey Artware jug, decorated in orange and yellow with Egyptian pattern, No. 140 in a limited edition of 200, 1997, 12in (30.5cm) high.
£90–100 PAC

A Staffordshire jug, depicting a circus, with lion handle and gold rim around base, c1840, 7in (18cm) high.
£150–165 SER

▶ A Hillstonia brown pottery jug, with double handle, 1922–30, 11in (28cm) high.
£55–65 Law

A Flaxman Ware jug, with double handle, decorated with stylized green and brown flowers and leaves on a burnt orange ground, 1930, 8½in (21.5cm) high.
£55–65 BEV

A Tuscan Decoro Pottery jug, by R. H. & S. L. Plant, decorated with purple and red flowers, c1940, 7½in (19cm) high.
£220–260 AOT

A brown salt-glazed character jug, 1870, 7in (18cm) high.
£100–120 COHU

A blue and cream-banded jug, damaged, late 19thC, 5½in (15cm) high.
£25–30 IW

A Swinnerton's pottery jug, with snake handle and base, decorated with blue-green leaves, 1930, 7½in (19cm) high.
£35–45 BEV

LUSTRE WARE

A Sunderland lustre child's mug, decorated in pink, c1820, 2in (5cm) high.
£55–65 SER

A Sunderland lustre jug, decorated in pink with a house and garden, gilt rim, c1830, 5¾in (14.5cm) high.
£100–120 SER

A Sunderland lustre wall plaque, with pink surround, inscribed 'Northumberland 74', impressed 'Dixon & Co', 1840, 7in (18cm) diam.
£230–260 IS

A copper lustre jug, with enamel decoration in yellow, pink and green, 1840, 6¼in (16cm) high.
£70–80 OD

A lustre scripture plaque, attributed to John Carr, North Shields Pottery, with pink and gilt surround, 1850, 9in (23cm) wide.
£200–220 IS

A lustre scripture plaque, attributed to Anthony Scott, Southwick, Sunderland, with pink and black border, 1860, 9in (23cm) wide.
£100–120 IS

A red iridescent lustre pottery mask, designed as a grotesque with ears forming handles, and mouth forming a bowl, attributed to Zsolnay, 1890–1900, 6¾in (17cm) wide.
£170–190 P(Ba)

A Howson flambé lustre jar and cover, decorated with a design of cats around base and rim, c1910, 25in (63.5cm) high.
£475–525 PAC

A Pilkington lustre vase, by Gordon Forsyth, decorated with a central band of figures in petrol blue on an amber ground, artist's mark and bee's mark for 1913, 7½in (19cm) high.
£200–250 P(Ba)

MALING

The history of Maling pottery dates back to 1762, when William Maling opened the North Hylton Pot Works in Sunderland. In 1815, the family transferred the business to Tyneside, and in the Victorian period, under the management of Christopher T. Maling, the company specialized in producing commercial containers for food and drink manufacturers, as well as pots and jars for ointments, medicines, ink and a host of other products. They turned over in the region of 80,000 articles a year, and it was estimated that 90 per cent of British jams and conserves were supplied in Maling's ceramic pots. From the 1890s, Maling expanded their production of decorative tableware and introduced Cetem Ware, the name being derived from the initials of C. T. Maling, and using a strong, white, semi-porcelain body. In the 1920s and 30s, Maling produced a whole range of ornamental ceramics and art pottery, becoming well-known for highly-coloured enamel painting and fine lustreware. Leading designers during this period included Harry Clifford Toft, C. N. Wright and Lucien Boullemier. The company was sold to Hoult's Estates and closed down in 1963.

A Maling plate, moulded with daisy pattern and decorated in blue, 1860, 6¼in (16cm) diam.
£40–45 OD

A Maling mug, decorated with Luxor pattern in green, blue, yellow and orange, with black handle and green rim, c1929, 4in (10cm) high.
£170–200 AOT

▶ A Maling rack plate, hand-painted with Harebells design, c1929, 11¼in (28.5cm) diam.
£360–440 AOT

A Maling rack plate, decorated with Luxor pattern in blue, green, red and black on a cream ground, c1929, 11¼in (28.5cm) diam.
£480–560 AOT

A Maling brown tree-trunk vase, 1930, 6in (15cm) high.
£55–65 COCO

◀ A Maling rack plate, embossed with Iris pattern on a green ground, c1929, 11¼in (28.5cm) diam.
£260–340 AOT

A Maling Cheeky Fox stirrup cup, c1929, 6in (15cm) high.
£480–560 AOT

This is from a set of 6 stirrup cups, made for the Haydon Hunt, of which C. T. Maling was Master. The fox sits symmetrically on his ears and nose.

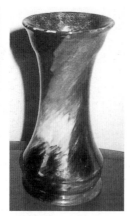

A Maling vase, decorated with Storm pattern in cobalt blue, yellow and turquoise, c1930, 10in (25.5cm) high.
£180–200 AOT

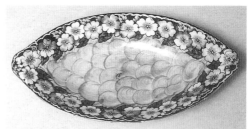

A Maling lustre dish, decorated with blue, pink and yellow flowers and a central pattern in green, c1935, 10in (25.5cm) wide.
£55–65 JACK

▶ A Maling charger, with embossed Flying Ducks pattern on a blue ground, c1936, 11¼in (28.5cm) diam.
£300–350 AOT

A Maling lustre jug, decorated with Blossom Bough pattern No. 6567, with blue flowers on a red ground, 1954, 3½in (9cm) wide.
£80–110 COCO

A Maling fruit bowl, decorated with Blossom Bough pattern No. 6576, decorated in pink, green and red, 1956, 11in (28cm) diam.
£145–155 COCO

A Maling lustre bowl, decorated with blue and yellow flowers and a central pattern in pink, c1940, 10in (25.5cm) wide.
£100–125 JACK

MASON'S

A Mason's Ironstone jug, decorated with Japan pattern in iron-red and blue, printed and impressed mark, c1820, 6½in (16.5cm) high.
£180–200 VH

A Mason's Ironstone dinner plate, decorated with Table and Flowerpot pattern, printed and impressed mark, c1815–20, 9½in (24cm) diam.
£80–100 VH

A Mason's Ironstone dinner plate, decorated with Japan pattern in iron-red and blue, c1815–20, 10in (25.5cm) diam.
£130–150 JP

A Mason's Ironstone dessert plate, decorated in iron-red and blue, impressed mark, c1815–20, 8in (20.5cm) diam.
£100–115 JP

A Mason's Ironstone miniature jug, decorated with Japan Fence pattern in iron-red and blue, gilt butterfly handle, c1815–25, 2¼in (5.5cm) high.
£450–500 JP

A Mason's plate, decorated with Tyburn Turnpike pattern, with clobbered border, c1820, 8in (20.5cm) diam.
£120–150 JP

Clobbering was a method of adding enamelled colours, usually in reds, greens, yellows and gilding, to embellish an existing design.

A Mason's Ironstone chamber pot, decorated with Table and Flowerpot pattern, 1820, 11in (28cm) wide.
£350–400 VH

◀ A Mason's Ironstone vase, decorated in iron-red and blue, with gilt handles, restored, c1820, 4½in (11.5cm) high.
£160–190 JP

A Mason's Ironstone inkstand, decorated in mazarine blue, richly gilded, complete with inkpot, lid missing, c1820–25, 3½in (9cm) diam.
£350–420 JP

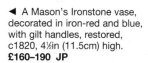

A Mason's Ironstone chamber stick, decorated with a cream and orange pattern on a cobalt blue ground, with a yellow handle, c1835, 6in (15cm) diam.
£270–300 JP

A C. J. Mason trio, decorated, in orange, green, yellow and brown, c1840, saucer 6in (15cm) diam.
£45–55 JP

MIDWINTER

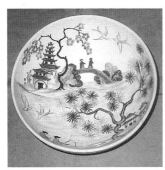

A Midwinter Handcrafts bowl, decorated with an Oriental scene in blue, red and green, c1950, 10in (25.5cm) diam.
£80–100 AND

Three Midwinter Stylecraft plates, from the Collectors' Series, designed by Terence Conran, printed in black on white, c1955, 3¼in (8.5cm) wide.
£25–30 each AND

A Midwinter Saladware bowl, designed by Terence Conran, decorated with vegetables in yellow and green, c1956, 8½in (21.5cm) wide.
£100–120 AND

A Midwinter black gravy boat, 1950s, 8½in (21.5cm) wide.
£25–30 BTB

Cross Reference
See Colour Review

A Midwinter Fashion hors d'oeuvre tray, decorated with Cannes pattern by Hugh Casson in blue, yellow and red on a white ground, c1960, 10in (25.5cm) wide.
£35–40 AND

A Midwinter coffee percolator, decorated with Creation pattern, and a coffee percolator and milk warmer, decorated with Fleur pattern, c1970s, percolators 10in (25.5cm) high.
£8–10 each AND

MOCHA WARE

A Mocha ware quart tankard, decorated with a tree and banded in green, blue and black, c1860, 6in (15cm) high.
£120–140 IW

A Mocha ware jug, decorated with black foliage, with honey-coloured glaze banded in black and white, 1880, 8in (20.5cm) high.
£230–260 OD

A Mocha ware mug, decorated with Four Trees pattern and banded in brown, blue and black, hairline crack, late 19thC, 5in (12.5cm) high.
£60–70 IW

A Mocha ware jug, by T. & G. Green, Derbyshire, decorated with black trees and banded in brown, blue and black, 1910, 6¼in (16cm) high.
£50–60 OD

MOORCROFT

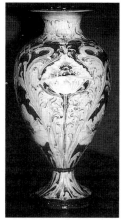

A Moorcroft Florian Ware vase, decorated with Cornflower pattern in blue and green on a mottled blue ground, c1900, 3in (7.5cm) high.
£900–1,000 GAK

A Moorcroft Florian Ware two-handled vase, decorated with Poppy pattern, made for Liberty & Co, minor rim chips, registration number, c1900, 3in (7.5cm) high.
£700–800 GAK

A Moorcroft vase, decorated with Cornflower pattern in dark blue on a blue flecked ground, 1920s, 6¼in (16cm) high.
£700–800 PAC

A Moorcroft Florian Ware vase, decorated with Poppy pattern in yellow, blue and green, c1902, 12in (30.5cm) high.
£2,500–3,000 RUM

◀ A collection of Moorcroft tableware, decorated in powder blue, 1913–63, saucer 5in (12.5cm) diam.
£20–24 each NP

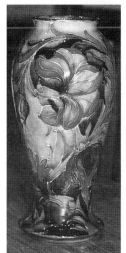

A Moorcroft vase, decorated with Spanish pattern in red, blue and yellow, c1916, 9in (23cm) high.
£1,600–1,800 RUM

A Moorcroft vase, decorated with Cornflower pattern in blue and green, c1916, 9in (23cm) high.
£2,500–2,800 RUM

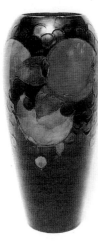

A Moorcroft plaque, decorated with berries and leaves in red and yellow with flambé glaze, c1920s, 10in (25.5cm) diam.
£600–700 PGA

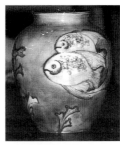

A Moorcroft vase, decorated with Fish pattern in blue and beige, c1930, 6in (15cm) high.
£1,100–1,300 RUM

A Moorcroft Caribbean mug, decorated with Palm Beach pattern in yellow, green and blue, mid-20thC, 4in (10cm) high.
£300–330 PCh

A Moorcroft vase, decorated with Pomegranite pattern in red, blue and dark green, signed, 1920s, 12in (30.5cm) high.
£900–1,100 PGA

A pair of Moorcroft vases, decorated with Anemone pattern in red and blue on a green ground, c1940, 3½in (9cm) high.
£500–600 PGA

A Moorcroft box and cover, decorated with Anemone pattern in red, green and yellow, 1970, 5in (12.5cm) diam.
£135–155 PAC

Cross Reference
See Colour Review

A Moorcroft two-handled vase, designed by Sally Tuffin, decorated with Blue Finch pattern in red, brown and green, 1988–96, 10in (25.5cm) high.
£500–600 NP

A Moorcroft jug, designed by Sally Tuffin, decorated with Buttercup pattern in orange and blue on a brown ground, 1992, 6in (15cm) high.
£260–300 NP

▶ A Moorcroft year plate, designed by Rachel Bishop, decorated with Morning Glory pattern in blue, red, green and brown, limited edition of 500, 1996, 8in (20.5cm) diam.
£125–145 NP

MYOTT

The Staffordshire firm of Myott, Son & Co was founded in 1897, and by the 1920s had developed a thriving business in moulded tableware. In addition to producing traditional designs, the company became well-known for flamboyant jugs and vases in the Art Deco style - the most collectable Myott products today.

Shapes are typically geometric, with squared angles and sharp lines, and the more complex the form, the more desirable the piece. Wares were hand-painted in brilliant contrasting colours, typically orange, brown, green, red and black. Value is affected by condition, and items should be checked carefully for cracks, chipped rims, flaking paint and any restoration.

A Myott vase, hand-painted in orange and black, 1930s, 9in (23cm) high.
£130–150 BEV

A Myott jug, decorated with flowers, hand-painted in red, blue and green, 1930s, 7½in (19cm) high.
£100–120 BEV

A Myott vase, in the form of Pierrot and Crinoline Lady, painted in orange, yellow and black, 1930s, 8in (20.5cm) high.
£100–120 HEW

A Myott stepped flower-holder, hand-painted in red, brown and cream, 1930, 8½in (21.5cm) high.
£120–140 BEV

A Myott Bow Tie jug, hand-painted in orange and green, 1930s, 7½in (19cm) high.
£125–145 BEV

▶ A Myott coaster, decorated with flowers, hand-painted in blue, beige and green, c1937, 4in (10cm) diam.
£20–25 BKK

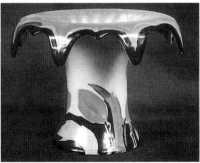

A Myott Downturn vase, hand-painted in orange, yellow and black, 1930s, 6¾in (17cm) high.
£175–195 BEV

NURSERY WARE

A creamware child's alphabet mug, printed in black, c1800, 2¾in (7cm) high.
£150–180 IW

A child's plate, decorated with red, yellow, green and blue flowers, with moulded border, c1820, 6½in (16.5cm) diam.
£65–75 IW

A child's plate, decorated with Girl on Wheelbarrow pattern in red, blue and green, with moulded daisy border, c1830, 4¾in (12cm) diam.
£60–70 IW

An earthenware child's plate, decorated with Cockatoo pattern in red, blue, green and yellow, with moulded daisy border, 1840, 5¾in (14.5cm) diam.
£30–35 OD

A pair of children's pearlware octagonal bowls, printed in black with figures and verses, with moulded daisy borders and purple lustre line rims, each marked 'Manufactured for Mrs R. Brandon, Kingston, Jamaica', c1840, 7½in (19cm) wide.
£750–850 DN

Apparently, Mrs Brandon commissioned a series of these pieces following her husband's death in 1838. The Jamaican subject matter makes them particularly rare.

A child's plate, depicting one of Benjamin Franklin's Maxims, 'He that hath a trade hath an estate, industry pays debts while despair increaseth them', transfer-printed in black, with moulded alphabet border, hairline crack, late 19thC, 6½in (16.5cm) diam.
£50–60 IW

Publisher, author, inventor and scientist, Benjamin Franklin (1706–90) helped draft America's Declaration of Independence and was one of the most admired men in the western world during the second half of the 18th century. In 1729, he published *Poor Richard's Almanack*, in which he coined numerous proverbs praising prudence, industry and honesty, known as 'Franklin's Maxims'.

A child's plate, transfer-printed in black, with moulded alphabet border, 1850, 6½in (16.5cm) diam.
£30–35 OD

◄ A child's mug, decorated with King of the Castle pattern in red yellow and green, some damage, c1880, 2¾in (7cm) high.
£35–40 IW

A child's mug, decorated with children at play, transfer-printed in red, yellow and brown, c1880, 4in (10cm) high.
£60–70 IW

A child's mug, transfer-printed in black 'T was a Tinker and mended a pot', c1880, 3in (7.5cm) high.
£55–65 IW

A Royal Doulton child's mug, designed by William Savage, decorated with Little Bo-Peep pattern, transfer-printed in pink, red and brown, 1910, 3in (7.5cm) high.
£50–60 WWY

A Royal Doulton Bunnykins porridge bowl, decorated with Visiting pattern in green, yellow, blue and red, signed 'Barbara Vernon', 1930s, 7½in (19cm) diam.
£50–60 MED

A Crown Ducal Nurseryware plate, designed by Charlotte Rhead, decorated with Little Boy Blue pattern, in red, blue, yellow and green, 1930s, 8in (20.5cm) diam.
£130–150 BDA

▶ A Crown Ducal Nurseryware plate, designed by Charlotte Rhead, decorated with Three Birds on a Branch pattern in pink and black, 1930s, 7in (18cm) diam.
£100–120 BDA

◀ A Staffordshire Noddy cup and saucer, decorated in red, blue, yellow and green, 1960s, saucer 3in (7.5cm) diam.
£16–20 WWY

A Wedgwood Beatrix Potter paperweight, decorated in red, blue, brown and green, 1970s, 3¾in (9.5cm) diam.
£16–20 WWY

A Wedgwood Beatrix Potter birthday plate, decorated in red, blue, brown and green, 1981, 8in (20.5cm) diam.
£20–25 WWY

PENDELFINS

A Pendelfin model entitled 'Lollipop', wearing a pink cape and eating a green lollipop, minor chips, 1961–66, 4in (10cm) high.
£160–200 PAC

Two Pendelfin models, entitled 'Mother Mouse', 1960s, 4¼in (11cm) high.
l. grey and turquoise **£300–350**
r. brown and turquoise **£200–250 DDM**

A Pendelfin model of a rabbit, entitled 'Pie Face', brown with blue cloth, 1960s, 4¼in (11cm) high.
£55–65 OD

PLATES

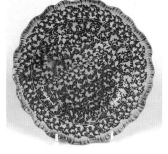

A Bristol delft plate, hand-painted in red, blue and green with flowers, c1725, 8¾in (22cm) diam.
£500–550 JHo

A Bristol delft plate, decorated with blue and white transfer-printed panels on a manganese ground, c1740, 8¾in (22cm) diam.
£320–360 JHo

A sponged creamware plate, with green shell rim, probably Yorkshire, 1780, 8in (20.5cm) diam.
£100–120 OD

A French faïence plate, decorated with fruit in orange, blue, green and brown, some damage, 1800, 8½in (21.5cm) diam.
£100–120 OD

A Hamilton plate, decorated with Philosopher pattern, transfer-printed in pink, 1820, 6in (15cm) diam.
£40–50 GN

A Social Hall plate, decorated with an illustration by H. S. Blood, transfer-printed in black, made for N. E. Janney & Co, c1860, 9in (23cm) diam.
£70–80 IW

A Berlin plate, decorated with a harbour scene, the pierced border detailed in blue and gilt, sceptre and impressed marks, 19thC, 9in (23cm) diam.
£100–120 WW

A pair of Coalport plates, from dessert service No. 4/412, painted with flowers in pink and green by Stephen Lawrence, with blue ground and gilt scroll border, 1840–50, 9in (23cm) wide.
£550–610 TMA

A Metlach charger, depicting Wartburg Castle, Germany, in brown, beige, green and blue, 1899, 17in (43cm) diam.
£350–400 DSG

A Grimwades Old Bill plate, decorated in sepia, by Bruce Bairnsfather, c1918, 10in (25.5cm) diam.
£120–135 LeB

A set of 6 Longchamps oyster plates and a server, decorated with white shells on a green ground, with brown moulded rope rims, c1920, server 13in (33cm) diam.
£250–285 MLL

A Sarreguemines plate, decorated with moulded and painted birds and leaves, in green, brown, yellow and red, c1900, 8in (20.5cm) diam.
£50–60 MLL

A Prinknash Pottery plate, transfer-printed in green, blue, yellow and brown, marked, 1945, 6¾in (17cm) diam.
£4–5 Law

A Fornasetti plate, depicting a navigation instrument, transfer-printed in black, with gilt rim, marked 'Christmas 1968' and 'Fornasetti Milano Made in Italy', 9½in (24cm) diam.
£60–75 DSG

◀ An Empire Porcelain Co plate, decorated with a harbour scene, transfer-printed in black, marked, 1960, 8½in (21.5cm) diam.
£8–9 Law

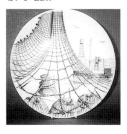

POOLE POTTERY

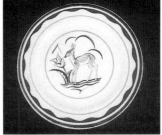

A Carter, Stabler & Adams charger, decorated with flowers, surrounded by a green and blue laddered border, designed by Erna Manners, c1921, 14¾in (37.5cm) diam.
£350–400 P(Ba)

A Carter, Stabler & Adams plate, painted by Ruth Pavely with a fawn and blue and black rim, 1925–35, 9in (23cm) diam.
£250–300 HarC

A Carter, Stabler & Adams model of an otter holding a fish, in blue-green, c1921, 5in (12.5cm) high.
£25–30 AnS

◀ A Carter, Stabler & Adams earthenware bowl, painted by Truda Carter with Leaping Deer pattern, c1930, 8in (20.5cm) diam.
£245–275 RUSK

Two Carter, Stabler & Adams children's plates, painted by Eileen Prangnell with a shepherdess and a lady gardener, late 1920s, 5in (12.5cm) diam.
£125–140 each HarC

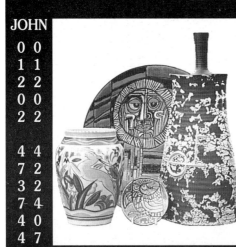

◀ A Carter, Stabler & Adams freestanding dog's head, in brown on a blue-green base, 1930s, 6in (15cm) high.
£350–400 HarC

Dogs' heads of this type are usually found as wall-hangings rather than freestanding busts, making this a very rare piece.

A Carter, Stabler & Adams salt and pepper set, decorated with flowers in blue, green, orange and pink, 1930s, tray 5in (12.5cm) wide.
£20–25 HarC

A Carter, Stabler & Adams vase, painted by Marian Jones with stylized flowers on a cream ground, c1934–36, 7in (18cm) high.
£200–250 ADE

A Carter, Stabler & Adams Contemporary vase, with a mottled beige glaze, c1955, 7in (18cm) high.
£30–35 ADE

A Poole Pottery olive-green Delphis vase, 1965–75, 4½in (11.5cm) high.
£35–40 DSG

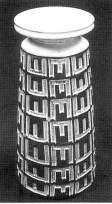

A Poole Pottery Studio vase, designed by Robert Jefferson, decorated with a geometric pattern in cream and brown, 1961–63, 8in (20.5cm) high.
£300–350 HarC

Pieces from the Studio period (1961–66) were made in much smaller numbers than the later Delphis/Atlantis/Aegean ranges.

A Poole Pottery bowl, decorated in blue and orange, early 1960s, 11in (28cm) diam.
£200–250 HarC

A Poole Pottery Atlantis vase, decorated in gold on a cream ground, by Guy Sydenham, 1970, 9in (23cm) high.
£300–350 HarC

The Atlantis range from the early 1960s consisted of one-off pieces until 1972–77, when a repeatable range of shapes became available. Hand-thrown and decorated by Guy Sydenham and his team of potters/designers, each of these later pieces is marked with a shape number on the base, always with the prefix 'A'. Atlantis was inspired by Guy Sydenham's love of the sea and coast.

▶ A Poole Pottery owl, by Barbara Linley Adams, c1980, 7in (18cm) high.
£65–80 DSG

A Poole Pottery Atlantis vase, by Jennie Haigh, decorated with a snake in brown on a dark cream ground, 1973–76, 7in (18cm) high.
£270–300 HarC

Animals, insects and sea creatures were sometimes used as decoration in the Atlantis series.

QUIMPER

Quimper, in northern France, has been a centre of faïence (tin-glazed earthenware) manufacture since the 17th century. It is best known, however, for the popular wares produced in the 19th and 20th centuries. Typical painted decoration includes milkmaids and country folk in traditional rural and Breton-style costumes, portrayed in a naïve style and surrounded by a border of simply-painted flowers. The decoration is in a traditional high-fired palette, with colours including blue, orange, yellow and green on a white or creamy ground.

A Quimper wall horn, by Adolphe Pourquier, decorated with 2 figures and flowers in blue, green and orange on a cream ground, marked, c1880, 4½in (11.5cm) high.
£100–120 VH

A Quimper wall horn, decorated with a woman, in blue and orange on a cream ground, chipped, c1970, 7½in (19cm) high.
£35–40 DSG

A Quimper cake stand, decorated with a man and a woman, with a floral border in blue, green and orange, marked 'HB', c1883, 9¾in (25cm) diam.
£325–365 VH

A Quimper oil and vinegar set, decorated with a man and a woman and flowers in blue, green, yellow and orange, marked 'HR Quimper', c1895, 6¾in (17cm) high.
£280–320 VH

◀ A Quimper pot, decorated with a woman and a moulded bow in green, blue, yellow and orange, marked 'HB Quimper', c1885, 3½in (9cm) high.
£200–220 VH

A Quimper bowl, by Adolphe Pourquier, decorated with a Breton man and flowers in blue, green, yellow and orange, c1895, 10¾in (27.5cm) diam.
£270–300 VH

A pair of Quimper knife rests, by C. Maillard, in the form of a reclining man and woman in brown, orange, green and blue, 1920, 5in (12.5cm) wide.
£180–200 VH

◀ A Quimper cigarette holder, in the form of a fish, hand-painted in orange and green on a deep cream ground, small chip to base, 1930s, 5½in (14cm) wide.
£35–40 BEV

FREDERICK & CHARLOTTE RHEAD

An Ellgreave pottery plate, designed by Charlotte Rhead, decorated in brown and yellow, stamped 'Lottie Rhead Ware', 1924, 8in (20cm) diam.
£150–180 BDA

A Bursley Ware plate, designed by Frederick Rhead, decorated with Amstel pattern in shades of blue, brown and black, c1924, 9in (23cm) diam.
£240–275 AOT

A Burleigh Ware vase, designed by Charlotte Rhead, decorated with gold, brown and yellow flowers, pattern No. 4106, 1927, 8½in (21.5cm) high.
£320–350 BDA

A Crown Ducal three-handled vase, designed by Charlotte Rhead, decorated with Hydrangea pattern in purple, red and green on a mottled cream ground, No. 3797, 1935, 7in (18cm) high.
£280–320 BDA

► A Crown Ducal pottery jardinière, by Charlotte Rhead, tube-lined and decorated with flowers in green, yellow, orange and blue on a trellis ground, 1930s, 13¾in (35cm) diam.
£180–220 AH

◄ A charger, designed by Charlotte Rhead, tube-lined and decorated with Wysteria pattern in shades of green and pink on a cream ground, 1930, 14in (35.5cm) diam.
£400–450 BEV

A Crown Ducal charger, by Charlotte Rhead, decorated with Indian Tree pattern in shades of orange and brown, No. 4795, c1936, 14½in (37cm) diam.
£280–320 BDA

A Crown Ducal wall plaque, designed by Charlotte Rhead, decorated in shades of brown, blue, orange and yellow, pattern No. 5983, c1938, 12½in (32cm) diam.
£290–330 PC

A Crown Ducal wall plaque, by Charlotte Rhead, decorated with Trellis pattern in blue and yellow, No. 5391, 1938, 12½in (32cm) diam.
£320–360 PC

A charger, by Charlotte Rhead, decorated with flowers, 1930s, 14½in (37cm) diam.
£280–320 WilP

A Bursley Ware two-handled dish, decorated with flowers in brown, orange and yellow on a caramel ground, pattern No. TL3, signed 'Charlotte Rhead', Second Period, 1940, 11in (28cm) wide.
£100–120 AOT

A Bursley Ware wall plaque, designed by Charlotte Rhead, decorated with flowers in brown, pink, blue and yellow on a cream ground, pattern No. TL76, Second Period, 1940, 12in (30.5cm) diam.
£300–330 PC

A Bursley Ware goblet vase, decorated with flowers, in pink, mauve and brown on a white ground with green rim and base, pattern No. TL76, designed by Charlotte Rhead, Second Period, 1940s, 8in (20.5cm) high.
£170–200 PC

A Bursley Ware coaching jug, decorated in shades of brown, orange and blue, pattern No. TL5, designed by Charlotte Rhead, Second Period, 1940s, 11in (28cm) high.
£200–220 PC

A Bursley Ware ewer, decorated in blue on white, pattern No. TL31, designed by Charlotte Rhead, Second Period, 1940s, 9in (23cm) high.
£250–300 PC

A Bursley Ware lamp base, designed by Charlotte Rhead, decorated with Daisy pattern No. TL37 in blue and pink with green base, Second Period, 1940s, 6½in (16cm) high.
£280–320 BDA

Cross Reference
See Colour Review

ROSENTHAL/RAYMOND PEYNET

A Rosenthal porcelain
vase, designed by
Raymond Peynet,
one side decorated with
a courting couple and
2 putti holding a pink
swag, the other with
2 putti on a flying bench,
1950s, 8¾in (22cm) high.
£140–160 P(Ba)

A set of 5 Rosenthal porcelain dishes, designed
by Raymond Peynet, decorated in brown and
black with courting and wedding scenes,
c1950–60s, large dish 5¾in (14.5cm) wide.
£130–150 RDG

A Rosenthal vase, designed by
Raymond Peynet, decorated with a
blue, pink and yellow balloon scene,
c1950–60s, 3½in (9cm) high.
£70–80 RDG

◄ A Rosenthal dish,
designed by Raymond
Peynet, decorated with
figures in a window with
blue curtains, c1950–60s,
8in (20.5cm) wide.
£40–45 RDG

A Rosenthal porcelain
vase, designed by
Raymond Peynet,
decorated with a bathing
scene, c1950–60s,
6in (15cm) high.
£130–150 RDG

**Raymond Peynet, French
artist and illustrator,
produced a range of
designs featuring his
famous drawings of
lovers for the German
company Rosenthal in
the 1950s and 1960s.**

A Rosenthal porcelain
vase, designed
by Raymond Peynet,
decorated in brown and
black with a couple on
a bridge, c1950–60s,
11¾in (30cm) high.
£250–300 RDG

A Rosenthal porcelain
group, designed by
Raymond Peynet,
entitled 'Musical Stockings',
the man wearing a lilac
hat, c1950–60s,
8in (20.5cm) high.
£450–500 RDG

A Rosenthal porcelain vase,
designed by Raymond
Peynet, decorated in
brown and black with a
couple in a boat, c1950–60,
6¼in (16cm) high.
£80–100 RDG

A Rosenthal porcelain
vase, designed by
Raymond Peynet,
with a blue whale and
mermaid, c1950–60s,
6¼in (16cm) high.
£65–75 RDG

Two Rosenthal porcelain dishes, designed by
Raymond Peynet, one decorated with a green
lizard and butterfly, the other with a winged blue
and brown tortoise, c1950–60s, 4in (10cm) diam.
£20–25 each RDG

Two Rosenthal porcelain month
dishes, designed by Raymond
Peynet, red 'Januar' and blue
'Februar', c1950–60s, 4in (10cm) diam.
£25–30 each RDG

ROYAL COPENHAGEN

A Royal Copenhagen vase, decorated with blue tulips, 1900, 8½in (21.5cm) high.
£200–250 FrG

A Royal Copenhagen bottle vase, decorated with bats on a grey ground, 1900, 6½in (16.5cm) high.
£400–450 FrG

A Royal Copenhagen frog and snake inkstand, decorated with brown leaves, 1900, 10¾in (27.5cm) wide.
£750–850 FrG

A Royal Copenhagen model of a brown owl, c1910, 5in (12.5cm) high.
£75–85 DAC

A Royal Copenhagen black and white lobster dish, c1920, 7½in (19cm) wide.
£150–180 FrG

A Royal Copenhagen figure of a Dutch woman knitting, with a blue shawl, 1950, 9in (23cm) high.
£120–140 FrG

A Royal Copenhagen figure of a girl with pigtails wearing blue dungarees, carrying a watering can, c1962, 8in (20.5cm) high.
£135–155 DAC

◄ A Royal Copenhagen figure of a girl wearing a blue skirt, with 2 goats, c1970, 9in (23cm) high.
£345–385 GSW

A Royal Copenhagen figure of a boy wearing blue holding a piglet, c1970, 7in (18cm) high.
£150–180 GSW

A Royal Copenhagen figure of a girl in riding dress, wearing a blue jumper, c1964, 7in (18cm) high.
£150–170 GSW

◄ A pair of Scottish pottery models of lions, 1880, 13in (33cm) long.
£300–350 OD

A ceramic piggy bank, with green and brown splashed decoration, early 20thC, 5in (12.5cm) long.
£40–50 OD

A Clews model of a chameleon tortoise, 1930s, 5½in (14cm) long.
£100–150 BEV

A French Mosanic dog, restored, c1900, 12½in (32cm) high.
£150–175 SER

A Beswick model of a dachshund, 1940s, 14in (35.5cm) long.
£80–95 BEV

Two Goebel models of rabbits, 1930–40s, 3½in (9cm) high.
£25–30 each EAS

A Bing & Grøndahl model of a spaniel, 1950, 4½in (11.5cm) long.
£30–40 FrG

A Szeiler studio model of a cow, 1980s, 7in (18cm) long.
£40–45 HarC

A Coalport model of Paddington Bear eating cake, 1976, 4¾in (12cm) high.
£40–50 WWY

A Beswick model of Winnie-The-Pooh, 1980s, 2½in (6.5cm) high.
£50–60 WWY

► A Cat Pottery model of a tabby cat, the extended front foot designed to overhang a shelf, 1990s, 9in (23cm) long.
£30–35 CP

A Dutch blue and white child's plate, hole filled, 1760, 6½in (16.5cm) diam.
£65–75 IW

The Dutch put holes in children's plates to enable them to be hung on a wall as a memento in the child's absence.

A Caughley blue and white custard cup and cover, decorated with Full Nankin pattern, printed in underglaze blue, c1785, 3in (7.5cm) high.
£350–400 JUP

A blue and white cream jug, decorated with Goldfinch pattern, 1820, 4in (10cm) high.
£225–245 GN

A blue and white platter, decorated with the Sundial pattern, 1820, 16in (40.5cm) wide.
£350–400 GN

A blue and white tankard, transfer-printed with a cockfight, after Henry Alken, late 19thC, 4¼in (11cm) high.
£175–220 OD

A pair of Spode blue and white ginger jars, the covers with knopped finials, decorated with Italian pattern, black mark, 19thC, 13in (33cm) high.
£80–100 each DDM

A Brannam pottery jug, by William Baron, sgraffito-decorated with a bird perched amid orange and green flowers on a blue ground, 1890, 14¼in (36cm) high.
£300–350 P(Ba)

A Brannam pottery figural jug, modelled as a puffin-like bird, decorated with a green glaze, heightened in yellow, 1899, 9½in (24cm) high.
£200–250 P(Ba)

A Brannam pottery candlestick, modelled as a horned grotesque seated with wings open and clasping a clover-shaped dish, decorated in blue, brown, green and cream slip, 1901, 6¼in (16cm) high.
£300–350 P(Ba)

A Brannam pottery twin-handled vase, sgraffito-decorated with panels of fish and flora, in green, brown and blue, the handles modelled as creeping lizards, 1911, 13¾in (35cm) high.
£400–450 P(Ba)

A pair of Bretby vases, 1890, 6½in (16.5cm) high.
£50–60 COHU

A Burleigh Ware jug, in the form of a wren on her nest, 1930s, 5in (12.5cm) high.
£145–165 BEV

A Burleigh Ware hand-painted pottery jug, the handle in the form of a golfer, 1930s, 8in (20.5cm) high.
£850–950 BEV

A Burleigh Ware Toby jug, modelled as Winston Churchill wearing a brown jacket and a blue bow tie, standing astride a bulldog, with the Union Jack draped behind him, impressed on base 'Bulldogs', factory mark and impressed 'John Bull Churchill 1940', 11¾in (30cm) high.
£230–260 P(Ba)

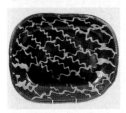

A Buckley pottery dish, decorated with slip, c1900, 13¾in (35cm) wide.
£150–200 IW

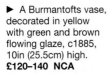

▶ A Burmantofts vase, decorated in yellow with green and brown flowing glaze, c1885, 10in (25.5cm) high.
£120–140 NCA

◀ A Burmantofts faïence pottery vase, incised with overlapping cellular shapes in a turquoise glaze, impressed 'Burmantoft Faïence', 1880–1904, 15¼in (38.5cm) high.
£170–200 P(Ba)

A Derby figure of a friar, c1880, 4½in (11.5cm) high.
£160–180 CAW

A candlestick and snuffer, in the form of a monkey on a lotus leaf, c1888, 5¼in (13.5cm) high.
£1,000–1,200 TH

A ceramic candle extinguisher, decorated with garlands of flowers, c1900, 3¼in (8.5cm) high.
£100–125 TH

A Royal Worcester candle extinguisher, in the form of a witch, c1912, 3½in (9cm) high.
£230–260 CAW

◀ Two Royal Worcester figures of Granny Snow, both chipped, 4½in (11.5cm) high.
l. c1924
£120–150
r. c1896
£230–260 CAW

◀ A Royal Worcester candle extinguisher, in the form of a Mandarin, c1925, 3¾in (9.5cm) high.
£300–350 TH

A Carlton Ware vase, decorated with a humming bird in enamel and gilt, 1920–30s, 7¾in (19.5cm) high.
£250–300 BEV

A Carlton Ware Handcraft vase, decorated with flowers, 1930, 6in (15cm) high.
£250–300 BEV

A Carlton Ware plate, decorated with Waggon Wheels pattern, 1930, 10¾in (27.5cm) diam.
£1,000–1,200 BEV

A Carlton Ware napkin ring, in the form of a clown, 1930s, 4½in (11.5cm) high.
£75–85 ChA

A Carlton Ware tea-for-two set, decorated with Yellow Buttercup pattern, comprising 10 pieces, c1940.
£720–800 AOT

A Carlton Ware money box, in the form of a train, 1970s, 7in (18cm) wide.
£30–40 AOS

A Carlton Ware teapot and cover, in the form of an RAF WWII aeroplane, decorated with the RAF circles and a pin-up 'Lucy May', the cover as a pilot, marked 'Carlton Ware Made in England', 1970–80s, 8½in (21.5cm) wide.
£300–350 P(Ba)

A Carlton Ware ceramic coffee pot and 4 mugs, 1960s, coffee pot 13in (33cm) high.
£85–95 AOS

A Royal Winton chintz ware lustre vase and pierced cover, decorated in orange and yellow flowers on a blue geometric ground, in a faint lustre glaze, 1930s, 7¾in (19.5cm) high.
£180–200 P(Ba)

◄ A Royal Winton chintz ware breakfast set, decorated with Marguerite pattern, 1950, tray 9in (23cm) wide.
£500–600 PAC

A Clarice Cliff vase, decorated with Xavier pattern, c1930–31, 7½in (19cm) high.
£1,700–1,900 BEV

A Clarice Cliff pot, decorated with Oranges pattern, c1930–31, 3½in (9cm) high.
£100–120 HEW

A Clarice Cliff Chester shape fern pot, decorated with Umbrellas and Rain pattern, 1930, 3½in (9cm) high.
£380–420 BKK

A Clarice Cliff vase, decorated with Aurea pattern, 1934, 9in (23cm) high.
£350–400 HEW

A Clarice Cliff Bizzare Lotus shape vase, decorated with Gayday pattern, impressed 'rd 668241', 1930s, 11⅛in (29cm) high.
£650–700 DDM

A Susie Cooper Nursery Ware plate, the three-sectioned plate decorated with a horse and cowboy, the rim with orange and yellow banding, with 'leaping deer' mark, 1930s, 8in (20.5cm) diam.
£220–250 P(Ba)

A Crown Devon hand-painted pottery jampot, in the form of a clown, 1930s, 5in (12.5cm) high.
£100–125 BEV

A Crown Ducal jug, 1930s, 8¼in (21cm) high.
£60–70 OD

A Crown Ducal hand-painted vase, depicting humourous golfing scenes, 1930s, 8in (20.5cm) high.
£400–450 BEV

A Doulton Burslem globular vase, decorated with pink and mauve flowers, 1880–1900, 5¾in (14.5cm) high.
£40–50 P(Ba)

A Doulton Lambeth ewer, by Eliza Simmance, 1895, 11¾in (30cm) high.
£500–600 JE

A Royal Doulton flambé vase, decorated in mottled red and blue, with printed factory mark to base and signed 'Noke, Sung', c1895, 11in (28cm) high.
£280–300 BLH

A Royal Doulton stone-ware vase, by Mark V. Marshall, c1905, 12in (30.5cm) high.
£1,200–1,500 JE

A Royal Doulton rack plate, decorated with Pansies pattern, c1930, 12in (30.5cm) diam.
£100–120 AOT

◄ A Royal Doulton moon flask, with Toby ware decoration designed by Harry Simeon, silver-mounted neck and blue-glazed stopper, stamped 'Asprey, London', impressed and incised marks to the underside 'Doulton Lambeth', hallmarked Birmingham 1929, 9½in (24cm) high.
£800–1,000 Mit

ROYAL WINTON

A Royal Winton lustre vase, 1930s, 10½in (26.5cm) wide.
£40–50 OD

A Royal Winton Olde England teapot, in the form of a cottage, decorated in yellow, green and red, c1940, 9½in (24cm) wide.
£150–180 AOT

A Royal Winton Chanticleer sugar sifter, painted in browns, 1930s, 6in (15cm) high.
£245–275 BEV

Chanticleer was the name of the cockerel in *Reynard the Fox*, Chaucer's *Nonnes Prestes Tale* and also Edmond Rostand's play, *Chanticleer*, produced in Paris in 1910.

A Royal Winton Pixie teapot, decorated with relief-moulded pattern, c1940, 9in (23cm) wide.
£250–280 AOT

A Royal Winton sugar shaker, in the form of a red rose in a green vase, 1930s, 5½in (14cm) high.
£60–70 BEV

A Royal Winton drainer and dish, decorated in green and red with Red Roof pattern, c1940, 8½in (22cm) wide.
£100–120 AOT

A Royal Winton character jug, in the form of a Native American, decorated with a yellow, orange and blue headband, 1930s, 3in (7.5cm) high.
£40–50 BTB

A Royal Winton yellow and green Iris vase, with handle, c1940, 13½in (34.5cm) high.
£200–220 AOT

A Royal Winton breakfast set for one, decorated in red and green, c1940, tray 12in (30.5cm) wide.
£200–220 AOT

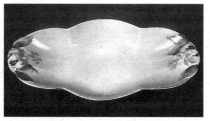

A Royal Winton serving dish, decorated with moulded flowers in red and yellow on a green ground, c1940, 11¼in (28.5cm) wide.
£35–40 DgC

A Royal Winton Olde England cheese dish, in the form of a cottage, decorated with relief-moulded pattern, c1940, 7in (18cm) wide.
£130–160 AOT

RUSKIN

A Ruskin brown-glazed ginger
jar and cover, decorated with
a green grapevine c1910,
4in (10cm) high.
£350–400 DSG

A Ruskin two-handled vase and
stand, decorated with flambé glaze
on ivory ground, impressed 'Ruskin,
England 1927', 12in (30.5cm) high.
£1,600–1,800 PAC

A Ruskin vase, decorated with
turquoise and amber crystalline
glaze, impressed 'W. Howson
Taylor, Ruskin, England 1932',
8in (20.5cm) high.
£350–400 RUSK

RYE POTTERY

A Rye Pottery green miniature
vase, c1900, 1¾in (4.5cm) high.
£40–50 NCA

A Rye Pottery bowl, decorated
with spiral bands in green,
black, yellow and red, 1960s,
8¾in (22cm) diam.
£40–50 MARK

A Rye Pottery brown miniature jug,
1910, 2¼in (5.5cm) high.
£30–35 NCA

A Rye Pottery pig, decorated in green and blue, with original box, 1950s,
5in (12.5cm) long.
£50–60 ADE

A Rye Pottery plate, decorated
in dark brown on a light brown
ground, 1960s, 12¼in (31cm) wide.
£35–40 MARK

SHELLEY

A Shelley bowl, decorated with Geisha Girl pattern in yellow, red, green and gilt on a dark blue ground, signed 'Walter Slater', 1930, 11½in (29cm) wide.
£350–400 BEV

A Shelley Harmony drip-ware ginger jar, decorated in orange and yellow, c1930, 9in (23cm) high.
£200–250 HEW

A Shelley Harmony drip-ware vase, decorated in green and brown, c1930, 6in (15cm) high.
£50–60 HEW

A Shelley cream jug, decorated with orange and yellow flowers, 1930, 3½in (9cm) high.
£25–30 DSC

▶ A Shelley tea-for-two, decorated with Daffodil Time pattern in yellow, blue, green and red, c1940, saucer 5in (12.5cm) diam.
£200–240 AOT

SHORTER & SON

A Shorter & Son vase, designed by Mabel Leigh, decorated with Autumn Leaves pattern in brown on a yellow ground, c1935, 10in (25.5cm) high.
£80–100 AOT

A Shorter & Son Daffodil vase, decorated in yellow and green on a beige ground, 1930s, 9in (23cm) high.
£100–115 BEV

A Shorter & Son Wave vase, decorated in orange and yellow, c1932, 11in (28cm) high.
£50–60 AOT

A Shorter & Son Cottage Ware coffee pot, designed by Mabel Leigh, from the Shantee series, decorated in yellow, orange, blue and green, c1935, 7½in (19cm) high.
£130–160 AOT

A Shorter & Son hand-painted dish, decorated with red flowers, c1930, 8½in (21.5cm) wide.
£30–35 CSAC

A Shorter & Son Old King Cole double-sided teapot, decorated in blue, red and brown, c1950, 5in (12.5cm) high.
£55–65 AOT

A Shorter & Son Pompadour chocolate pot with pink handle, the cover decorated with moulded apples and foliage, c1950, 7in (18cm) high.
£80–90 AOT

A Shorter & Son Gilbert & Sullivan figure, Buttercup from *HMS Pinafore*, decorated in red, blue and yellow, c1949, 10in (25.5cm) high.
£220–260 AOT

A Shorter & Son preserve jar and cover, decorated with a grey glaze, the cover with purple and red fruit, c1950, 4in (10cm) high.
£16–20 CSA

In the 1950s, Shorter reintroduced its embossed fruit designs from the 1920s and 1930s, but in new, contemporary colour-ways designed to appeal to the modern market.

A Shorter & Son Gilbert & Sullivan figure, Sir Joseph Porter from *HMS Pinafore*, decorated in black, gold and orange, c1949, 10in (25.5cm) high.
£220–260 AOT

A Shorter & Son King Neptune jug, decorated in green, pink, yellow and purple, 1950, 8in (20.5cm) high.
£60–70 AOT

A Shorter & Son Gilbert & Sullivan figure, Dick Deadeye, decorated in blue and yellow, c1949, 10in (25.5cm) high.
£220–260 AOT

Around 1940, Shorter & Son obtained permission from the D'Oyly Carte Opera Company to produce a series of figures inspired by Gilbert & Sullivan operettas. Designed by Clarice Cliff in association with Shorter designer and modeller Betty Sylvester, the series went into production in 1949. Figures were modelled on members of the cast captured in mid-gesture, each wearing an exact copy of the original stage costume. This character is from *HMS Pinafore*.

A Shorter & Son Harmony cheese dish, decorated in red and green on a yellow ground, c1950, 6½in (16.5cm) wide.
£70–80 AOT

A Shorter & Son Pompadour salad bowl and servers, decorated in green, brown and blue, c1950, 10in (25.5cm) wide.
£80–100 AOT

A Shorter & Son Fish set, comprising 3 of 8 pieces, decorated in green and yellow, c1960, largest dish 13in (33cm) wide.
£80–90 AOT

STAFFORDSHIRE

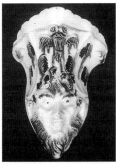

A Staffordshire wall vase, with moulded decoration in blue and green, solid red earthenware back, repaired, c1765, 6¾in (17cm) high.
£850–950 JHo

A Staffordshire whistle, in the form of a rabbit, decorated in green and yellow, 18thC, 2¾in (7cm) wide.
£600–700 JHo

A Staffordshire figure, entitled 'Juno and the Peacock', Juno wearing a yellow cape and floral-patterned dress, c1800, 5¾in (14.5cm) high.
£200–250 SER

A Staffordshire model of a rabbit, decorated in blue and orange, c1780, 2¼in (5.5cm) wide.
£500–600 JHo

A Staffordshire figure of Iphigenia, with red, blue and yellow dress, on a green base, 1790–1800, 7¾in (19.5cm) high.
£200–250 SER

A Staffordshire model of a brown bear, on a green base, c1800, 3½in (9cm) high.
£600–700 JHo

A Staffordshire figure of a woman, one of Four Seasons series, with brown robe, on a green base, c1780, 7in (18cm) high.
£200–225 SER

A Staffordshire figure of Bacchus, with pink robe, on a green base, slight damage, c1780, 7¼in (18.5cm) high.
£215–235 SER

A Staffordshire model of a hen, decorated in black, on a green base, early 19thC, 3¼in (8.5cm) high.
£700–800 JHo

A Staffordshire gardener group, the woman carrying a rake and the man a scythe, both figures decorated in yellow and red, on a green base, c1820, 9½in (24cm) high.
£350–400 JO

A Staffordshire porcellaneous model of a dog, in brown and white, c1840, 4½in (11.5cm) high.
£200–230 JRc

A Staffordshire Prattware figure of a huntsman, wearing a green tunic, c1800, 5in (12.5cm) high.
£125–150 SER

A Staffordshire model of a poodle, c1840, 4½in (11.5cm) high.
£130–150 JO

A Staffordshire two-part folly, decorated in blue, pink, red, yellow and gilt, c1840, 7½in (19cm) high.
£450–500 JO

A Staffordshire figure of Falstaff, decorated in brown and iron-red, on a green base, c1810, 8¾in (22cm) high.
£350–400 JO

A Staffordshire spill vase, in the form of a boy and dog before a tree-trunk, the boy wearing a red coat and spotted breeches, c1810, 8¾in (22cm) high.
£350–400 JO

A pair of Staffordshire models of sheep, with gilt rim line to base, c1830, 3¼in (8.5cm) wide.
£450–500 JO

A pair of Staffordshire models of poodles, with pink tongues, gilt rim line to base, c1835, 3½in (9cm) high.
£300–340 JO

▶ A Staffordshire figure of a girl sitting on a goat, possibly Princess Royal, wearing a blue dress, c1850, 4in (10cm) high.
£100–125 SER

A pair of Staffordshire figures of Victoria and Albert, decorated in blue, red, and yellow, c1850, 11½in (29cm) high.
£500–550 JO

A Staffordshire watch holder, modelled as a castle, decorated in red, blue, green and yellow, c1855, 10¾in (27.5cm) high.
£200–220 JO

A Staffordshire model of a cat, in orange and white, 1850–60, 6½in (16.5cm) wide.
£200–250 SER

A Staffordshire figure of the Prince of Wales dressed as a sailor, wearing a black-spotted shirt and scarf, on a brown and green base, 19thC, 13in (33cm) high.
£300–350 DHA

A Staffordshire figure of Sir William Wallace, wearing a plumed hat and carrying a sword and shield, decorated in red, blue and orange, 1860s, 17in (43cm) high.
£350–400 AnS

Sir William Wallace (1270–1305) was one of Scotland's great heroes. He defeated an English army of 50,000 men at Stirling in 1297, and drove the English from Scotland. Edward I, however, pursued him, and his army was defeated at Falkirk in 1298. Wallace went into hiding, but was betrayed by fellow Scot, Sir John Monteith. He was executed in London on 22 August 1305, and his quartered body was dispatched north, being displayed on gibbets in Newcastle, Berwick, Stirling and Perth.

► A Staffordshire group, entitled 'Soldier's Return', the soldier wearing a red hatched sash and the woman a striped skirt in red, blue and green, c1860, 9¼in (23.5cm) high.
£170–200 JO

A Staffordshire figure of Lord Kitchener, riding a horse, in white on a green base, c1900, 12in (30.5cm) high.
£170–200 AnS

STUDIO POTTERY

A Michael Buckland pottery bowl, decorated in red and green, c1920, 7½in (19cm) diam.
£170–200 DSG

A Michael Cardew stoneware bowl, made at Wenford Bridge, decorated with an incised line pattern in brown and green, 1950s, 14in (35.5cm) diam.
£600–700 RUSK

A Derek Clarkson pottery vase, decorated with a crystalline-effect pattern in green and yellow, c1980, 7½in (19cm) high.
£180–200 PGA

A Joanna Constantinidis stoneware vase, decorated in brown and speckled grey, red mark, c1990, 9in (23cm) high.
£300–350 PGA

A Dartington Pottery high-fired stoneware bowl, designed by Roger Law and Janice Tchalenko, with moulded carp decoration in brown and blue, limited edition of 100, 1996, 11¾in (30cm) diam.
£200–230 RDG

A Dennis China Works Autumn jug, designed by Sally Tuffin, decorated with brown leaves on a yellow and green ground, 1996, 10in (25.5cm) high.
£200–250 NP

◀ A David Frith stoneware ginger jar, decorated in green and brown, 1980, 6½in (16.5cm) high.
£35–40 IW

A John Dunn exhibition-piece vase, decorated in shades of beige, c1990, 16½in (42cm) high.
£650–800 DSG

▶ A Walter Keeler teapot, decorated with black speckled glaze, 1985–90, 12in (30.5cm) wide.
£500–600 DSG

A David Leach slipware tankard, made at St Ives, decorated with a shield pattern in black on a brown ground, small chip, early 1930s, 5½in (14cm) high.
£130–160 OD

A Leach Pottery standardware bowl, decorated with a bird and banded in green and brown, impressed 'St Ives', c1960, 5in (12.5cm) diam.
£80–100 RUSK

A Dennis Moore Green Dean pottery bowl, decorated in blue, green and brown, c1950, 7in (18cm) diam.
£200–250 DSG

A Ray Marshall coffee pot, decorated in shades of brown, 1963, 9¾in (25cm) high.
£20–25 IW

A pair of Mary Rich pottery miniature vases, decorated in Persian style with gilded bands, c1986, largest 4in (10cm) high.
£125–150 each PGA

An Ursula Marley-Price pinched stoneware bowl, the irregular wavy rim covered in oatmeal slip, 1990s, 9½in (24cm) diam.
£400–450 PGA

▶ A Bernard Rooke vase, decorated with a pattern of circles in green and brown, 1960s, 7in (18cm) high.
£65–80 MARK

A John Ward vase, decorated with vertical stripes in green on a cream ground, c1990, 7in (18cm) high.
£500–600 DSG

A Troika Coffin vase, decorated in brown and grey, 1970s, 6¾in (17cm) high.
£65–75 MARK

A Geoffrey Whiting pottery teapot, decorated with brown glaze, c1975, 7½in (19cm) wide.
£450–500 DSG

A Winchcombe bowl, by Sid Tustin, decorated in black on a green ground, 1950–60s, 6in (15cm) diam.
£16–20 IW

SYLVAC

The pottery, founded in Stoke-on-Trent by William Shaw and William Copestake in 1894, began using the name SylvaC in the mid-1930s. Products included tableware, vases, wall pockets and novelty items ranging from household fancies to garden gnomes. In the late 1920s, the company began to produce animal models and, at around the same time, developed the range of low-fired matt glazes that would become associated with the SylvaC name – typical muted colours include beige, green, blue and brown. A large variety of animals was manufactured, most notably dogs, which are very popular with collectors today. Most pieces are impressed on the base with the model number, factory name and 'England'.

A pair of SylvaC brown and blue candlesticks, 1930, 7in (18cm) high.
£75–85 BEV

A SylvaC Budgie vase, decorated with a blue budgerigar on a pink ground, 1930s, 9in (23cm) high.
£60–70 BtB

A SylvaC model of a terrier, No. 145, 1930s, 5in (12.5cm) wide.
£35–40 TAC

A SylvaC beige model of a dog, No. 2938, c1930, 4in (10cm) high.
£20–25 TAC

Miller's is a price GUIDE not a price LIST

A SylvaC model of a brown dog and yellow basket, 1930s, 5½in (14cm) wide.
£25–30 TAC

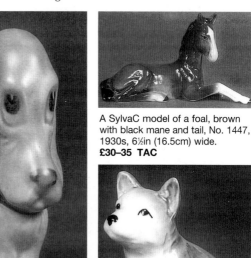

A SylvaC model of a foal, brown with black mane and tail, No. 1447, 1930s, 6½in (16.5cm) wide.
£30–35 TAC

A SylvaC model of a brown corgi puppy, 1930–50, 3in (7.5cm) high.
£20–25 TAC

A SylvaC model of a black, brown and white collie dog, in No. 2502, 1930–50, 8in (20.5cm) long.
£45–55 TAC

TEAPOTS & TEA SETS

A Derbyshire brown salt-glazed teapot, cover replaced, c1840, 7½in (19cm) wide.
£50–60 IW

A Staffordshire tortoiseshell teapot, in green and black, standing on 3 feet, restored, c1765, 4½in (11.5cm) high.
£1,000–1,150 JHo

The unglazed creamware body of tortoiseshell ware is sponged with several colours of metallic oxide, then overglazed with a transparent lead glaze.

A Wedgwood stoneware teapot, decorated with blue flowers and foliage on a brown smear-glazed ground, 1830, 4in (10cm) high.
£70–80 IW

▶ A Japanese Banko teapot, decorated with applied white birds and blue and yellow flowers, c1900, 6in (15cm) wide.
£100–125 JaG

A Doulton Lambeth tea set, decorated in shades of brown, c1895, teapot 7in (18cm) wide.
£450–500 JE

A Victorian Rockingham-style tea service, comprising teapot, covered sugar bowl, milk jug, slop bowl, 18 cups, 12 saucers and 2 bread plates, the borders painted with lyre and acanthus motifs in turquoise, blue and gilt, saucer 4¾in (12cm) diam.
£550–650 DA

A Jackson & Gosling porcelain cube tea set, decorated with flowers in red, green and yellow, 1920–30, teapot 3¼in (8.5cm) high.
£100–125 PGA

The cube pot was patented in 1916 by R. C. Johnson as a 'safety' teapot. It was used on the Cunard liners, because it was easy to stack and did not tip over in high seas. Despite the fact that the spout dribbled, cube pots were purchased in their thousands by the Lyons Corner Houses and tea shops that sprang up in the inter-war period, when tea drinking was at its height in the UK. Cube pots were produced by many companies during this period, and the shape is considered a classic example of Art Deco design.

A Doulton Royle's Patent Self-Pouring Teapot, decorated with Spray pattern in blue with silver-plated mounts and cover, 1886–1900, 9in (23cm) high.
£170–200 DDM

The Royle's Patent Self-Pouring Teapot was manufactured in Doulton's Burslem factory for J. J. Royle of Manchester. A metal collar attached to the underside of the lid trapped 'a cupful' of air. When the lid was pressed down into the pot, tea was forced out through the spout and into the cup.

A novelty brown squirrel teapot, by Tony Wood, 1970–80, 7¼in (18.5cm) high.
£8–10 MED

Teapots & Tea Sets • CERAMICS 163

TILES

A pair of German tiles, depicting Caesar and Rex Davit, decorated in blue, brown and orange on a green ground, c1530, 11¼in (28.5cm) high.
£3,500–4,000 JHO

A Liverpool tile, transfer-printed in manganese with St. Andrew, restored, 1760, 5¼in (13.5cm) high.
£55–65 JHO

A Bristol tile, transfer-printed in manganese with a lady in a landscape, slight damage, c1760, 5in (12.5cm) square.
£85–95 JHO

A Dutch blue and white tile, with cattle and herdsmen in a landscape, 18thC, 5in (12.5cm) square.
£30–50 JHO

A Victorian tile, decorated with a black pattern on a white gound, 1880, 6in (15cm) square.
£7–10 GIN

A Delft tile, decorated with brown flowers in a vase on a white ground, slight damage, 19thC, 5in (12.5cm) square.
£18–22 AOH

A pair of Minton tiles, in black, blue and white, designed by John Moyr Smith, one inscribed 'Elaine', c1875, 6in (15cm) square.
£100–120 DSG

These tiles are from a series based on Alfred Lord Tennyson's _Idylls of the King_ (1859).

A Rozenburg tile, decorated in brown with a painting after J. W. van Borselen, 1893, 13in (33cm) high, framed.
£500–600 OO

A tile, decorated with a photograph of US President Theodore Roosevelt, in black and grey, c1910, 6in (15cm) high.
£35–40 WAB

TORQUAY POTTERY

A Hele Cross parrot jug, decorated in blue, green, orange and yellow, 1905–18, 6in (15cm) high.
£25–30 PC

A Lemon & Crute posy vase, decorated in the Alexander Rose pattern in pink, green and black on a white ground, c1914, 3¾in (9.5cm) high.
£20–30 TPCS

A pair of Royal Torquay Pottery vases, decorated with orange and green pattern on a blue ground, c1920, 9¼in (23.5cm) high.
£85–100 DSG

A Longpark vase, in the form of a tree-trunk in dark brown, c1920, 7½in (19cm) high.
£35–45 IW

▶ A Barton sugar bowl, decorated with pink blossom and green leaves on a blue ground, 1922–38, 3in (7.5cm) diam.
£10–15 TPCS

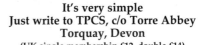

A Watcombe jam dish, decorated in shades of orange, blue and green, inscribed 'Take a little jam', 1930s, 5¼in (13.5cm) wide.
£10–15 OD

A pair of Torquay vases, decorated with kingfishers in blue, brown and yellow on a brown ground, 1930s, 6in (15cm) high.
£40–50 BTB

A Longpark bowl, decorated with Crocus pattern in shades of red, green and yellow, with mauve fluted edge, c1930–40, 5¾in (14.5cm) diam.
£12–15 PC

A Lynmouth motto bowl, decorated with brown and green pattern on a cream ground, 1940, 4in (10cm) diam.
£30–35 RAC

WADE

The Wade group of potteries, founded in the second half of the 19th century, produced tableware and industrial ceramics. The 1930s saw the establishment of an art pottery, and the manufacture of a large range of ornamental and novelty ware. During the 1950s, the company introduced its most famous novelty line, the Wade Whimsies. Launched at the British Industries Fair in the spring of 1954, and designed as pocket money toys, the little animal models sold in sets of five for 5s 9d (about 28p) and were an instant hit. Wade controlled production so that the porcelain miniatures would not flood the market, and to increase demand some figures were only manufactured for a limited period. Between 1954 and 1961, Wade produced one set of four, and nine sets of five miniatures, and today these First Whimsies are very sought-after. The success of this new line spawned a host of other models, including Minikins – small, white-glazed animals that sold for one shilling (5p) each, and the Hat Box series, characters from

Walt Disney films, beginning with *Lady and the Tramp* in 1956, packaged in round, striped, cardboard boxes resembling hat boxes.

As well as figures for retail, Wade also manufactured a vast amount of promotional ware, ranging from Christmas cracker favours for Tom Smith & Co to the famous Gollies for Robertson's preserves. In 1967, Red Rose Tea, Canada, commissioned Wade to produce a series of animals as free gifts to go with packages of teabags. The long-running campaign was extended to the USA and proved so successful that Red Rose estimates that over 150 million Wade models have been distributed with their tea in North America, while in the UK, Brooke Bond also offered Wade figures as a free gift with teabags.

Prices for Wade depend above all on rarity. While the most unusual sets and models can fetch hundreds of pounds and more, the commonplace miniatures that were produced in their millions can be picked up for a couple of pounds or less, and are still popular collectables with children.

A Wadeheath group, Snow White & the Seven Dwarfs, Snow White decorated in yellow, Dwarfs decorated in red, green, blue and browns, c1938, largest 7in (18cm) high.
£1,200–1,500 GOR

This is one of the most sought-after of all Wade sets.

A Wade Comic Penguin Family, Mr & Mrs Penguin, Benny and Penny, cream with grey backs, blue hats and scarf, 1940s, largest 3¾in (9.5cm) high.
£400–450 PC

Five Wade Minikins from various sets, decorated with green, red and yellow markings, c1955–58, 1in (2.5cm) high.
£8–12 each MRW

A Wade squirrel, fawn with a brown nut, 1940–50s, 3in (7.5cm) high.
£100–150 PC

Four Wade First Whimsies, from the African Jungle Animals series, Lion, Monkey & Baby, Rhinoceros and Crocodile, decorated in browns and grey, c1955–58, largest 1¾in (4.5cm) wide.
£10–30 each McG

Two Wade First Whimsies, Foxhound, fawn and white, and Swan, from Farm Animals set No. 10, each on a green ground, c1959, 2in (5cm) wide.
£120–150 each MRW

Two Wade First Whimsies, shire horses from Farm Animals set No. 10, one fawn and one grey, c1959, 2in (5cm) high.
£130–150 each MRW

Two Wade Disney Hat Box series animals, Baby Pegasus grey with white wings and mane, Dumbo cream with pale pink ears, 1956–65, largest 1¾in (4.5cm) high.
£30–40 each PC

A Wade Pearly Queen, from the British Character set, pink, grey and white, 1959, 2¾in (7cm) high.
£70–80 PC

Four Wade Disney Hat Box series animals, Si and Am, fawn with black paws and tails, Toughy, beige with red mouth, and Jock with green and red tartan coat, 1956–65, largest 2in (5cm) high.
£25–45 each McG

Four Wade Disney Hat Box series animals, Peg, with a yellow fringe, Dachie, with dark brown ears, Flower the skunk, black and white, and Thumper holding red and yellow flowers, 1956–65, largest 1¾in (4.5cm) high.
£20–30 each PC

Four Wade First Whimsies, Husky, fawn with white chest and tail, Lion Cub, tawny, Retriever, golden yellow on a green base, and Snowy Owl, cream with yellow eyes,1950s, largest 1¼in (3cm) high.
£15–25 each McG

Three Wade TV Pets, from *Bengo and his Puppy Friends*, Mitzi, blue-grey and white with pink mouth, Bengo, light brown and white with grey muzzle, and Pepi, white with tan patches, 1959–65, largest 2¼in (5.5cm) high.
£30–35 each McG

Four Wade TV Pets, from *Bengo and his Puppy Friends'*, Droopy Junior, with white chest and grey ear tips, Percy, beige with orange patches, Bruno, with brown rump, head and ears with red tongue, Whisky, beige with white face, chest and paws and red tongue, 1959–65, largest 2¼in 5.5cm) high.
£80–100 each PC

A Wade First Whimsies St. Bernard dog, from Pedigree Dogs set No. 7, brown and white, 1957, 2in (5cm) long.
£60–70 HarC

Three Wade TV Pets from *Bengo and His Puppy Friends,* Simon, white with black spots, Chee-Chee, beige with white face, chest and paws, and Fifi, grey and white with red bow, 1959–65, largest 2¼in (5.5cm) high.
£15–25 each McG

A Wade hedgehog with lid, light chestnut body and dark brown quills and nose, 1961, 4in (10cm) wide.
£25–30 PC

A Wade First Issue animal, The Girl Squirrel, beige and white with honey-brown tail and black eyes, on a green base, 1956–65, 2in (5cm) high
£75–80 HarC

A Wade Blow Up Disney Tramp, with grey and white face, neck and chest, and red tongue, 1961–65, 6in (15cm) high.
£230–250 PC

A Wade pottery plaque, Marty Wilde from the Teenage Pottery Series, flesh colour, brown hair, yellow and green collar, on dark brown ground, 1950s, 3¾in (9.5cm) high.
£100–120 McG

A Wade Blow Up model of Thumper, holding red and yellow flowers, 1961–65, 5½in (14cm) high.
£180–200 PC

Thumper is one of the most difficult figures to find.

◀ A Wade Blow Up Polar, copy of a smaller model Whimsy, cream and white on a blue and white base, 1961–62, 5¾in (14.5cm) high.
£150–180 McG

◀ A Wade Blow Up Disney dog, Scamp, grey with pink ears, 1961–65, 4½in (11cm) high.
£100–130 PC

A Wade Disney owl, Archimedes, brown with red beak and yellow eyes, 1956–65, 2in (5cm) high.
£70–80 PC

Five Wade Nursery Favourites figures, Tom Tom the Piper's Son with brown jacket, Mary Had a Little Lamb with blue bonnet, Mary Mary with blue dress, Wee Willie Winkie with grey nightshirt, and Little Jack Horner with green jacket, 1972–1974, largest 3in (7.5cm) high.
£25–40 each McG

A pair of Wade Disney animals, Tom, blue with white chest and muzzle, and Gerry, fawn with white chest and muzzle, 1973–79, largest 3½in (9cm) high.
£55–65 DDM

These models originally retailed at 95p for the pair.

A Wade Disney group, Snow White and the Seven Dwarfs, Second Version, in yellow, red, blue and brown on green bases, 1981–84, largest 3¾in (9.5cm) high.
£700–750 McG

The original price of this set in 1981 was £39.50.

◄ A Wade bell-shaped whisky decanter, commemorating the wedding of Prince Charles and Lady Diana Spencer, gilt banding, full, sealed and boxed, 1981, 10¼in (26cm) high.
£400–500 PC

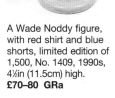

A Wade Noddy figure, with red shirt and blue shorts, limited edition of 1,500, No. 1409, 1990s, 4½in (11.5cm) high.
£70–80 GRa

A Wade, black and white Bertie Badger, designed for the St John's Ambulance Brigade, limited edition of 5,000, 1989–94, 4in (10cm) high.
£120–140 PC

A Wade Childhood Favourites series model, Rupert and the Snowman, No. 4, Camtrak limited edition of 2,000, No. 1363, 1997, 5in (12.5cm) high.
£60–70 HarC

A Wade Big Ears figure, with red and white shirt, blue jacket and red hat and nose, No. 1409, limited edition of 1,500, 1990s, 6in (15cm) high.
£70–80 GRa

▶ Two Wade models of Arthur Hare, for C&S Collectables, the left fawn, limited edition of 200, the right blue, limited edition of 2,000, 6in (15cm) high.
l. £100–150 r. £50–60 HarC

C&S Collectables commissioned Arthur Hare in late 1993. They are the first of a series of comic animals based on the characters from a British storybook, *The Adventures of Arthur Hare and the Silent Butterfly*.

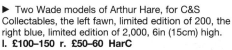

WEDGWOOD

A Wedgwood black basalt crocus pot, modelled as a hedgehog, some restoration, 1790, 10in (25.5cm) wide.
£380–420 OD

A Wedgwood cane ware honey pot, straw-coloured, c1800, 5in (12.5cm) high.
£180–200 HUM

A Wedgwood egg cup, decorated with green, mauve and black design on white ground, c1820, 2¼in (5.5cm) high.
£75–85 AMH

Cross Reference
See Colour Review

A Wedgwood jasper ware honey pot, decorated with white pattern on a dark blue ground, c1910, 5in (12.5cm) diam.
£250–280 HUM

A Wedgwood model, Tiger and Buck, by John Skeaping, cream-glazed, from a series of 10 animal subjects, marked, 1927–30, 13½in (34.5cm) wide.
£130–160 P(Ba)

A Wedgwood majolica game dish, with applied rabbit finial, moulded with game and flowers, incised mark, late 19thC, 10½in (26.5cm) wide.
£330–360 GAK

A Wedgwood pottery vase and bowl, by Keith Murray, with cream Moonstone glaze, the vase moulded with vertical fluting, the bowl with silver-coloured banding, 1930–35, bowl 9½in (24.5cm) diam.
£170–200 P(Ba)

A Wedgwood earthenware bowl, by Alfred Powell, decorated with deer in gold lustre, c1930, 12½in (32cm) diam.
£450–500 RUSK

A Wedgwood Beatrix Potter jam pot, decorated with Peter Rabbit in brown, green and blue, 1970s, 4½in (11.5cm) high.
£25–30 WWY

◄ A Wedgwood model of Taurus the bull, by Arnold Machin, with gilt signs of the zodiac on a black ground, limited edition of 250, marked, 1987, 13½in (34.5cm) wide.
£140–160 P(Ba)

KATHIE WINKLE

Kathie Winkle (b1932) started work in the potteries of Shorter & Son at the age of 15, then in 1950 joined the Stoke-on-Trent firm of James Broadhurst & Sons. Initially employed as a paintress, she began to produce her own designs in 1958. Winkle worked in the 'contemporary' style, and her geometric patterns in fashionable browns, greens, yellows and oranges appealed to the new generation of baby-boomers furnishing their 1960s homes with Scandinavian-style furniture, abstract textiles and modern tableware. Following the lead of potteries such as Midwinter, who made a feature of designers' names, Broadhurst included Kathie Winkle's signature on the backstamp as an added selling point. The company also expanded into new areas, selling direct to supermarkets and producing boxed sets for the growing mail order catalogue business.

Kathie Winkle ceramics were marketed as stylish but affordable crockery. Designs were printed with semi-automatic rubber stamping machines and then hand-coloured, a technique that permitted mass production since, with such simple designs, an experienced paintress could decorate over a thousand pieces a day. Nevertheless, by the late 1970s mechanisation overtook most methods of hand decoration. Kathie Winkle switched from designing ceramics to quality control in 1978, finally retiring in 1992.

In 1999, the first book about Kathie Winkle was published, compiled by an enthusiast who came across an example of her work in the 1996/97 *Miller's Collectables Price Guide*, and then having tracked down her ceramics in boot fairs, charity shops and auctions, decided to research and record their history.

Thanks in part to the efforts of such dedicated collectors, interest in 1960s and 1970s decorative arts continues to grow, and these ceramics are a perfect example of works that are currently making the move from the second-hand shop to the antiques market.

A Kathie Winkle plate, decorated with Pedro pattern in yellow, blue and green, c1958, 5½in (14cm) diam. £12–15 PC

Three Kathie Winkle pieces, decorated with Albany pattern in grey, yellow and turquoise, c1959. Plate 7in (18cm) diam. £10–12 Sugar bowl 4in (10cm) diam. £18–20 Vegetable dish with cover 9½in (24cm) diam. £45–50 KWCC

A Kathie Winkle mark.

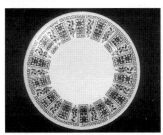

A Kathie Winkle plate, decorated with Apollo pattern in red, blue, yellow, green and black, c1963, 7in (18cm) diam. £6–7 PC

A Kathie Winkle gravy boat and stand, and an oval plate, decorated with Newlyn pattern in yellow, red and green, c1963, plate 12in (30.5cm) wide. £20–25 each PC

A Kathie Winkle plate, decorated with Harebell pattern in blue and yellow, 1964, 6¾in (17cm) diam. £2–3 Law

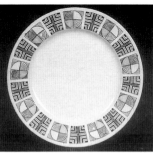

A Kathie Winkle 22-piece tea set and coffee pot, decorated in yellow and red with Rushstone pattern, c1965.
Plate 7in (18cm) diam.
Coffee pot 9in (23cm) high.

£180–200
£35–45 KWCC

A Kathie Winkle 21-piece tea set, decorated with Concord pattern in blue and red, c1965, tea plate 7in (18cm) diam.
£185–200 PC

Two Kathie Winkle plates, decorated with Rushstone pattern in brown and yellow, 1965, largest 9½in (24cm) diam.
£5–7 Law

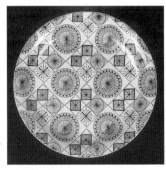

A Kathie Winkle plate, decorated with Compass pattern in blue and yellow, c1968, 9½in (24cm) diam.
£25–30 KWCC

A Kathie Winkle plate, decorated with Electra pattern in olive green and black, 1969, 6¾in (17cm) diam.
£3–4 Law

A Kathie Winkle plate, decorated with Renaissance pattern in orange and olive green, 1970, 9½in (24cm) diam.
£5–6 Law

A Kathie Winkle plate, decorated with Versailles pattern in orange and brown, 1970, 9½in (24cm) diam.
£5–6 Law

A Kathie Winkle 21-piece coffee set and plate, decorated with Mexico pattern in orange and brown, c1970, plate 9½in (24cm) diam.
£200–220 PC

A Kathie Winkle plate, decorated with Carousel pattern in blue and yellow, 1971, 9½in (24cm) diam.
£5–6 Law

Two Kathie Winkle plates, decorated with Wild Flowers pattern in pink and green, c1975,
8in (20.5cm) diam. **£8–10**
7in (18cm) diam. **£4–6 KWCC**

A Kathie Winkle cup, saucer and plate, decorated with Wayfarer pattern in red, c1976, plate 9½in (24cm) diam.
£10–14 KWCC

WORCESTER

A Worcester potted meat tub, shape No. 22, painted with Cannonball pattern in underglaze blue, c1760, 5¼in (13.5cm) diam.
£350–400 JUP

A Worcester cream jug, shape No. 29, painted in underglaze blue with flowers and gilt highlights, c1780, 3½in (9cm) high.
£220–250 JUP

A Royal Worcester egg cup, decorated with blue flowers and gilt rim, 1894, 2½in (6.5cm) high.
£45–50 AMH

A Royal Worcester pedestal bowl, shape No. 1807, the rim moulded with foliate scrolls, the body decorated in colours with butterflies and foliage, on a blush ground with gilded detail, small repair to foot and minor rim chip, printed mark and date cipher for 1895, 10in (25.5cm) high.
£370–420 GAK

A pair of Royal Worcester blush porcelain sweetmeat dishes, each modelled as a scallop shell, painted with floral sprays with gilt rims, on rustic silver-plated stands with loop handles surmounted by a cherub, c1900, 6in (15cm) high.
£430–480 AH

A Royal Worcester jug, hand-decorated with pink, green, blue and gilt flowers, gilt handle and rim, 1895–1915, 3¾in (9.5cm) high.
£100–125 BEV

◀ A Royal Worcester vase, hand-decorated with birds in blue, brown and gilt, and gilt handles, 1895–1915, 7in (18cm) high.
£280–320 BEV

▶ A Royal Worcester vase, hand-decorated with red, yellow, green and gilt flowers, gilt rim, 1895–1915, 6¾in (17cm) high.
£165–185 BEV

A Royal Worcester coffee pot, hand-decorated with pink, blue, orange and green flowers, gilt handle and rim, 1895–1915, 9in (23cm) high.
£440–480 BEV

A Royal Worcester pepper pot, modelled as Bonzo, pink with a red nose and black spot, 1920–30s, 3in (7.5cm) high.
£450–550 BEV

A Royal Worcester brooch, in the form of a foxhound, with black and tan markings, 1932, 1¾in (4.5cm) wide.
£200–225 TH

A Royal Worcester brooch, in the form of a bull terrier, white with pink inner ears, 1932, 2in (5cm) high.
£200–225 TH

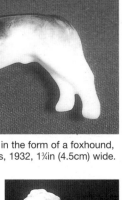

A Royal Worcester figure, Spain, from the Children of the Nations series, by Freda Doughty, with pink dress and yellow and green flowers to apron, marked, 1934–59, 5½in (14cm) high.
£250–280 JEA

A Royal Worcester figure, Holland, from the Children of the Nations series, by Freda Doughty, with blue and pink dress and yellow clogs, marked, 1934–59, 5½in (14cm) high.
£250–280 JEA

A Royal Worcester figure, England, from the Children of the Nations series, by Freda Doughty, with blue dress and yellow hair, marked, 1934–59, 6in (15cm) high.
£250–280 WAC

A Royal Worcester figure, Wales, from the Children of the Nations series, by Freda Doughty, with pink dress and yellow flowers, marked, 1935–59, 5½in (14cm) high.
£250–280 JEA

▶ A Royal Worcester model, Bears, decorated in brown, c1942, 5½in (14cm) wide.
£600–680 CAW

This model is quite rare in the UK and was mainly exported to USA.

◀ A Royal Worcester model, Happy Days, in green, rey, cream and brown, by Freda Doughty, marked, 1948–55, 7½in (19cm) high.
£1,000–1,250 CAW

A Royal Worcester figure, Pick-a-Back, modelled by Phoebe Stabler, decorated in mauve, green and blue, puce mark, c1930, 8½in (21.5cm) high.
£750–850 JEA

Phoebe Stabler also worked for the Royal Doulton factory.

A Royal Worcester figure, Burma, by Freda Doughty, c1960, 5in (12.5cm) high.
£140–160 GRI

A Royal Worcester figure, March, from the Months of the Year series, by Freda Doughty, with pink dress and blue hat, marked, c1950–85, 6in (15cm) high.
£200–230 JEA

▶ A Royal Worcester figure, September, from the Months of the Year series, by Freda Doughty, with and trousers and white cat, marked, 1950–61, 4½in (11.5cm) high.
£200–225 WAC

A Royal Worcester figure, January, from the Months of the Year series, by Freda Doughty, marked, c1950–85, 6¼in (16cm) high.
£180–200 CAW

Christmas Collectables

A Christmas postcard, decorated with a lady in red, on a yellow and blue ground, c1905–10, 5½ x 3½in (14 x 9cm).
£4–5 JMC

A Christmas postcard, decorated in red, green and silver, 1905–10, 5½ x 3½in (14 x 9cm).
£1–2 JMC

A Christmas postcard, decorated in green, red and blue, 1905–10, 5½ x 3½in (14 x 9cm).
£1–2 JMC

A Christmas postcard, decorated in green, red and orange, 1908, 5½ x 3½in (14 x 9cm).
£1–2 JMC

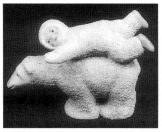

A German ceramic snow baby on a polar bear, white with a pink face and yellow boots, 1920–30, 4in (10cm) long.
£70–80 HUX

A German ceramic snow baby, with a pink face and red shoes, 1920–30, 2¼in (5.5cm) high.
£70–80 PC

A German ceramic snow baby, white with a pink face, 1920–30, 4¼in (11cm) high.
£70–80 HUX

A German Father Christmas cake decoration, with a red coat and hat and pink face, 1920–30, 3¼in (8.5cm) high.
£45–50 PC

A Christmas stocking, in red felt with green trim to top, 1950s, 15in (38cm) high.
£16–18 SMAM

A Santa Claus Christmas decoration, green, red and gold, 1950s, 5in (12.5cm) high.
£15–20 AnS

A G. L. Wilsons Santa Claus Club 1958 badge, red and black, 1¼in (3cm) diam.
£3–4 SVB

Cocktails

The word 'cocktail' first appeared in the USA at the beginning of the 19th century, but it was in the 1920s and '30s that the cocktail truly came into its own, ironically inspired by Prohibition (1919–33). In order to beat the ban, huge amounts of illicit alcohol were manufactured. To conceal its often poor taste, Americans took to mixing their drinks and the cocktail, colourful and frivolous, became the drink of the Jazz Age. American barmen, escaping the Depression, took the art of mixing cocktails to Europe – US-born Henry Craddock opened London's first cocktail bar at the Savoy Hotel, which soon became a Mecca for the bright young things.

The cocktail inspired a host of new accoutrements and fashions. The cocktail party was all the rage and the cocktail cabinet became the centrepiece of the Art Deco living-room. As well as liqueurs, this contained cocktail shaker, cocktail glasses in every shape, ice bucket, swizzle and cocktail sticks. The concept of miniaturized cocktail food also emerged in the same period and, in 1933, the Fortnum & Mason's catalogue proudly announced the arrival of the cocktail sausage.

Cocktail-drinking went out during WWII, but came back in the 1950s and '60s, with the addition of plastic fittings, pin-up-style decorative motifs, and new cocktail cabinet essentials such as the Sparklet's soda syphon.

A chrome cocktail shaker, with red Bakelite top, and 6 glasses with red bases, 1930s, shaker 11½in (29cm) high.
£100–125 SpM

A brass and copper champagne bottle, with cranberry glass decanter and 3 glasses inside, 1920–30, 12in (30.5cm) high.
£450–500 BEV

A silver-plated cocktail shaker, 1930s, 9in (23cm) high.
£100–125 BEV

A silver-plated cocktail shaker, 1930s, 9in (23cm) high.
£50–60 BEV

◄ A silver-plated cocktail shaker, with lemon-squeezer in the lid, 1930s, 8in (20.5cm) high.
£50–60 BEV

▶ A hand-bell cocktail shaker, with chrome and wood handle, 1930s, 11¼in (28.6cm) high.
£100–120 BEV

A Bakelite cocktail shaker, with silver-plated top showing recipe for a Tom Collins, 1930s, 11in (28cm) high.
£250–300 BEV

A silver-plated hip flask, with raised panel and Art Deco decoration, 1930s, 3¾in (9.5cm) high.
£40–45 BEV

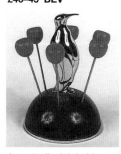

A cocktail stick holder, with chrome penguin and 6 sticks with Bakelite 'cherry' tops, 1930s, 3½in (9cm) high.
£60–70 BEV

A silver-plated ice bucket, with stepped lid and black finial, 1930s, 7in (18cm) high.
£85–95 BEV

A silver-plated hip flask, with raised panel, 1930s, 5¾in (14.5cm) high.
£45–55 BEV

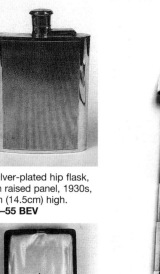

A set of Walker & Hall silver cocktail sticks, with red Bakelite tops, in original case, 1930s, 3½in (9cm) high.
£40–50 BEV

A silver-plated ice bucket, with rope-twist decoration on rim, handles and base, 1930s, 10in (25.5cm) high.
£145–165 BEV

A French advertising novelty telescopic cigarette holder, in the shape of a champagne bottle, 1930s, 1½in (4cm) high.
£85–95 LBe

A silver-plated champagne bucket, with ring handles, 1930s, 6¾in (17cm) high.
£85–95 BEV

A silver-plated cocktail measure, in the shape of a cat, 1930s, 4in (10cm) high.
£55–65 BEV

A silver-plated double measure, with a golf ball centrepiece, 1930s, 4¾in (12cm) high.
£30–35 BEV

A WMF cocktail stick holder, the sticks in the shape of swords, 1930s, 6in (15cm) high.
£35–40 BEV

Three Austrian bottle-stoppers, modelled as figures with moving heads and arms, in blue, green, red and brown, 1930s, 5in (12.5cm) high.
£35–40 each EMC

A Huntley & Palmers Football Wafers tin, with red, cream and black lettering on brown ground, c1930, 6in (15cm) high.
£15–20 HUX

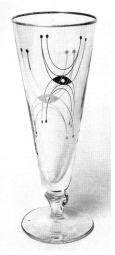

A set of 4 American beer glasses, with gilt decoration, 1950s, 8¼in (21cm) high.
£30–35 SpM

A set of 4 Martini glasses with yellow plastic mermaid cocktail sticks, 1940s–50s, glass 5¾in (14.5cm) high.
£20–25 SpM

A chrome globe-shaped combined soda syphon and ice bucket, 1950s, 16in (40.5cm) high.
£250–280 ZOOM

A Planters Cocktail Peanuts tin, in yellow and white on a dark blue ground, full and unopened, 1950s, 3in (7.5cm) high.
£8–10 HUX

> **Cross Reference**
> See Colour Review

An aluminium cocktail tray, painted with bottles, lemons, cherries and a cocktail glass, in red, blue, yellow and green, 1950s, 9¼in (23.5cm) wide.
£24–27 SpM

A glass cocktail shaker with chrome lid, and 2 glasses, with printed cocktail recipes in red and blue, 1950s, shaker 6½in (16.5cm) high.
£30–35 set SpM

▶ A Sparklets Globemaster soda syphon, blue and chrome, 1960s, 12in (30.5cm) high, with box.
£60–75 ZOOM

A set of 4 drinks pourers, made for pub use, modelled as birds, in blue, green, red and yellow, c1950, 5in (12.5cm) high.
£30–35 DAC

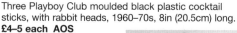

A Wink-A-Drink Liquor Pourer, in the form of an eye, inscribed 'Have an Eye Opener', 1962, 2¾in (7cm) high, with original box.
£10–15 SpM

Three Playboy Club moulded black plastic cocktail sticks, with rabbit heads, 1960–70s, 8in (20.5cm) long.
£4–5 each AOS

A Sparklets Hostmaster soda syphon, dark blue with black top and base, 1960s, 13in (33cm) high, with box.
£35–50 ZOOM

A packet of cocktail mats, napkins and plastic sticks, in original package, decorated with mice and glasses in pink, lilac and green, 1960s, 8½in (21.5cm) wide.
£10–12 SpM

A chrome soda syphon, with green bands and top, 1960s, 11¾in (30cm) high.
£20–25 ZOOM

A German plastic ice bucket, modelled as a top hat, Nortec, Danish design by Ole M. Jensen 1960–70s, 13in (33cm) wide.
£50–60 ZOOM

A soda syphon, red with black top, 1970s, 12¾in (32.5cm) high.
£10–15 ZOOM

A soda syphon, decorated with silver circles on a white ground, 1970s, 13¼in (33.5cm) high.
£15–20 ZOOM

Two glass Martini cocktail mixers, decorated with logo and cocktail recipes, 1970, 6in (15cm) high.
£2–3 each AL

A plastic ice bucket, modelled as a pineapple in cream with gilt foliage, 1970, 13¼in (33.5cm) high.
£85–95 ZOOM

Comics

The past year has been an exciting time for British comics. Recent auction records include £6,820 ($11,050) for the *Beano* comic No. 1 with free Whoopee Mask (1938), and just under £5,000 ($8,000) for *Dandy* comic No. 1 (1937). 'It's all a question of rarity,' explains Malcolm Phillips from Comic Book Postal Auctions. 'Only about eight No. 1 issues are known to exist of each of these comics, and everybody wants one. The reason for this is that *Beano* and *Dandy* have remained popular, and in publication, for over 50 years and so appeal to a broad age-range. That record-breaking *Beano* sold to an enthuusiast who was only 25. Whereas there used to be just one or two people bidding for something, now numbers can be far greater.'

Increased competition has not only pushed prices up – *Beanos* No. 2 and 3 can both fetch over £1,000 ($1,600) – but has also expanded the collectable market. '*Beezer, Topper, Lion, Tiger, Eagle* and especially *TV 21* are also beginning to make some strong prices,' says Phillips. 'A lot of people are getting into the 1960s.' It was during this time that US Comics (*Amazing Spiderman, Fantastic Four*, etc) began to be widely distributed in the UK. 'The period from c1959 when these American super-hero comics first came over, until the early 1970s, is known as the Silver Age of US Comics,' says Phillips. 'They can certainly be valuable but condition is absolutely critical. A comic worth $10,000 (£6,000) in mint condition might fetch $5,000 (£3,000) in fine condition, $500 (£300) in good but worn condition, and so on downwards. Everything is carefully graded.' Phillips is very keen to point out, however, that collecting comics is not all about super-hero-type prices. 'The bulk of the comic business is people buying an old favourite for £1–2 ($2.5–3.5). The old story papers from the 1930s, *Hotspur, Rover, Wizard, Triumph, Champion*, can still be picked up for this sort of money. That is what makes comics so much fun. There is something for everybody in every price range.'

Twenty issues of *Adventure* comic, Nos. 664, 695, 698–700, 702, 703, 705–708, 718, 720, 721, 737, 738, 740, 757, 768, 774, Issue 774 good condition, balance very good condition, 1934–36.
£250–280 CBP

▶ Eighteen *Beano* comics, Nos. 445, 446, 451–453 Easter issue, 461, 463, 468–70, 474, 477, 478, 480, 484–487, 1951, very good condition.
£170–200 CBP

The Boys' Friend, August 26th 1916.
£5–6 DPO

The Dandy comic, No. 1,
first adventures of Korky The Cat
and Desperate Dan, one of only
8 copies known to exist, 1937.
£4,900–5,200 CBP

**Founded in 1937, *Dandy* is
now the longest-running comic
in the world.**

The Dandy Monster Comic annual,
restored, very good condition, 1939.
£2,700–2,900 CBP

The Dandy's Desperate Dan, first
annual, very good condition, 1954.
£125–150 CBP

Flash Comics, No. 1, Shelly
Moldoff cover art, restored, 1940.
£2,300–2,500 CBP

**With all comics, first issues
are usually more valuable than
later issues.**

The Gem comic,
10th September 1921.
£3–4 DPO

The Incredible Hulk comic, No. 1,
very good condition, 1962.
£370–400 CBP

The Midget Comic, cover illustration
by Dudley Watkins, 1930s.
£90–110 CBP

Merry and Bright comic,
September 22nd 1917.
£4–5 DPO

The Popular comic, 7th May 1921.
£2–3 DPO

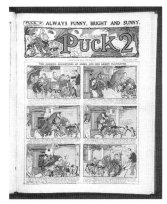

Puck 2 comic, March 26th 1927.
£3–4 DPO

Strange Adventures comic, No. 1, very good condition, 1950.
£300–350 CBP

Strange Tales comic, No. 7, slightly worn, 1952.
£200–220 CBP

Sub-Mariner comic, No. 38, starring Syd Shores marine super-hero, last pre-code issue, very good condition, 1955.
£320–380 CBP

The Sunbeam comic, No. 579, March 6th 1927.
£4–6 DPO

Tales of Suspense comic, No. 39, Iron Man is Born, fine condition, 1963.
£240–260 CBP

Century TV21 Annual, published by City Magazine Ltd and AP Films, 1965, 11in (28cm) high.
£8–10 J&J

The Union Jack Library comic, No. 927, July 16th 1921.
£3–4 DPO

The Wizard comic, No. 1797, July 23rd 1960.
£3–4 DPO

Commemorative Ware

MILITARY & NAVAL

A Wedgwood creamware teapot, transfer-printed in black with the Marquis of Granby, after the engraving by Richard Houston, the reverse with a battle scene within a scrolling cartouche, c1766, 4¼in (11cm) high.
£3,200–3,500 SAS

John Manners, Marquis of Granby, succeeded as Commander-in-Chief in 1766, having previously achieved a spectacular victory at Warburg in 1760, prompting Horace Walpole to refer to him as 'the mob's hero'. The expression 'going bald-headed' derives from Granby losing his wig when charging at the Battle of Minden in 1759.

A black basalt teapot, commemorating Wellington and Vittoria, moulded with mask-head spout and panels with figures beneath a laurel-leaf band, 1813, 5¾in (14.5cm) high.
£270–300 SAS

▶ An octagonal pottery jug, commemorating the Crimea, transfer-printed in black and enamelled in red, green, blue and yellow, with gilt rim, chip to spout, 1854, 6¼in (16cm) high.
£140–160 SAS

A Prattware plaque, moulded with a portrait of Admiral the Earl Howe flanked by trophies of war in blue, yellow, brown and green with a yellow moulded border, with blue scrolling above and below, some repair and flaking, c1794, 8¼in (21cm) high.
£1,600–1,800 SAS

A pottery mug, commemorating the Crimea, transfer-printed in black, the reverse with a scene entitled 'The Sailor's Return', cracked, 1854, 5in (12.5cm) high.
£70–80 SAS

A Staffordshire creamware mug, commemorating Duncan's Victory at Camperdown, transfer-printed in black with 2 sailing ships, inscribed 'De-Winters Ship Vryheid' and 'Duncan's Ship Venrable', restored, 1797, 5in (12.5cm) high.
£2,000–2,400 SAS

A brown treacle-glazed jug, in the form of The Duke of Wellington, 1854, 7in (18cm) high.
£75–85 COHU

◀ A pottery jug, commemorating Sir George Brown and the Battle of the Alma, transfer-printed in black with a battle scene, the reverse with a view entitled 'Sebastopol', 1854, 8¼in (21cm) high.
£350–400 SAS

A Copeland Parian bust of Nelson, slight damage, the reverse with impressed mark, c1855, 11½in (29cm) high, on a socle base.
£800–1,000 SAS

A spelter bust of General Charles George Gordon, on a named plinth base, c1885, 12¾in (32.5cm) high.
£200–220 SAS

Cross Reference
See Militaria

A glass picture, depicting the tomb of the unknown warrior, Westminster Abbey, inscribed for the 1914–18 war, 10 x 8in (25.5 x 20.5cm), framed.
£80–90 SAS

A Robinson & Leadbeater parian bust of Lord Roberts, the reverse inscribed 'by W. C. Lawton Sculpt. copyright Jan. 1900', on a named base, 8in (20.5cm) high.
£100–120 SAS

▶ A mug, commemorating the Great War, printed in colours with Kaiser Bill and Franz Josef II, c1918, 3in (7.5cm) high.
£35–40 MGC

A brown-glazed tile, commemorating the Boer War, moulded with a portrait of Lord Roberts, 1899–1902, 6in (15cm) square.
£30–40 MGC

A beaker, commemorating the Boer War, transfer-printed in brown and enamelled in colours with Lord Kitchener, Sir Redvers Buller and Lord Roberts, blue crown mark, 1899–1902, 3½in (9cm) high.
£80–90 StC

▶ An 'Old Bill' Tank Bank money box, with purple glaze, 1918, 4in (10cm) wide.
£40–45 MGC

POLITICAL

A jug, commemorating Colonel Gwyllym Lloyd Wardle, the yellow ground printed in grey with named portraits of Colonel Wardle and Miss Taylor, each within a black painted cartouche, black rim line, c1809, 6¾in (17cm) high.
£650–750 SAS

Colonel Wardle was elected MP of Okehampton in 1807. On 27th January 1809 he brought a motion against Frederick, Duke of York, alleging indiscretions with Mary Anne Clarke. Miss 'May' Taylor was a key witness to the investigations by the House of Commons committee in 1809.

A creamware jug, commemorating Henry Brougham, transfer-printed in grey with a named portrait of a youthful Henry Brougham above a seven-line loyal address, the reverse with a scene of African slavery, lined in blue, c1811, 4¾in (12cm) high.
£2,000–2,400 SAS

Brougham's Felony Act of 1811 made the shipping and trafficking of slaves a felony punishable by transportation.

A jug, commemorating Henry Hunt, transfer-printed in black with a portrait and inscribed on the reverse, banded in pink lustre and decorated with red, green and mauve around the rim, c1819, 6in (15cm) high.
£550–650 SAS

Henry Hunt (1773–1835) was a staunch Radical, who devoted much of his life to the repeal of the Corn Laws and parliamentary reform. On 6th August 1819 he was speaking to a crowd of some 50,000 at St Petersfield, Manchester. The authorities tried to arrest him, his audience fought back, and the cavalry charged into the crowd killing 11 people and injuring 400. The incident became known as the Peterloo Massacre and Hunt was imprisoned for 3 years.

A pottery jug, depicting Sir Robert Peel, transfer-printed in blue with named portrait, the reverse with a view of Drayton Manor, spout restored, 1850, 5¾in (14.5cm) high.
£150–180 SAS

A porcelain vase, depicting William Pitt the younger, painted with a portrait on a profusely gilded white ground, the reverse with floral panel, restored rim, inscribed in iron-red 'Pitt No. 262', c1821, 5¼in (13.5cm) high.
£380–420 SAS

Cross Reference
See Colour Review

A plaque, transfer-printed with portrait entitled 'Hon. Charles Pelham Villiers, M.P.', lined in black, c1846, 6½in (16.5cm) diam.
£400–450 IS

Charles Villiers and Richard Cobden repealed the Corn Laws in 1846.

◄ A brass plaque, cast with a portrait of Earl of Beaconsfield, c1881, 9½in (24cm) high.
£50–60 SAS

A Doulton Lambeth stoneware tyg, commemorating Henry William Wyndham-Quin, in brown with blue and brown bands to handles, inscribed with his electoral success, crest of the Dunraven family and flowers of the Union, impressed marks, 1895, 6½in (16.5cm) high.
£400–450 SAS

A pottery plate, commemorating the National Health Insurance Act 1912, transfer-printed in green with portrait of Rt. Hon. David Lloyd George, 10¾in (27.5cm) diam.
£110–130 SAS

A plate, commemorating The Borough of Richmond Yorks Charter Celebration 1329–1929, transfer-printed in blue, with ox roast and crest, 8¼in (21cm) diam.
£50–55 MAC

A jug, moulded with a portrait of William Ewart Gladstone and 'G.O.M', green and yellow, 1880–90, 9in (23cm) high.
£55–65 MGC

A pottery plate, printed in black and decorated in colours with a caricature of Herbert Asquith on a black ground within a blue and gilt border, c1915, 10¾in (27.5cm) diam.
£180–200 SAS

An Ashtead Potters buff-coloured caricature jug depicting Stanley Baldwin, with facsimile signature, the underside numbered 28 of edition of 1,000, c1931, 7½in (19cm) high.
£170–200 SAS

A Doulton Lambeth brown stoneware plaque, moulded with a portrait and entitled 'William Pitt 1806–1906', the reverse inscribed 'Doulton Lambeth 1.1.06 J Broad Sc.', 7¾in (19.5cm) high.
£170–200 SAS

A pottery jug, transfer-printed with a picture of the Houses of Parliament, Belfast, in black with green and blue, the ground with pink and black crazed-effect pattern, c1920, 3½in (9cm) high.
£15–17 MLa

A tile, transfer-printed in magenta with Joseph Chamberlain, chipped, 1900–10, 6in (15cm) square.
£30–40 MGC

A Staffordshire pottery caricature of Herbert Henry Asquith, painted in brown, black and red, blue line to base, c1911, 5½in (14cm) high.
£120–150 SAS

Asquith succeeded Henry Campbell-Bannerman as Prime Minister in 1908. He encountered a number of difficulties. Following the 'People's Budget' of 1909, the Parliament Act of 1911 removed the right of veto from the Lords. The Suffragette Movement, Industrial Strife, Irish Home Rule and subsequent outbreak of WWI all confronted him.

A Chiswick Ceramics mug, commemorating Margaret Thatcher, transfer-printed in blue, produced for Britannia, Gray's Antique Market, 1979, 3½in (9cm) high.
£10–15 HUX

Political • COMMEMORATIVE WARE 187

ROYALTY

A commemorative jug, transfer-printed in purple with King William IV and Queen Adelaide flanking a crown entitled 'Crowned Sep 8 1831', 19thC, 8in (20.5cm) high.
£170–200 CGC

A cup and saucer, commemorating Queen Victoria's Diamond Jubilee, decorated with a portrait in yellow, blue and red, 1897, 3in (7.5cm) high.
£50–60 AnS

A Copeland mug, commemorating Queen Victoria's Diamond Jubilee, the moulded portrait on a dark ground, 1897, 3in (7.5cm) high.
£80–100 MGC

▶ A Copeland pottery mug, commemorating Queen Victoria's Diamond Jubilee, transfer-printed in brown with portrait and inscription 'God Bless Our Queen Long May She Reign', 1897, 3in (7.5cm) high.
£75–85 GwR

A Staffordshire nursery plate, commemorating the coronation of Queen Victoria, transfer-printed in blue with her portrait and inscribed 'Victoria Regina, Born 25th May 1819 Proclaimed 20th of June 1837', the border moulded with flowers and foliage, 1837, 6½in (16.5cm) diam.
£350–400 SAS

Interestingly, the birth date on this plate is incorrect – Queen Victoria was born on 24th May.

A Royal Worcester plate, commemorating Queen Victoria's Golden Jubilee, transfer-printed in blue with a portrait within an inscribed wreath, the border printed with thistles and roses, 1887, 10½in (26.5cm) diam.
£85–95 GwR

A *sucrier* and cover, blue with cream moulded busts of Victoria and Albert, cream banding to bowl and cover, c1840, 4¾in (12cm) high.
£80–100 IW

An Aller Vale mug, commemorating Queen Victoria's Diamond Jubilee, brown and green on a yellow ground, inscribed '1837' 'VR' and '1897', 4½in (11.5cm) high.
£220–250 MGC

A Crown Staffordshire jug, commemorating the coronation of King Edward VII, moulded with portraits and crest, with gilt lion handle, No. 33 from a limited edition of 500, 1902, 8in (20.5cm) high.
£250–300 MGC

A Paragon porcelain mug, commemorating the Silver Jubilee of King George V and Queen Mary, transfer-printed in brown with portraits, the crown and union flag in colours, with flower-moulded handle in pink, green and blue, 1935, 3¾in (9.5cm) high.
£60–70 GwR

A Wedgwood beaker, commemorating the coronation of King George VI and Queen Elizabeth transfer-printed in blue and pink, 1937, 4½in (11.5cm) high.
£50–60 MGC

A Minton two-handled loving cup, commemorating the coronation of Queen Elizabeth II, decorated in gilt, 1953, 4in (10cm) high.
£110–130 MGC

A Wedgwood beaker, commemorating the coronation of Edward VIII May 1937, transfer-printed in blue and pink with portrait and crown, 4½in (11.5cm) high.
£45–55 MGC

A pair of display busts, depicting King George VI and Queen Elizabeth, painted in realistic colours with blue clothes and gilt, on square bases, late 1930s, 22in (56cm) high.
£600–700 BTB

A mug, commemorating the coronation of Queen Elizabeth II, transfer-printed in brown with red, green and yellow, gilt rim line, 1953, 4in (10cm) high.
£12–16 AnS

A mug, commemorating the coronation of Edward VIII transfer-printed in red, blue, green and yellow, with gilt rim line, 1937, 3in (7.5cm) high.
£30–40 AnS

A jug, by E. T. Bailie, moulded with scenes of the coronation of Queen Elizabeth II, the handle with moulded crown, light brown and pale green, 1952, 8½in (21.5cm) high.
£50–60 DSG

Miller's is a price GUIDE not a price LIST

An Aynsley plate, commemorating the visit of HRH Princess Margaret to Canada, transfer-printed in brown, with gilt rim line, 1958, 6½in (16.5cm) wide.
£40–50 MGC

Corkscrews

A double-action corkscrew, of the type patented by Sir Edward Thomason in 1802, decorated with embossed autumn fruits, bone handle and brush, c1820, 7¼in (18.5cm) high.
£330–350 CS

A Thomason four-pillar brass corkscrew, with signed collar and bone handle and brush, 1820, 5in (12.5cm) high.
£600–700 EMC

A two-pillar brass corkscrew, with open frame, turned walnut handle and brush, c1830, 8¼in (21cm) high.
£85–90 CS

A half-bottle or small Thomason-type double-action corkscrew, with ringed brass barrel and royal coat-of-arms badge, turned bone handle and brush, wire helix, early 19thC, 7in (18cm) high.
£220–250 P(B)

A folding bow corkscrew, 1860, 3in (7.5cm) high.
£200–250 EMC

A silver-plated figural corkscrew, the handle and shaft modelled as a standing putti with a bunch of grapes in each hand, wire helix, possibly Scandinavian, 1890–1920, 6½in (16.5cm) high.
£240–280 P(B)

A Thomason-type double-action corkscrew, the ringed bronze barrel with royal coat-of-arms marked 'ne plus ultra', with large turned-wood handle, possibly old replacement, wire helix damaged, some marks to barrel, early 19thC, 7in (18cm) high.
£130–160 P(B)

A Holborn champagne screw, with turned wooden handle, 1880, 6½in (16.5cm) high.
£200–250 EMC

A corkscrew, black with brass plate inscribed 'C. Hull Birmingham Royal Club Corkscrew' and with coat-of-arms, 1864, 9½in (24cm) high.
£1,500–1,700 EMC

A champagne bottle top, to pour and seal, 1920, 5½in (14cm) high.
£75–85 EMC

A brass corkscrew, modelled as a cat, 1930s, 4in (10cm) long.
£50–60 EMC

A brass corkscrew, modelled as a motor-cycle and rider, 1930s, 3½in (9cm) long.
£40–50 EMC

◄ A silver-plated corkscrew, modelled as a dog, 1930, 2½in (6.5cm) long.
£28–32 BEV

► A silver-plated bottle opener, in the form of a donkey, 1930, 3½in (9cm) high.
£30–40 BEV

An American table corkscrew, depicting Senator Volstead and inscribed 'Old Snifter', marked with maker's name 'Demley', c1935, 6¾in (17cm) high.
£50–60 CS

An American soroco-wood corkscrew, in the form of The Old Codger, the head detachable from the body and fitted with corkscrew with bell cap, c1940, 8½in (21.5cm) high.
£35–40 CS

◄ A Scandinavian corkscrew, modelled as a pair of seahorses, 1940s, 5¼in (13.5cm) high.
£65–75 EMC

Cosmetics & Hairdressing

A tortoiseshell comb, by Murrle Bennet, with gold decoration, 1900, 5in (12.5cm) wide.
£150–180 CHAP

A Carlton Ware orange powder bowl, the finial in the form of a lady wearing a black dress and holding a red rose, 1920, 5in (12.5cm) high.
£160–200 LeB

A powder box, the cover in the form of a ceramic Spanish dancer, wearing a brown dress trimmed with black lace, red painted fan and headdress, registration number to base and incised mark 'Germany', 1920s, 5in (12.5cm) high.
£160–200 LeB

A ceramic powder bowl, in the form of a flapper, the legs forming the handle of the powder puff, decorated with gilt, 1920s, 7in (18cm) high.
£200–220 LeB

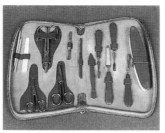

A manicure set, with green handles, in a tan leather case, 1930, 12in (30.5cm) wide.
£15–20 UTP

A silver dressing set, with pink enamel backs, in original blue case, 1931, 14in (35.5cm) wide.
£130–150 JACK

A silver hairbrush, by Wilson & Sharpe, Edinburgh, with yellow enamel back, 1931, 9in (23cm) long.
£50–60 JACK

A plastic fold-up comb, the handle forming the case, 1930s, 4½in (11.5cm) long.
£12–15 CHU

◀ A French base-metal powder compact with green shading, marked 'Beauté', 1930s, 2in (5cm) square.
£10–15 PC

▶ A base-metal compact, with black decoration, marked 'Naturelle', 1930s, 2in (5cm) diam.
£5–7 PC

A pair of silver hair brushes, with green enamel backs, Birmingham 1934, 9in (23cm) long.
£90–110 JACK

A brown plastic comb, with incised brass cover, 1950–60, 5in (12.5cm) long.
£18–20 CHU

◀ An Ormond Bakelite hairdryer, in original case, 1930s, 10in (25.5cm) wide.
£20–30 MED

MEN'S TOILETRIES

A silver travelling shaving brush, Birmingham 1804, in a leather case, 11in (28cm) long.
£180–200 HUM

A Victorian brass double-sided shaving mirror, on a tripod base, 15in (38cm) high.
£170–190 RUL

◀ An American condom tin, decorated in brown and yellow, 1930s, 2in (5cm) wide.
£40–50 HUX

A steel and Bakelite cut-throat razor, in a wooden box, engraved 'Chas Clements King of Diamonds', unused, 1920–30, 6in 15cm) wide.
£45–50 DHO

A Lund's steel and Bakelite cut-throat razor, in a leather case, unused, 1920–30s, 6½in (16.5cm) long.
£30–35 DHO

Condoms

'Something for the weekend, sir?', barbers would ask their male customers after the weekly cut and shave. Condoms are said to be named after a Colonel Condom, an 18thC British Guards officer who was anxious to protect his men from venereal disease. In use for centuries, protective sheaths were manufactured from materials including linen, leather and animal intestines. The 19thC saw the introduction of rubber and in 1932 the London Rubber Company launched the most famous brand in the world, Durex, named after its three prime requisites, 'Durability, Reliability and Excellence'.

A packet of Durex, 1964, 4⅛in (11.5cm) wide.
£8–10 HUX

Disneyana

A set of 13 Disney children's plates, with brightly-coloured transfer-printed pictures telling the story of the circus coming to town, French, early 1930s, largest 11in (28cm) diam.
£800–960 Bon(C)

A Paragon child's mug, decorated with Mickey Mouse, the base marked 'Wishing you a Happy Christmas from HRH Duchess of York, Dec 25th 1932', signed 'Walter E. Disney' 3in (7.5cm) high.
£500–600 AAV

This mug was given to a young boy in the TB ward at Mearnskirk Hospital, Newton, Mearns, Glasgow.

A Phillip Segal figure of Minnie Mouse, her green dress with yellow flowers, slight damage, 1947, 2¾in (7cm) high.
£170–200 S(S)

Phillip Segal was refused permission to market his Mickey and Minnie Mouse figures. Very few are known to exist.

A Mickey Mouse rubber composition toy, with red trousers, yellow top and blue bow, c1950, 9in (23cm) high.
£25–30 RAR

A set of Snow White picture bricks with cards, decorated in bright colours, c1950, box 8in (20.5cm) wide.
£25–35 GAZE

A Urago diecast and plastic ⅛th scale model of a Bugatti Type 59, with Goofy driving, green, red and orange, c1980, 11in (28cm) long.
£20–25 MED

A Beswick figure of Peter Pan, with green jerkin and black trousers, 1965, 4¾in (12cm) high.
£200–250 WWY

A Duanny Sylvester and Tweetie Pie hot water bottle, black, yellow, orange and red, 1984, 14in (35.5cm) high.
£5–8 MED

A Royal Doulton group, Patch, Rolly and Freckles from *101 Dalmations*, No. 2437 from a limited edition of 3,500, 1997, 7in (18cm) wide.
£155–185 PAC

Dolls

BISQUE

A Simone bisque-headed doll, with blonde hair, wearing a brown and black dress, c1870, 18in (45.5cm) high.
£1,200–1,500 DOL

A Bru bisque-headed doll, with blonde wig and gussetted fabric body, slight damage, c1875, 17½in (44.5cm) high.
£1,500–1,800 S

A pair of Bähr & Pröschild bisque-headed dolls, wearing white dresses with red cloaks, mould No. 309, c1890, largest 30in (76cm) high.
£650–750 DOL

A Kestner bisque-headed doll, with blonde wig, wearing a cream lace dress with pink sash, c1890, 24in (61cm) high.
£2,300–2,600 DOL

An Alt, Beck & Gottschalk bisque shoulderheaded doll, with fixed blue glass eyes, dressed in a dark grey changeable satin skirt and jacket with lace skullcap, apron and collar, and a trunk of clothes, c1895, 18½in (47cm) high.
£550–600 S

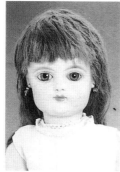

An Eden bisque-headed *bébé* doll, with fixed blue paperweight eyes and brown wig, dressed in white cotton underclothes, slight damage, c1890, 23½in (60cm) high.
£1,200–1,400 S

▶ An S.F.B.J. bisque-headed doll, with black eyes, wearing a pink spotted cream dress and cream hat, marked, 1902, 21in (53.5cm) high.
£160–180 BGC

A Gebrüder Heubach bisque-headed doll, dressed in brown suit with white collar and cap, c1900, 24in (61cm) high.
£1,400–1,700 DOL

A bisque-headed baby doll, with painted hair and face and blue glass sleeping eyes, dressed in original cream christening gown, the head marked 'A.M. Germany', c1900, 12in (30.5cm) high.
£100–120 BLH

A Heubach bisque-headed doll, with blonde wig, brown glass sleeping eyes, wearing a grey-blue dress, marked 'Heubach 250.44/09 Köppelsdorf', clothes worn, c1900, 16in (38cm) high.
£80–100 BLH

◀ A Kämmer & Reinhardt bisque-headed doll, with weighted blue glass eyes and long brown mohair wig, wearing a peach silk and cream lace dress and straw hat, incised 'K and R', c1910, 25½in (62cm) high.
£900–1,100 Bon(C)

A Kämmer & Reinhardt bisque-headed doll, with auburn hair, wearing a cream dress with lace cap, c1910, 14in (35.5cm) high.
£1,000–1,200 DOL

▶ A German fully-jointed all-bisque googly-eyed doll, with weighted blue glass eyes and long dark brown mohair wig, probably Kestner, c1915, 4¾in (12cm) high.
£800–1,000 S

An Armand Marseille bisque-headed sailor doll, dressed in black with cream hat and collar, c1920, 13in (33cm) high.
£200–250 DOL

A German bisque-headed character doll, with fixed brown almond eyes, wearing a cream silk dress and lawn pinafore, probably by Armand Marseille, damaged, c1910, 29½in (75cm) high.
£700–800 S

A German all-bisque piano baby, c1920, 6¼in (16cm) high.
£50–60 YC

A Kämmer & Reinhardt bisque-headed character doll, wearing a pale green and white dress and bonnet, mould No. 121, 1915, 22in (60cm) high.
£550–650 DOL

▶ A Max Handwerke *bébé élite* doll, wearing a cream dress and pink bow, with extra clothes in basket, c1920, doll 17in (43cm) high.
£580–650 DOL

An Armand Marseille bisque-headed dream baby hand puppet, in pink and cream lace bed, c1925, bed 11in (28cm) wide.
£300–350 DOL

CELLULOID

A Schultz celluloid character doll, wearing a white dress, c1930, 24in (61cm) high.
£350–420 DOL

◀ A South African celluloid baby doll, dressed in Zulu costume with beaded anklet, necklace and bracelet, maker's mark to back, 1920–30, 6in (16cm) high.
£40–50 BLH

A Kämmer & Reinhardt celluloid doll, with long blonde wig, wearing a pink and white pattern dress and white cape, together with trunk and trouseau, c1920, 19in (50cm) high.
£600–700 Bon(C)

COMPOSITION

A Heubach Kopplesdorf composition doll, with a red and white striped dress, 1930, 15in (38cm) high.
£250–275 DOL

A composition doll, with blonde hair, wearing a white dress and cream shawl, probably Schilling, Germany, c1890, 22in (60cm) high.
£350–400 DOL

A pair of composition twin baby dolls in a pull-along bed, German, 1920s, bed 11in (28cm) long.
£200–220 BGC

> Miller's is a price GUIDE not a price LIST

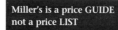

▶ A Käthe Kruse composition doll, with blonde wig, in original cardboard box, stamped 'made in Germany US Zone', 1957, 18in (46cm) high.
£350–400 S(S)

▶ A composite walking doll, with applied wig, wearing a lilac dress with white collar and cuffs, 1950–60, 23in (58.5cm) high.
£25–30 BLH

PLASTIC

A Pedigree hard plastic baby doll, with open and shut eyes, dressed in blue jacket, trousers and hood, 1940s, 14in (35.5cm) high.
£70–80 GRa

A Tudor Rose hard plastic doll, dressed in Fairy Glen Brownie outfit, 1950s, 7½in (19cm) high.
£30–40 GRa

A Pedigree hard plastic doll, with flirty eyes, wearing original white dress, 1940–60, 16in (40.5cm) high.
£50–60 BGC

A Gene Marshall Ashton Drake doll, Blue Goddess, dressed in 'Goodbye New York' outfit in brown and white, 1996, 15in (38cm) high.
£70–80 PC

◄ A St Lucia plastic doll, dressed in blue skirt, and red and orange cap, 1960s, 10in (25.5cm) high.
£14–18 GRa

A hard plastic Asian boy doll, dressed in original blue, white and brown striped trousers, 1950s, 6in (15cm) high.
£18–22 GRa

A Pedigree plastic pin-up doll, with blonde hair and pink bows, wearing original red, brown and white checked dress and white jacket, 1952, 14in (35.5cm) high.
£65–75 GRa

ACTION MAN

In 1964, the American company Hasbro introduced GI Joe, a doll for boys. His manly visage was based on photographs of 20 decorated US veterans and the toy soldier was an instant success. Palitoy secured the UK rights and changed the scar-faced hero's name. Action Man was launched in January 1966 and by the 1970s it was estimated that there was one Action Man for every boy in Britain. As with Barbie and Sindy, it was the multifarious outfits and accessories that attracted children, and still appeal to adult collectors today.

In the early years, uniforms were made from a thick twill material, with insignia either being stitched to the material or produced as metal or plastic badges and buttons. Accessories tended to be made in plastic. By the late 1970s, much thinner cotton was being used, insignia were generally printed and the use of plastic for badges, etc. increased. The price ranges shown here are for mint, or near mint, unboxed items. As with many toys, the presence of the original box or packaging can double, or even treble, the value of an object.

An Action Man, with painted head, original Field Jacket and pack set, and metal dog-tag, 1966, 12in (30.5cm) high.
£100–120 CY

An Action Man, with green Russian Infantry uniform and gun, 1968, 12in (30.5cm) high.
£95–105 CY

A Palitoy Action Man German Storm Trooper uniform, 1975, box 14 x 10in (35.5 x 25.5cm).
£150–170 TOY

An Action Man, with painted head, in khaki American MP uniform with red collar and yellow truncheon, 1966, 12in (30.5cm) high.
£75–85 CY

An Action Man horse, with saddle and bridle, stirrups missing, 1970s, 13in (33cm) high.
£45–55 UNI

An Action Man Mercury Astronaut and Capsule, with blue interior, American flag on underside, 1970, 13in (33 cm) long.
Figure   £65–70
Capsule £30–35 CY

The Mercury Space Capsule and Astronaut was introduced to the range in 1970 following the 1969 Apollo moon landing.

An Action Man Police Motor Cyclist, in Police Patrol Uniform, black with red sash and belt, 1979–80, 14in (35.5cm) wide.
£20–25 CY

Although issued later in the range, good examples of the white motorcycle are difficult to find as they are often discoloured, turning yellow due to sunlight.

BARBIE

Barbie was launched in 1959, when Ruth and Elliot Handler, founders of the US company Mattel, came up with the concept of a teenage fashion doll, named after their daughter Barbara and inspired by her love of playing with cut-out paper dolls. Although toy stores were initially reluctant to stock a doll with breasts, children were captivated. 'It was the clothing and accessories that did it,' says Elizabeth Lee, President of the UK Barbie Collectors Club. 'Ruth Handler deliberately didn't give the doll a specific personality, she wanted children to create their own Barbie characters through dressing her up.'

Over 40 years on, Barbie is now a very grown-up business indeed, worth an estimated $1.9 billion (£1.2 billion) a year. Two Barbies are purchased every second, and since 1959 over one billion Barbie dolls have been sold – placed head-to-toe, they would circle the earth more than seven times.

For adult enthusiasts, the most collectable dolls are the vintage Barbies, ie those produced before 1971. 'Vintage divides into two periods, the Ponytail Era, 1959–66, and the Mod Era, 1967–72,' explains Elizabeth. 'A good identification trick is to look at Barbie's bottom. She's marked on the right buttock. Don't go by date, since that might just refer to the copyright year, but anything collectable will be marked 'Japan', where the early dolls were made.' Condition is very important to value, check for missing hair, broken little fingers and other signs of juvenile damage, and a doll that's never been removed from its box can be worth three times as much as a doll that is in excellent, but played-with condition.

In the 1960s Barbie fashions were inspired by every major designer from Givenchy to Mary Quant, and each change in Barbie's life or multi-faceted career involved a new dress. These vintage clothes (particularly complete outfits with all the associated accessories) can be highly collectable, since for many adult collectors, as for children, the main attraction of Barbie and her friends is dressing them up.

A Barbie No 3, with blonde hair, dressed in striped bathing suit, and with red finger and toe nails, 1960, 11½in (29cm) high.
£400–500 ELe

A Bubblecut Barbie, with blonde hair, dressed in grey and white striped Movie Date dress, 1961–67, 11½in (29cm) high.
Barbie   £70–90
Dress   £15–20 PC

A Second Issue Ken doll, with moulded hair, dressed in red shorts and red and white striped shirt, in original box, 1962, 12in (30.5cm) high.
£80–90 TBCC

Barbie's boyfriend Ken was named after Ruth and Elliot Handler's son.

A Swirl Ponytail Barbie, with blonde hair, dressed in After Five black dress, with white hat and collar, mint condition, 1964, 11½in (29.5cm) high.
Barbie   £120–150
Outfit   £25–30 ELe

A straight-leg Skipper Barbie, dressed in Lounging Lovelies set, in pale blue with white lace trim and ribbon, mint condition, 1964–67, outfit 1966, 9¼in (23.5cm) high.
Skipper £40–50
Outfit £25–30 PC

Skipper is Barbie's little sister.

A Fashion Queen Barbie, with moulded plastic hair, dressed in 'Pak' red and white striped T-shirt and navy jeans, with 3 different wigs and a wig stand, 1965, 11½in (29cm) high.
£80–100 TBCC

'Pak' is the term for budget mix-and-match clothes, sold separately and not just in full outfits.

A bend-leg Skipper Barbie, dressed in Outdoor Casuals set, with turquoise sweater and trousers, white gloves and shoes, mint condition, 1965–66, 9¼in (23.5cm) high.
Skipper £60–70
Outfit £35–40 ELe

A Skooter Barbie, dressed in Ballet Lessons set, with pink tutu, and white shoes, 1965, 9¼in (23.5cm) high.
Skooter £35–40
Outfit £35–40 PC

Skooter is a friend of Barbie's little sister Skipper.

A European Issue Skipper, dressed in Town Togs, with green coat and dress, yellow sweater, and black and white checked stockings and hat, mint condition, 1971 reissue, outfit 1965–66, 9¼in (23.5cm) high.
Skipper £130–150
Outfit £40–50 TBCC

A Chris Barbie, dressed in Ship Shape set, with white spotted blue dress with white collar and trim, mint condition, 1967, outfit 1966, 6¼in (16cm) high.
Chris £40–50
Outfit £30–35 ELe

Chris is the best friend of Tutti, Barbie's youngest sister.

A Francie straight-leg Barbie, dressed in Pink 'n' Pretty set, with pink mini-dress with white lace inset, mint condition, 1966, outfit 1972, 11¼in (28.5cm) high.
Francie £100–120
Outfit £20–25 TBCC

Francie is Barbie's cousin.

A Black Francie, with white dress and flowered hem, fair condition, 1967, 11¼in (28.5cm) high.
£280–300 PC

Black Francie was not a successful doll, since the US public were not yet ready to accept that Barbie could have a black cousin – as such this is a rare doll and if not removed from box could be worth over £900.

SINDY

An Active Sindy, dressed in Pony Club outfit, with navy jacket and beige johdpurs, 1980s, 12½in (32cm) high.
£28–32 CMF

A Sindy with a pram, dressed in Dell Fun Time blue and white dress, pram 1982, outfit 1984, pram 6in (15cm) high.
Pram   £15–20
Outfit   £30–35 CMF

A Sindy ballerina, dressed in pink tutu and shoes, 1975, 12in (30.5cm) high.
£40–50 CMF

▶ A Sindy doll, and a quantity of clothes and furniture, in original packaging, 1970s.
£250–300 S(S)

PAPIER MACHE

A German papier mâché shoulder-headed huntsman doll, with wooden lower limbs, in original beige knee breeches, waistcoat and scarlet felt jacket, c1830, 10¾in (26cm) high.
£500–600 S

A German papier mâché shoulder-headed doll, dressed as a pedlar in original green cotton dress and white apron, with painted features and real hair wig, carrying a tray showing a selection of wares for sale, c1850, 15in (38cm) high.
£2,000–2,500 Bon(C)

A Greiner papier-mâché shoulder-headed doll, dressed in original brown and white checked dress with red trim and flowered cream pinafore, 1860s, 33in (84cm) high.
£1,800–2,000 DOL

WAX

A poured wax shoulder-headed doll, with cloth body, in whitework dress, c1880, 26in (66cm) high.
£600–700 S(S)

A poured wax doll, depicting Queen Victoria as a child, with blue glass eyes, inserted blonde hair, wearing a grey silk dress, damaged, c1830, 22in (56cm) high.
£600–700 Bon(C)

◄ A Montinari poured wax baby doll, dressed in original white gown with cream and white bonnet, c1860, 17in (43cm) high.
£500–600 DOL

DOLLS' FURNITURE & CLOTHING

A Victorian doll's silk parasol, the pommel in the form of a dice, 10in (25.5cm) high.
£75–85 DOL

A Victorian pine doll's bed, with carved legs and finials, 28in (71cm) wide.
£180–200 OLM

A *faux* bamboo doll's chair, 1900, 12in (30.5cm) high.
£65–75 MLL

◄ A doll's trousseau and trunk, containing a collection of dresses, hats, jerkins, pyjamas and accessories, c1925, for a 13in (33cm) high doll.
£250–300 GrD

Three Happy House Fashion Doll outfits, one leopard-print coat, one yellow and pink dungarees, one red and white striped ski costume, c1960, for an 11½in (29cm) high doll.
£3–5 each HUX

DOLLS' HOUSES

Many of the more expensive dolls' houses in this section were the property of Vivien Greene who, after more than half a century tracking down and restoring miniature houses, finally, in her 90s, decided to auction her extensive collection at Bonhams.

The wife of novelist Graham Greene, Vivien purchased her first dolls' house during WWII, when her marriage was going through difficulties and she and her family had just been bombed out of their own home and were living at Trinity College, Oxford. Wanting to make at least one domestic haven, she purchased an old dolls' house from a local dealer for virtually nothing. 'They weren't considered antiques,' she remembers, 'nobody could understand why I was interested. You might as well have said do you collect bicycle clips?'

Vivien started both to collect and research dolls' houses and furniture. No books had been written on the subject, so Vivien travelled the country, seeking out and drawing dolls' houses in British collections and compiling her first book *English Dolls' Houses of the 18th and 19th Centuries*, published by Batsford in 1955.

Greene established herself as one of the world's leading historians in the field, and created a famous dolls' house museum, the Rotunda, in the gardens of her Oxfordshire home.

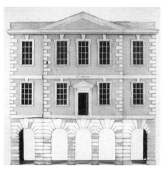

A Palladian mansion dolls' house, Van Haeften, on original arcaded base, painted to simulate stone with quoining, opening into 2 wings with 4 rooms on 2 levels, 1740–50, 49in (125cm) high.
£20,000–25,000 Bon

A wooden model of a dolls' house, painted in maroon, with decorative wooden door surround and window frames, surrounded by flowers and pines, 1800s, in a case 13 x 18in, (33 x 46cm).
£200–250 Bon(C)

The Dower House, the outer walls painted sandstone, the façade opening in 2 wings revealing 4 rooms on 2 levels, c1750, 37in (69cm) high.
£8,000–9,000 Bon

THE ORIGINAL SWAN

Durward's Hall, the one-piece façade detaches to reveal 3 spacious rooms on 3 levels, the exterior painted sandstone, with mahogany front door, c1810, 58in (147cm) high.
£4,000–5,000 Bon

◄ A dolls' house, converted into a country hotel, The Original Swan, the front façade painted bright yellow and marked to represent stonework, with 5 working sash windows, the back open to reveal 4 rooms, hallway and stairs leading to 2 landings, 1865–70, 64in (162.5cm) high.
£7,000–8,000 Bon

Ivy Lodge, painted in red brick effect, the front opening in 3 sections to reveal 6 rooms, hallway and landing on 3 levels, with original wallpaper, on original stand, 1886, 78in (198cm) high.
£6,000–7,000 Bon

A wooden dolls' house, flat-fronted with red and cream brick-effect paper, hinged front revealing 4 rooms, together with a quantity of furniture and effects, 1900, 22in (56cm) high.
£650–750 S(S)

The Cedars, Woodbridge, painted in dark brown with black roof and white painted cornice, c1890, 48in (122cm) high.
£4,500–5,000 Bon

An Egyptian dolls' house, with painted sandstone façade, green-painted tin shutters, and dark brown front door, the front opening in 2 wings to reveal 4 rooms on 2 levels, 1907, 44in (112cm) high.
£2,000–2,500 Bon(C)

> **Cross Reference**
> See Colour Review

The Edwardian Villa, with painted white façade, stencilled and black-painted half-timber effect, the turret topped with a clock tower and weathercock, the front and rear opening in 5 wings to reveal 12 rooms on 2 levels, some damage, c1905, 45in (114cm) wide.
£11,500–13,000 Bon

A wooden chalet dolls' house, with some fittings, painted cream façade with green trimmings and grey roof, 1920s, 21in (53.5cm) high.
£30–40 GAZE

A mahogany open dolls' house, with 5 rooms, hall, staircase and landing, containing miniature silver furniture, c1932, 24in (61cm) wide.
£3,400–3,800 S(S)

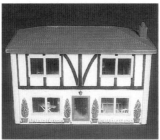

A wooden dolls' bungalow, on casters, with original lino and glass in windows, painted red roof and chimney, white walls and green base, 1930s, 25in (63.5cm) wide.
£45–55 UNI

A dolls' house, with white and black façade, yellow window trim and green trees, red plastic roof and opening windows and doors, 1970s, 21in (53.5cm) wide.
£35–45 UNI

A wooden dolls' house, with white painted walls, 5 bay windows and castellated flat roof, opening in 2 wings revealing 4 rooms and 3 landings, 1960–80, 29in (74cm) high.
£1,500–1,800 Bon

DOLLS' HOUSE FURNITURE

A mahogany piecrust table, with hinged top and tripod base, c1750, 4in (10cm) high.
£1,400–1,600 Bon

A mahogany cradle, with shaped rockers, the pitched canopy with turned supports, c1810, 4in (10cm) long.
£700–800 Bon

A cast-iron fireplace, with moulded decorative foliate surround and cast ornaments to top, on a cast-iron base, c1810, 10¾in (27.5cm) high.
£350–400 Bon(C)

A painted-metal chair, with moulded 'cane' seat, top-rail with painted floral design, probably by Evans & Cartwright, with another similar chair, c1820, 3½in (9cm) high.
£500–600 Bon

A dolls' house sampler rug, in red, yellow and green, dated '1828', 4in (10cm) wide.
£80–100 HUM

A rosewood piano, with 8 keys, and hinged top opening to reveal the internal workings, early 19thC, 5in (12.5cm) square.
£1,000–1,200 Bon

Three German cake-stands, 2 with pewter stands and one with a gilt stand, late 19thC, largest 4in (10cm) high.
£500–550 Bon

◄ A Queen Anne-style walnut and yew chest-on-stand, with 6 drawers, the stand with cabriole legs, 1800–50, 6in (15cm) high.
£275–325 Bon

◄ A Queen Anne-style walnut and yew chest-on-stand, with 6 drawers, the stand with cabriole legs, 1800–50, 6in (15cm) high.
£275–325 Bon

A brass table, with turned stand and 3 legs, c1910, 3½in (9cm) high.
£25–30 DOL

◄ A Victorian mahogany centre table, the turned shaft on 3 ball feet, paper label 'Made at Settle by Uncle Wilhain Pierson, 1856', 3¼in (8cm) high.
£250–300 Bon

Ephemera

AUTOGRAPHS

Neil Armstrong, a signed colour photograph, trimmed down from a larger photograph of the Apollo 11 crew, c1979, 6in (15cm) high.
£120–140 VS

The Beatles, a signed programme, together with a ticket stub, 11th July 1963.
£3,000–3,500 Bon

Enrico Caruso, a pen and ink self-caricature, some damage, 1905, 8½ x 5½in (21.5 x 14cm).
£700–775 VS

Leonardo di Caprio, a signed colour photograph, half-length in dinner jacket from the film *Titanic*, 1990s, 10 x 8in (25.5 x 20.5cm).
£80–90 VS

Diana, Princess of Wales, a signed photograph from the preview of Christies' 1997 sale of her dresses, dedicated to 'Dearest Audrey, Lots of love from Diana x', 12½in (32cm) high.
£1,400–1,600 Bon

Audrey was the dressmaker who made this dress, which was designed by Catherine Walker.

Judy Garland, a photograph signed in green, 1970s, 9 x 7in (23 x 18cm).
£400–450 VS

Jimi Hendrix, a clipped piece of paper signed in black ballpoint 'Stay Kool Jimi Hendrix EXP', and a colour machine print of Jimi on stage, mounted, 1960s, 19in x 13in (48.5 x 34.5cm).
£450–500 Bon

Alfred Hitchcock, a signed note on headed paper, framed and glazed with original envelope and promo photo, 1969, 15½in (39.5cm) wide.
£300–350 TBoy

Lawrence of Arabia, a collection of material from the film, including a copy of the soundtrack album signed by Peter O'Toole, David Lean and Maurice Jarre, 1962.
£240–280 Bon

Led Zeppelin, a gatefold album sleeve signed by Robert Plant, John Paul Jones, Jimmy Page and John Bonham, October 22nd 1969, 7¼in (18.5cm) square.
£230–260 Bon

Little Richard, a signed full-length photograph, performing with the band in the back-ground, 1960s, 8 x 10in (20.5 x 25.5cm).
£80–100 VS

Marilyn Monroe, a signed cheque, 1961.
£1,800–2,000 TBoy

▶ Madonna, a signed colour photograph, from *Evita*, 1990s, 8 x 10in (20.5 x 25.5cm).
£100–120 VS

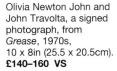

Olivia Newton John and John Travolta, a signed photograph, from *Grease*, 1970s, 10 x 8in (25.5 x 20.5cm).
£140–160 VS

Pablo Picasso, a signed etching entitled 'Pour Roby', with certificate of authenticity, 1950s, 12 x 10in (30.5 x 25.5cm).
£650–750 VS

Pierre Auguste Renoir, one page letter to an unidentified friend, in French, with photo showing Renoir at work, 1892, 16½ x 14½in (42 x 37cm).
£1,000–1,200 VS

Frank Sinatra, a signed postcard, half-length in suit and tie, with lit cigarette in one hand, 1950s.
£275–325 VS

U2, a signed black and white newspaper advertisement for a Wembley Stadium concert, 12/13th June 1987, 16 x 12in (40.5 x 30.5cm).
£325–375 FRa

Keith Richard, a signed letter handwritten to a fan in green ink, 1964–65, 7 x 5½in (18 x 14cm).
£275–325 Bon

Charles Schultz, a hardback edition of *I Need All The Friends I Can Get*, signed and inscribed on flyleaf with an original pencil sketch of Snoopy holding a tennis racket, 1964.
£275–325 VS

Mike Tyson, a signed colour photograph, 1980s, 10 x 8in (25.5 x 20.5cm).
£50–60 VS

Michael Schumacher, a signed colour photograph, 1990s, 10 x 8in (25.5 x 20.5cm) high.
£70–80 VS

Gene Kelly, Donald O'Connor and Debbie Reynolds, a signed colour postcard, reproduction of the film poster of *Singin' in the Rain*, 1950s.
£120–140 VS

Mark Hamill, Harrison Ford, and Carrie Fisher, a signed colour photograph, dressed in costumes from *Star Wars*, 1970s, 8 x 10in (20.5 x 25.5cm).
£170–200 VS

CIGARETTE & TRADE CARDS

Gallaher Ltd, Royalty Series No. 1, set of 50, 1902.
£100–120 VS

W. D. & H. O. Wills, Scissors, Sporting Girls, set of 30, 1913.
£170–200 JACK

▶ Godfrey Phillips, Flags, 20th Series, set of 120, c1915.
75p–£1 each LCC

John Player & Sons, Countries' Arms & Flags, set of 50, 1905.
£30–40 JACK

W. D. & H. O. Wills, Garden Life, set of 50, 1914.
£15–20 MUR

Cope Bros & Co Ltd, Music Hall Artistes, set of 50, 1913.
£325–375 JACK

Godfrey Phillips, Clan Tartans, set of 65, c1915.
75p–£1 each LCC

John Player & Sons, British Live Stock, set of 25, 1915.
£40–50 MAr

Godfrey Phillips, League Colours,
silk, postcard size, 1920.
£4–5 each JACK

John Player & Sons,
Cries of London, Second Series,
set of 25, 1916.
£15–20 MAr

Carreras Ltd, Types of London,
set of 80, 1919.
£60–85 MAr

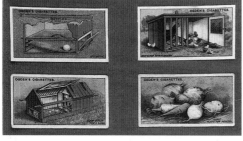

Ogden's, Poultry Rearing & Management,
Second Series, set of 25, 1923.
£55–60 MAr

Salmon & Gluckstein's
Cigarettes, Magical
Series, set of 25, 1923.
£70–80 VS

W. D. & H. O. Wills,
Lucky Charms,
set of 50, 1923.
£20–25 MUR

W. D. & H. O. Wills, Flower Culture in Pots,
set of 50, 1925.
£15–20 MAr

John Player & Sons, Footballers, Caricatures by 'RIP',
set of 50, 1926.
£50–60 MUR

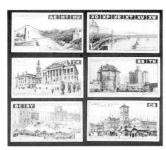

Lambert & Butler, Motor Index Marks, set of 50, 1926.
£100–120 JACK

Ogden's, Trainers and Owners' Colours, Second Series, set of 25, 1926.
£40–55 MAr

W. A. & A. C. Churchman, Famous Cricket Colours, set of 25, 1928.
£40–50 JACK

W. D. & H. O. Wills, English Period Costumes, set of 50, 1929.
£40–45 MUR

R. & J. Hill Ltd, Scientific Inventions and Discoveries, set of 35, 1929.
£25–35 MAr

John Player & Sons, Cricketers, set of 50, 1930.
£40–50 JACK

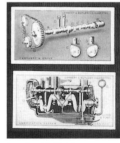

John Player & Sons, Portals of the Past, set of 25, 1930.
£40–50 MAr

Lambert & Butler, How Motor Cars Work, set of 25, 1931.
£50–60 JACK

W. D. & H. O. Wills, albums of Safety First and Birds & Their Young, and John Player & Sons, album of RAF Badges, 1930s.
£5–10 each LCC

John Player & Sons, Wild Animals' Heads, set of 50, 1931.
£25–35 MAr

W. D. & H. O. Wills, Garden Flowers, set of 50, 1933.
£20–25 MAr

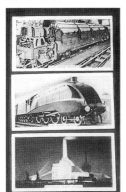

Radio Stars album, part-filled, 1935, 7 x 4¼in (18 x 11cm).
£8–10 MAC

Ogden's, By the Roadside, set of 50, 1932.
£40–50 JACK

John Player & Sons, Hints on Association Football, set of 50, 1934.
£20–25 MAr

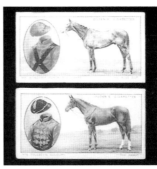

Ogden's, Prominent Racehorses of 1933, set of 50, 1933.
£55–65 JACK

John Player & Sons, Decorations & Medals, set of 50, c1935.
£80–100 JACK

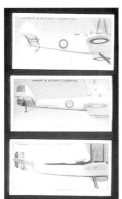

Godfrey Phillips, This Mechanized Age, set of 50, 1936.
£10–12 LCC

Lambert & Butler, Aeroplane Markings, set of 50, 1937.
£60–70 JACK

W. D. & H. O. Wills, Famous British Authors, set of 40, 1937.
£50–65 MAr

W. D. & H. O. Wills, Racehorses & Jockeys, 1938, set of 40, 1938.
£60–70 MAr

John Player & Sons, Speedway Riders, set of 50, 1937.
£65–70 MAr

Rothmans Ltd, Beauties of the Cinema, set of 24, 1939.
£70–80 JACK

W. A. & A. C. Churchman, In Town Tonight, set of 50, 1938.
£10–12 MUR

Cope Bros & Co Ltd, Cathedrals, set of 25, 1939.
£28–32 MUR

John Player & Sons, Cycling, set of 50, 1939.
£30–40 MAr

Primrose, Popeye, First Series, set of 50, 1960.
£220–250 VS

Barratt & Co Ltd, Walt Disney Characters, Second Series, set of 50, 1957.
£70–80 VS

An Arcadian model of the Queen's Dolls' House, with British Empire exhibition crest, 1924, 3½in (9cm) wide.
£50–60 CCC

A Carlton model, 'Tommy in his dugout somewhere in France', with Boston Spa crest, 1918, 3½in (9cm) wide.
£80–90 CCC

A Clifton model of the *Beta* airship, with Inverness crest, 1914–18, 3in (7.5cm) wide.
£80–90 MGC

A Swan model of a donkey, with Irthlingborough crest, c1910, 5in (12.5cm) long.
£80–100 CCC

An Arcadian charabanc, with Eastbourne crest, 1910–20, 5in (12.5cm) long.
£40–50 MGC

A Carlton figure of a bathing belle, 'Washed up by the tide', on an oyster-shell dish with Flamborough crest, c1925, 4in (10cm) wide.
£160–180 CCC

A Goss Manx cottage, 1890–1920, 3½in (9cm) wide.
£130–150 MGC

A Swan model of a black cat in a well, with 'Arms of Duke of Bedford' and crest, 1930s, 2½in (6.5cm) high.
£65–75 MGC

A Carlton figure of a child, 'I'm Forever Blowing Bubbles', with City of Cardiff crest, c1920, 4½in (11.5cm) high.
£90–100 MGC

A Goss figure of Edyth, 1930s, 6in (15cm) high.
£250–280 MGC

A Goss taper jug, with crest depicting 7 flags of the Allies of the Great War and 'L'Union fait la Force, Eendracht Maakt Macht', 1917, 3½in (9cm) high.
£85–95 MGC

◄ A Willow Art model, black boy playing a drum, with Ashington crest, 1920s, 3in (7.5cm) high.
£150–175 MGC

CERAMICS • COLOUR REVIEW 217

A Gouda wall plate, decorated with a kiwi, made for Gibsons & Pattersons Ltd, New Zealand, 1915, 10½in (26.5cm) diam.
£350–400 OO

A Gouda two-handled vase, decorated with Samarat pattern, c1929, 8½in (21.5cm) high.
£300–350 OO

A Gouda humidor, decorated with Westland pattern, 1920, 8in (20.5cm) high.
£275–325 OO

A Gouda vase, decorated with Syncap pattern, 1929, 7¼in (18.5cm) high.
£40–50 OO

A Limoges porcelain vase, c1790, 6½in (16.5cm) high.
£300–330 ChA

A copper lustre cup and saucer, decorated with blue pattern, c1840, saucer 5½in (14cm) diam.
£55–65 SER

A Garrison Pottery lustre wall plaque, attributed to Dixon & Co, Sunderland, 1830, 9in (23cm) wide.
£340–380 IS

A lustre wall plaque, depicting 'The Gauntlet Clipper Ship', attributed to Anthony Scott, Southwick Pottery/Moore & Co, Sunderland, 1860, 9in (23cm) wide.
£200–220 IS

A Maling creamware wall plaque, decorated with 'Prepare to meet thy God' within pink lustre border, impressed mark 'Maling' Newcastle, c1825, 6½in (16.5cm) diam.
£340–380 IS

◀ A Maling bowl, decorated with Lantern & Butterfly lustre pattern, 1930, 8½in (21.5cm) diam.
£200–250 BEV

▶ A pair of Maling rack plates, hand-painted with Harebells pattern, c1929, 11¼in (28.5cm) diam.
£380–440 AOT

Two Mason's Ironstone jugs, **l.** decorated with Ivy pattern, c1820, 3½in (9cm) high.
£150–180
r. decorated with flowers, c1880, 2in (5cm) high.
£250–280 JP

A William Moorcroft
vase, decorated with
Hazledene pattern,
c1913, 8in (20.5cm) high.
£1,400–1,600 RUM

A Myott hand-painted flower-holder,
1930, 11in (28cm) wide.
£100–135 BEV

A pair of Victorian Potichomania vases and
covers, transfer-decorated with chinoiserie
patterns, 16¼in (41.5cm) high.
£4,000–4,500 AH

◄ A Parrot ware jug, moulded and hand-
painted with Johnny Appleseed pattern,
1930s, 8½in (21.5cm) high.
£85–95 BEV

An Onnaing cachepot, moulded
with birds and flowers, c1880,
8in (20.5cm) high.
£345–385 MLL

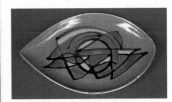

A Poole Pottery vase, decorated
with Bird pattern, 1930,
11in (28cm) high.
£1,800–2,000 HarC

**This large vase was designed by
Truda Adams as a centrepiece
for the Poole Pottery stand at
one of the British Industry fairs.**

A Poole Pottery model of a fish,
1930s, 9in (23cm) high.
£350–400 HarC

A Poole Pottery tea-for-two,
in green and beige, 1960s,
tray 14½in (37cm) wide.
£80–90 ZOOM

A Poole Pottery vase, decorated
with curves and arches, marked
'Carter, Stabler & Adams',
c1940–50s, 7in (18cm) high.
£275–300 P(Ba)

► A Quimper plate, with floral
border, marked 'HR', c1890,
9¾in (25cm) diam.
£170–190 VH

A Poole Pottery spear dish,
decorated with Delphis pattern,
c1966, 12in (30.5cm) wide.
£18–20 MED

A Foley Intarsio clock, designed by Frederick Rhead, modelled as a pavillion, decorated with a lady and a gentleman bowing and 'The Time o' Day', the clock face bordered with gilt, c1890, 11in (28cm) wide.
£650–750 PGA

A Crown Ducal flagon, designed by Charlotte Rhead, decorated with floral pattern No. 3797, shape No. 146, by Richardson's, 1935, 8½in (21.5cm) high.
£250–280 PC

A Gardener-Rosenthal figure group, designed by Raymond Peynet, depicting a boy watering flowers on a girl's hat, slight damage, 1950–60s, 6in (15cm) high.
£180–200 RDG

A Wileman Intarsio charger, designed by Frederick Rhead, decorated with 2 women sitting on a bench, one sewing, one playing a lyre, with floral border, c1897, 14in (35.5cm) diam.
£1,600–1,800 AOT

A Crown Ducal nursery ware cup and saucer, designed by Charlotte Rhead, decorated with Chick in a Field pattern, 1930s, saucer 3in (7.5cm) diam.
£150–180 BDA

A Royal Winton Pixie Ware clock, moulded with pixies, mushrooms and a tree, 1930s, 8½in (21.5cm) wide.
£100–125 BEV

▶ A Sadler teapot, in the form of a racing car, with mottled yellow glaze, 1930s, 4in (10cm) high.
£80–100 CGC

A Crown Ducal pedestal flower vase, designed by Charlotte Rhead, decorated with Primula pattern No. 2033, 1931, 8in (20.5cm) high.
£220–260 BDA

A Rozenburg clog, decorated in blue and brown pattern, by Sam Schellink, 1911, 4¾in (12cm) wide.
£75–100 OO

A St Ives two-handled vase, decorated with galena glaze, attributed to Bernard Leach, c1930, 10in (25.5cm) high.
£380–420 RUSK

A Shelley Harmony drip-ware ginger jar, c1930, 8in (20.5cm) high.
£125–150 HEW

A Shorter seven-piece Fishware set, design attributed to Clarice Cliff, 1927, largest plate 14in (35.5cm) wide.
£140–160 DEC

A Staffordshire figure of Peace, by Ralph Wood, decorated in gilt, c1800, 25in (63.5cm) high.
£2,250–2,500 JO

A Staffordshire group, entitled 'Romulus & Remus', c1820, 6½in (16.5cm) wide.
£3,000–3,300 JO

A Staffordshire figure of John Liston as Paul Pry, c1820, 6in (15cm) high.
£350–400 JO

A Staffordshire Walton group of a man and a woman playing instruments, with sheep, before bocage, c1820, 10in (25.5cm) high.
£1,600–1,800 JO

A Staffordshire figure, wearing a kilt, and with 2 sheep, 1870, 10¾in (27.5cm) high.
£100–120 OD

A pair of Staffordshire Walton sheep with lambs, decorated in brown, before bocage, c1820, 6in (15cm) high.
£550–650 SER

Two SylvaC monkeys, 1930–50s.
Large 7in (18cm) high.   £65
Small 5in (12.5cm) high.   £35 UNI

◄ A Victorian Staffordshire porcelain dessert service, the centres decorated with various flowers, within gilt border, comprising a pair of rectangular comports, 4 oval comports and 12 plates, slight damage, impressed Design Registry diamond and pattern No. 'A2063', plates 9in (23cm) diam.
£800–1,000 CAG

A Wadeheath pottery
jug, hand-painted with
a windmill in a rural
landscape, 1930s,
11½in (29cm) high.
£100–115 BEV

An Upsala-Ekerby platter,
decorated with zigzag pattern
by Mari Simulson, 1950s,
11½in (29cm) wide.
£40–50 MARK

A Wade lustre coffee set, comprising
6 cups and saucers, coffee pot, cream
jug and sugar bowl, 1950–60s, coffee pot
6½in (16.5cm) high.
£170–190 SLL

A Wade model of a
woodpecker on a branch,
1950, 7in (18cm) high.
£160–190 PAC

A Wade Betty Boop
Beach Belle, No. 537
from a limited edition
of 2,000, 1990s,
6¼in (16cm) high.
£65–75 GRa

A Wedgwood model of
Ferdinand the Bull, by
Arnold Machin, c1941,
12¼in (31cm) wide.
£500–600 DID

▶ A Wade Rupert Bear,
model No. 2, 1996,
5in (12.5cm) high.
£90–100 HarC

A Wedgwood egg, decorated with
a group of Beatrix Potter rabbits,
1970s, 4¼in (11cm) wide.
£20–30 WWY

A Kathie Winkle plate, decorated
with Wild Flowers pattern, 1975,
9½in (24cm) diam.
£6–7 Law

◀ A Worcester teapot, with floral
decoration, the spout, handle and
lid gilt, 1895, 5½in (14cm) high.
£335–365 BEV

A Royal Worcester figure of Pansy,
modelled by Anne Acheson, 1940,
4in (10cm) high.
£250–280 CAW

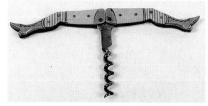

A novelty folding corkscrew, in the form of a pair of lady's legs, marked 'Germany', late 19thC, 5in (12.5cm) wide.
£170–190 P(B)

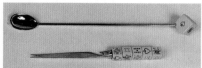

A silver-plated cocktail set, with Bakelite dice-shaped handles, 1930s, largest 6in (15cm) long.
£35–40 BEV

A Bakelite cocktail shaker, with silver-plated top and recipe for a Manhattan cocktail, 1930s, 11in (28cm) high.
£270–300 BEV

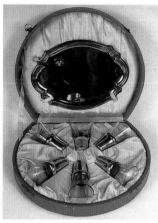

A silver-plated liqueur set and tray, in original case, 1930s, 12½in (32cm) wide.
£125–145 BEV

A set of chrome cocktail sticks with Bakelite tops, in a chrome wheelbarrow holder, 1930, 5in (12.5cm) wide.
£40–50 BEV

A Huntley & Palmers Cocktail Assorted Biscuits tin, 1950s, 9in (23cm) wide.
£12–14 HUX

An Austrian cranberry glass liqueur decanter, in the form of a duck, with silver-plated head, 1930s, 6in (15cm) high.
£220–245 BEV

► A box of Beverage Thermometers, made in Ohio, 1950s, 8¾in (22cm) wide.
£30–40 SpM

A box of plastic mermaid cocktail sticks, 1950s, 3½in (9cm) high.
£15–20 SpM

◄ A box of Pink Lady plastic cocktail glass markers, 1950s, 6½in (16.5cm) wide.
£30–35 SpM

A wooden cat cocktail stick holder, 1950s, 4½in (11.5cm) high.
£15–20 LBe

An enamel on copper miniature, depicting a caricature of the enjoined left half of Charles James Fox's face and the right half of Lord North's, reverse inscribed, 1783, 2in (5cm) high, in an oval mahogany frame.
£5,300–5,800 SAS

Lord North was Tory MP for Banbury 1754–90 and Prime Minister 1770–82 when he resigned following the failure of his policy with regard to American colonies. Fox and North met on 14th February 1783 and on 24th February the Whig Prime Minister, the Earl of Shelburne, resigned and the unlikely coalition between North and Fox was sealed on 2nd April. It was short-lived for they both resigned following rejection of the India Bill by the House of Lords at the instigation of the King.

A Foley Intarsio teapot and cover, with caricature of Lloyd George, chip to spout, printed mark to base, c1901, 4¾in (12cm) high.
£380–420 SAS

A painted tin cut-out, depicting Jack Tar holding the Union flag, paint chips and rust, early 19thC, 2½in (6.5cm) high.
£550–600 SAS

An Edward Smith & Co pottery tile, moulded with the head of the Marquis of Salisbury, small chips, c1880, 6in (15cm) wide.
£35–40 SAS

A mug, commemorating the Silver Jubilee of George V and Queen Mary, 1935, 4in (10cm) high.
£20–25 AnS

◀ A J. Kent, Longton, Staffordshire, sweetmeat dish, commemorating the coronation of George VI, 1937, 9¾in (25cm) wide.
£25–30 IW

A mug, transfer-printed with a portrait of Mathew Bell, with pink lustre bands and 'Bell For-Ever True Blue', some damage, c1826, 5¼in (13.5cm) high.
£600–675 SAS

▶ A Hancock & Whittingham pottery jug, with hinged pewter cover, printed with named statues and 'Free Trade', printed mark to base, c1875, 9½in (24cm) high.
£70–90 SAS

A Windsor China porcelain mug, commemorating the coronation of George VI and Queen Elizabeth, 1937, 3in (7.5cm) high.
£60–70 GwR

A Mercian China plate, commemorating the visit to Japan of Queen Elizabeth II and HRH The Duke of Edinburgh, 1975, 10½in (26.5cm) diam.
£30–35 MGC

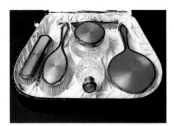

An Edwardian cut-glass and pink
enamel vanity set, in original case,
c1910, case 17in (43cm) wide.
£250–300 JACK

A glass powder bowl, with
enamelled roses and daisies,
c1920s, 7in (18cm) diam.
£45–55 LeB

A Mascarade powder box,
by L. T. Piver Paris, decorated
with theatrical masks, unopened,
1920s, 3in (7.5cm) diam.
£65–75 LeB

A German powder bowl,
in the form of a lady with a
fan, 1920s, 4½in (11.5cm) high.
£100–125 LeB

A silver-thread wig, 1920s.
£450–500 RUL

Three celluloid hair combs, 1920s,
largest 5in (12.5cm) high.
£20–30 each LeB

A Dubarry Bakelite powder bowl,
1930s, 4in (10cm) diam.
£15–20 MRW

A German base-metal and enamel
compact, decorated with a
butterfly, 1930s, 3in (7.5cm) wide.
£55–65 LBe

A Gala of London 'Lipstick
Wardrobe' box of 4 lipsticks,
1950s, box 4in (10cm) wide.
£35–40 LeB

A Birmingham silver and enamel hand mirror, 1934,
10in (25.5cm) wide.
£80–90 JACK

A plastic comb, the cover forming a handle, 1940s,
3½in (9cm) wide.
£10–14 CHU

COSMETICS & HAIRDRESSING • COLOUR REVIEW 225

A *Mickey Mouse Weekly* comic,
No. 254, 1940, 14 x 11in
(35.5 x 28cm).
£10–15 TOY

A Mickey Mouse sweet tin, 1950s,
6in (15cm) diam.
£30–35 GAZE

A Mickey Mouse eraser,
marked BIMBO©W.D.P.,
late 1940s, 6¾in (17cm) high.
£75–85 CWO

A Minnie Mouse Ideal Home
Fantasy Light, 1970s,
9in (23cm) high, with original box.
£20–25 MED

A Minnie Mouse rubber lamp,
1970s, 14in (35.5cm) high.
£20–25 MED

A Donald Duck hot water bottle,
c1965, 14in (35.5cm) high.
£40–50 BTB

▶ A Schmid ceramic musical
figure of Goofy in an open-top
sports car, 1970–80s,
6in (15cm) wide, in original
box with packaging.
£80–90 MED

A Urago diecast and plastic
1:18 scale model of a Jaguar
SS100, with Donald Duck figure,
c1980, 10in (25.5cm) long.
£20–25 MED

A set of 7 Snow White Dwarfs rubber squeeze toys, with original clear
PVC carry case, 1980–90s, 5½in (14cm) high.
£25–30 MED

A Gebrüder Heubach bisque-headed doll, in sailor dress, with jointed composition body, square Heubach mark, 1910–15, 19in (48.5cm) high.
£250–300 BGC

A German 'Little Boy' Easter Surprise egg, with coloured nursery rhyme print, c1910, 6in (15cm) high.
£90–110 GrD

A Welsch & Co bisque-headed doll, with blonde hair and silk dress, 1911–28, 16in (40.5cm) high.
£150–180 BGC

A French pierrot doll, with wax head and dressed in silk, c1920, 28in (71cm) high.
£350–400 DOL

A Schultzmeister & Quendt bisque-headed doll, with composition body, in a muslin dress, marked 'S&Q', 1920, 16in (40.5cm) high.
£170–200 BGC

A German all-bisque piano baby, c1920, 7in (18cm) high.
£40–50 YC

A Dressed Cupid doll, c1920, 7in (18cm) high, with original box.
£75–85 DOL

This doll bears its original price tag of 1s 11d.

A pair of Lenci 300 series pressed felt dolls, with painted eyes and mouths, c1930, 17in (43cm) high.
£900–1,100 each Bon(C)

A Schultz celluloid doll, with flirty eyes, original dress and extra dress, c1930, 22in (56cm) high.
£325–375 DOL

A Lenci felt doll, in original clothes, c1930, 20in (51cm) high.
£200–250 DOL

▶ A vinyl Shirley Temple doll, in original clothes, 1973, 19in (48.5cm) high.
£80–100 BGC

A Barbie carrying case,
1960s, 14in (35.5cm) high.
£12–15 PC

A Barbie American Girl
doll, wearing Fraternity
Dance outfit, 1965–66,
11½in (29cm) high.
£100–125 PC

A Tutti doll, Barbie's
smallest sister, wearing
Clowning Around outfit,
1966–67, 6¼in (16cm) high.
£40–50 PC

A Palitoy Action Man,
wearing Underwater
Explorer uniform, with
realistic hair, fixed eyes
and hard fixed hands,
1972, 12in (30.5cm) high.
£55–60 CY

A Palitoy Action Man,
wearing Red Devil uniform,
1973, 12in (30.5cm) high.
£50–55 CY

**This Red Devil uniform
was used on dolls
produced between 1973
and 1976. The dolls had
realistic hair, rubber
gripping hands, and
fixed eyes.**

Kenner Designer Collection fashions for Jaime
Sommers, the Bionic Woman doll, 1974, in original
packaging, 12in (30.5cm) wide.
£10–15 TOY

A set of Palitoy Action Man
Commando uniform, 1975,
in original packaging,
14 x 10in (35.5 x 25.5cm).
£145–160 TOY

A Sunshine Sindy, wearing Casual Dress, and
a Sindy scooter, 1982, doll 12in (30.5cm) high.
£20–35 each CMF

A Sleeping Sindy, wearing
Sweet Dreams outfit,
1980s, 12in (30.5cm) high.
£40–50 CMF

A Gene Marshall King's Daughter
doll, limited edition of 5,000, 1997,
15in (38cm) high.
£220–250 PC

A doll's house, Farnham House, brick effect façade, restored, late 18thC, 49in (124.5cm) high.
£20,000–22,000 Bon

Ex-Vivien Greene (widow of Graham Greene) collection.

A doll's house, Strawberry Hill Gothick, with 4 bedrooms, hallway and landing, some restoration, 1820–30, 25in (63.5cm) high.
£4,000–4,500 Bon

Ex-Vivien Greene collection. The pink paintwork is a reference to Horace Walpole's Gothick Villa on Strawberry Hill, Twickenham.

A set of German wooden doll's house furniture, decorated with flowers, cherubs and birds, slight damage, mid-19thC, sofa 3in (7.5cm) high.
£600–700 Bon

Two pairs of German bisque-headed dolls, with moulded hair, cloth bodies with bisque lower arms and legs, moulded shoes, one in original dress, c1900, 5½in (14cm) high.
£500–700 each Bon

Ex-Vivien Greene Collection.

A Nouveauté de Paris set of dolls' dressing table accessories, c1890, on original presentation card, 9¼ x 5½in (23.5 x 14cm).
£225–245 G&D

A doll's tin washstand, with mirror, jug, bowl and pail, some damage, c1915, 21in (53.5cm) high.
£130–150 DOL

Five miniature all-bisque dolls, with glass eyes, mohair wigs, fixed necks, jointed arms and legs, all wearing original clothes, and another with composition body, and 2 hand-painted tinplate prams, c1910, dolls 3½in (9cm) high.
£1,400–1,600 Bon

Ex-Vivien Green collection.

A Triang double-fronted doll's house, with electric lights, timbered gables and opening windows and doors, 1950s, 26½in (67.5cm) wide.
£275–325 RAR

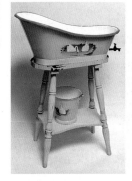

▶ A doll's tin bath and bucket on a wooden stand, transfer-decorated with pictures of swans, c1920, 22in (56cm) high.
£150–200 DOL

A Tudor Toys doll's house, with balcony and shutters, late 1960s, 17½in (44.5cm) wide.
£40–45 UNI

A Daily Express Easter card, with a yellow pop-up chicken, 1901, 7in (18cm) wide.
£15–18 WAB

A French paper fan, painted with seaside scene, 1920s, 6in (15cm) wide.
£10–12 HUX

Mikhail Gorbachov, a signed photograph for the Nobel Peace Prize, June 1991, 10 x 8in (25.5 x 20.5cm).
£400–450 FRa

▶ Ardath Tobacco Co, Film, Stage and Radio Stars, set of 50 cigarette cards, excellent condition, 1935.
£35–40 JACK

A Mabel Lucie Attwell calendar, inscribed 'I'se still on the shelf', 1928, 11in (28cm) high.
£40–50 WWY

Apollo 11, Armstrong, Aldrin and Collins, a signed photograph, July 1979, 8 x 10in (20.5 x 25.5cm).
£3,250–3,500 FRa

John Player & Sons, Kings & Queens of England, set of 50 cigarette cards, 1935.
£55–65 MUR

A Cameo Flower Perfumed Calendar, by Dubarry, c1940, 4¼in (11cm) diam, in original box.
£20–25 HUX

Helena Christensen, a signed photograph, first name only, c1996, 10 x 8in (25.5 x 20.5cm).
£20–25 VS

Fleer 95 Ultra, American Bat Man For Ever, set of 120 trade cards, 1995.
£8–10 LCC

A Roman phallic badge, 1st–2nd century AD, 1½in (4cm) wide.
£75–95 GRa

A Continental silver cigarette case, with a concealed enamel nude scene, c1910, 3¾in (9.5cm) wide.
£3,000–3,400 THOM

A silvered alpaca cigarette case, with enamel portrait of a nude lady on the lid, 1920, 3½in (9cm) high.
£1,250–1,450 PT

A Japanese Butt Snuffer, 1950s, 2½in (6.5cm) wide, in original box.
£20–25 SpM

A French miniature brass cigar-cutter, in the form of a lady on a pot, 1900, 1¼in (3cm) high.
£145–165 EMC

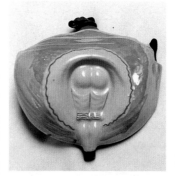

An ashtray, in the form of a Japanese lady, entitled 'The Yellow Peril', the reverse showing a bare behind, c1930, 5in (12.5cm) wide.
£65–75 HT

A set of 4 glass tumblers, each with a naked lady on the reverse, 1950s, 4in (10cm) high.
£55–65 SpM

A Continental silver cigar case, with an enamel portrait of a naked lady on the lid, 1920, 5in (13cm) high.
£800–900 PT

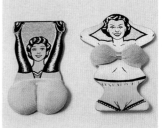

Two cardboard cut-out figures, with moving padded breasts and posterior, 1930s, 3½in (9cm) high.
£18–22 each SpM

A watercolour portrait of Jayne Mansfield, 1960s, 12in (30.5cm) high.
£400–450 ZOOM

A Vizagapatam ivory chess set, c1780, king 5in (12.5cm) high.
£2,500–3,500 TMi

A selection of 'onion skin' glass marbles, in various colours, c1850, largest ½in (12mm) diam.
£50–60 each MRW

A Jaques horse-racing game, Minoru, c1910, 15in (38cm) wide.
£70–80 GAZE

A wooden table game, Squails, c1870, 12in (30.5cm) wide.
£60–70 J&J

A Märklin horse-racing game, with 9 hand-painted figures of horses and riders, operated by a lever mechanism to side, c1900, 14in (35.5cm) square.
£250–300 BLH

A Spear's Comical Tivoli Game, 1920s, 11 x 8in (28 x 20.5cm).
£80–100 J&J

A GWR jigsaw, entitled 'Locomotives Old and New', complete, c1934, 9½ x 19½in (24 x 49.5cm).
£100–120 RAR

An eastern European painted wood chess set, c1950, king 3¾in (9.5cm) high.
£100–120 TMi

A James Bond Thunderball jigsaw, 1966, 11 x 7in (28 x18cm).
£40–50 TOY

◄ A Spear's Games Noddy's Ring Game, 1960, 6 x 13in (15 x 33cm) wide.
£20–25 GAZE

The Reel to Reel Picture Show, 007 Movie Trivia Game, 1997, 8in (20.5cm) diam.
£10–12 GRa

Erotica

A Roman phallic badge, 1st–2nd century AD, 1in (25mm) long.
£45–95 GRa

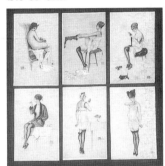

A set of 6 illustrations by Leonnec, entitled 'Intimités de Boudoir', Nos. 74, 76–80, signed, c1914–18.
£75–90 SpP

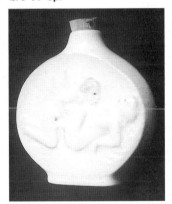

A Sitzendorf perfume bottle, depicting Leda and the Swan, c1920–30s, 2½in (6.5cm) high.
£75–85 HT

A Foxfield Ceramics teapot, in the form of a Bunny Girl, 1984, 17in (43cm) wide.
£30–40 GRa

A Swiss quarter-repeating automaton verge watch, in a gold case with concealed erotic scene, c1810, 22½in (57cm) diam.
£10,500–11,500 PT

A porcelain box, with an erotic decoration on the cover and interior, c1930s, 1½in (4cm) wide.
£55–65 HT

John Lennon/Yoko Ono, 'Unfinished Music No 1: Two Virgins', LP stereo release, May 1968.
£200–250 MTM

When this was first released, a brown paper sleeve covered the nudity allowing only John and Yoko's heads to appear.

▶ A leg stand, inspired by Allen Jones, c1970, 28in (71cm) high.
£125–150 LBe

A pewter snuff box, with a ceramic panel depicting an erotic scene, Scottish or Continental, c1830, 2in (5cm) diam.
£125–145 IW

A cigarette case, decorated with a nude scene depicting The Three Graces, 1920s, 3in (7.5cm) high.
£650–700 JBU

Fans

A French painted paper leaf fan, decorated with a scene of lovers in the countryside, with carved ivory sticks and painted columns of leaves, c1780, 10¼in (26cm) wide.
£500–550 P

A black chantilly lace leaf fan, backed with ivory silk, decorated with flowers and blossom, with mother-of-pearl sticks, c1870, 11in (28cm) wide.
£260–300 P

A Brussels *point de Gaze* lace fan, the leaf with a painted vellum cartouche depicting a young lady and cupid in a garden, pierced and gilded mother-of-pearl sticks, signed 'G. Silvain', c1890, 13in (33cm) wide.
£450–500 P

A jet brooch, in the form of a fan, with carved decoration, 1880–1910, 2in (5cm) wide.
£6–8 VB

A mosaic picture frame, in the form of a fan, decorated with small blue flowers, 1880–1910, 2½in (6.5cm) wide.
£55–65 VB

An orange ostrich feather fan, with Bakelite sticks, 1920s, 27in (68.5cm) wide.
£60–70 PC

A French advertising fan, inscribed 'Bière du Fort Carré', 1920s, 10in (25.5cm) high.
£15–18 HUX

► A BOAC advertising fan, decorated with images from various countries, 1960s, 15in (38cm) wide.
£8–10 HUX

A French advertising fan, inscribed 'Cie Gle Transatlantique, 1940s, 11in (28cm) wide.
£12–15 HUX

Fifties

A Swan Brand metal teapot, commemorating the Festival of Britain, c1951, 4½in (11.5cm) high.
£15–20 HUX

A chrome bottle opener, stamped 'Kobe Ship Repair Co, Ltd', with flag motif, 1954, 10½in (26.5cm) long.
£10–15 BTB

An Ice-O-Matic ice crusher, 1950s, 9in (23cm) high.
£35–40 BTB

◄ A three-tier imitation wood and chrome cake stand, 1950s, 14½in (37cm) high.
£50–60 ZOOM

A Hovis Coronation Periscope, 1953, 14½in (37cm) high.
£20–22 HUX

A chrome bottle opener, in the form of a hand, decorated with toasts in various languages, c1950s, 9½in (24cm) long.
£10–15 BTB

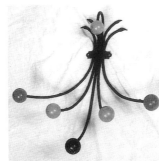

A metal coat hook, with red, yellow and green knobs, 1950s, 19in (48.5cm) wide.
£35–40 BTB

A wooden-handled kettle, by Piqot, 1950s, 10in (25.5cm) wide.
£45–50 BTB

A French wooden-handled kettle, with fluted sides, 1950s, 11in (28cm) high.
£30–35 ChA

A painted-metal standing lamp, in the form of a palm tree, with 6 glass shades in the form of buds and flowers, 1950s, 71in (180.5cm) high.
£500–600 E

A Royal Brierley blue and green glass Rainbow ware vase, c1950, 8in (20.5cm) high.
£80–100 RUSK

▶ A Finnish Iittala blue glass carafe, by Timo Sarpaneva, marked on base 'Timo Sarpaneva – 5288', designed 1959, 10¾in (27.5cm) high.
£145–165 FF

A two-tone Formica sideboard, 1950s, 66in (167.5cm) wide.
£120–150 RAT

A diary/memo pad, boxed, 1950s, 10in (25.5cm) high.
£10–12 MRW

CERAMICS

A Bavarian porcelain coffee set, black with white polka dots, decorated with poodles, 1950s, coffee pot 7in (18cm) high.
£90–110 LBe

A Beswick Ballet fruit bowl, 1950s, 9in (23cm) wide.
£20–25 RAT

A Burleigh Ware hand-painted vase, white with red interior, 1950, 6in (15cm) high.
£45–50 RAT

Further Reading

Miller's Collecting the 1950s, Miller's Publications, 1997

▶ A ceramic cheese stand, signed 'Vallauris', 1950s, 15in (38cm) wide.
£15–18 Law

An ashtray, advertising Woodbine cigarettes, 1950s, 4½in (11.5cm) wide.
£10–12 HUX

◀ A Carlton Ware dish, green with gilt rim, 1950s, 12in (30.5cm) wide.
£24–26 CHU

HOMEMAKER

Designed by Enid Seeney (b1932) Homemaker is probably the most famous British tableware design of the 1950s. Manufactured by Ridgways in Staffordshire, it was sold exclusively through Woolworths between c1955 and 1967. The fashionable black and white pattern provides a ceramic catalogue of contemporary home furnishings, including the boomerang table, spindly plant stand, Robin Day armchair, Gordon Russell-style sideboard – everything the young 1950s homemaker might desire.

Homemaker was marketed as affordable china. Cups, saucers and plates were mass-produced in their thousands and can still be picked up for very little cost today. Other items, such as tea and coffee pots and serving dishes, were manufactured in fewer numbers and these rarer pieces can command far higher prices.

A Homemaker trio, 1957, plate 7in (18cm) diam.
£20–22 HarC

Two Homemaker bowls, c1957, largest 7in (18cm) diam.
£10–15 HarC

Four Homemaker plates, 1957, largest 10in (25.5cm) diam.
£6–12 each HarC

A Homemaker vegetable dish, 1955–57, 9in (23cm) diam.
£60–70 GIN

A Homemaker meat plate, c1957, 15in (38cm) wide.
£125–150 HarC

A Homemaker sandwich plate, 1957, 9in (23cm) wide.
£75–90 HarC

A Homemaker Metro coffee pot, 1957, 9in (23cm) high.
£150–175 HarC

◄ A Homemaker Metro teapot, c1957, 5in (12.5cm) high.
£250–275 HarC

A Homemaker Cadenza jug, 1957, 4in (10cm) high.
£95–125 HarC

Games

Three multicoloured glass marbles, with transparent swirls with central cores, 1850, ¾in (18mm) diam.
£10–15 each MRW

Two Victorian ceramic marbles, banded with red, green and black, ¾in (18mm) diam.
£30–40 each MRW

A Wheeling board game, by J. Jacques & Son London, 'The Anchor at Ripley', 1900, 14in (35.5cm) square.
£100–120 J&J

A Gymnastic Bubbles game, complete and unused, 1910, box 6 x 5in (15 x 12.5cm).
£40–50 J&J

A Spin Round the Country game, 1910–20, 8 x 10in (20.5 x 25.5cm).
£40–50 J&J

A Winkle's Wedding game, 1920s, box 6¼ x 4in (16 x 19cm).
£7–8 CMF

A Chinese Mahjong set, with bone and bamboo tiles, 1920, in a wooden box, 9in (23cm) wide.
£200–250 TMi

A Selcol Satellite Game, with cardboard back and perspex front, 1950s, 4 x 7in (10 x 18cm).
£25–30 UNI

A BGL Funny Things Happen! board game, 1950s, box 11 x 10in (28 x 25.5cm).
£15–20 J&J

A Marx Super Crow Shoot game, c1960, box 18 x 13in (45.5 x 13cm).
£25–30 J&J

▶ A Spear's Games James Bond 007 Secret Service Game, 1965, box 14 x 7in (35.5 x 18cm).
£8–10 MED

CARD GAMES

◄ A Spear's Games card game of Snap, 1910.
£20–25 J&J

► An Old Maid card game, 1910.
£20–25 J&J

An H. P. Gibson & Sons Peter Pan card game, based on the book by J. M. Barrie, 1920s.
£20–25 J&J

A Chas Goodall & Son box of Patience playing cards, 1940s.
£5–6 CMF

A Snap card game, featuring outdoor pursuits, 1950.
£5–6 J&J

CHESS

A Behampor ivory chess set, one side stained black, the other natural, mid-19thC, king 4in (10cm) high.
£1,200–1,500 TMi

A French Régence bone chess set, red and white, 19thC, king 3½in (9cm) high.
£350–400 TMi

A Jacques & Son In Statu Quo Chess Board, with red and white bone pieces, hinged wooden board and black carrying case, 1890, 12in (30.5cm) wide.
£500–600 TMi

Cross Reference
See Colour Review

A Castleford Staffordshire chess set, with blue and grey figures, 1830, king 3½in (9cm) high, in a wooden box.
£1,400–1,600 TMi

A Victorian pub chess board, with gilt-decorated surround and oak frame, 22in (56cm) square.
£180–200 TMi

JIGSAWS

The jigsaw puzzle was invented in 1760 by London map maker John Spilsbury, who applied a map to a mahogany board, and cut round the countries. He called his creation a dissection and, throughout much of the 19th century, dissections were predominantly designed as learning tools for upper- and middle-class children, featuring themes such as geography, history and religion. Dissections were cut in simple patterns from hard woods using a hand-held saw. The work was laborious and puzzles were expensive, costing as much as a guinea each, more than the average labourer's weekly wage.

In the 1870s came the invention of the power scroll saw, known as the jigsaw, from which the jigsaw puzzle gained its now familiar name. Thanks to improved technology, puzzles could be made more quickly and affordably. Designs became more complex, subjects more entertaining, and for the first time jigsaws were popular with adults.

The 1900s saw a puzzle craze among high society in the USA, and in the UK the 1920s and '30s were a golden age for the jigsaw puzzle. Favourite subjects included trains, ocean liners and popular art, as well as the more traditional children's themes.

Up until the 1930s, puzzles were generally made from wood. After WWII cheap, mass-produced cardboard reigned supreme, and the introduction of television to the family home inspired a wealth of TV-oriented puzzles. Wooden puzzles are the most desirable. Prices depend, above all, on age and subject matter, 1920s and 1930s transport pictures, for example, are sought after both by puzzle collectors and transport enthusiasts. Do not buy a loose puzzle until you have seen it made up, since any missing pieces will affect both the value of the jigsaw and the pleasure of playing with it.

A Victorian Superior Dissected Map of Ireland, box 11 x 9in (28 x 23cm).
£80–90 ChA

A News Chronicle Publications wooden jigsaw puzzle, The Noah Family, 1920, 9 x 7in (23 x 18cm).
£50–60 J&J

A wooden jigsaw puzzle, Watch Your Step, painted in green, orange and grey, 1910–20, box 22 x 13in (56 x 33cm).
£80–100 J&J

◄ A wooden hand-cut jigsaw puzzle, Christmas Eve, 1920, 18 x 16in (45.5 x 40.5cm).
£50–60 J&J

► A Frederick Warne & Co wooden jigsaw puzzle, Peter Rabbit, 1920s, 9in (23cm) square.
£60–70 J&J

A Chad Valley wooden jigsaw puzzle, Mickey Mouse, 1930s, box 7 x 8in (18 x 20.5cm).
£85–100 J&J

A Waddington's cardboard circular jigsaw puzzle, depicting painted military scenes, 1960, box 8 x 10in (20.5 x 25.5cm).
£8–10 J&J

A Victory wooden jigsaw puzzle, Rock-a-Bye Baby, from the Nursery Rhyme series, 1930s, 12 x 9in (30.5 x 28cm).
£15–20 J&J

Further Reading

Miller's Toys & Games Antiques Checklist, Miller's Publications, 1995

▶ A wooden jigsaw puzzle 'Teddy Tar Goes to Sea', 1960, box 10 x 12in (25.5 x 30.5cm).
£10–12 J&J

A Victory wooden jigsaw puzzle, 1950s, 36½ x 30in (93 x 76cm).
£70–80 ZOOM

Garden Collectables

A wrought-iron stand, early 19thC, 29in (73.5cm) wide.
£200–250 NET

A pair of reconstituted stone figures of putti, on square bases, damaged, late 19thC, 35½in (91cm) high.
£1,800–2,000 DN

An Irish pine and maple grain shovel, with brass edge, c1890, 66in (167.5cm) long.
£30–35 EON

An Armenian clay storage jar, c1830, 28in (71cm) high.
£250–275 NET

A cast-iron garden urn, painted white, c1870, 30in (76cm) high.
£500–575 NET

A pair of Victorian wirework garden chairs, painted white, 34in (86.5cm) high.
£400–450 SPU

A wooden barrow, with metal wheel, 1840s, 67in (170cm) long.
£225–250 A&H

A French high-backed hand-turned wheelbarrow, in original green paint, with removable sides and metal-rimmed wheel, late 19thC, 78in (198cm) long.
£260–300 GaB

A pine flax cutter, c1880, 36in (91.5cm) long.
£85–95 BAB

A cast-iron garden bench, with scroll ends, metal seat frame and wooden slats, marked 'Robert Hall and Sons. Makers, Bury', 19thC, 53½in (136cm) wide.
£600–700 DN

A cast-iron bench, with wooden slats, painted green, 19thC, 60in (152.5cm) wide.
£325–365 NET

A Brown's of Leighton Buzzard wood and metal hand plough, 1900, 58in (147.5cm) long.
£60–70 BYG

A pair of wooden dibbers, early 20thC, 14in (35.5cm) high.
£9–12 each GaB

◄ A ground-breaking metal spade, with ribbed blade and wooden handle, c1910, 35in (89cm) high.
£25–30 GaB

A metal combination hand rake and trowel, c1950, 11in (28cm) long.
£8–10 GaB

A set of 4 metal-framed folding garden chairs, with wooden slats, painted green, c1900.
£100–120 NET

A turfing iron, with Ace of Spades head and wooden handle, c1900, 52in (132cm) high.
£30–35 GaB

A Sankey terracotta rhubarb forcing and blanching pot, c1900, 24in (61cm) high.
£225–275 NET

A marble group of Adam and Eve, with tree stump and serpent, early 20thC, 32in (94cm) high.
£1,900–2,200 DN

A cast-iron seed drill, c1900, 60in (152.5cm) high.
£60–70 BYG

Miller's is a price GUIDE not a price LIST

A wood and wire riddle, early 20thC, 20in (51cm) diam.
£12–15 GaB

A Sussex trug, early 20thC, 22in (56cm) wide.
£30–35 GaB

A French grape picker's wooden trug, early 20thC, 18in (45.5cm) wide.
£30–35 GaB

A Kentish hop fork, early 20thC, 35in (89cm) high.
£20–25 WO

An Abol No. 5 garden insecticide sprayer, c1913, 27in (68.5cm) long.
£25–30 GaB

Two metal watering cans, with copper nozzles, one painted red and one black, c1920, largest 15in (38cm) high.
£15–18 each AL

A metal watering can, 1930, 18in (45.5cm) high.
£15–18 UTP

Two weeding forks with twisted metal prongs, 1920–40, largest 17in (43cm) high.
£8–10 each GaB

A child's wooden wheelbarrow, painted green and brown, marked 'Sandy', 1930, 27in (68.5cm) long.
£140–160 SMI

A Bees Seeds display stand, painted light green, c1950, 26in (66cm) long.
£25–30 AL

◄ Two terracotta figures of dwarfs, from *Snow White and the Seven Dwarfs*, 1940–50, 7in (18cm) high.
£35–40 each HarC

A set of red and black sack weighing scales, 1930s, 19in (48.5cm) high.
£80–90 BYG

Don't Throw Away A Fortune!
Invest In
Miller's Price Guides

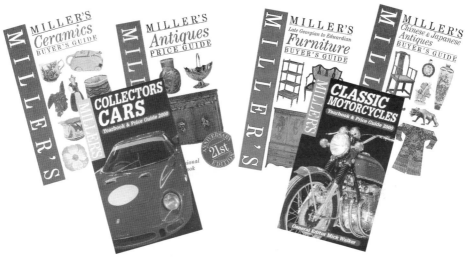

Please send me the following editions

❑ **Miller's Antiques Price Guide 2000** – £22.50
❑ **Miller's Classic Motorcycles Yearbook & Price Guide 2000** – £14.99
❑ **Miller's Collectors Cars Yearbook & Price Guide 2000** – £19.99
❑ **Miller's Ceramics Buyer's Guide** – £19.99
❑ **Miller's Late Georgian to Edwardian Furniture Buyer's Guide** – £18.99
❑ **Miller's Chinese & Japanese Antiques Buyers Guide** – £19.99

If you do not wish your name to be used by Miller's or other carefully selected organisations for promotional purposes, please tick this box ❑

I enclose my cheque/postal order for £..................post free (UK only)
Please make cheques payable to *'Octopus Publishing Group Ltd'*
or please debit my Access/Visa/Amex/Diners Club account number

Expiry Date............/............

NAME Title *Initial* *Surname*

ADDRESS

Postcode

SIGNATURE

Photocopy this page or write the above details on a separate sheet and send it to Miller's Direct,
27 Sanders Road, Wellingborough, Northants. NN8 4NL or telephone the Credit Card Hotline 01933 443863.
Lines open from 9:00am to 5:00pm. Registered office: 2-4 Heron Quays, Docklands, London E14 4JP.
Registered in England number 3597451

Glass

A cut-glass butter dish, cover and stand, c1800, 7½in (19cm) wide.
£475–525 CB

A blue bonnet glass, the honeycomb-moulded double ogee bowl on a conical foot with petal-shaped edge, c1750, 2¾in (7cm) high.
£230–260 SOM

A blue glass sugar bowl, with opalescent rim, gilt rim line worn, 1790, 4¾in (12cm) high.
£100–120 COHU

Bonnet glasses were used for sweetmeats.

An Irish heavy glass celery vase, with bands of flute, strawberry, diamond, sunburst and stiff-leaf cutting, short knopped stem and star-cut foot, c1810, 9in (23cm) high.
£340–380 SOM

A pair of Bohemian green and white opaque overlay glass lustre vases, the flared rims with shaped edges enamelled with vignettes, hung with cut prismatic drops, chipped, 19thC, 13in (33cm) high.
£650–750 CAG

A baluster glass celery vase, on ball knop stem, c1830, 10in (25.5cm) high.
£50–60 FD

A Bohemian clear and amber glass goblet and cover, moulded with hunting scenes, c1845, 10½in (26.5cm) high.
£1,200–1,500 ALiN

A peach-tinted glass bowl, on 6 glass feet, 1860–80, 3½in (9cm) high.
£20–25 OD

▶ A glass lily vase, the purple base fading to pale pink petals with clear green leaves, 1860–80, 7½in (19cm) high.
£80–90 BHA

◀ A milk glass vase, decorated with gilt, enamel and 'jewels', c1875, 9in (23cm) high.
£200–250 GRI

A blow-moulded clear glass bird feeder, with blue stopper, c1870, 6in (15cm) high.
£80–95 CB

A clear glass and silver-plated cruet set, by Dr Christopher Dresser, c1875, 9in (23cm) high.
£500–600 ChA

◄ A vaseline glass cruet set, on silver-plated stand, c1890, 6in (15cm) high.
£150–170 AnS

A George Davidson primrose Pearline glass bonbon dish, No. 176566, 1891, 5in (12.5cm) diam.
£50–60 AnS

A James Powell, Whitefriars, clear glass preserve dish, trailed with dark green, on a silver-plated base, c1880, 7in (18cm) high.
£100–120 AnS

A shaded pink satin glass vase, with enamel decoration in gold, yellow and blue, on 6 clear glass feet, c1890, 7in (18cm) high.
£170–190 GRI

A pair of amethyst over white glass Jack-in-the-pulpit vases, c1895, 7in (18cm) high.
£220–250 GRI

A Jack-in-the-pulpit vase resembles the shape of the American woodland flower of the same name.

A pair of Stevens & Williams vaseline glass trumpet vases, with folded feet, c1900, 13in (33cm) high.
£400–450 GRI

Vaseline glass contains a small amount of uranium which imparts a yellowish-green, opalescent effect. Named after the famous petroleum jelly, vaseline glass was extremely popular in the Victorian period.

A Daum glass vase, decorated with 4 etched panels of spiky flowers and leaves, applied with green, marked 'Daum, Nancy', c1900, 4¼in (11cm) high.
£300–350 WW

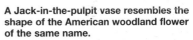

A yellow vaseline glass double-gourd vase, c1900, 5in (12.5cm) high.
£175–190 AnS

A frilled clear glass salt, with green marvering, in a silver-plated holder, c1900, 3in (7.5cm) diam.
£100–110 GRI

A Continental glass biscuit barrel, with silver-plated top, the cover with a swan finial, c1900, 5½in (14cm) diam.
£280–320 GRI

A Stourbridge frilled clear glass preserve dish, with amethyst edge, c1900, 5⅛in (14cm) diam.
£90–100 GRI

A cut-glass bowl, on a short stem and square base, 1900, 8in (20.5cm) diam.
£65–75 OD

A James Powell, Whitefriars, vaseline glass comport, c1900, 2in (5cm) high.
£150–175 GRI

A John Walsh Walsh mother-of-pearl glass lily leaf, on a clear green stem, 1903, 5in (12.5cm) high.
£110–120 GRI

A Stevens & Williams amber cameo glass vase, c1900, 5in (12.5cm) high.
£1,500–1,700 GRI

An Austrian amber-coloured iridescent glass vase, 1900–1910, 9¼in (23.5cm) high.
£300–350 BTB

A Stevens & Williams citrine over clear glass sundae dish, engraved with fruiting vines, c1910, 5in (12.5cm) high.
£160–180 GRI

Cross Reference
See Colour Review

Two Venetian opaque glass lily vases, one with green and one purple rim and foot, 1910–20, tallest 21in (53.5cm) high.
£65–85 each BHA

◄ A Millersburg Little Stars green glass bowl, 1909–11, 7in (18cm) diam.
£100–120 ASe

◄ A Schneider yellow and black cameo glass vase, marked 'Berlinpot', 1918–20, 3in (7.5cm) high.
£300–350 AOH

A set of 6 blue glass dessert bowls, 1920s, 5in (12.5cm) diam.
£16–18 Law

A blue pressed glass jug, 1920–30s, 7¼in (18.5cm) high.
£5–6 Law

A Monart amethyst glass bowl, with blue and black speckles, c1924–61, 9¼in (23.5cm) diam.
£125–150 TCG

A French crystal vase, indistinct mark on base, c1920, 17¼in (44cm) high.
£200–220 AOT

An American pressed glass two-handled bowl, 1920–30s, 7in (18cm) wide.
£4–5 Law

A Gray-Stan footed glass bowl, with swirled apricot pattern, 1926–38, 5¼in (13.5cm) high.
£150–180 TCG

A Bimini white glass figurine, on a black and white glass base, 1930s, 8in (20.5cm) high.
£150–170 GRI

▶ A Loetz iridescent gold and crackle glass vase, 1930s, 7in (18cm) high.
£300–350 BTB

A Gray-Stan clear glass vase, decorated with trailing turquoise festoons, 1930s, 8¼in (21cm) high.
£120–140 TCG

A Czechoslovakian pressed green glass trumpet vase, the stem in the form of 2 maidens, c1930, 12in (30.5cm) high.
£90–110 BKK

A French black glass vase, 1930s, 11¾in (30cm) high.
£450–500 BTB

A Powell cobalt blue glass bucket vase, 1930s, 6in (15cm) high.
£50–60 TCG

A pressed glass vase, decorated with amethyst roses, c1930, 8in (20.5cm) high.
£175–200 TCG

A Sowerby iridescent marigold glass cream jug, moulded with Thorn & Thistle pattern, 1925–35, 3in (7.5cm) high.
£5–10 ASe

A Baccarat crystal bowl, by Jean Puiforçat, with silver and gilt rim, c1930, 5in (12.5cm) diam.
£340–380 ChA

A French moulded black glass vase, 1930s, 9½in (24cm) high.
£400–500 BTB

A Daum Nancy blue glass dish, the lid with acid-etched decoration, signed, c1930, 5in (12.5cm) diam.
£400–450 ART

► A Murano red and grey banded glass vase, maker's sticker 'Sent Murano Made in Italy', c1950, 7¾in (19.5cm) high.
£40–50 AOT

A Murano brown glass pitcher, by Venini, 1950s, 8½in (21.5cm) high.
£150–175 MARK

A Whitefriars grey-shaded glass vase, 1960–70, 10in (25.5cm) high.
£25–30 Law

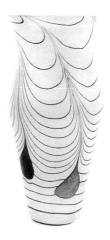

A green and beige textured glass vase, 1960s, 7in (18cm) high.
£2–3 Law

These vases were sold by Woolworths in the 1960s. Although superficially similar to Whitefriars, they are lighter in weight, and cruder in colour and definition.

A Whitefriars pewter glass log vase, designed by Geoffrey Baxter, 1966, 7in (18cm) high.
£20–25 Law

Cross Reference
See Colour Review

A pearl glass vase, decorated with swirls of iridescent blue, purple and green, signed, No. 4399, 1995, 11in (28cm) high.
£100–130 GLA

A brown and clear glass bud vase, 1970s, 24¾in (63cm) high.
£130–150 ZOOM

CRANBERRY

Cranberry glass is among the most collectable of all Victorian glassware. With the repeal of excise duty on glass in 1845, British manufacturers were able to experiment more freely with new techniques and colours.

Cranberry glass was produced in the Midlands, in Sunderland, Warrington and most notably in the Stourbridge area, and was also imported from the Continent. The other main centre of production was the USA, from where this distinctive, reddish pink glass gained its name.

While drinking glasses and functional pieces could be comparatively simple in design, as the 19th century progressed cranberry glass became increasingly ornamental, decorated with trailing, enamelling and contrasting clear glass, and shaped into every form from huge elaborate epergnes to tiny novelties. Cranberry glass was almost always hand-blown but, with the development of pressed moulded glass and increasing mechanisation at the turn of the century, production tailed off, coming to a virtual end with the start of WWI in 1914.

A cranberry glass salt, with uranium glass curled feet and prunt, c1880, 3in (7.5cm) diam.
£80–90 AnS

◄ A Bohemian cranberry glass fruit comport, the bowl with shaped rim and floral painted panels alternating with diamond cut panels, with a portrait of a woman on a gilded scrolling foliate ground and flared base, 19thC, 11in (28cm) high.
£250–300 AH

► A cranberry glass oval cut vase, on circular base, c1885, 8in (20.5cm) high.
£170–190 GRI

◀ A cranberry glass vase, decorated in Mary Gregory style, c1885, 13in (33cm) high.
£450–550 GRI

A cranberry glass jug, with frilled top and clear glass handle, c1885, 8in (20.5cm) high.
£200–250 GRI

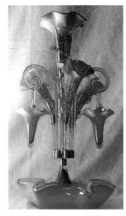

A cranberry and milk glass trumpet epergne, with central vase, 3 smaller trumpet-shaped vases, 3 clear glass canes, supporting further trumpet basket vases, the whole raised on a hexagonal bowl-shaped base, c1885, 19¼in (49cm) high.
£750–850 DDM

A cranberry glass bell, 1890, 12¾in (32.5cm) high.
£90–100 CB

▶ A cranberry glass custard cup, with clear glass handle and foot, c1895, 3in (7.5cm) high.
£45–55 GRI

A Thomas Webb cranberry glass salt, on a silver-plated stand, c1900, 3in (7.5cm) diam.
£100–125 GRI

A cranberry glass epergne, on a mirrored base, c1900, 11in (28cm) high.
£850–950 GRI

A cranberry glass vase, with frilled crystal top, the neck decorated with white threading, on a clear base, c1890, 9in (23cm) high.
£200–250 GRI

A pair of cranberry glass vases, with crimped edges, probably by Smart Brothers, c1895, 12in (30.5cm) high.
£500–600 GRI

▶ A Stourbridge four-trumpet cranberry glass epergne, c1910, 20in (51cm) high.
£700–800 GRI

A cranberry glass ribbed trumpet vase, probably by Stevens & Williams, on a folded foot, c1900, 17in (43cm) high.
£450–500 GRI

DECANTERS

A brown glass spirit flagon, with metal mount, stopper missing, c1840, 7½in (19cm) high.
£65–80 SOM

A glass decanter, the tapering body flute-cut at the base and diamond facet-cut round the neck, cut spire stopper, c1780, 10in (25.5cm) high.
£320–360 SOM

A glass toddy lifter, with flute-cut base, the neck with 3 bands of prism cutting, annulated lip, c1820, 6½in (16.5cm) high.
£160–180 SOM

A cranberry glass decanter, c1895, 11in (28cm) high.
£200–240 GRI

▶ A glass claret jug, with silver mounts by William Comyns, London 1903, 8in (20.5cm) high.
£750–850 CHAP

DRINKING GLASSES

A baluster wine glass, the bell bowl on a cushioned knop above central and basal knops, c1730, 6in (15cm) high.
£800–900 BELL

A gin glass, the bowl with moulded flutes, the stem with flattened shoulder knop and folded foot, c1745, 4½in (11.5cm) high.
£160–175 GS

A balustroid wine glass, the ogee bowl with basal flutes over a centre knopped stem and folded stem, c1745, 6½in (16.5cm) high.
£235–265 GS

A wine glass, the round funnel bowl supported on an opaque twist stem, c1760, 6¼in (16cm) high.
£175–210 GS

A small dram glass, with firing foot, double series opaque twist stem and engraved ogee bowl, c1760, 4in (10cm) high.
£350–400 GS

An ale glass, with moulded bowl, 1800, 4½in (11.5cm) high.
£25–30 OD

A Bristol blue bowl wine glass, on clear stem, c1880, 5½in (14cm) high.
£75–85 JAS

A wine glass, the round funnel bowl supported on a double series opaque twist stem, restored foot chip, c1765, 6¼in (16cm) high.
£165–185 GS

A glass, the bowl cut with bands, the stem with central knop, early 19thC, 3¼in (8.5cm) high.
£20–25 OD

An ale flute, engraved with hops and barley, 1800, 4½in (11.5cm) high.
£40–50 OD

An incurved bucket bowl rummer, decorated with a cut diamond band, with bladed knop stem, c1820, 4½in (11.5cm) high.
£80–90 GS

◄ A pair of tall ale glasses, with drawn trumpet bowls engraved with hops and barley, teared stems and domed and folded feet, 19thC, 8in (20.5cm) high.
£380–420 TMA

► A cranberry glass stirrup glass, modelled as a boot, c1880, 8in (20.5cm) high.
£140–160 GRI

A wrythen ale flute, 1800, 5in (12.5cm) high.
£15–20 OD

Wrythen means decorated with spiral or swirling vertical reeding.

A glass tankard, with acid-etched floral decoration, dated '1873', 6in (15cm) high.
£130–150 JHa

A cranberry glass mug, by Moser, decorated with enamel and gilt, c1900, 2½in (6.5cm) high.
£100–110 GRI

A Stevens & Williams amethyst loving cup, engraved with fruiting vines, 1900–10, 7in (18cm) high.
£250–275 GRI

A Richardson's amethyst bowl wine glass, on faceted hollow stem, c1885, 6in (15cm) high.
£100–110 GRI

A Stevens & Williams wine glass, cased blue and amber over clear, c1910, 8in (20.5cm) high.
£270–320 GRI

> **Cross Reference**
> See Cocktails

▶ A glass goblet, with a model of a bi-plane enclosed in the knop, c1930, 7in (18cm) high.
£60–70 GRI

◀ A Danish wine glass, by Holmegaard, c1950, 8in (20.5cm) high.
£35–40 BRU

LALIQUE

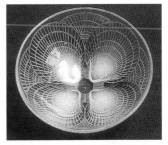

A Lalique opalescent glass bowl, entitled 'Coquilles' etched mark, c1930, 9in (23cm) diam.
£400–450 RUSK

A Lalique glass dish, entitled 'Poissons', moulded with fish, c1925, 10in (25.5cm) high.
£450–500 AOH

A Lalique glass bowl, the cover engraved with flowers and leaves, 1920–30, 3¼in (8.5cm) diam.
£400–450 ASA

> **Cross Reference**
> See Colour Review

▶ A Lalique square glass box, the cover engraved with flowers, 1920–30, 4in (10cm) wide.
£450–500 ASA

PAPERWEIGHTS

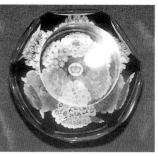

◄ A Richardson's desk set, comprising 2 paperweights and a bottle, in red, yellow and blue millefiori pattern, 1913–16, bottle 6in (15cm) high.
£1,300–1,500 SWB

A Whitefriars paperweight, pink, white and pale blue on a dark blue ground, 1953–78, 3in (7.5cm) diam.
£150–175 SWB

A Perthshire hollow paperweight, the centre with a swan on a green pond, signed on wing 'P', limited edition of 250, 1973, 3in (7.5cm) diam.
£300–350 STG

A Perthshire paperweight, the multicoloured centre with a purple surround, 1974, 2¾in (7cm) diam.
£300–350 SWB

A Wedgwood green glass paperweight, modelled as a wren, 1970s, 3¾in (9.5cm) high.
£16–18 Law

A Whitefriars red, white and blue paperweight, to commemorate the US bicentenary, 1976, 3in (7.5cm) diam.
£255–285 SWB

A paperweight, modelled as a horse, 1970s, 6¼in (16cm) high.
£10–15 Law

A Powell Whitefriars brown glass paperweight, filled with air bubbles, 1970s, 2⅛in (6.5cm) diam.
£10–12 Law

LOCATE THE SOURCE

The source of each illustration in Miller's can be found by checking the code letters below each caption with the Key to Illustrations, pages 476–484.

► A mauve and green Peony paperweight, by David Salazan, Lundberg Studio, USA, 1988, 2¾in (7cm) diam.
£150–175 SWB

A Perthshire paperweight, with pink, blue, red, green and yellow flowers, 1991, 3in (7.5cm) diam.
£250–285 SWB

Five flat landscape paperweights, blue, red, purple and yellow, signed 'J. Ditchfield, Glasform', 1995, largest 4in (10cm) wide.
£100–120 each GLA

A Perthshire paperweight, with close-pack millefiori magnum pattern, by P. McDougal, signed, 1997, 4¼in (11cm) diam.
£1,800–2,000 STG

A Caithness Temptation paperweight, pink, green and red, 1997, 3½in (9cm) high.
£250–275 SWB

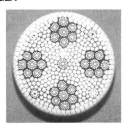

A Perthshire millefiori paperweight, red, blue, yellow and white, 1998, 3in (7.5cm) diam.
£100–120 SWB

A William Manson black glass paperweight, with flowers and a butterfly in green, white, yellow and brown, 1998, 3in (7.5cm) diam.
£200–225 SWB

A St Louis paperweight, Feuilles d'Olivier, pink, yellow and green, 1998, 3in (7.5cm) diam.
£575–625 SWB

A frosted glass eagle paperweight, on a clear glass base, 4½in (11.5cm) high.
£35–45 EAS

◀ A White Crane paperweight, by David Salazan, Lundberg Studio, USA, blue, green and white, 1998, 3¼in (8.5cm) diam.
£275–325 SWB

Handbags

A chainmail purse, with enamel clasp and chain handle, c1900, 8in (20.5cm) long.
£45–55 ChA

A silver beaded purse, with lilac beaded pattern and fringe, 1920s, 6in (15cm) square, with box.
£70–80 L&L

Cross Reference
See Colour Review

◀ A French white Bakelite fish purse, with whte metal frame, 1900, 2¾in (7cm) wide.
£75–85 LBe

A silver and gold beaded purse, with gold and mauve pattern and fringe, 1920s, 5in (12.5cm) long.
£70–80 L&L

An Irish green and yellow beaded evening bag, with tassles, lined in silk, 1920s, 10in (25.5cm) long.
£120–150 JVa

A green leather clutch bag, with blue enamel and chrome motif on flap, 1930s, 10in (25.5cm) wide.
£25–30 PC

◀ A printed cloth handbag, with brown, blue and orange abstract design, c1930, 10¼in (26cm) wide.
£35–45 PC

A brown leather handbag, 1930s, 10in (25.5cm) wide.
£15–20 HarC

A navy blue *roulet* clutch bag, c1950, 9in (23cm) wide.
£10–12 CCO

Further Reading

Miller's Collecting the 1950s, Miller's Publications, 1997

A handbag, made from an orange patterned paisley shawl, with leather handles and brass rings, 1950s, 9in (23cm) wide.
£110–125 LBe

PLASTIC HANDBAGS

The hard plastic or lucite handbag was a by-product of WWII plastics technology and perfectly summed up the whimsical spirit of the fifties style. Bags were manufactured in the USA, around New York and Miami. Designs came in both clear and coloured plastics, often tortoiseshell or pearl colours in black, white and grey. Surfaces could be carved or decorated with rhinestones, some bags were manufactured from glitter plastic or perspex set with lace.

Today these examples of fifties frivolity are highly collectable. It is important, however, to check condition, and beware of cracked or crizzled plastic. Principal manufacturers include Llewellyn, Rialto, Willardi, Florida Handbags and Patricia of Miami, and some bags retain their original label or a maker's mark.

A sparkle lucite handbag, the carved panels set with rhinestones, c1950, 8in (20.5cm) wide.
£325–365 ArD

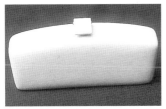

A white plastic clutch handbag, with plastic fittings, 1950s, 5in (12.5cm) wide.
£75–85 LBr

A white hard plastic handbag, with brass fittings, 1950s, 10in (25cm) wide.
£140–160 LBr

A Tyrolean lucite handbag, with clear carved lid and caramel coloured base, 1950s, 10in (25.5cm) wide.
£130–150 ArD

A white pearlized lucite handbag, decorated with pink, green and yellow shells, 1950s, 9in (23cm) wide.
£275–300 ArD

▶ A grey lucite handbag, with clear plastic handle, 1950s, 12in (30.5cm) wide.
£200–220 ArD

A Magestic lucite handbag, with black lid and gilt criss-cross pattern, 1950s, 10in (25.5cm) wide.
£180–200 ArD

A Wilardy white lucite handbag, with silver beaded clasp, maker's label, 1950s, 10in (25.5cm) wide.
£280–320 ArD

A clear lucite handbag, with carved flower pattern and black beaded handle, 1950s, 8in (20.5cm) wide.
£450–500 ArD

A caramel-coloured lucite handbag, with carved clear lid and handle, 1950, 9in (23cm) wide.
£250–280 ArD

A tortoiseshell lucite shell-shaped handbag, with brass chain handle, 1950s, 7in (18cm) wide.
£85–95 ArD

A clear lucite handbag, with inset lace design, 1950s, 6in (15cm) wide.
£280–300 ArD

A Patricia green mottled lucite handbag, with clear carved lid and sides, 1950s, 10in (25.5cm) wide.
£300–350 ArD

A silver-coloured confetti lucite handbag, with carved clear lid, 1950s, 9in (23cm) wide.
£220–230 ArD

LOCATE THE SOURCE
The source of each illustration in Miller's can be found by checking the code letters below each caption with the Key to Illustrations, pages 476–484.

A carved clear lucite basket bag, 1950s, 10in (25.5cm) wide.
£35–45 LBr

A Wilardy white pearlized lucite compact/handbag, with gilt fittings, 1950s, 7in (18cm) wide.
£180–200 ArD

A grey lucite handbag, with heavily carved clear lid, button fastener, 1950s, 10in (25.5cm) wide.
£220–250 ArD

A clear and tortoiseshell carved lucite handbag, 1950s, 10in (25.5cm) wide.
£275–300 ArD

Insets

Although these tiny creatures can inspire a fear that is out of all proportion to their size, insects have appeared in the fine and decorative arts since ancient times. The Egyptians wore scarab amulets, made from semi-precious stones or clay, as they thought the scarab concealed the secret of eternal life. They also believed that all scarabs were male. Spiders, however, were often thought of as female, because of the female spider's habit of devouring its mate and also the spinning of the web. The word 'arachnid' comes from Arachne, champion weaver of Greek mythology, who rashly challenged the goddess Minerva to a weaving contest and was changed into a spider. Finding a spider on one's clothes, particularly a money spider, was traditionally believed to bring good fortune, hence one of the reasons why spiders often appear in the form of brooches. Butterflies too have been a popular subject in jewellery from the time of the Aztecs onwards and, along with dragonflies, were one of the favourite motifs of the Art Nouveau period.

Insects were employed in the applied arts both for ornamental and symbolic reasons. In religious art, a beehive is used as the symbol of saints renowned for their eloquence, suggesting that their words are sweet as honey. In ceramics, the honey pot is one of the most decorative pieces of tableware, often modelled in the form of a beehive. The bee itself was a symbol of industry and the chosen emblem of Napoleon, the self-made emperor. Although we might spend much of our lives plotting how to get rid of bugs and beetles, this section looks at the collectable insect and its various manifestations in the decorative arts.

CERAMICS

A Bodley porcelain plate, decorated with a dragonfly, butterfly, bee and foliage in green, blue and red, 1880, 9in (23cm) diam.
£50–55 OD

A Lemon & Crute butterfly posy vase, painted with a green butterfly and leaves on a pink ground, 1914–26, 3in (7.5cm) high.
£10–15 PC

A Wemyss button, painted with a dragonfly with blue wings within a black border, impressed mark 'WEMYSS', early 20thC, 1¼in (3.5cm) diam.
£1,000–1,200 S

◄ A Royal Worcester bowl, decorated with 3 blue, green and gilt butterflies, on a mottled blue ground, c1930, 12in (30.5cm) diam.
£300–350 Mit

▶ A Fishley-Holland vase, painted with a grey butterfly on a mottled brown ground, 1950–60, 3¼in (8.5cm) high.
£10–15 Law

GLASS

A Lalique perfume bottle, Muguet by Coty, with moth design on the stopper, 1920s, 3½in (9cm) high.
£250–300 LBe

A Webb Corbett paperweight, with engraved dragonflies in ruby and clear glass, 1975, 3in (7.5cm) diam.
£35–40 SWB

An Orrefors glass vase, engraved with a flying insect and flowers, 1960s, 5in (12.5cm) high.
£200–250 ZOOM

HONEY POTS

A pearlware honey pot, with blue pattern and brown lid handle, c1810, 5in (12.5cm) high.
£200–220 HUM

A Wemyss honey pot and stand, hand-painted with bees and hive on a cream ground, late 19thC, pot 3in (7.5cm) high.
£180–200 HUM

A Belleek honey pot and cover, decorated with grass teaware pattern, with coloured bees and foliage, black transfer-printed mark on base and cover, 1863–91, 6¼in (16cm) high.
£800–900 HOK

A Crown Devon honeycomb pot, the beige body moulded to create a honeycomb texture, decorated with hand-painted bees, 1930s, 5in (12.5cm) square.
£70–80 OD

A Marutomo Ware relief-moulded honey pot, hand-painted in brown with green leaves and yellow bees, and a yellow bee finial, 1920–30, 4½in (11.5cm) high.
£45–55 COCO

Two Marutomo Ware yellow and red honeycomb-moulded honey pots, decorated with blue and yellow bees, c1950, 3½in (9cm) high.
£30–35 HarC

JEWELLERY & METALWARE

A Japanese *tsuba,* decorated with gilt locusts, late 18thC, 3in (7.5cm) wide.
£400–450 GRa

A brass and white metal brooch, the centre stamped with a bee, with decorative border, 1880–90, 1½in (4cm) diam.
£35–45 TB

A dragonfly brooch, with red stone eyes, 1910, 2in (5cm) long.
£10–12 OD

A Victorian butterfly bar brooch, set with a moonstone and red gemstone eyes, 1in (2.5cm) wide.
£80–100 FHF

A yellow metal fly brooch, with turquoise body, 1910, ¾in (20mm) long.
£5–7 OD

A yellow metal bee brooch, early 20thC, ¾in (20mm) long.
£3–5 OD

A scarab brooch, made from the body of a real beetle, with metal legs and fitting, 1910, 1½in (4cm) long.
£15–20 OD

Jewellery using the bodies of real beetles was produced both in South America and India. The iridescent carapaces and wings have also been incorporated into textiles and other decorative items.

▶ A Czechoslovakian gilt-metal dragonfly cloak or cardigan clip, set with red, green and amber rhinestones, 1930s, 2½in (6.5cm) wide.
£55–65 LBe

A silver, gold leaf and black Bakelite cicada brooch, 1930s, 3in (7.5cm) long.
£30–35 LBe

A black Bakelite bug brooch, set with white rhinestones, 1930s, 2½in (6.5cm) long.
£45–55 LBe

A marcasite and silver leaf flying insect brooch, 1930s, 3in (7.5cm) long.
£30–35 LBe

A carved wood butterfly brooch, painted yellow with black wingtips, 1930s, 3in (7.5cm) long.
£40–45 LBe

A Lea Stein laminated plastic bee brooch, in red, 1930–40, 2in (5cm) wide.
£45–50 HT

A Czechoslovakian gilt-metal spider brooch, with orange faceted glass body and blue head, 1930s, 1in (2.5cm) long.
£40–45 LBe

A silver spider brooch, with banded agate body, 1940s, 3in (7.5cm) long.
£85–95 LBe

A brass spider brooch, with red Bakelite body, 1940s, 2in (5cm) long.
£40–45 LBe

A gilt-metal bee brooch, signed 'Joseff of Hollywood', 1940s, 2in (5cm) long.
£40–45 LBe

A Joseff of Hollywood gilt-metal bee necklace, 1940s.
£180–200 LBe

A sterling silver butterfly brooch, set with red stones, signed 'Valsran Brody-Baiardi', late 1940s, 4in (10cm) wide.
£130–150 LBe

An Italian 18ct yellow gold grasshopper brooch, with yellow, green and red enamelled wings and head, 1950s, 1½in (4cm) long.
£210–230 DuM

An 18ct yellow gold bee brooch, set with emeralds, rubies, a sapphire and diamonds, 1950s, 1¼in (3cm) wide.
£800–1,000 BHA

A Victorian green glass dump, on a wooden base, 7in (18cm) high.
£325–350 OCAC

A pair of ruby glass candlesticks, with gilt decoration, c1880, 7in (18cm) high.
£500–550 GRI

Two Victorian glass tumblers, 1880, 3¾in (9.5cm) high.
Green tumbler **£5–10**
Cranberry tumbler **£20–25 OD**

A green glass posy vase, 1880, 4in (10cm) high.
£40–45 BHA

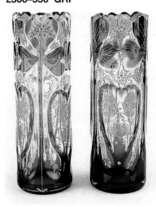

Six green cut glass overlay posy vases, decorated with shamrocks and gilt, c1890, 5in (12.5cm) high.
£750–850 GRI

◄ A Continental cranberry glass vase, with gilt decoration and a painted cameo portrait, c1885, 13in (33cm) high.
£350–400 GRI

A Clutha glass vase, made for Liberty, design attributed to George Walton, c1890, 4in (10cm) high.
£675–750 NCA

Three Continental amethyst glass vases, decorated with Mary Gregory-style enamelled figures, and gilt, c1890, tallest 9in (23cm) high.
£1,800–2,000 GRI

► A cranberry glass bell, with vaseline handle, c1890, 13½in (34.5cm) high.
£200–250 CB

A satin blue glass vase, decorated with gilt and enamel, c1890, 9in (23cm) high.
£200–220 GRI

► A cranberry glass vinegar bottle, decorated with gilt and enamel, c1890, 7in (18cm) high.
£200–220 GRI

A Stourbridge basket, in cased crystal over opalescent glass, c1890, 7in (18cm) high.
£170–190 GRI

A red glass vase, with cameo cyclamen pattern, c1900, 4½in (11.5cm) high.
£1,200–1,500 GRI

A Tiffany iridescent bowl and saucer, c1900, saucer 6in (15cm) diam.
£550–650 AOH

A miniature glass cheese dish, decorated with enamel and gilt, c1900, dish 2½in (6.5cm) diam.
£75–90 GRI

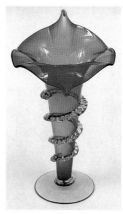

◄ A *latticino* glass plate, decorated with pink and gilt, c1900, 8in (20.5cm) diam.
£120–130 GRI

A cranberry glass jack-in-the-pulpit vase, with citrine glass trail and foot, c1900, 10in (25.5cm) high.
£220–250 GRI

A Moser cobalt blue glass vase, decorated with coloured oak leaves, and gilt, c1900, 11in (28cm) high.
£200–225 GRI

A Stevens & Williams blue glass urchin-shaped posy vase, with air trap design, reg No. 55693, 1911, 2in (5cm) high.
£90–100 GRI

A Northwood amethyst carnival glass mug, decorated with Singing Birds pattern, 1910–15, 3½in (9cm) high.
£80–110 ASe

A three-piece glass toilet set, with silver and turquoise blue enamel tops, Birmingham 1911, 4in (10cm) high.
£125–145 JACK

A ruby glass flask, decorated with acid-etched cameo sporting scenes, marked 'St Louis', c1920, 6in (15cm) high.
£400–450 GRI

A yellow crackle glass wall pocket, 1930s, 10in (25.5cm) high.
£45–55 RUL

An Art Deco crackle glass lamp-shade, 1930s, 6in (15cm) high.
£20–25 OD

A blue glass jug, decorated with etched floral pattern, 1930s, 7½in (19cm) high.
£10–15 Law

A Vasart glass vase, with orange and red pattern, 1948–63, 8in (20.5cm) high.
£120–140 TCG

A James Powell & Sons, Whitefriars, ruby glass jug, with flint-coloured grass-twist handle, c1955, 6in (15cm) high.
£40–50 RUSK

A James Powell & Sons, Whitefriars, ruby glass log vase, designed by Geoffrey Baxter, 1966, 7¼in (18.5cm) high.
£25–30 Law

A James Powell & Sons, Whitefriars, textured vase, designed by Geoffrey Baxter, in kingfisher blue cased crystal, 1967, 7in (18cm) high.
£12–15 Law

► An iridescent glass vase, decorated with gold feathering, signed and numbered '4469', 1995, 4½in (11.5cm) high.
£100–120 GLA

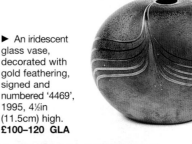

◄ A Siddy Langley glass vase, decorated with Navajo pattern, 1997, 5in (12.5cm) high.
£80–90 NP

A blue glass paperweight, decorated with a sulphide of a winged figure, probably by Baccarat, c1890, 3½in (9cm) diam.
£280–320 HUM

A Baccarat glass paperweight, decorated with a blue and green flower, numbered edition, signature and date cane, also engraved on base, 1973, 3in (7.5cm) diam.
£550–650 STG

◀ A Paul Stankard glass paperweight, from an edition of 50 lampwork 'Trailing Arbutus', signed 'S' cane and inscribed with date and edition, 1985, 3in (7.5cm) diam.
£1,500–1,800 STG

▶ A Lundberg Studios glass paperweight, with coloured butterfly wings pattern, 1996, 3in (7.5cm) diam.
£135–155 SWB

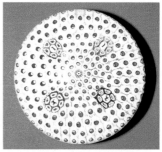

A St Louis glass paperweight, with red and white carpet ground pattern, 1978, 3¼in (8.5cm) diam.
£330–360 SWB

A Wemyss pottery honey pot, hand-painted with bees and hive, late 19thC, 5in (12.5cm) high.
£150–180 HUM

A Marutomo ware hand-painted Butterfly preserve pot, the cover with flower finial, 1920–30s, 2¼in (5.5cm) high.
£45–55 COCO

A Czechoslovakian bee brooch, gilt metal with blue and crystal stones, 1930–40s, 2in (5cm) long.
£40–45 LBe

A Triffari ladybird brooch, white metal with red and black body, 1950s, 1¾in (4.5cm) long.
£40–45 LBe

A letter card, decorated with pop-up bee in blossom, 1910, 4in (10cm) high.
£20–30 MRW

A Mackintosh's Beehive Toffee tin, c1930, 4in (10cm) high.
£40–50 HUM

A white metal and malachite spider brooch, 1940s, 2½in (6.5cm) long.
£50–55 LBe

A hand-painted pottery honey pot, in the form of a house, the cover with bee finial, 1920–30s, 4in (10cm) high.
£35–45 COCO

A Bakelite flying bug brooch, decorated with gold and silver leaf, 1930s, 3in (7.5cm) long.
£30–35 LBe

A Weiss butterfly brooch, yellow metal with rhinestones, 1950, 2in (5cm) long.
£55–65 LBe

◄ A leather and Bakelite compact, with zip closure, decorated with a spider on a web, 1940s, 3in (7.5cm) wide.
£50–55 LBe

A gold pin, in the shape of a flower, with central opal, c1840, 1in (2.5cm) diam.
£150–170 WIM

A Scottish silver pin, inset with slate, c1850, 2in (5cm) diam.
£225–275 WIM

A gold cross pendant, pavé set with turquoises, 1870, 4in (10cm) long.
£350–400 JSM

A 9ct rose gold charm bracelet, with 8 charms, 1890–1920, 7in (18cm) long.
£350–400 BND

A silver and marcasite set of earrings, bracelet, ring and pendant, inset with jade, 1920s, earrings 2in (5cm) long.
£230–260 DAC

A silver dress clip, set with marcasite and amazonite, 1930s, 1in (2.5cm) long.
£35–40 JSM

A French yellow metal and Bakelite bangle, decorated with sea horses, 1930s, 2in (5cm) high.
£55–65 LBe

l. A silver palette ring by Veral Marshall, with gold, amethyst, tour-maline, lolite, citrine and aquamarine, 1990s.
£250–300
r. An 18ct gold ring with 3 bands by Simon Marshall, set with central lolite, with aquamarine, amethyst, peridot and tourmaline, 1990s.
£800–900 STG

A Swiss ring, by Gilbert Albert, with 7 interchangeable stones, c1960s.
£750–850 DID

A Deakin & Francis gold and amethyst pendant, with a chain, 1976, 2¾in (7cm) high.
£650–750 DID

◀ A yellow metal bracelet, possibly by Butler & Wilson, with white diamanté, green marquise and red cabochon, c1980.
£75–85 PKT

A brass cheese grater, c1880,
13in (33cm) long.
£135–150 SMI

A wooden box containing
Wileman's Plate Powder,
with 32 original contents, c1910,
10in (25.5cm) wide.
£140–160 SMI

▶ A Belgian vegetable bucket,
c1920, 9in (23cm) high.
£40–50 B&R

A set of 3 French enamel jars,
inscribed 'Sucre', 'Chicorée',
'Café', 1930s, 6in (15cm) high.
£70–80 B&R

A Garrison tin spice rack, with 6 screw-
top jars, c1930, 7in (18cm) wide.
£40–45 SMI

A wooden bread board,
the border carved with
roses and wheat, late 19thC,
12in (30.5cm) diam.
£70–80 B&R

A Japanese salt and pepper,
modelled as corn cobs, 1970s,
5in (12.5cm) high.
£15–20 BTB

A Grimwade cheese dish and milk
jug, printed with 'I'm going a
milking, Sir, she said', c1890–1910,
jug 6½in (16.5cm) high.
£60–70 SMI

An Arnold milk shake mixer, with
cup, 1923, 18in (46cm) high.
£100–120 EKK

▶ A Maruhon
ware pottery
lemon squeezer,
moulded with
flowers, 1920–30s,
4in (10cm) wide.
£25–30 COCO

A plastic peanut butter man,
made in Hong Kong, 1980s,
9½in (24cm) high.
£15–30 BTB

Three Victorian brass table lamps, with fluted columns, square bases and coloured etched shades.
l. 30½in (77.5cm) high.
£650–750
c. 28¼in (72cm) high.
£180–220
r. 31½in (80cm) high.
£600–700 AH

A Litlux headboard light, with fan-shaped pleated silk shade and fringed tassle, Bakelite switches and wooden plug, in original box, 1934, 4½in (11.5cm) high.
£20–30 BKK

A Glasform coral and blue glass lampshade, 1995, 6¼in (16cm) high.
£25–30 GLA

► A Wombles plastic bedside lamp, 1980s, 11in (28cm) high.
£10–12 CMF

A brass French harp hanging oil lamp, with blue glass fount and shade, and Kosmos burner, 19thC, 24in (61cm) high.
£240–270 LIB

► A chrome lamp, with mottled pink and orange shade, rewired, c1930, 9in (23cm) high.
£180–200 BTB

A phenolic lamp, with glass shade, rewired, 1930s, 19in (48.5cm) high.
£120–150 BTB

An Italian lamp shade, in the style of Tiffany, with inserted shells, c1890, 13½in (34.5cm) wide.
£170–200 SER

A chrome wall light, with green shade, 1940s, 13in (33cm) long.
£130–150 BTB

A child's painted wooden bedroom light, modelled as a rainbow and moon, 1950s 18in (45.5cm) wide.
£100–125 DHAR

► Two cast resin lamp bases, and laminated fabric shade, 1960s, largest with shade 19in (48.5cm) high.
£100–125 ZOOM

A Russian enamelled brass crucifix/icon, 19thC, 8¾in (22cm) high.
£80–100 GRa

A brass and copper tea urn, of pedestal form with large domed lid, and mask-mounted ring handles, 19thC, 19¼in (49cm) high.
£60–70 DOM

A copper and brass classical shaped hot water urn, with angular mask-mounted handles, 19thC, 20½in (52cm) high.
£70–90 DOM

A bargeware water carrier, painted by George Nurser, 1890–1900, 11in (28cm) high.
£270–300 MRW

George Nurser was a canal artist on the Grand Union canal.

A hand-painted metal fringed purse, 1950s, 5in (12.5cm) wide.
£40–50 JPr

A London Transport enamel target sign for Victoria Station, 1930s, 21in (53.5cm) wide.
£550–600 RAR

A German silver-plated cigar box, decorated with enamelled portrait of a German officer, c1914–18, 5in (12.5cm) high.
£60–70 AnS

An Edward VII 9th Lancers tunic, 1901–10.
£150–175 Q&C

▶ A brass trench art ashtray, inscribed and with Reims cathedral, 3½in (9cm) high.
£20–25 AOH

Three WWI medals, 1914–15 Star, British War Medal and Victory Medal, with ribbons.
£16–25 each RMC

◀ A Lifeguards full ceremonial uniform, with silver-plated cuirass, post-1952.
£4,000–5,000 Q&C

A colour lithograph, 'Folies Bergere', by Jules Cheret, 1893, 48 x 43in (122 x 109cm).
£4,000–4,500 BSL

A Daly's linen poster, 'A Country Girl', 1920s, 28 x 19in (71 x 48.5cm).
£175–225 Do

A poster, by Otto Treumann, for the Kröller-Müller Museum, 1919, 20in (50.5cm) square.
£85–100 VSP

A colour lithograph, by Théophile Steinlen, 'Affiches Charles Verneau', 1896, 92 x 119in (233 x 302cm).
£10,000–12,000 BSL

An Alf Cook linen theatre poster, 'Robinson Crusoe', by Jim Affleck, 1920s, 30 x 20in (76 x 51cm).
£225–250 Do

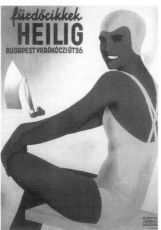

A coloured lithograph, 'Heilig', by Pokorny Hofbauer, c1930, 49½ x 36½in (125 x 92cm).
£1,000–1,200 BSL

A colour lithograph, 'Le Journal', by Théophile Steinlen, some repair, 1899, 73 x 49in (185 x 125cm).
£1,400–1,800 S

An LMS coloured lithograph, 'Sunny Rhyl', by Septimus Scott, c1925, 40 x 50in (101.5 x 127cm).
£4,000–4,500 BSL

A coloured lithograph, 'PKZ', by Herbert Matter, 1928, 50 x 36in (127 x 91.5cm).
£3,600–4,000 BSL

An RKO poster, 'King Kong', by Rene Peron, 1933, 63 x 47in (160 x 119.5cm).
£6,000–7,000 S

A German film poster, *'Titanic'* by Hans Wendt, 1953, 33 x 23in (84 x 58.5cm).
£600–700 REEL

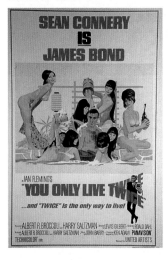

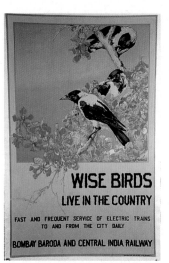

A Bombay Railway linen poster, 'Wise Birds Live in the Country', by K. I. Nixon, 1930s, 40 x 25in (101.5 x 63.5cm).
£325–375 Do

A London Underground linen poster, by Bainbridge, 1953, 40 x 25in (101.5 x 63.5cm).
£325–375 Do

◀ An American poster, *'You Only Live Twice'*, 1967, 41 x 27in (104 x 68.5cm).
£350–400 REEL

▶ An American poster, *'Blade Runner'*, 1982, 41 x 27in (104 x 68.5cm).
£200–250 REEL

A Spanish linen poster, 'Cognac Quevedo', 1930s, 33 x 24in (84 x 61cm).
£325–375 Do

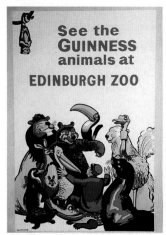

A Guinness linen poster, 1960s, 30 x 20in (76 x 50.8cm).
£300–350 Do

SOUTHPORT
BY
FORTUNINO MATANIA R.I.

HYÈRES RM
ET SES ILES *(PORQUEROLLES ET PORT-GROS)*
La station la plus au sud de la Côte d'Azur

The
Vintage
Poster
Specialist

CACHOU LAJAUNIE

SCOTLAND FOR YOUR HOLIDAYS

A papier mâché glove puppet, 1950s, 10in (25.5cm) high.
£40–50 AnS

A Shillabeer wooden circus horse string puppet, 1960, 13in (33cm) long.
£180–200 STK

◀ A Pelham Big Ears string puppet, 1950s, 12in (30.5cm) high.
£50–60 ARo

A Pelham frog string puppet, with original box, 1960s, 12½in (32cm) high.
£40–50 ARo

A Pelham Mother Dragon string puppet, 1960s, 20in (51cm) long.
£40–50 ARo

A Pelham string puppet, 1960, 12in (30.5cm) high.
£30–40 J&J

A Pelham Womble string puppet, with original box, 1970s, 8in (20.5cm) high.
£25–30 ARo

A Pelham Beatles string puppet, with original box, 1960s, 12½in (32cm) high.
£60–70 ARo

A Pelham Gretel string puppet, with plastic arms and legs, restrung, 1970s, 11in (28cm) high.
£10–15 J&J

▶ A Pelham Indian Snake Charmer string puppet, with original box, 1970s, 13in (33cm) high.
£40–50 ARo

A Beatles wig, made by Lowell Toy Manufacturing Corp, with original packaging, 1960s, 10 x 9in (25.4 x 23cm).
£80–100 MTM

Two Beatles 340-piece jigsaw puzzles, by Nems Enterprises, 1960s, 17 x 11in (43 x 28cm).
£175–200 each MTM

A Beatles beach towel, made by Canon, 1960s, 59 x 35in (150 x 89cm).
£180–200 MTM

◄ A set of 4 Beatles 'Sergeant Pepper' dolls, 1988, 22in (56cm) high.
£180–200 BTC

Five Beatles 'Long Eating Liquorice Records', with original box, 1960s, box 10 x 5in (25.5 x 12.5cm).
£1,300–1,500 MTM

These 4in (10cm) diameter liquorice records were covered in a square paper sleeve with black and white paper photo insert, one of each Beatle and one of the group. Being edible, they are very hard to find complete and in their original box.

A 'Sergeant Pepper's Lonely Hearts Club Band' picture disc, in die cut sleeve, 1978, 12in (30.5cm) square.
£35–50 MTM

A French EMI Records Beatles 'Abbey Road' picture disc, 1979, 12in (30.5cm) square.
£25–30 MVX

A Royal Doulton John Lennon character jug, by Stanley James Taylor, No. 663 of a limited edition of 1,000, 1987, 5½in (14cm) high.
£600–700 MTM

Cream 'Disraeli Gears' record, 1967, 12¼in (31cm) square.
£125–150 ZOOM

► A Palace Videos 'Jimi Hendrix plays Berkeley' VHS music video, 1981, 8in (20.5cm) high.
£20–30 MVX

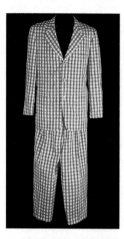

◀ Elton John's red gingham two-piece suit, by Gianni Versace, with trademark buttons and lining, as seen in the documentary on Elton, *Tantrums and Tiaras*, 1990s.
£1,400–1,600 S

Madonna's blouse, from the Girlie Show tour, labelled 'Dolce & Gabbana', with letter of authenticity, 1992.
£6,000–7,000 S

George Michael 'Careless Whisper' extended mix, Epic Records, 12in single picture disc, 1984.
£25–35 MVX

A Mexican EMI Records Pet Shop Boys 'Very' picture disc album, signed, 1993, 12in (30.5cm) diam.
£180–200 MVX

'At Home With Screamin' Jay Hawkins', Epic Records, 1958, 12in (30.5cm) diam.
£700–800 MVX

A page of handwritten lyrics, by Elvis Presley, for 'Music Makin' Mama from Memphis', with 2 colour prints of Elvis in uniform, mounted, framed and glazed, 1960, 23 x 26in (58.5 x 66cm).
£3,000–3,500 Bon

The page comes from a personal notebook kept by Elvis while serving with the US army and stationed in Germany. The book was left with Frau Pieper, Elvis's landlady there, when he returned to the US in 1960. At that time, this particular song was very special to Elvis as it reminded him of his greatly-missed mother Gladys.

Spice Girls CD, Virgin Records, signed edition, 1996.
£100–125 MVX

Frank Zapper 'You Are What You Is', CBS Records, single picture disc, 1981, 12in (30.5cm) diam.
£10–12 MVX

A Wurlitzer Model 1050 jukebox, restored, 1973, 50in (127cm) high.
£5,500–6,000 CJB

▶ A Seeburg 100 Select-o-Matic jukebox, 1953, 55in (139.5cm) high.
£8,000–9,000 JU

Jewellery

BRACELETS

A 9ct yellow and rose gold charm bracelet, 1880, 7in (18cm) long.
£240–280 BND

Charm bracelets have been popular from the 19thC onwards. At the top of the range, Victorian and Edwardian charms were made from cast rather than stamped gold and decorated with tiny jewels. For the lower end of the market, they were produced in cheaper metals and in the 20thC, the charm bracelet became a favourite tourist souvenir. Values of charms depend on age, material and novelty.

A Trifari bangle, with blue step-cut glass crystal set in chrome-plated articulated mountings and pavé set white baguette diamanté, signed, 1940s.
£650–750 GLT

▶ A Weiss silver-metal bracelet, set with square, faceted glass beads, with a safety chain, signed, c1960, 7in (18cm) long.
£85–95 PKT

A gold charm bracelet, 1890–1930, 7in (18cm) long.
£400–450 BND

A French base metal bangle, set with green Bakelite, the centre segment a compact, 1940s, 7in (18cm) long.
£300–350 LBe

◀ An Elsa Peretti sterling silver cuff bangle, for Tiffany & Co, New York, 1975, 3in (7.5cm) diam.
£450–500 DID

BROOCHES

A Scottish silver and grey agate strap brooch, c1860, 2½in (6.5cm) diam.
£350–400 BWA

A 15ct gold Etruscan brooch, c1860, 1¼in (3cm) wide.
£350–400 WIM

A silver and cairngorm plaid brooch, c1880, 4½in (11.5cm) diam.
£250–300 BWA

Cairngorm is a variety of yellowish quartz, originally found in the Cairngorm mountain range in Scotland and used in Scottish jewellery. Demand exceeds supply so the stone has also been imitated with heat-treated Brazilian amethyst.

A Scottish silver and green, blue and yellow agate knot brooch, c1860, 2in (5cm) diam.
£250–300 BWA

A cameo brooch, carved with a classical figure scene in a yellow metal mount, 19thC, 3¼in (8.5cm) high.
£550–600 AH

Four silver name brooches, Lizzie, Lilly, Pollie and Louie, 1900–20, 1½in (4cm) wide.
£40–50 each EXC

◄ A turtle brooch, the shell made from tortoiseshell-coloured agate, set in silver and gold, with diamond head and gilt and ruby eyes, c1880, 1¼in (3cm) long.
£1,000–1,100 WIM

A 15ct gold brooch, the centre with a *pietra dura* mosaic of flowers in pink and green on a black ground, c1860, 2in (5cm) wide.
£750–850 WIM

***Pietra dura* was a form of decorative inlay practised in Italy since the 16thC, using marbles and other stones to produce table tops, furniture panels and various items. Miniature *pietra dura* panels were manufactured in Italy in the 19thC and were often exported and mounted abroad. Flowers are the most frequently found *pietra dura* designs. Shading on the leaves, to give a three dimensional effect, is a sign of quality and the inlay should be well fitted with no stones missing.**

Four silver name brooches, Marian, Christina, Sissie and Dinah, 1880–1900, 1¼in (3cm) diam.
£40–50 each EXC

Name brooches were made for nannies and maids to wear on their uniform so that the family knew their name. A tremendous number were produced in silver, some with initials in a gold overlay. Prices for name brooches depend on how popular the name is today, and with the current resurgence of Edwardian names, Lilly, Rose, etc., these brooches are once again in demand.

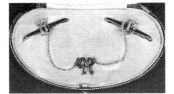

A gold, pearl and green enamel brooch, in the form of 2 bars with pearl and gold initials attached by gold chains to a green bow set with a diamond, given as a gift by King Edward VII, c1910, 1½in (4cm) wide, in original fitted case.
£2,000–2,250 SHa

A French silver paste-set plaque brooch, 1930s, 3in (7.5cm) wide.
£180–200 JSM

A 15ct gold, pearl and enamel brooch, in the form of an open roundel, in original fitted case from James Aitchison Edinburgh, c1910, 20mm diam.
£500–550 HofB

▶ A Lea Stein laminated plastic brooch, in the form of a brown fox, 1930–40, 3½in (9cm) high.
£30–35 HT

A Miriam Haskell 3 flowered pink paste and crystal pin with pink bead tassels, 1940s, 3in (7.5cm) long.
£175–195 MAU

A Lea Stein laminated plastic brooch, in the form of a cockney man with brown hair and red, black and white tartan cap and tie, 1930–40, 2in (5cm) high.
£40–45 HT

A Lea Stein laminated plastic brooch, in the form of a dog with black ears and nose and brown collar, 1930–40, 3½in (9cm) high.
£45–50 HT

Lea Stein

Lea Stein began producing plastic jewellery in Paris in the 1930s. Her husband was a plastics chemist, and what distinguishes her brooches is not only the novelty of their various designs but the high quality of the material itself. Shapes were cut from a sheet composed of some 30 layers of plastic, which gave the brooches strength and lustre. On many examples the back is a different colour from the front and typically pieces are marked 'Lea Stein Paris'. Retailers were supplied with the unmounted designs together with three different fittings – tie clip, hair clip and brooch pin. Once purchasers had chosen the design and the fittings they wanted, the retailer would then attach the chosen clip, which explains why these can vary in quality of application.

An 18ct gold, sapphire and diamond clip brooch/pendant, c1950, 2in (5cm) long.
£1,000–1,250 WIM

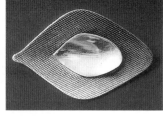

A Norwegian sterling silver brooch, designed by Grete Prytz Kittelsen, c1950, 2¾in (7cm) wide.
£100–120 DID

A Georg Jensen silver brooch, modelled as a deer, No. 256, 1950, 2in (5cm) wide.
£200–225 DAC

An American 14ct gold and cultured pearl brooch, in the shape of an atom, 1960s, 1½in (4cm) wide.
£400–450 DID

A Gobilin 18ct gold brooch, in the form of a skier, with ruby head, 1950s, 1¾in (4.5cm) high.
£1,100–1,300 WIM

An amoebic sterling silver brooch, by Karen Strand for Aage Drasted, c1955, 2¼in (6cm) wide.
£170–200 DID

An 18ct gold abstract brooch, by Gilbert Albert, Geneva 1960s, 2¾in (7cm) wide.
£650–750 DID

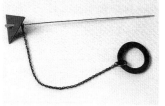

A Mikela Naur oxydized silver and 14ct gold pin, for Anton Michelsen, 1970s, 4in (10cm) wide.
£100–150 DID

An American Black Landstrom Hills 9ct gold brooch, in the form of a bird of prey, hallmarked 10K, imported mark 375, 1989, 2½in (6.5cm) long.
£300–350 BND

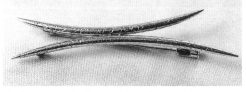

An 18ct gold brooch, by Andrew Grima, designed to suggest the initials 'JK', to commemorate the life of President J. F. Kennedy, 1980s, 2½in (6.5cm) wide.
£650–750 DID

The original brooch won the Duke of Edinburgh's Prize for Elegant Design in 1966 and was presented to Mrs Jacqueline Kennedy by Andrew Grima.

A hand-soldered brooch, by Iradj Moini, set with antique Austrian crystals, in the form of grapes above 3 leaves and a stalk, 1980s, 4½in (11.5cm) long.
£400–450 CRIS

EARRINGS

A pair of silver and paste drop earrings, late 1920s, 3in (7.5cm) long.
£225–250 JSM

A pair of 14ct gold and turquoise earrings, by Anni and Bent Knudsen 1950s.
£450–500 DID

A pair of Nana Ditzel sterling silver earrings, for Georg Jensen, c1953.
£200–250 DID

Cross Reference
See Colour Review

A black plastic and diamanté pendant perfume bottle and matching earrings, 1960s, earrings 3in (7.5cm) long.
£140–160 GLT

A white-painted yellow metal brooch and earrings set, in the form of snakes with open mouths and red glass eyes, signed, c1970, brooch 3in (7.5cm) long.
£50–60 PKT

A Vivienne Westwood diamanté orb brooch and earrings, set with coloured stones, 1990s, brooch 1½in (4cm) wide.
£120–150 ID

MEN'S ACCESSORIES

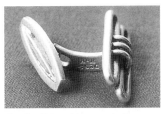

A pair of Hans Hansen sterling silver cufflinks, hallmarked, 1940s.
£100–120 DID

A pair of Hans Hansen sterling silver cufflinks, c1940s.
£100–120 DID

A pair of 9ct gold, onyx and diamond cuff links, 1980s.
£570–620 BND

A 9ct gold tie slide, 1970s, 2¾in (7cm) long.
£70–80 BND

A gold money clip, 1980s, 2in (5cm) long.
£100–120 BND

NECKLACES & PENDANTS

A 15ct gold heart-shaped pomander, c1790, 20mm long.
£400–475 WIM

A Miriam Haskell necklace, with blue disc-shaped cut-glass crystals and brass chain-link spacers, signed, 1930s, 20in (51cm) long.
£500–600 GLT

A Chanel white *pâte de verre* necklace and earrings set, signed 'France', 1930s, necklace 14in (35.5cm) long.
£1,800–2,000 GLT

◄ A crystal bracelet, earrings and necklace set, 1940s.
£400–450 GLT

A pinchbeck chain necklace, 1790, 34in (86.5cm) long.
£600–675 WIM

Pinchbeck, an alloy of copper and zinc, was invented by London watchmaker Christopher Pinchbeck, c1720. Although it looked like gold, it was much lighter, and was developed for watch cases. It soon became popular for creating inexpensive jewellery such as chains, chatelaines, buckles, clasps, etc. It was much used in the 18th and early 19thC, but became more or less obsolete after 1854 when it became legal to sell 9ct gold, and with the introduction of cheaper substitutes such as rolled gold and electroplating.

A French Art Deco chrome and green Bakelite necklace, 1930s, 15in (38cm) long.
£75–85 GLT

An Eisenberg crystal bracelet, earrings and necklace set, signed, 1940s.
£750–850 GLT

A Victorian gold pendant, enamelled and set with cabochon garnets and pearls, on a gold chain, 1860, 20in (51cm) long.
£750–850 BHA

A cornelian and cut-glass necklace, 1930s, 26in (66cm) long.
£30–35 DEC

A Henning Koppel sterling silver abstract amoebic bracelet and necklace set, for Georg Jensen, c1945, necklace 15in (38cm) long.
£3,000–3,500 DID

A Boucher opaque pink and green glass and diamanté earrings and necklace set, 1950s, 15in (38cm) long.
£250–280 GLT

A Weiss silver-metal necklace, set with faceted glass beads with white diamanté overlays, signed, c1955, 14in (35.5cm) long.
£160–185 PKT

A Danish chalcedony and sterling silver necklace, by N. E., c1960, 15in (38cm) long.
£300–350 DID

A white and blue diamanté necklace, attributed to Norman Hartnell, c1955, 17in (43cm) long.
£90–100 PKT

A Miriam Haskell two-strand baroque pearl necklace, with gilt leaf pendant surrounded by seed pearls, 1960s, 13in (33cm) long.
£400–450 MAU

◄ A Knud V. Andersen star-burst sterling silver pendant and chain, for Anton Michelsen, 1960s, pendant 2¼in (6cm) wide.
£180–200 DID

▶ An Oscar de la Renta gilt pendant, with black glass drop set in gilt leaves, signed, 1960s, 20in (51cm) long.
£250–300 GLT

A Bent Gabrielsen Pedersen gilt and silver torque, for Hans Hansen, 1960s, 14in (35.5cm) long.
£500–550 DID

A Tapio Wirkkala Finland sterling silver kinetic pendant and chain, by KultaKesus oy Hämeenlinna, c1970, pendant 4¾in (12cm) high.
£750–850 DID

A Vivienne Westwood white metal 'SEX' choker necklace, with matching earrings, 1990s, choker 12in (30.5cm) long.
£150–175 ID

RINGS

A silver ring, with plain elliptical band and domed glass stone covering paste stones of red, blue, green and orange, late 16thC.
£220–250 ANG

A Faller of Galway gold Claddagh ring, c1885.
£320–350 WELD

Claddagh rings are often in the form of 2 hands clasping a heart and are given as a token of eternal love. Claddagh is a small fishing village on the edge of Galway city.

An Art Deco 18ct white gold, emerald and diamond ring, 1930s.
£700–800 AnS

An 18ct gold ring, set with 4 square sapphires, diamonds and platinum, 1930.
£600–700 JSM

▶ An Anni and Bent Knudsen 14ct gold and turquoise ring, c1950.
£350–400 DID

> **Miller's is a price GUIDE not a price LIST**

◀ A French Art Deco paste ring, 1930s.
£80–90 AnS

◀ A Kupittaan Kulta rock crystal and silver kinetic ring, with a carnelian bead rolling around under the crystal, 1960s.
£220–250 DID

An Elis Kauppi sterling silver and goldstone ring, for Kupittaan Kulta, 1970.
£150–200 DID

A Just Andersen sterling silver and cabochon amethyst ring, import marks, 1973.
£220–250 DID

Kitchenware

A glass egg timer, in a metal frame with a bell, c1880, 6in (15cm) high.
£90–100 SMI

As the sand runs out, the glass timer twists, and when the process is completed the metal weight hits the bell.

An Oven Mop cooker cleaner, red with yellow text, c1920s, 13in (33cm) long.
£10–12 WAB

Two Hygene glass pourers, with red and blue plastic lids, 1950, 6in (15cm) high.
£4–5 each AL

◀ Six Homepride 'Fred' black and white pastry cutters, c1970s, 4⅛in (11.5cm) high.
£18–20 MED

A tin Household Wants Indicator, c1910, 13 x 11in (33 x 28cm).
£80–100 SMI

A Main Mainservor No 78 four-burner gas cooker, enamelled in mottled grey and white, 1936, 59in (150cm) high.
£40–50 VGC

◀ A German metal and green-painted wood coffee grinder, c1940, 8in (20.5cm) high.
£25–35 CPA

Three Prestige orange, white and red plastic milk indicators, 1960, largest 3½in (9cm) wide.
£2–3 each AL

CERAMICS

A Scottish yellow and brown ceramic bread crock, the sides with moulded decoration, c1880, 14in (35.5cm) wide.
£350–400 B&R

A ceramic bread plate on feet, moulded in blue with 'Eat thy Bread with Joy and Thankfulness', painted with ears of corn and with gilt rim, c1880, 12in (30.5cm) diam.
£130–150 SMI

A ceramic storage jar and lid, with white moulded label and impressed 'Tapioca' in black, c1880, 9in (23cm) high.
£50–55 SMI

A brown salt-glazed ceramic colander, c1880, 10in (25.5cm) diam.
£60–70 SMI

A white ceramic cheese slab, with black lettering, c1900–10, 13in (33cm) square.
£180–200 SMI

A white ceramic bucket, transfer-printed in blue with cows and 'Pure Milk', c1910, 12in (30.5cm) high.
£500–600 B&R

A Gourmet & Co, London, white ceramic Eddystone Milk Boiler, with printed blue crest, c1910, 6¼in (16cm) high.
£65–75 B&R

A Grimwades white ceramic rolling pin, transfer-printed in green and with wooden handles, c1910, 18in (45.5cm) long.
£500–550 SMI

A white ceramic oven thermometer, advertising 'Yeatman's Yeast Powder', c1910, 6in (15cm) high.
£75–85 SMI

▶ A white ceramic cream carrier, with brass and steel top, some damage, early 20thC, 6in (15cm) high.
£80–100 SMI

A Carforth, Leeds, white ceramic dish, printed in black, early 20thC, 11in (28cm) wide.
£90–100 SMI

Two Scottish stoneware storage jars, the labels printed in blue, c1920, largest 10in (25.5cm) high.
£50–55 SMI

A Marutomo ceramic toast rack, with butter and jam wells, painted in yellow and green with red, yellow, purple and green moulded fruit and vegetables, 1920–30s, 7½in (19cm) wide.
£35–45 COCO

Two ceramic storage jars and lids, with moulded white and black labels, c1930, largest 10in (25.5cm) high.
£40–45 SMI

A Continental ceramic mustard pot, in the form of a chef, painted details in green, red and brown, 1920s, 3½in (9cm) high.
£25–35 COCO

A T. G. Green Cornish Ware mixing bowl, with blue banding, 1920s, 4¾in (12cm) high.
£30–40 UNI

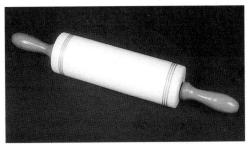

A T. G. Green white ceramic rolling pin, with grey handles, 1930s, 17in (43cm) long.
£65–75 UNI

A Heatmaster white ceramic coffee pot, with chrome cover and Bakelite ball feet and finial, 1940s, 9in (23cm) high.
£20–25 OD

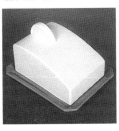

A T. G. Green Cornish Ware China Tea storage jar, with blue banding, c1930, 6in (15cm) high.
£225–240 SMI

The value of Cornish Ware storage jars depends on the inscription – China Tea is a rare example hence its price range is far higher than for more common products such as sugar.

◀ A Poole Pottery cheese dish, with white lid and coral base, 1950, 7in (18cm) wide.
£18–20 AL

ENAMEL WARE

A J. & J. Siddons speckled grey enamel cast-iron eight-pint kettle, with brass lid and handle, c1880, 13in (33cm) high.
£70–80 SMI

Six white enamel spice tins, with red and black lettering, 1920, in a wooden rack, 12in (30.5cm) wide.
£55–65 SMI

Two dark blue enamel milk cans, one with wooden handle grip, c1920, largest 10½in (26.5cm) high
£10–20 each AL

Two white enamel hot water jugs, with blue lettering, the French with lid, the English with wicker handle, c1920, 13in (33cm) high.
£40–50 each B&R

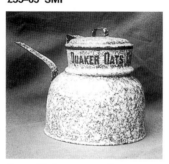

A speckled grey enamel Quaker Oats Cooker, c1920, 10½in (26.5cm) high.
£60–70 B&R

This enamel porringer was offered by Quaker in return for Quaker Oats box lids, and is desirable both as a piece of kitchenware and an example of 1920s advertising memorabilia. To make porridge in a porringer, the top section of the pan is filled with oats and water, and the bottom with water, which is brought to the boil and then simmered so that the porridge will not burn.

Two Continental enamel utensils racks, hand-painted with pink, yellow, green and brown flowers, c1920, 19in (48.5cm) high.
£70–80 B&R

A cream enamel flour tin, with red lettering and handles, 1930s, 12in (30.5cm) wide.
£25–30 SMI

Lids on enamel tins often become chipped, but as long as the interior is undamaged these containers can still be used for storing food products. This shape is traditionally associated with enamel bread bins, produced in large numbers from the 1920s to the 1950s. The hole under the handle is for ventilation, as air helps to maintain the freshness of the contents and preventing it from going mouldy.

A cream enamel teapot, with dark green spout, handle and rim line, 1950, 7in (18cm) high.
£12–15 AL

▶ Two French white enamel towel holders, with blue and red lettering, c1950, 14in (35.5cm) wide.
£35–45 each B&R

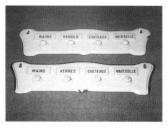

METALWARE

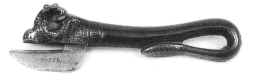

A steel tin opener, modelled as a bull, c1880,
6in (15cm) long.
£10–12 SMI

A cast-iron tin opener, modelled as a lion, c1880,
6in (15cm) long.
£70–80 SMI

A Golden Syrup Best Treacle
dispenser, c1900, 17in (43cm) wide.
£250–300 B&R

A wire egg basket, c1920,
9in (23cm) diam.
£14–16 AL

A Morton's Patent Household
Whisk, in a black tin with brass
handle and name plate, c1920,
10in (25.5cm) high.
£60–70 SMI

A Hinks copper and brass hot plate, with 2 burners,
c1930, 30in (76cm) wide.
£200–235 NET

A metal Ideal Cream
Maker, with wooden
handle in green, 1930,
9in (23cm) high.
£10–15 AL

A Spong mincer,
with a green stand and
wooden handle, 1940,
9in (23cm) wide.
£16–18 UTP

MOULDS

Before the 18th century jellies were principally a savoury dish, made from meat or fish-based products, but with the increasing importation of sugar from the West Indies, sweet jellies became popular.

At grand dinner parties jellies were a favourite centrepiece, designed for show as much as consumption, hence the development of elaborate jelly moulds, in shapes ranging from animals to fruit to flowers. Victorian moulds were produced in ceramic, copper, pewter, tin and other materials and were used for jellies, blancmanges, ice-cream and a wide range of savoury mousses and aspics. Famous retailers included Victorian cookery writer Mrs Agnes B. Marshall, who ran a school and a shop for cooks in London, and whose *Illustrated Catalogue of Moulds and Kitchen Equipment* (published 1886) describes over a thousand mould designs, and is an essential tool for the collector.

Values of moulds depend on medium, design and condition. Moulds tend to be used as decorative rather than practical items, particularly antique metal examples, since some materials (ie lead-lined ice-cream moulds) do not meet current health and safety regulations.

A brown salt-glazed jelly mould, based on a Staffordshire original, c1840, 3in (7.5cm) wide.
£40–50 IW

A Derbyshire brown salt-glazed mould, c1840, 6¾in (17cm) wide.
£25–30 IW

A copper mould, in the form of a cockerel, by Kirkham, New York, c1920, 10¾in (27.5cm) high.
£220–250 MSB

Three Grimwade The Paragon blancmange and jelly moulds, green transfer-printed with advertisements, c1910, largest 6½in (16.5cm) diam.
£60–70 SMI

A Peek Frean & Co metal biscuit mould, 1950, 9in (23cm) wide.
£8–9 AL

A pewter ice-cream mould, in the form of a basket, c1900, 8in (20.5cm) wide.
£450–525 MSB

A metal mould, with 8 shapes of calves, 1960, 6 x 4in (15 x 10cm).
£12–15 AL

UTENSILS

A black wire whisk, late 19thC, 8in (20.5cm) long.
£4–5 No7

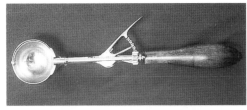

An ice-cream scoop, with chrome bowl, brass workings and wooden handle, 1920s, 10in (25.5cm) long.
£50–55 EKK

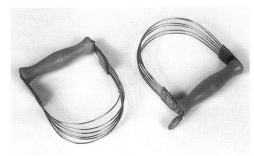

Two pastry blenders, with red and green wooden handles, c1950, 5½in (14cm) wide.
£3–4 each AL

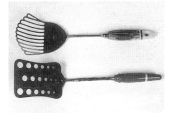

▶ Two metal food slices, with green and yellow wooden handles, 1950s, 13in (33cm) long.
£3–4 each AL

◀ An aluminium lemon squeezer, 1950, 8in (20.5cm) long.
£3–4 AL

WASHING & IRONING

A Ewbank Treasure green and red painted cast-iron and wood mangle, c1900, 43in (109cm) high.
£300–350 BYG

The Jolly Molly ironing board cover, in original packet, 1930–40s, 12 x 42in (30.5 x 106.5cm).
£8–10 PC

A Clayton, Lewis & Miller Clem travelling iron, blue with black handle, 1940, 4½in (11.5cm) wide.
£18–20 UTP

WOOD

A metal-banded wooden barrel, late 19thC, 8½in (21.5cm) high.
£55–65 ChA

A set of boxwood spice drawers, the bottom drawer for nutmeg grater, c1880, 11in (28cm) high.
£165–185 B&R

A circular wooden spice box, with 8 spice containers, c1880, 9½in (24cm) diam.
£180–200 SMI

A pine fruit bowl, late 19thC, 11in (28cm) diam.
£45–55 ChA

A metal-banded wooden butter churn, c1890, 24in (61cm) high.
£200–250 AL

Breadboards

Ornately carved breadboards were popular in the Victorian period. Typical inscriptions included religious and moral mottoes and messages wishing happiness and long life, since breadboards were traditionally given as wedding presents. Decoration often includes ears of corn, a reference both to the bread and a symbol of fertility. Stained boards can be cleaned by scrubbing carefully with an abrasive powder then polishing the board with beeswax. Prices vary depending on the amount of carving and the rarity of the inscription.

A wooden breadboard, carved with 'Waste not Want not' and ears of corn, late 19thC, 12¾in (32.5cm) diam.
£70–80 B&R

An eastern European wooden marriage board, decorated with red, yellow, white and green flowers, painted blue with '1920' and 'Rose', 25¼in (65cm) diam.
£80–90 B&R

A wooden breadboard, the ceramic centre decorated with flowers in blue and green, with carved border, c1920, 12in (30.5cm) diam.
£80–100 SMI

A wooden flour barrel, c1930, 10in (25.5cm) high.
£55–65 SMI

Lighting

CEILING LAMPS

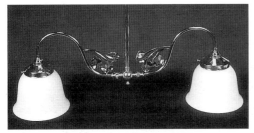

A brass down rod double lamp, with opaque glass shades, originally gas, early 1900s, 31in (78.5cm) wide.
£380–420 LIB

A Müller Frère *pâte de verre* chandelier, with mottled purple and red central *plafonnier*, the 3 smaller shades suspended by wrought-iron framework, each shade with etched mark 'Müller Frère, Lunéville', c1920, 36in (91.5cm) high.
£800–1,000 Mit

An opaque glass hanging lamp, with brass rim, fittings, chain and rose, 1920s, 13½in (34.5cm) high.
£180–200 LIB

> **Miller's is a price GUIDE not a price LIST**

A pink and green marbled glass ceiling bowl, in the shape of a jelly mould, 1930s, 12in (30.5cm) diam.
£50–60 TWa

A brass down rod lamp, with holophane shade, originally gas, early 1900s, 31in (78.5cm) high.
£180–200 LIB

A pair of hanging lamps, with brass chain and rose, cut glass galleries, 1920s, 9½in (24cm) high.
£240–280 LIB

▶ A lampshade, in the form of a shell, late 1950s, 20in (51cm) diam.
£350–400 ZOOM

A pair of brass down rod lamps, with opaque glass shades, originally gas, early 1900s, 23in (58.5cm) wide.
£250–300 LIB

A Coronet Purse chandelier, with brass rim and clear and purple crystal lustres, 1920s, 10in (25.5cm) high.
£175–195 LIB

A hanging light, with 5 yellow and white striped glass shades, 1960s, 21in (53.5cm) wide.
£40–50 TWa

An orange plastic and perspex hanging light, 1960s, 16in (40.5cm) diam.
£170–200 ZOOM

A three-branch glass hanging light, with glass shades, 1960–70s, 16in (40.5cm) wide.
£60–70 TWa

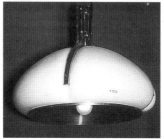

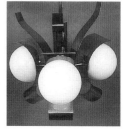

A five-branch hanging light, with white and brown smoked plastic discs forming the shades, 1960–70s, 25in (63.5cm) wide.
£60–70 TWa

A Harvey Guzzini chrome hanging light, with white plastic shade, 1970s, 19in (48.5cm) diam.
£400–450 ZOOM

A chrome hanging light, with 3 ball shades, 1960–70s, 14in (35.5cm) wide.
£60–70 TWa

DESK & TABLE LAMPS

A Sitzendorf oil lamp, the porcelain fount decorated with pink and green flowers and supported by 3 cupids, the brown base decorated with flowers, 19thC, 17½in (44.5cm) high.
£380–420 LIB

A brass oil lamp, with original etched glass globe, the burner marked 'In Lux Nay', the fount 'Thermidor Belge, Pat.', 19thC, 21in (53.5cm) high.
£420–480 LIB

A spelter oil lamp, with drop-in fount and opaque glass shade, c1890, 22in (56cm) high.
£100–120 TWa

An oil lamp, with a copper fount, wrought-iron stand, Veritas burner, replacement glass globe, 19thC, 25¼in (64cm) high.
£130–160 LIB

Oil lamps

From ancient times, men have used a wick floating in oil to create illumination, but it was not until the 18th century that technological changes revolutionized the hitherto smelly and smoky oil lamp. In 1784, Swiss scientist Ami Argand invented a new burner with a circular wick, which allowed air to pass up through the lamp. A glass funnel was subsequently added to protect the flame and created a far brighter light than candles.

The oil lamp became one of the most common forms of lighting in the 19th century. Up until c1840, whale oil was the usual fuel. Vegetable-based oils such as Colza (made from rape seed) were also used, but in the second half of the century paraffin (distilled from minerals) became the favourite choice, and a huge variety of different lamps was produced, suitable for everywhere from the maid's bedroom to the mistress's drawing room.

An oil lamp is composed of four main parts: the base, containing the fount or reservoir for fuel, the wick and carrier, the glass chimney and the glass shade.

A Doulton Lambeth oil lamp, with yellow relief floral swag and bird design, frilled cranberry-edged shade with rosette mark, maker's mark EP, c1890, 22½in (57cm) high.
£450–500 WiLP

An brass oil lamp, with pink edged frilled glass shade, the ceramic fount decorated with fruit and flowers, c1900, 24in (61cm) high.
£140–160 TWa

An oil lamp, with Vesta opaline shade, fount and base, early 1900, 22in (56cm) high.
£90–110 LIB

A brass tilley lamp, early 1900s, 21in (53.5cm) high.
£80–90 LIB

A fuel pump is housed in the base which supplies vapourized fuel to the incandescent mantle.

A Trench Art copper table lamp, 1916, 14in (35.5cm) high.
£225–250 RUL

◄ An adjustable brass desk lamp, 1920s, 11½in (29cm) high.
£220–240 LIB

A brass table lamp, the white glass shade bordered with pansies in orange and green, 1920, 18in (45.5cm) high.
£150–180 LIB

An adjustable brass table lamp, with crackle glass shade, 1920, 21½in (54.5cm) high.
£220–250 LIB

A chrome desk light, with black wooden base, rewired, c1930s, 10½in (26,5cm) high.
£90–120 BTB

An aluminium table lamp, in the form of a seal balancing a glass ball, on a marble base, 1950s, 22in (56cm) high.
£475–525 ZOOM

A Bakelite oil lamp, with Aladdin fittings, shade missing, c1930s, 23½in (59.5cm) high.
£90–100 DHAR

An Anglepoise chrome lamp, on a square base, rechromed and reconditioned, 1940s, 36in (91.5cm) high.
£100–125 BTB

A National green desk lamp, 1950s, 12¾in (32.5cm) high.
£80–100 ZOOM

A mushroom lamp, with Bakelite base and chrome shade, c1935, 12in (30.5cm) high.
£200–220 BTB

A Bursley Ware pink, mauve, green and brown lamp base, designed by Charlotte Rhead, pattern No. TL76, 1940s, 7in (18cm) high.
£140–165 PC

An Antennalite Telerection table lamp, with an integral television aerial, cream base and red shade, damaged, 1950s, 23in (58.5cm) high.
£125–150 ZOOM

A wrought-iron table lamp, with patterned frosted glass shade, 1930s, 14½in (37cm) high.
£250–300 BTB

A green cast resin table lamp, with matching green shade, 1960s, 25in (63.5cm) high.
£150–175 ZOOM

Colourful cast resin bases were a 1960s favourite. In 1968, British Home Stores offered similar plastic lamp bases in amber, green or blue, retailing for 49s 11d (just under £2.50). Shades were sold separately and it is unusual to find these lights with a matching coloured shade.

◀ A lava lamp, with a copper base, early 1960s, 18in (45.5cm) high.
£75–100 **ZOOM**

The lava or bubble lamp was pioneered by British engineer Craven Walker. Launched in 1963, it initially bemused retailers, but as psychedelia took off sales boomed and the lava lamp became a hippy icon.

A Rye Pottery white ceramic lamp base, decorated with a brown bison, 1960s, 13½in 34.5cm) high.
£65–75 **MARK**

A gilt plaster lamp, in the form of a nude supporting a pink fringed silk shade, for Biba, 1960s–70s, 34in (86.5cm) high.
£300–350 **ZOOM**

◀ A fibre optic lamp, 1970s, 20in (51cm) high.
£80–100 **ZOOM**

The craze for fibre optic lamps took off in the 1970s. Made from tiny filaments of glass, they must be treated with care and placed in a safe position. If you brush against the glass the fronds snap, creating a host of tiny, invisible and painful splinters.

> **Cross Reference**
> See 1960s

LANTERNS

A Lucas King of the Road No. 43 rear lamp, 1910, 13in (33cm) high.
£130–150 **JUN**

◀ An Irish lead and glass convent lamp, 1820, 33in (84cm) high.
£280–300 **EON**

A pair of wooden converted temple lanterns, southern China, late 19thC, 19in (48.5cm) high.
£425–475 **GHC**

A brass and steel miner's oil lamp, incomplete and unrestored, 1940s, 11in (28cm) high.
£50–60 **DOM**

Luggage & Travel Goods

A Victorian leather trunk, handle missing, 27in (68.5cm) wide.
£200–250 NET

A Louis Vuitton yellow stained leather and metal bound wardrobe trunk, brass fittings stamped with maker's name or initials, leather carrying handles stamped 'Louis Vuitton, Paris, London', interior fitted with hangers and shelves, label No. 742229, c1930, 40in (101.5cm) high.
£1,000–1,200 MCA

A Barrett & Sons two-person wicker picnic set, with wicker covered bottles, 1903, 14in (35.5cm) wide.
£275–325 DRJ

A Drew & Sons two-person 'en route' wicker picnic set, 1930s, 18in (45.5cm) wide.
£350–400 PC

A leather half music case, c1920, 15in (38cm) wide.
£10–15 AL

A brown leather suitcase, initialled 'D.D.H.', c1930, 24in (61cm) wide.
£100–125 BYG

A brown leather suitcase, with reproduction stickers, initialled 'H.C.', c1950s, 22in (56cm) wide.
£30–35 BYG

A leather music case, c1950, 15in (38cm) wide.
£10–12 AL

◀ A blue and white plastic picnic set, 1970s, in a fitted case, 11in (28cm) wide.
£20–25 PC

A Brexton six-person wicker picnic set, with red plastic storage containers, c1960s, 24in (61cm) wide.
£100–120 PPH

Medals

COMMEMORATIVE

A silver medal, commemorating the Embarkation at Scheveningen, by Peter van Abeele, with bust of Charles II, on the reverse Fame with trumpet over the fleet, 1660, 77mm diam.
£775–850 BAL

A bronze medal, by J. Hancock, commemorating John Philip Kemble, 1798, 52mm diam.
£100–125 BAL

John Philip Kemble (1752–1823) was an actor, and brother of Sarah Siddons. He was manager of Covent Garden at the time of the 'Old Price' Riots. His last performance was in 1817 after which he retired to Lausanne for health reasons.

A bronze medal, with a draped bust of Pope Paul II, the reverse with the frontal elevation of the Palazzo Venezia, 1465, 33mm diam.
£100–120 DNW

A silver satirical medal, Order of the Gorgomans, with bust of Chin Quan, the sun in splendour on the reverse, c1800, 75mm high.
£220–250 DNW

◄ A white metal medal, commemorating Clapham Rise British Orphan Asylum, Surrey, the reverse inscribed, 1872, 38mm diam.
£40–50 BAL

A bronze uniface plaque, with long-haired armoured bust of Charles I, probably by J. Obrisset, c1700, 72mm high.
£150–180 BAL

A silvered-lead medal, commemorating the death of Jonathan Swift, by W. Mossop, with three-quarters facing bust, a scratched legend on the reverse, 1745, 77mm high.
£130–150 BAL

◄ A bronze medal, commemorating the siege of Corfu, with armoured bust of General Schulemburg, on the reverse an overhead plan of Corfu with details of the siege, 1716, 49mm diam.
£240–280 Gle

A silver medal, commemorating the Highland Society of Scotland, to Gilbert McBlain, by J. McKay, with an engraving of a plough and furrows on the reverse, Edinburgh hallmark, and 'J.M.', 1833, 45mm diam.
£140–160 DNW

A bronze medal, commemorating the Inauguration of the Memorial of the Great Exhibition, by C. Wiener, with bust of Prince Albert and inscription on the reverse, 1863, 68mm diam.
£40–50 BAL

LOCATE THE SOURCE

The source of each illustration in Miller's can be found by checking the code letters below each caption with the Key to Illustrations, pages 476–484.

A brass and blue enamel medal, commemorating the Masonic Provincial Grand Lodge, East Perthshire, with St. Andrew on the cross, the reverse plain, with suspension loop, c1880, 70mm high.
£60–70 DNW

A silver province medal, commemorating the instituting of the Royal Caledonian Curling Club on 25th July 1838, a curling scene on the reverse, the suspension formed by thistles and a crown, 25th July 1838, 55mm high.
£80–90 DNW

A silver medal, commemorating the Zoological Society of London 1826, with various birds, edge engraved 'To Mr Abraham Dee Bartlett in Acknowledgement of Services Rendered to the Society 5th November 1872', in original Wyon case, 77mm diam.
£1,250–1,450 BAL

The Wyons were a famous family of medal makers who came to England from Cologne in the 18thC, and continued trading throughout the 19thC.

◄ A brass and blue enamel medal, commemorating the Masonic Provincial Grand Lodge, East Perthshire, with St. Andrew on the cross, the reverse plain, with suspension loop, c1880, 70mm high.
£60–70 DNW

A white metal medal, commemorating the Majority of Princess Victoria, by T. Halliday, with face of Princess Victoria within an open rose and British lion with a foul anchor on the reverse, 1837, 38mm diam.
£25–30 BAL

A silver prize medal, inscribed on reverse 'The Cat Club Won by Mrs H. V. James' "Blackwell Jogram" for the Best Long-Haired Male Smoke Cat, Jan 9th & 10th 1900, St. Stephen's Hall Westminster', 1900, 54mm diam.
£120–150 BAL

A 9ct gold and enamel medal, by Fattorini & Son, Bradford, prize for Pigeon Fancying, Yorkshire, with pigeon and surrounding field in colours and 'Cudworth D.F.S.' engraved 'Best Turbit in Show, H. E. Veale, 1901' on the reverse, Birmingham 1901, 30mm diam.
£100–120 DNW

A bronze medal, commemorating the opening of the Coal Exchange, by B. Wyon, with central portrait medallion of Queen Victoria, surrounded by Prince Albert, the Prince of Wales and Princess Royal, the interior of the Coal Exchange on the reverse, 1849, 89mm diam.
£220–250 BAL

A silver medal, commemorating Leith Academy 1889–1900, engraved with the façade, to Margaret I. Johnson, Edinburgh hallmark and for Hamilton & Inches, 45mm diam.
£110–130 DNW

A silver challenge medal, for the Stockbridge (Edinburgh) Draughts Club, by R. & H. B. Kirkwood, with black enamel squares, 1901, 52mm square.
£100–120 DNW

A silver medal, commemorating Sandyford Burns Club instituted 1883, with two dogs, the reverse 'John Bruce 1902', by John Boyd Glasgow, inset with a portrait of Burns surrounded by floral and scroll mount, 1902, 44mm high.
£200–220 DNW

A silvered bronze medal, commemorating Joseph Chamberlain's visit to South Africa, by J. Fray, with bust facing wearing a monacle, inscribed 'I go to S. Africa with the most earnest desire to bring together the people into one great African nation under the British flag' on the reverse, 1903, 51mm diam.
£35–45 BAL

A bronze prize medal, commemorating The Lincolnshire Red Shorthorn Association, by A. Lowentall, with a bull standing with Lincoln Cathedral in the distance, blank on the reverse, c1910, 63mm diam.
£80–100 BAL

A silver medal, commemorating the Aberdeenshire Bee Keepers' Association, with a bee in high relief, inscribed Associaton show 1919, awarded to W. M. Kennedy, 1st prize for display of honey & bees wax' on the reverse, 1919, 45mm diam.
£220–250 DNW

◄ A silver prize medal, commemorating the British Empire Games, England, 1934, inscribed 'Swimming 100 Yds Back 2nd' on the reverse, 51mm diam.
£120–140 DNW

A bronze medal, commemorating the Nice War Memorial, by André Lavrillier, inscribed 'Hommage de la Cité 29 janvier 1928' on the reverse, 1928, 72mm diam.
£120–150 DNW

A bronze medal, commem-orating the International Colonial Exposition, Paris, 1931, by E. Blin, with conjoined busts of 3 French colonials, 2 elephants wearing decorative coverings facing each other, and a view of the colonial exhibition buildings on the reverse, 68mm diam.
£140–160 DNW

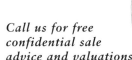

A platinum medal, commemorating William Shakespeare, 400th anniversary, 1964, by P. Vincze, with a bust, 2 figures kneeling and inscribed 'We shall not look upon his like again' on the reverse, No. 13 of limited edition of 100, with damaged certificate, 52mm diam, in original box.
£480–530 Gle

MILITARY

A Naval General Service 1793–1840 medal, with 3 bars, Algiers, Trafalgar and Copenhagen 1801, awarded to Francis Leonard.
£3,000–3,500 Gle

A Punjab campaign medal, with Mooltan and Goojerat bars, 1848–49.
£225–275 Q&C

A South Africa war medal, 1853.
£250–300 Q&C

An Indian Mutiny medal, 1857–58, awarded to 3rd Bengal European Regiment.
£80–100 RMC

A Naval General Service Medal, with Syria bar, 1840, and a St Jean d'Arc medal, 1840.
£350–400 Q&C

A Volunteer Long Service Medal, with bust of Queen Victoria, awarded to Cpl. W. G. Gibson, West Yorkshire Volunteer Artillery, 1894–1901.
£40–50 RMC

A group of 3 medals, awarded to Sergeant J. H. Newton, of Damant's Horse and Corps of Guides.
£2,200–2,500 Gle

A Queen's South Africa 1899–1902 medal, with Belfast, Orange Free State and Cape Colony bars, and the King's South Africa medal, with South Africa 1901 and South Africa 1902 bars, awarded to Cornet W. A. N. Heygate, South African Constabulary, Late Lord Strathcona's Horse.
£2,400–2,700 Gle

A 15ct gold Boer War Tribute medal, presented to Private J. Dearnley of the West Riding Regiment, in leather case, the lid embossed in gold with 'Holmfirth & District 1900–01'.
£500–550 Gle

A Queen's South Africa Medal, awarded to Pte. C. W. Smith, Uitenage Town Guard, 1899–1902.
£35–45 RMC

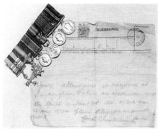

Six miniature award medals, Military Cross, G.VI.R. with 3 bars, 1914–15 Star with Mons Bar, British War Medal, Victory Medal with MID oakleaf, Defence Medal, War Medal, awarded to Captain F. V. Wallington, Royal Field Artillery.
£1,900–2,200 Gle

Four WWI medals, Military Medal, G.V.R with second award bar, 1914–15 Star, British War and Victory Medal, and certificate for an MID dated 19 March 1919, awarded to Sjt. E. Briggs, Royal Artillery.
£450–500 Gle

Five medals, MVO, OBE, British War Medal, Victory Medal with MID, George V Delhi Durbar medal, awarded to Major K. O. Goldie, 10th Lancers (Hodson's Horse), 1911–19, in presentation case.
£1,000–1,200 Q&C

◀ Three medals, George V British Empire Medal, Defence Medal, and War Medal, awarded to F/Sgt. G. L. Martin, Royal Air Force, 1940s.
£140–175 RMC

▶ An Imperial Service Medal, George VI, awarded to Mabel L. Sullivan, 1937–52.
£12–15 RMC

Three medals, Queen Elizabeth II, General Service Medal with Arabian Peninsula bar, Campaign Service Medal with Borneo bar, R.A.F. Long Service and Good Conduct Medal, awarded to Chief Technician K. Woodhead, Royal Air Force.
£125–140 RMC

▶ An Order of the Rising Sun medal, breast star in silver and enamels, with Japanese characters to reverse, c1900, 90mm diam.
£300–350 WAL

Metalware

A Tiffany & Co copper and silver bowl, 1890, 13½in (34.5cm) diam.
£225–275 ChA

A whistle, J. Hudson, Birmingham, with leather strap, dated '1915', 3½in (9cm) long.
£12–15 AOH

A Lister brass and tin engine-oil filler, 1930s, 9in (23cm) high.
£30–35 SMI

A William Foster & Co cast-iron tank plaque, c1918–20, 39in (99cm) long.
£600–700 JUN

◀ A Spratts iron gin trap, with ground pin, early 20thC, 5½in (14cm) diam.
£40–50 ET

BRASS

A brass paper clip, applied with a bunch of grapes and leaves, 1880, 6in (15cm) wide.
£150–175 CHAP

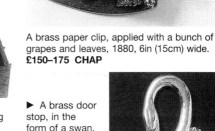

A set of brass weights, by Young Son & Marlow, in a mahogany case with brass handles, c1860, 17¾in (45cm) wide.
£1,600–1,800 INC

▶ A brass door stop, in the form of a swan, 19thC, 15½in (39.5cm) high.
£300–350 CHAP

A pair of brass petal-based candlesticks, mid-18thC, 7½in (19cm) high.
£425–475 ANT

◀ A pair of Victorian brass door knockers, modelled as stylized dolphins, 8in (20.5cm) long.
£300–350 CHAP

A brass and copper paraffin heater, c1890, 17in (43cm) high.
£70–80 RUL

A brass and copper water carrier, by Hick Brothers, Leeds, 1900, 20in (51cm) high.
£180–200 SMI

A Victorian brass chestnut roaster, with crest on the handle, 22in (56cm) long.
£175–195 CHAP

A brass paper clip, 1880, 6in (15cm) high.
£85–95 CHAP

▶ A brass grape-hod umbrella stand, decorated with a tavern scene, 1920s, 35in (90cm) high.
£125–145 DQ

A set of brass postal scales, the base with pierced foliate cast border, c1900, 10¼in (26cm) wide.
£350–400 P

Three brass butcher's weights, c1935, largest 8in (20.5cm) high.
£75–90 JUN

BRONZE

A bronze paper clip, modelled as 2 bears on a see-saw, 1890, 5in (12.5cm) wide.
£500–550 CHAP

A French bronze figure of a cherub, c1850, 11in (28cm) long.
£125–150 HUM

A pair of Viennese bronze models of deer, 1860–80, 4in (10cm) high.
£235–265 BND

An Austrian bronze nib-wipe, modelled as a rat, c1890, 3¾in (9.5cm) long.
£150–180 ChA

▶ A bronze figural dish, surmounted by a maiden and child, by Peter Tereszczuk, signed and monogrammed, early 20thC, 6in (15cm) high.
£90–100 AH

A bronze model of a saddled stallion, cast from a model by John Willis-Good, signed and with 'Cire Perdue, Bronze' on base, early 20thC, 12in (30.5cm) wide.
£1,300–1,500 Bri

PEWTER

A Sadware pewter plate, 18thC, 8in (20.5cm) diam.
£30–40 AnSh

A Victorian pewter coffee pot, 9in (23cm) high.
£50–60 AnS

A Victorian pewter one-pint tankard, with monogram, 5in (12.5cm) high.
£40–45 AnSh

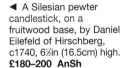

◀ A Silesian pewter candlestick, on a fruitwood base, by Daniel Eilefeld of Hirschberg, c1740, 6½in (16.5cm) high.
£180–200 AnSh

A Continental pewter demi-litre mug, 19thC, 4¾in (12cm) high.
£40–45 AnS

A Victorian pewter quart mug, 6in (15cm) high.
£60–70 AnS

A pewter chamberstick with snuffer, c1840, 4½in (11.5cm) high.
£70–80 ChA

▶ An early Victorian pewter pint measure, 5in (12.5cm) high.
£50–60 AnS

A pewter plate, c1850,
10in (25.5cm) diam.
£60–70 ChA

A Derbyshire pewter mug,
1910–36, 5in (12.5cm) high.
£60–70 AnS

A pewter teapot, with acorn finial,
late 1920s, 8in (20.5cm) high.
£15–20 AnSh

POCKET KNIVES

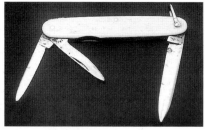

An ivory three-bladed penknife, 1870,
3½in (9cm) wide.
£60–70 MB

A Sheffield mother-of-pearl
folding pocket knife, 1825–98,
2in (5cm) long.
£35–45 AnS

A Sheffield chequered
mother-of-pearl and
silver-bladed fruit knife,
1896, 3in (7.5cm) long.
£20–25 AnS

A hunting knife, with
antler handle, 1900,
5in (12.5cm) long.
£30–35 MB

▶ A German lady's
pocket knife, by Elosi,
with perfume bottle
corkscrew, 1930s,
1in (2.5cm) long.
£15–20 AnS

An Italian brass barrel knife,
engraved with a coat-of-arms
and wine flask, inscribed
'Forniture di S.S. Pio XI', 1890,
3¼in (8.5cm) wide.
£50–60 EMC

**This type of knife was used to
cut the seal on barrels of wine.**

◀ A miniature
penknife, with
simulated
tortoiseshell
handle, 1920s,
1¼in (3cm) long.
£60–70 MRW

Militaria

A bronze signal cannon, with swollen muzzle, bulbous cascabel and stepped trunnions, on stepped iron garrison carriage with pierced sides, early 19thC, barrel 24½in (62cm) long.
£1,100–1,300 WAL

A 2nd Battalion Hampshire Regiment half cheese drum, 1880, 14in (35.5cm) wide.
£850–1,000 Q&C

A 9th Lancers silver-plated miniature kettledrum, with embossed crest, c1900, 8in (20.5cm) diam.
£650–750 Q&C

◀ An Imperial German cigarette tin, the lid decorated with a Kriegsmarine flag and a Naval Officer smoking a cigarette, inscribed 'Constanin Kaisepreis', c1914, 4¼in (11cm) wide.
£50–60 BOS

A brass rifle-barrel inspector, c1920s, 4½in (11.5cm) long.
£15–20 WAB

ARMOUR & UNIFORMS

A composed half-armour, with Italian closed helmet, breastplate and backplate, late 16thC, German arms, mid-16thC, and gauntlets 19thC, some damage.
£5,000–6,000 TEN

A lobster-tailed helmet, with pierced single-plate cheek-pieces, probably 1625–50, and a pair of German fingered gauntlets, 1550–90.
Helmet £700–800
Gauntlets £800–900 Bon

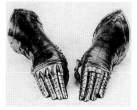

▶ Two north German gauntlets, late 16thC, longest 16in (41cm).
£1,300–1,500 S(S)

A James II lobster-tailed helmet, stamped with mark on peak, restored, c1685.
£1,400–1,600 WSA

Soldiers were popularly referred to as 'lobsters' because they turned red (ie wore red coats) when they enlisted. The term was first used during the Civil War when a troop of Parliamentary horse soldiers were described by Royalists as 'the regiment of lobsters' because of their bright, iron armour which covered them like a shell. The lobster-tailed helmet was so-called because of its protective neck flap.

A Rifles Brigade silver-mounted cross-belt, 1890.
£350–400 Q&C

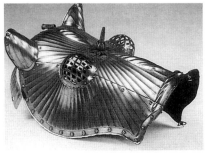

A copy of a 16thC Maximillian-style horse armour, late19th/early 20thC.
£1,500–1,800 SK

A Persian chiselled and gold-damascened steel Kulah Khud helmet, with 2 fitted horns and later silver-mounted hardstone finial, 19thC, 9½in (24cm) high.
£600–700 Bon

A Boer War officer's field service cap, in khaki cotton material with thin leather chin strap, 1899.
£170–200 BOS

An officer's green cloth spiked helmet, of the Kings Shropshire Light Infantry, post-1902.
£700–800 WAL

A Grenadier Guards bearskin, with horse-hair plume, c1920, 14in (35.5cm) high.
£200–250 Q&C

A King's Royal Irish Hussars trooper's cavalry busby, pre-1922.
£300–350 Q&C

A Gloucestershire blue cloth regimental band helmet, post-1952.
£200–225 Q&C

Five regimental forage caps, c1950.
£35–40 each Q&C

▶ A Scottish piper's feather bonnet, with ostrich feather, post-1952, 13in (33cm) high.
£250–300 Q&C

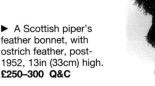

EDGED WEAPONS

A European fighting axe, possibly 16thC,
head 7½in (19cm) wide, with later wooden haft.
£170–190 WAL

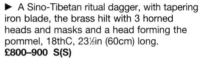

A Spanish elbow-length parrying gauntlet, combined with
a dagger blade, the gauntlet decorated with scrollwork,
late 17thC, 37½in (95cm) long.
£1,700–2,000 S(S)

A Scottish composite
basket-hilted broadsword,
late 18thC, with earlier
blade, 32in (81.5cm) long.
£750–850 Bon

▶ A Sino-Tibetan ritual dagger, with tapering
iron blade, the brass hilt with 3 horned
heads and masks and a head forming the
pommel, 18thC, 23½in (60cm) long.
£800–900 S(S)

An infantry officer's sabre, with bronze stirrup
hilt, c1800, blade 28½in (72.5cm) long.
£200–240 ASB

A 1796 pattern infantry officer's sword, complete with
original black leather scabbard.
£400–450 BOS

A William IV infantry officer's 1822 pattern sword,
with brass four-bar basket hilt incorporating the
royal cypher, in original brass-mounted black
leather scabbard, 1830–37, blade 32in (81.5cm) long.
£250–280 ASB

An Arab Nimcha, with rhino horn grip and leather-
covered wooden scabbard, early 19thC,
39in (99cm) long.
£550–650 GV

A Burmese Dha, decorated with copper and silver,
with brass-mounted wooden scabbard, 19thC,
33⅓in (85cm) long.
£130–150 GV

A Scottish dirk, with basket-weave hilt, orange stone
mounts and plain nickel scabbard mounts,
20thC, blade 12in (30.5cm) long.
£300–350 GV

FIREARMS

An Italian stonebow, the walnut tiller carved with decorative mouldings, early 17thC, 37in (94cm) long.
£1,100–1,300 S(S)

An American .32 four-shot rim-fire pocket pistol, No. 2950, stamped 'C. Sharps Patent Jan. 25.1859', 5in (12.5cm) long.
£450–500 Bon

A pair of officer's flintlock pistols, by Whateley, with full walnut stocks with iron ramrods under, the lockplates signed, the butts mounted with a silver shield-shaped plaque with engraved cursive initials, c1820, 13in (33cm) long.
£1,800–2,000 TEN

A French military percussion pistol, with walnut half stock and bird-head butt cap, 19thC, 14in (35cm) long.
£450–500 GV

A flintlock box-lock tinderlighter, with flat-sided walnut butt chequered along the spine, late 18th/early 19thC, 8¾in (22cm) long.
£350–400 Bon

◄ An Indian all-steel combined walking stick and percussion gun, with tiger-head handle, decorated with gold-damascened flowerheads, mid-19thC, 40¼in (102.5cm) long.
£3,500–4,000 Bon

A North African 24 bore silver-mounted Kabyle Snaphaunce jezail, with silver barrel bands, the butt with silver scrolls and ivory plaques, 19thC, 65in (165cm) long.
£400–450 WAL

A .44 six-shot Remington New Model Army SA percussion revolver, No. 48155, 19thC, 13½in (34.5cm) long.
£700–800 WAL

POWDER FLASKS

An east European Carpathian Basin polished natural staghorn powder flask, with silver mount, engraved with 'Found After The Battle of Ooderpoor Decr. 2nd.1858', 7¼in (19.4cm) high.
£550–600 Bon

An eastern European Carpathian Basin natural staghorn powder flask, engraved with scrolls and triangles, 18thC, 8in (20.5cm) high.
£400–450 Bon

> Miller's is a price GUIDE not a price LIST

An embossed copper gun flask, by Hawksley, c1840, 8¼in (21cm) long.
£65–75 WSA

An American brass-mounted powder flask, by Frary, Benham & Co, embossed on one side with a covey of partridges in a landscape, 19thC, 8¼in (21cm) long.
£450–500 Bon

TRENCH ART

A pair of 18lb shells, engraved with flowers and birds, 1914–18, 11in (28cm) high.
£70–80 AOH

A caricature of an army officer reading the *Balkan News*, dated '1918', 5in (12.5cm) high.
£25–30 AnS

A brass pot, 1914–18, 2in (5cm) high.
£10–15 AnS

A German brass lighter, embossed with a crown and inscribed 'Gott Mit Uns', 1914–18, 2in (5cm) diam.
£15–20 AnS

A brass shell, engraved with 'Souvenir Boiry Notre Dame 1919, 397 P.O.W.', 1914–18, 9in (23cm) high.
£30–32 AOH

Did You Know?

Trench Art, as its name suggests, derives from the trenches in the 1914–18 war, when soldiers transformed shell cases, bullets and other military waste into everyday domestic objects from vases to umbrella stands to lighters. Pieces were often inscribed or pricked with date and place name (frequently a battlefield), and provide a humble, poignant and increasingly collectable reminder of the Great War.

Money Boxes

A green, orange, blue and white agateware pig money box, c1820, 4in (10cm) long.
£100–120 HUM

A Continental yellow and orange pottery money box, impressed '1842', 4in (10cm) high.
£85–100 IW

A Buckley Sebastapol brown-glazed money box, 1860, 10in (25.5cm) wide.
£240–260 IW

◀ A Yorkshire pottery brown-glazed savings bank, modelled as a chest of drawers, late 19thC, 7in (18cm) wide.
£125–145 IW

▶ A Bristol brown-glazed stoneware money box, in the shape of an urn, impressed 'Alice Pearce', late 19thC, 6in (15cm) high.
£30–40 IW

A copper top hat money box, inscribed 'NE', c1930, 4¾in (12cm) wide.
£25–30 OD

A Midland Bank elephant money box, red with white lettering, 1970s, 8in (20.5cm) high.
£15–20 Law

A plastic Chicken Feeding Money Box, in red, orange, yellow and green, made in Hong Kong, c1960, 4½in (11.5cm) high.
£15–18 CMF

Money Collectables

First issued by Henry VII, the sovereign was superseded by the guinea in 1663 but was revived in 1817. The sovereign was worth 20s (£1) and because the gold coin was attractive to forgers, portable money scales were often used to test its weight.

Prince Albert popularized the habit of wearing a watch chain attached horizontally from pocket to pocket, and a new fashion began of attaching items such as vestas and sovereign cases to the end of Albert chains. These sovereign cases were adapted both for full and half sovereigns, and were produced throughout the Victorian and Edwardian periods up until WWI. However, in 1917 gold became worth more than the face value of the coin, and the sovereign was replaced in common currency by paper money.

A set of coin scales, in a black painted tin decorated with the figure of justice in red, brown and white, c1800, tin 5in (12.5cm) wide.
£120–140 HUM

A Harrison Improved Sovereign Balance, to weigh half and full sovereigns, c1840, mid-19thC, 4in (10cm) wide, in original box.
£30–35 HUM

A Victorian gun-metal half and full sovereign case, with copper interior, 2in (5cm) wide.
£120–140 BHA

A silver-plated sovereign case, with stamp holder in cover, 1875, 1¼in (3cm) square.
£25–30 BHA

A W. Haseler silver sovereign case, marked for Birmingham 1913, 2½in (6.5cm) wide.
£350–400 THOM

A brown crocodile skin sovereign case, 1885, 1½in (4cm) diam.
£100–125 BHA

A silver-plated sovereign case, 1890, 2½in (6.5cm) wide.
£50–60 BHA

LOCATE THE SOURCE

The source of each illustration in Miller's can be found by checking the code letters below each caption with the Key to Illustrations, pages 476–484.

A white metal sovereign case, initialled 'A. W. J. V.', 1890, 1¼in (3cm) wide.
£65–75 BHA

Newspapers & Magazines

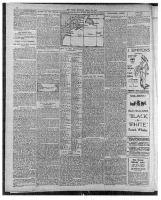

The Times, dated August 7th, 1793, 18 x 12½in (45.5 x 32cm).
£40–50 HaR

John Bull, issue No. 1, dated June 9th, 1906, 11¾ x 8in (30 x 20.5cm).
£20–25 HaR

The Times, April 16th, 1912, with headline 'Titanic Sinks – No Deaths, 1st Report – Page 10', 24 x 18in (61 x 45.5cm).
£80–100 HaR

Two *La Mode du Jour* magazines, printed in brown, dated '25 Decembre 1930' and '10 Septembre 1931', 14 x 11in (35.5 x 28cm).
£10–15 each DRJ

The Guide, The Official Organ of the Girl Guides Association, August 12th, 1933.
£2–3 SVB

Daily Herald, the cover with the first photo of Edward and Mrs Simpson, inside the story of the Hindenburg disaster, May 8, 1937, 21 x 17in (53.5 x 43cm).
£4–5 HaR

Picture Post, dated January 20, 1940, 13 x 10½in (33 x 26.5cm).
£2–3 RAD

The Illustrated, with full colour cover, August 28, 1948, 12 x 10in (30.5 x 25.5cm).
£2–3 RAD

The Motor magazine, with full colour cover, June 5, 1957, 11 x 8in (28 x 20.5cm).
£3–4 SVB

Harper's Bazaar magazine, with full colour cover, May 1959, 12¾ x 10¾in (32.5 x 27.5cm).
£8–9 RAD

Osbornes

An Osborne plaque, entitled 'Mr Pickwick', in shades of brown, stamped 'A. Osborne', 1909, 5in (12.5cm) high.
£35–40 PC

An Osborne plaque, entitled 'The Gleaners', brown, yellow and green, marked '©AO', c1913, 9¼in (23.5cm) wide.
£25–30 JMC

An Osborne plaque, entitled 'Shakespeare's House', in brown, yellow and green, 1910–39, 4½in (11.5cm) wide.
£12–16 GIN

An Osborne plaque, entitled 'Mr Pecksniff', brown, cream and blue, damaged, 1914, 3in (7.5cm) high.
£5–10 RAC

An Osborne plaque, entitled 'Sir Walter Scott's Monument, Edinburgh', grey, brown and green, 1920s, 11½ x 7½in (29 x19cm).
£50–55 JMC

An Osborne plaque, entitled 'Brig O'Balgowrie, Aberdeen', brown and grey, 1930s, 7 x 10½in (18 x 26.5cm).
£40–50 JMC

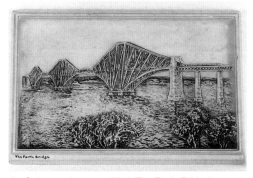

An Osborne plaque, entitled 'The Forth Bridge', blue, green and cream, 1930s, 7½ x 11½in (19 x 29cm).
£45–50 JMC

An Osborne figure of a Welsh lady, entitled 'Off to Market', red, green and blue, late 1940s, 5in (12.5cm) high.
£60–70 JMC

An Osborne figure, entitled 'The Grandfather', red, yellow and green, from a set of 8 Dickens characters, 1940s, 5in (12.5cm) high.
£55–65 JMC

Paper Money

A French 5 livres note, 1793, 4¼in (11cm) wide.
£10–15 NAR

A Jersey £1 note, unissued, 1810–19.
£550–600 P

A 10/- Mafeking Siege Note, signed by Capt. Greener, March 1900, 6¼in (16cm) wide.
£85–95 WP

A United Kingdom of Great Britain and Ireland 10/- note, with Dardanelles overprint, 1915, 5¼in (13.5cm) wide.
£270–300 WP

A Confederate States of America $500 note, 1864.
£400–450 NAR

A National Bank of Egypt £1 note, 1924, 6¼in (16cm) wide.
£345–365 NAR

A Hibernian Bank Limited, Republic of Ireland £1 note, 1933, 6in (15cm) wide.
£50–60 WP

A States of Guernsey £1 note, 1938, 6in (15cm) wide.
£800–900 WP

A Palestine Currency Board £1 note, 1939, 6¼in (16cm) wide.
£200–250 NAR

A Mongolian 5 Tugrik note, 1941, 6in (15cm) wide.
£40–50 NAR

A Bank of Jamaica £1 note, 1960s, 6in (15cm) wide.
£40–45 NAR

A Union Bank of Scotland Limited £100 note, dated 18 February 1947, part of final issue of 1,000 notes.
£650–700 P

A National Commercial Bank of Scotland £100 note, 1959, 7in (18cm) wide.
£160–180 WP

A Central Bank of Ireland £5 note, known as a Lady Lavery note, 1975, 6½in (16.5cm) wide.
£15–20 WP

An Isle of Man Government £10 note, dated 23 June 1972, 6in (15cm) wide.
£250–300 WP

An Isle of Man Government £20 note, 1979.
£180–200 NAR

A Bank of England £1 note, miscut and with extra paper, 1981.
£60–70 WP

◀ A Bank of England £20 note, missing Romeo and Juliet and George and the Dragon, 1988–91.
£160–180 P

▶ An Iraq 10 dinars note, 1992, 6¾in (17cm) wide.
£1–2 NAR

Plastics

A pair of brown Bakelite candlesticks, with silver-plated necks, 1930s, 7in (18cm) high.
£65–75 BEV

A brown Bakelite Air Clear air purifier, 1930s, 8in (20.5cm) wide.
£330–370 YAN

A beige celluloid comb and cover, 1930s, 4in (10cm) long.
£14–18 CHU

Five orange and brown Bakelite kohl bottles, 1930s, largest 4in (10cm) high.
£80–100 YAN

◀ A Bakelite picture frame, with black base, 1938, the postcard c1950s, 6½in (16.5cm) high.
£25–30 BKK

A red Bakelite thermometer, 1930s, 4½in (11.5cm) high.
£35–40 BEV

A black and brown plastic clothes brush, in the form of a duck, 1940–50s, 12in (30.5cm) high.
£12–15 TWa

A green Bakelite knitting needles case, 1930s, 15¼in (38.5cm) wide.
£15–20 PC

A red plastic dice jewellery case, 1940s, 5in (12.5cm) square.
£40–50 BTB

A John Corby Ltd brown Bakelite tie press, the 'Countess Mara', 1940s, 5in (12.5cm) high.
£35–40 DHAR

A red plastic lemonade jug and 6 beakers, designed by Pierre Cardin, 1960–70s, jug 10¼in (26cm) high.
£40–45 MARK

Police

The foundations of the police force as we know it today were laid out in the 19th century. In 1829, Home Secretary Sir Robert Peel established the Metropolitan Police in London, hence the slang terms for policemen: 'Peeler' and 'Bobby'. By 1857, similar forces were created across Britain.

Police uniform was gradually refined in the Victorian period. In the 1860s the Metropolitan Police introduced a dark blue tunic with white metal letters on the collar and replaced the leather reinforced top hat with what was to become the famous policeman's helmet. Police whistles were first issued in 1884, and the most common weapon was the truncheon.

The turn of the century saw a host of technological advances in the art of detection, most notably the introduction of fingerprinting, adopted by Scotland Yard in 1901, and new inventions such as the telephone, the telegraph and the automobile soon became essential to police work.

A Metropolitan Police whistle and chain, No. 36746, c1930s.
£25–30 WAB

A Doland patent bull's eye police lantern, c1850, 8in (20.5cm) high.
£50–60 AOH

Police whistles were marked with the number of the officer.

A police cap, from Mysore state, India, pre-1947.
£80–90 Q&C

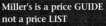

Miller's is a price GUIDE not a price LIST

A Dinky Toys police hut, motorcycle patrol and policemen, No. 42, boxed, 1936–40.
£130–150 DDM

Two cork police helmets, bearing the Queen's crown, c1950s.
£60–65 each Q&C

A metal battery-powered lamp, sign depicting police force and area missing from front, c1950s, 7in (18cm) high.
£15–20 DDM

Two police helmet badges, c1950, 3in (7.5cm) wide.
£15–20 each AOH

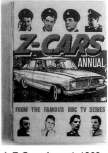

A Z-Cars Annual, 1963, 10 x 8in (25.5 x 20.5cm).
£5–7 YR

Postcards

An Italian black and white postcard commemorating polar explorers, 1899.
£35–45 Pln

A French postcard, with a man and a lady playing billiards, used, 1904.
£20–25 Pln

A French postcard, by Raphael Kirchner, in yellow, brown and black, unused, 1900–10.
£55–60 SpP

A sepia postcard, 'The Start of the Isle of Wight Motor Omnibuses, April 13, 1905', used, stamp removed.
£25–30 SpP

◄ A postcard, 'With Best Wishes for Your Birthday', in mauve, blue, green and red, 1906.
£1–2 THA

A woven postcard, 'Palais de Justice Bruxelles', printed in red, 1907.
£20–25 SpP

An Australian postcard, 'Visit of the United States Fleet To Melbourne Australia', in red, white, blue and gold, unused, dated 'Sept 1908'.
£20–25 SpP

An American photo portrait postcard of Ripon College Basket Ball Team, Wisconsin, used, 1909.
£30–35 Pln

A photo postcard of the New Zealand Expeditionary Force, signed on front, 1915.
£35–40 Pln

► Two postcards, embroidered in silk with flowers in pink, green, mauve and yellow, 1915.
£2–3 each MAC

An embroidered postcard, with The Manchester Regiment Egypt, 1916.
£45–50 SpP

An American postcard, 'American Legion Convention Oct 6–9 1930, Welcome Comrade', Boston, 1930.
£50–60 Pln

A Louis Wain postcard, 'At The Cat Show', series I.
£160–180 VS

Three money postcards, 1920, 1940 and 1950.
£3–4 each WP

Posters

The colourful advertising poster emerged in the second half of the 19th century, coinciding with the rise of Art Nouveau, and resulting from new techniques in lithography and printing. France pioneered the development of the poster, notable early figures ranging from the painter Toulouse-Lautrec, perhaps the most collectable name in the field, who produced only 31 poster designs, to commercial artist Jules Cheret, who founded L'Imprimerie Chaix in 1866 and created over 1,000 different posters.

Among the first major clients for this bright and effective form of advertising were theatres and food and drink manufacturers. Whatever the product on offer, a favourite feature was often a beautiful woman, her feminine curves complementing the swirling lines of Art Nouveau graphics.

With the explosion of travel in the 20th century, railway companies, shipping lines and automobile manufacturers all exploited the power of the poster. Art Deco, streamlined and modern, was the perfect style for capturing the speed, excitement and luxury of new forms of transport, and the 1920s and '30s saw a host of brilliant designs. French poster artist Cassandre created celebrated Art Deco images both for the railways and for the Normandie ocean liner, whilst in the UK the Shell Oil company, the major railways and London Underground, under the management of Frank Pick, all commissioned influential series of posters.

Cinema was another 20th century invention that relied largely on the poster to publicize its offerings. As with rock and pop posters that flourished from the 1950s onwards, film posters were created as ephemeral items and were often simply thrown away once the movie had finished its run, hence the rarity and worth of surviving examples.

Values of posters depend on subject, artist and size, since the same image could be printed in different dimensions. As posters were mass produced, rarity is a crucial factor, as is condition. Minor creases and tears can be acceptable, but more serious damage will certainly affect the desirability of all but the very rarest posters.

A coloured lithographic poster 'Fête des Fleurs', by Jules Cheret, 1890, 48 x 33in (122 x 84cm).
£2,300–2,500 BSL

A French coloured lithographic poster 'La revue blanche', by Henri de Toulouse-Lautrec, 1895, 50 x 36in (127 x 91.5cm).
£18,000–20,000 BSL

▶ A poster, for the Diamond Jubilee of Queen Victoria, June 22, 1897, 33 x 13in (84 x 33cm), framed.
£70–80 WAB

A coloured lithographic poster, 'Fanny Davenport', by Alphonse Mucha, 1897, 85 x 28in (216 x 71cm).
£5,500–6,500 BSL

Further Reading

Miller's Collecting Prints & Posters,
Miller's Publications, 1997

A linen poster, 'Fine Monis', by Clerice Frères, printed in yellow, red and black, 1911, 17 x 13in (43 x 33cm).
£130–160 Do

A coloured lithographic poster, 'Eno's Fruit Salt', by Claud Lovat Fraser, printed by Curwen Press, London, minor damage, 1920s, 30 x 20in (76 x 51cm).
£240–280 S

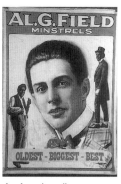

An American linen poster, 'AL. G. Field Minstrels', printed in red, blue and brown, 1920s, 25 x 19in (63.5 x 48.5cm).
£250–275 Do

A linen poster, 'Epping Forest', by Nancy Smith, printed in orange, yellow, green and brown, 1920s, 40 x 24in (101.5 x 61cm).
£500–550 Do

An American First National poster, *Her Wild Oat*, by Beckoff, printed in red, blue and beige, 1922, 41 x 27in (104 x 68.5cm).
£350–400 S

A coloured lithographic poster, 'Kulm Hotel', by Otto Ernst, 1925, 39 x 27in (99 x 68.5cm).
£2,000–2,200 BSL

A linen poster, 'Continent via Harwich', by Tom Purvis, printed in yellow, green and black, c1925, 40 x 24in (101.5 x 61cm).
£550–650 Do

A linen poster, 'Siemens Gasfilled Lamps', printed in red, yellow and black, c1925, 18 x 12in (45.5 x 30.5cm).
£145–165 Do

A coloured lithographic poster, 'Chapeaux Mossant', by Olsky, c1928, 62 x 47in (157.5 x 119.5cm).
£2,200–2,500 BSL

An American RKO film poster, *The Sin Ship*, printed in red, green and brown, 1930, 41 x 27in (104 x 68.5cm).
£350–400 S

A coloured lithographic poster, 'Garston, LMS', by Norman Wilkinson, c1930, 50 x 40in (127 x 101.5cm).
£1,700–1,900 BSL

A coloured lithographic poster, 'Rayon Des Soieries', by Maurice Dufréne, printed by Chaix, Paris, 1930, 46¾ x 31¼in (119 x 79cm).
£600–700 S

St IVES CORNWALL
Glorious Sands   Ideal Bathing
TRAVEL BY TRAIN

A British Rail linen poster, 'St Ives, Cornwall', printed in blue, yellow, red and green, 1930s, 40 x 25in (101.5 x 63.5cm).
£375–425 ONS

A French coloured lithographic poster, 'Wagons Lits Cook', by Adolphe Mouron Cassandre, 1933, 39 x 24½in (99 x 62cm).
£4,100–4,500 BSL

An American RKO film poster, *The Gay Diplomat*, printed in red, blue and black, 1931, 41 x 27in (104 x 68.5cm).
£350–400 S

Ivan Lebedeff had been an officer in the Czar's army but fled to Germany after the Bolshevik revolution. He began playing character parts in films in 1922 and moved to Hollywood in 1925. His looks ensured he played a long line of suave villains or gigolos securing him a certain amount of popularity.

A London Transport poster, 'London's Leisure Hours Study, The Artist's Masterpieces Travel by Underground', by Austin Cooper, printed in yellow red, blue and brown, 1933, 40 x 25in (101.5 x 63.5cm).
£120–150 ONS

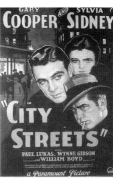

An American Paramount film poster, *City Streets*, printed in green, pink and black, 1931, 41 x 27in (104 x 68.5cm).
£3,500–4,000 S

A linen poster, 'Ryvita Crispbread', by E. Byatt, in yellow, brown and green, 1930s, 15 x 10in (38 x 30.5cm).
£135–155 Do

A French linen poster, 'Cirque Pinder ses Fauves', by G. Soury, printed in yellow, orange and brown, c1930, 21 x 15in (53.5 x 38cm).
£130–150 Do

An American Fox poster, *Skyline*, printed in red, blue and brown, 1931, 41 x 27in (104 x 68.5cm).
£800–900 S

An RKO film poster, *King Kong*, printed in red and brown, by Roland Coudon, 1933, 63 x 47in (160 x 119.5cm).
£8,000–8,500 S

Posters of the most famous films tend to attract the highest prices, and few movies are more celebrated than King Kong. The 1933 horror classic provided a dramatic reinterpretation of the Beauty and the Beast story. King Kong, a gargantuan ape living on Skull Island, falls in love with Fay Wray and goes on the rampage, finally meeting his spectacular end on top of the Empire State Building, New York. Both King Kong's death and Fay Wray's screaming have passed into movie legend, and memorabilia associated with this vintage film is highly desirable.

A coloured lithographic poster, 'Turnberry, on the Ayrshire Coast', in green, yellow and orange, by W. T. N., McCorquodale Studio, printed by Wellington Printers, London, 1930s, 40 x 50in (101.5 x 127cm).
£1,000–1,200 S

A coloured lithographic poster, 'Lowestoft, L.M.S.', in green, red and blue, by Austin Cooper, printed by McCorquodale & Co, London, minor damage, 1930s, 40 x 49in (101.5 x 124.5cm).
£600–700 S

A Belgian poster, 'Socovel', printed in red, yellow, green and black, 1930s, 24 x 33in (61 x 86.5cm).
£275–325 Do

A coloured lithographic poster, 'Cunard White Star Cruises', by Jarvis, c1934, 40 x 25in (101.5 x 63.5cm).
£800–950 BSL

A poster, 'Norway Orient Line Cruises', by Kalvert Booth, printed in orange, yellow, green and black, c1935, 40 x 24in (101.5 x 61cm).
£475–525 Do

A Belgian poster, 'Archidur', in red, green and black, on linen, c1935, 12 x 33in (30.5 x 84cm).
£150–175 Do

A poster, 'Help your Neighbour', printed in red, blue and black, 1935, 23 x 16in (58.5 x 40.5cm).
£120–150 Do

A Belgian poster, 'Citron Belgo Orangeade', printed in yellow, grey and blue, on linen, c1935, 24 x 16in (61 x 40.5cm).
£25–275 Do

An American RKO window card, *Top Hat,* printed in red, black and grey, 1935, 14 x 11in (35.5 x 28cm).
£1,400–1,600 S

A poster, 'Armagnac Ryst', by Savignac, printed in yellow, brown, grey and black, 1930s, 13 x 10in (33 x 25.5cm).
£80–90 Do

▶ A French poster, 'Favor', by Bellenger, printed in red, blue, orange and black, 1937, 15 x 23in (38 x 58.5cm).
£170–200 Do

A Danish Paramount film poster, *Angel*, printed in pink, blue and black, 1937, 35 x 27in (89 x 68.5cm).
£1,500–1,700 S

A coloured lithographic poster, 'Paris', by Eugene Beaudoin and Marcel Lods, 1937, 39 x 24in (99 x 61cm).
£800–900 BSL

An American RKO film poster, 'Walt Disney's Snow White and the Seven Dwarfs', by Gustave Tenngren, in red, green brown and blue, 1937, 41 x 27in (104 x 68.5cm).
£3,800–4,200 S

A British Gaumont poster, The Lady Vanishes, printed in pink, green and black, 1938, 40 x 27in (101.5 x 68.5cm).
£4,300–4,800 S

Hitchcock topped his time in Britain with this film which won him the Best Director award from the New York Film Critics. As soon as the picture was completed Hitchcock was signed by producer David O. Selznick to direct in America.

A coloured lithograph, 'New York', by Karel Maes, printed in red, blue and black, by Plakkaat Marci, Brussels, 1939, 39 x 24½in (99 x 62cm).
£600–700 S

A Swedish MGM poster, *Dr Jekyll and Mr Hyde*, in red, yellow, blue and black, 1941, 40 x 54in (101.5 x 137cm).
£400–450 S

A Swedish Tobis poster, *Titanic*, printed in red, blue and black, 1943, 39 x 28in (99 x 71cm).
£550–600 S

An American MGM censored full colour lobby card, *The Postman Always Rings Twice*, 1946, 11 x 14in (28 x 35.5cm).
£1,800–2,000 S

This is a very rare lobby card, to date only 2 others are known to have survived destruction by MGM.

A coloured lithographic poster, 'Trooping the Colour', by Christopher Clark, c1950, 40 x 50in (101.5 x 127cm).
£1,300–1,500 BSL

► A poster, 'Chivers Jams', printed in yellow, green and brown, on linen, c1950, 18 x 16in (47.5 x 40.5cm).
£150–175 Do

A British Railways coloured lithographic poster, 'Yorkshire', by Leonard Russell Squirrell, printed by Jordison & Co Ltd, London, some damage, 1954, 40 x 25in (102 x 64cm).
£240–280 S

A Belgian travel poster, 'Middelkerke', printed in blue, green, yellow and brown, early 1950s, 39 x 24in (99 x 61cm).
£120–140 RAR

A Palace Theatre Leicester poster, *The King and I*, printed in black and red, 1950s, 15 x 10in (38 x 25.5cm).
£15–20 MRW

A British Railways poster, 'Norfolk', printed in blue, green, brown and yellow, 1960, 40 x 25in (101.5 x 63.5cm).
£160–180 RAR

An American poster, 'Terrytoons', printed in red, yellow, blue and brown, 1957, 41 x 27in (104 x 68.5cm).
£250–300 REEL

▶ A Rank Organisation coloured lithographic poster, *A Night to Remember*, printed by Charles & Reed Ltd, on linen, 1958, 30 x 40in (76 x 101.5cm).
£650–720 ONS

An American Paramount Pictures insert, *Funny Face*, 1957, 36 x 14in (91.5 x 35.5cm), framed and glazed.
£100–120 Bon

◀ A French Specta poster, 'Mon Oncle', by P. Etaix, in pink and black, on linen, 1958, 33 x 23in (84 x 58.5cm).
£350–400 S

A United Artists linen poster, 'The Magnificent Seven', in red, yellow and brown, 1960, 30 x 40in (76 x 101.5cm).
£450–500 S

A poster, *Exodus*, by Saul Bass, printed in yellow, orange and blue, 1960, 30 x 40in (76 x 101.5cm).
£200–250 REEL

A British Railways poster, 'Clapham Junction', by T. Cuneo, printed in full colour, 1960s, 42 x 52in (106.5 x 132cm).
£140–160 RAR

An American Paramount poster, *Breakfast at Tiffany's*, in red and black, 1961, 81 x 41in (206 x 104cm).
£1,200–1,400 S

An Italian United Artists poster, *West Side Story*, printed in red, blue and yellow, on linen, 1961, 78 x 55in (198 x 140cm).
£450–500 S

A Rank Organisation poster, *This Sporting Life*, by Renato Fratini, printed in red, yellow, brown and black, 1963, 41 x 27in (104 x 68.5cm).
£200–250 REEL

An American United Artists poster, *Goldfinger*, printed in black, yellow and orange, 1964, 41 x 27in (104 x 68.5cm).
£450–500 REEL

► A United Artists special premiere poster, *From Russia With Love*, by Renato Fratini, printed in pink, blue and black, 1963, 30 x 40in (76 x 101.5cm).
£850–950 S

This very rare poster was used at a regional premiere screening.

A poster, *Repulsion*, by Jan Lenica, printed in blue, green and black, 1965, 30 x 40in (76 x 101.5cm).
£350–400 REEL

A French poster, 'Le Mans', by Ferracci, in red and browns, 1971, 31 x 24in (78.5 x 61cm).
£250–300 REEL

An American poster, *The Jungle Book*, in green, brown and blue, 1967, 41 x 27in (104 x 68.5cm).
£250–300 S

An MGM poster, *Blow Up*, printed in full colour, 1967, 30 x 40in (76 x 101.5cm).
£350–400 REEL

◄ A United Artists poster, *The Graduate*, printed in red, black and green, 1968, 30 x 40in (76 x 101.5cm).
£370–420 S

► A United Artists poster, *Diamonds Are Forever*, printed in red, blue, yellow and black, 1971, 40in (101.5cm) square.
£170–200 REEL

An American 20th
Century Fox poster,
*The Rolling Stones
Gimme Shelter*, in black,
yellow and red, 1971,
41 x 27in (104 x 68.5cm).
£300–350 REEL

A Hammer Production
poster, *Scars of Dracula*,
c1971, 40 x 27in
(101.5 x 68.5cm).
£90–110 Bon

A Warner Bros poster,
Enter The Dragon,
printed in red, yellow
and blue, 1973, 41 x 27in
(104 x 68.5cm).
£200–250 REEL

An American poster,
The Sting, by Richard
Amsel, printed in red,
orange and brown, 1974,
41 x 27in (104 x 68.5cm).
£130–150 REEL

A Universal poster, *Jaws*,
printed in red, blue and
black, 1975, 60 x 40in
(152.5 x 101.5cm).
£250–300 S

An American United
Artists poster, *One Flew
Over The Cuckoo's Nest*,
in red and black, 1975,
41 x 27in (104 x 68.5cm).
£250–300 REEL

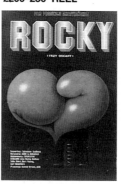

A Polish United Artists
poster, *Rocky*, by
Edward Lutczyn, printed
in red and blue, 1976,
37 x 27in (94 x 68.5cm).
£180–220 S

An American Warner Bros
poster, *The Outlaw Josey
Wales*, printed in orange
and brown, 1976,
41 x 27in (104 x 68.5cm).
£300–350 REEL

> **Cross Reference**
> See Colour Review

An American poster,
Andy Warhol's BAD,
printed in red, green and
blue, 1977, 41 x 27in
(104 x 68.5cm).
£250–300 REEL

An American United
Artists poster, *A View
to a Kill*, printed in pink,
blue and black, design
by Vic Fair, illustration
by Brian Bysouth, 1985,
41 x 27in (104 x 68.5cm).
£350–400 S

An American Orion
Pictures poster,
Robocop, printed in red,
blue and black, 1987,
41 x 27in (104 x 68.5cm).
£65–75 REEL

A Spanish poster,
Tacones Lejanos, printed
in red and black, 1991,
39 x 27in (99 x 68.5cm).
£40–50 REEL

Puppets

A Pelham reindeer string puppet, white with brown markings and black feet, c1950s, 5in (12.5cm) high.
£25–30 J&J

A Pelham monkey string puppet, with green jacket and striped trousers, late 1950s, 11in (28cm) high.
£70–80 J&J

A Pelham Puppet Kit No. 1, c1950, box 6in (15cm) square.
£30–35 GAZE

A Pelham giraffe spring-mounted string puppet, yellow with brown markings, 1960s, 32in (81.5cm) high, ex-shop display model.
£200–250 UNI

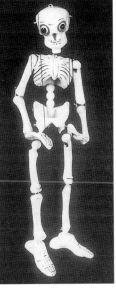

◄ A Chad Valley Sooty glove puppet, yellow with black ears, 1960s, 9½in (24cm) high.
£15–18 CMF

Two Pelham string puppets, Wolf and Giant, in original yellow boxes, c1960s, 12in (30.5cm) high.
£125–150 DN

► A skeleton string puppet, white with red and black eyes, 1970s, 14in (35.5cm) high.
£45–55 ARo

Four Pelham string puppets, Clown, Minstrel, Girl and Witch, c1970s, 13in (33cm) high, in original boxes.
£35–40 each TOY

Radios & Sound Equipment

A Graves Vulcan two-valve receiver, with wooden case and black controls, 1926, 9in (23cm) high.
£100–120 OTA

An American General Radio Co amateur radio wavemeter, type 358, with instructions, in original wooden box, 1930s, 12in (30.5cm) wide.
£60–70 ET

◄ A German VE301 people's radio, with Nazi eagle motif, 1935, 15in (38cm) high.
£200–250 OTA

A GEC AC4 black Bakelite cabinet radio, 1935, 17in (43cm) high.
£130–150 OTA

A Philco black Bakelite people's radio, c1937, 15in (38cm) high.
£300–350 OTA

A Murphy AD94 radio, with black Bakelite cabinet, slight moulding fault, 1940, 13in (33cm) high.
£100–120 OTA

An Ekco AC74 black Bakelite and chrome radio, designed by Serge Chermayeff, 1933, 17¾in (45cm) high.
£300–350 OTA

The interest of this radio is enhanced by the fact that it was designed by Serge Ivan Chermayeff. Born in Russia in 1900, Chermayeff moved to London in 1910 where he became one of Britain's foremost modern designers. In the 1920s and '30s he pioneered the acceptance of tubular steel furniture in the UK and created furnishings for Waring & Gillow, Pel, and his own company, Plan. In 1933 he started his own architectural practice and, together with Erich Mendelsohn, produced some of the most significant British modernist buildings of the pre-war period. Along with architecture and interior decoration, he also experimented with industrial design, producing lighting and Bakelite radio housings for Ekco. In 1939 Chermayeff moved to the USA where he became Professor of Architecture first at Harvard, then Yale.

◄ A Murphy A98 black Bakelite radio, with beige Oriental pattern fabric panel, 1945, 24in (61cm) high.
£100–120 GM

A Defiant radio, with cream grille and tuners, c1950, 15in (38cm) wide.
£10–30 OTA

Defiant was the Co-Op's own brand.

A Cossor cream and brown radio 1950s, 12in (30.5cm) wide.
£50–60 JUN

A Cossor Melody Master radio, model 523, with 4 wavelengths and 7 valves, in wood-effect cabinet, c1953, 20in (51cm) wide.
£50–60 DAC

A Cossor radio, with wood effect cabinet, 1950s, 20in (51cm) high.
£25–30 SAF

A black and white Solid State AM New Panda Radio, 1950s, 6in (15cm) high, in original green box.
£20–25 MED

A black Poodle Radio, with gold collar and lead, 1950s, 10in (25.5cm) wide.
£170–200 SpM

This fluffy poodle contains a working radio, and the dog's chain enables you to hang it from your wrist.

▶ A Perdio Piccadilly model PR721 red and grey, coat-pocket transistor radio, 1959, 6½in (17.5cm) wide.
£35–45 OVE

◀ A Japanese Olympic model 666 blue coat-pocket transistor radio, with delta-wing motif on tuning dial, 1959, 6½in (17.5cm) wide.
£65–75 OVE

▶ A Bush radio, cream and navy with red and chrome dial, 1960s, 13in (33cm) wide.
£40–45 PPH

An American General Electric model P831C shirt-pocket blue transistor radio, 1960, 4½in (12cm) high.
£45–55 OVE

A Toshiba Cat's Eye model 7TP–303 shirt-pocket ivory and chrome transistor radio, 1961, 4½in (12cm) high.
£60–75 OVE

An American Zenith Royal model 3000–1 Trans Oceanic multi-band radio, with fold-down front incorporating world maps, c1962, 10½in (27cm) high.
£120–140 PC

A Toshiba Concentric Ring model 8TP–90 shirt-pocket black transistor radio, 1962, 4½in (11.5cm) high.
£275–300 OVE

◄ A Leader clear-plastic bag radio, with carrying handle, 1970s, 7in (18cm) high.
£30–35 PLB

► A Japanese Aristo-Tone model AP–122 micro-sized pocket transistor radio, in original box with 'clamshell' case and instructions, 1962, 2in (5cm) square.
£40–45 OVE

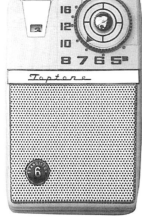

A Roberts model RM33 mains only transistor radio, finished in polished wood, c1975, 4½in (11cm) high.
£30–35 PC

A Golden Eagle Hi-Fi 6 shirt-pocket black transistor radio, made in Hong Kong, c1970, 4¼in (11cm) high.
£5–10 OVE

A Crompton Vidor battery plastic radio, 1980s, 5in (12.5cm) high.
£15–20 PLB

GRAMOPHONES

A German Symphonion, brass and steel movement, in simulated rosewood case with transfer design to lid, and a collection of 36 discs, late 19thC, 14in (35.5cm) wide.
£240–280 DDM

A German Puck phonograph, with tin horn and cast iron lyre base, c1900, 13in (33cm) wide.
£200–250 HHO

A Mikiphone pocket phonograph, with original needle tin and nickel-plated case, 1925, 5in (12.5cm) diam.
£300–350 HHO

An HMV model 130 Table Grand gramophone, in wooden case, c1930, 18in (45.5cm) wide.
£120–150 HHO

An Edison Gem phonograph, spun aluminium horn and 10 cylinders, dated May 31st 1891, 9¼in (23cm) wide, with oak carrying case.
£450–500 DDM

A phonograph reproduces sound by means of the vibration of a stylus or needle following a spiral groove on a revolving disc or cylinder. Although experimental prototypes appeared as early as the 1850s, general credit for the invention of the phonograph is given to US inventor, Thomas Edison, in 1877.

A Gramophone & Typewriter Co Triple Spring Monarch, with brass horn and oak base, c1905, base 13in (33cm) square.
£1,300–1,500 HHO

A Gramophone Company brass horn, in contemporary wicker carrying case, c1904, 29in (73.5cm) high.
£300–350 HHO

An Edison model D Standard phonograph, with original horn and ICS language teaching attachment, 1908, oak base 13in (33cm) wide.
£400–450 HHO

A Decca gramophone, in black carrying case, 1930s, 17in (43cm) wide.
£65–75 JUN

◄ A Bing Bebephone child's gramophone, on a wooden base, c1925, 12in (30.5cm) wide.
£200–220 HHO

Railwayana

A GER bridge number plate, with '808' in raised white numerals on black, restored, c1860–80, 9½in (24cm) wide.
£25–30 SOL

A Bassett-Lowke ¾ scale Burrell-type brass traction engine, with carrying case and instructions, c1910, 12in (30.5cm) long.
£650–700 BKS

◄ A Bing vertical single cylinder steam engine, with *faux* tile floor, c1900, 16in (40.5cm) wide.
£420–480 BKS

◄ A cast-iron railway ticket vending machine, navy and black, c1900, 85in (213cm) high, with later signs.
£850–1,000 JUN

A Polish State Railways steam locomotive cab-side plaque, with white Polish eagle on red ground, restored, post-1919, 9¾in (24.8cm) high.
£35–40 SOL

A German Doll & Cie single cylinder vertical steam engine, in brass and tin with black painted fire and cast stand with red trim, c1920, 14in (35.5cm) high.
£500–600 BKS

A Railway Centenary Shildon teapot stand, with portrait of Timothy Hackworth, Inventor of the Steam Blast Pipe, with yellow and red crests, 1925, 6in 15cm) diam.
£130–150 SRA

A Bowmanmodel E101 horizontal single cylinder steam engine, in brass with copper piping, on a black and green base, 1920s, 10in (25.5cm) wide, with original wooden box and instructions.
£240–280 BKS

A GWR wooden coach ventilator, with emergency instructions and restaurant car services, c1920, 20in (51cm) wide.
£125–150 RAR

A Southern Railway Co cast-iron Private Road sign, in white on green ground, 1923–47, 25in (63.5cm) wide.
£65–75 RAR

Miller's is a price GUIDE not a price LIST

A brown-painted metal railway hand lamp, marked 'LMS', c1925, 12in (30.5cm) high.
£60–70 JUN

A GWR booklet, *The Unrivalled Holiday Lands of the G.W.R.*, 1928, 8½in x 5½in (21.5cm x 14cm).
£4–5 HAX

An LNER locomotive pressure gauge, with wooden back and base and brass mount, 1920s, 9in (23cm) high.
£8–10 HAX

A Southern Railway Lord Nelson class nameplate, 'Lord Collingwood', in red, gold and blue, 1929, 61½in (156cm) wide.
£16,000–18,000 SRA

A German Doll & Cie cast based steam-driven horizontal engine, 1930s, 9in (23cm) wide.
£140–160 GAZE

A William Allchin of Northampton scale model traction engine, No. 3251 1930s, 18in (45.5cm) wide.
£1,600–1,800 BKS

A London Transport Underground red, white and blue enamel sign, 'High Barnet', c1935, 60in (152.5cm) wide.
£300–350 CAB

An LNER Hunt Class locomotive nameplate, 'The Albrighton', 1934, 32in (81.5cm) wide.
£13,500–15,000 SRA

► A BR(S) totem station sign, 'London Road (Guildford)', white on green, 1950s, 36in (91.5cm) wide.
£350–400 RAR

An LMS Jubilee Class locomotive nameplate, 'Vindictive', gold on a red ground, 1936, 34in (86.5cm) wide.
£8,500–9,500 SRA

A Bowman LMS live steam gauge 0 4-4-0 and tender, box revarnished, 1950s, 8in (20.5cm) wide.
£120–140 BKS

A Stuart Turner Babcock boiler, No. 501, with mill engine, 1950s, base 11in (28cm) wide.
£200–220 RAR

A BR(W) brown and cream enamel doorplate, 'Ladies', minor chips, 1950s, 18in (45.5cm) wide.
£90–100 SRA

A BR Standard Class 5 locomotive nameplate, 'Elaine', gold on red ground, 1955, 31in (78.5cm) wide.
£5,500–6,500 SRA

A blue glass overlay double scent bottle, with waisted centre and silver tops, c1890, 5⅞in (14.5cm) wide.
£130–150 MED

A Georgian red and white spiral-banded glass scent bottle, with original finger chain, 2in (5cm) high.
£250–300 LeB

A Murano glass red and black vertical banded scent bottle, with clear glass stopper, c1890, 5in (12.5cm) high.
£80–90 AnS

Two St Louis acid-etched cameo scent bottles, c1900, 6in (15cm) high.
£250–270 each GRI

A cranberry glass scent bottle, decorated with enamel and gilt, with faceted stopper, c1910, 6in (15cm) high.
£200–250 GRI

A Samson Mordan & Co blue glass scent bottle, the top modelled as an owl's head with yellow eyes, 1895, 3in (7.5cm) high.
£1,500–1,700 THOM

◄ A Bourjois blue mottled Bakelite novelty scent bottle, modelled as an owl, 1930s, 4in (10cm) high.
£110–130 LBe

A Vigny scent bottle, modelled as a golly, made in France for the US market, 1920s, 4in (10cm) high, in original box.
£300–350 LBe

Four Bakelite scent bottles, modelled as totem poles, 1930–35, 5in (12.5cm) high.
£170–190 each YAN

A Houbigant Chantilly scent bottle, with contents, on a chair, 1950s, 3¾in (9.5cm) high.
£80–100 LBe

A Victorian beaded pin cushion, with beaded fringe, 6in (15cm) diam.
£40–45 L&L

A Tartan ware pin wheel, c1860, 2in (5cm) diam.
£70–80 HUM

A needle book, decorated with a rose print, 1870, 3in (7.5cm) wide.
£35–40 VB

A red leather combination sewing box, 1884, 9in (23cm) long.
£65–75 DHA

A pair of Mauchline ware pin wheels, transfer-printed with 'Folkestone, looking West' and 'The Pier, Bognor', late 19thC, 1½in (4cm) diam.
£60–70 TMA

Three lengths of Russian artificial silk, c1900, in original box, 9in (23cm) wide.
£40–50 MRW

◄ A velvet pin cushion, made for a Jubilee exhibition, dated '1887', 4in (10cm) diam.
£50–60 HUM

A Gordes Vale silver pin cushion, modelled as a rabbit, Birmingham 1907, 2⅛in (6.5cm) long.
£750–825 THOM

A box of 36 reels of C. A. Rickards black button hole silk twist, 8½ x 5in (21.5 x 12.5cm), and a package of Brook's Prize Thread, both complete and unused, c1920s.
£7–12 each WAB

A Lady's Companion, including patterns for camisole and knickers and embroidery transfers, dated '26th January 1924', 12 x 9½in (30.5 x 24cm).
£10–12 RAD

Two Abacus Designs Coronation St Counted Cross Stitch Kits, designed by Christine Silvester, 1996, 8 x 7in (20.5 x 18cm).
£25–30 each KEN

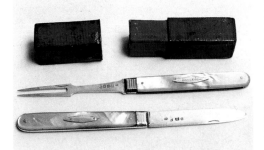

A silver travelling knife and fork set, with mother-of-pearl handles, engraved 'James Norton', 1822–29, 6in (15cm) long, with original box.
£125–165 JBU

An N. Mills silver gilt vinaigrette, in the shape of a pocket watch, Birmingham 1829, 1in (2.5cm) diam.
£670–720 THOM

A William Hutton & Son silver and enamel photo frame, London 1903, 8 x 5½in (20.5 x 14cm).
£2,300–2,650 THOM

A silver seal, with hollow handle and hinged lid, London 1875, 3in (7.5cm) high.
£230–260 HUM

A gilt case for half and full sovereigns, 1880, 2in (5cm) wide.
£100–120 BHA

An silver and enamel compact, hand-painted with roses and gilt, Birmingham 1912, 2in (5cm) diam.
£165–185 JACK

A Cohen & Charles silver cigar snips, modelled as a peg doll, some damage to face, London 1924, 3½in (9cm) high.
£550–625 JBU

◄ A Tiffany sterling silver pocket barometer, engraved 'H.W.B.',1900, 4½in (11.5cm) high.
£250–280 REG

A Grey & Co silver and tortoiseshell book mark, Birmingham 1906, 4½in (11.5cm) high.
£280–320 THOM

A set of silver and enamel coffee bean spoons, retailed by T. & J. Perry, Birmingham 1936, in original case, 6 x 5in (15 x 13cm).
£200–225 JACK

A pair of Linda Spotlignt nylon stockings, in original packet, 1960s, 9½ x 7in (24 x18cm).
£6–7 RAD

A Rowntrees chocolate bar shop display, 1960, 19 x 10in (48.5 x 25.5cm).
£35–45 YR

◄ A fibreglass prototype umbrella/stick stand, designed by Emma Schweinberger-Gismondi, normally made in plastic, 1966, 14in (35.5cm) high.
£160–180 MARK

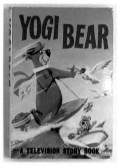

Yogi Bear Annual, 1962, 12 x 9in (30.5 x 23cm).
£5–7 YR

A red plastic bean bag, 1960s, 28in (71cm) high.
£250–300 ZOOM

The Dalek Book, 1964, 10 x 8in (25.5 x 20.5cm).
£20–25 YR

A disco mirror ball, 1960s, 12in (30.5cm) diam.
£180–200 ZOOM

◀ Tom Smith's Indoor Fireworks, the box in the form of a London bus, 1960s–70s, 7in (18cm) long.
£20–25 GAZE

A pair of silver leather platform sandals, 1970s.
£30–35 HarC

A Bay City Rollers shop display box of 48 packs of bubble gum, with picture cards, 1974, 8in (20.5cm) wide.
£100–125 YR

A Biba poster advertising cosmetics, 1970s, 34 x 20in (86.5 x 51cm).
£75–85 PLB

A pair of flared trousers, with floral pattern, 1970s.
£20–30 HarC

A brass vesta, in the form of a clenched fist, late 19thC, 2½in (6.5cm) long.
£60–80 GH

A Samson Mordan silver vesta, with enamelled scene of a carriage with horses, c1895, 2½in (6.5cm) wide.
£2,000–2,250 THOM

A white metal vesta, engraved and inset with Scottish granites, late 19thC, 1½in (4cm) high.
£100–125 GH

A John Player 'Country Life' Smoking Mixture tin, c1920, 3¼in (8.5cm) wide.
£30–35 WAB

A lady's silver and enamelled vesta case and cigarette case, Birmingham 1933, 6 x 5in (15 x 12.5cm).
£150–175 JACK

A green Bakelite cigarette holder, in original case, 1930s, 3in (7.5cm) wide.
£35–40 HarC

A wooden novelty cigarette box, with duck cigarette holder, 1930s, 7in (18cm) wide.
£15–20 HarC

A plastic and chrome pedestal ashtray, 1960s, 22in (56cm) high.
£50–60 ZOOM

◀ A box of 'Dandy' Special Virginia cigarettes, each cigarette personalized with name and address, 1930s, box 3½in (9cm) wide.
£20–25 LBe

◀ A Murano glass ashtray, 1950–60s, 6in (15cm) diam.
£80–100 ZOOM

A J. Bains Bradford 'Colne' shield-shaped trade card, slight damage, 1897, 3in (7.5cm) high.
£45–55 KNI

A New Table Game of Midget Golf For the Drawing Room, c1910, 13½in (34.5cm) wide.
£60–70 ARo

A Lenci ceramic golfing figure, 1932, 8in (20.5cm) high.
£350–380 HarC

A German porcelain figure, after Kinsella 'Cockney' Boy Cricketer, inscribed 'The Hope of his Side', early 1900s, 5in (12.5cm) high.
£180–200 KNI

A ceramic tobacco jar, in the form of a golfer, 1925, 7½in (19cm) high.
£270–300 HUX

A South African One Day International baseball-style cap, by Albion C & D of Australia, with embroidered crest of the Protea flower of South Africa, 1997–98.
£60–70 KNI

A J. Jaques & Son Ping Pong or Gossima game, c1910, 18in (45.5cm) wide.
£100–120 ARo

A Limoges parasol head, in the shape of a golf club, decorated with a seated lady, c1910, 2½in (6.5cm) wide.
£100–125 WaR

A tin of Dunlop Fort Tennis Balls, c1930, 8½in (21.5cm) high.
£8–10 AL

A Topps Gum card, depicting Bobby Orr, 1966–67.
£850–950 HALL

A Steiff golden mohair teddy bear, with orange glass eyes and black stitched nose, mouth and paws, fully jointed, with large hump, filled with straw, button on left ear, repaired, c1920, 20in (51cm) high.
£1,400–1,600 Bon(C)

A teddy bear, with velvet pads, possibly French, 1920s, 18in (45.5cm) high.
£120–140 BGC

A mohair teddy bear, with Rexine paws and plastic eyes, wearing a contemporary shirt, mid-1950s, 15in (38cm) high.
£40–50 TED

A Merrythought beach donkey, late 1960s, 15½in (39.5cm) high.
£20–25 UNI

◀ A Steiff golden plush Waldi, 1950s, 21in (53.5cm) long.
£130–150 GrD

▶ An American Muppet Show character, Miss Piggy, with cloth body, plastic head and realistic hair, 1981, 13½in (34.5cm) high.
£18–25 UNI

Religion

Churches have always been major centres of craftsmanship in every medium from wood to textiles, metalware and glass. The Victorian period saw the creation of many new churches and the refurbishment of existing religious buildings, predominantly in the Gothic taste, inspired by the medieval past and regarded as the most fitting style for devotional architecture and furnishings. In the present day, with the development both of secularisation and a multi-cultural Britain embracing a host of different faiths, many church buildings, particularly in urban areas, have been deconsecrated, and the religious fixtures and fittings that were once a part of people's daily lives, both in church and at home, are now turning up in antique shops.

According to Durham House Antiques, in Stow-on-the-Wold, what attracts collectors to such items is not only their religious and historical significance, but the standard of material and craftsmanship at prices that are often very affordable. 'You can find some truly beautiful artefacts, and they might be three or four times cheaper than secular objects of the same period and quality,' agrees Bath dealer David Payne. One of Payne's specialities is 19th-century bibles, many purchased from eastern European countries. 'People like them because they are decorative,' he explains. 'A typical example is an American lady who was getting married and bought an ivory covered bible to carry down the aisle. It was in Czech, and she couldn't read it, but she wanted it as an accessory!' His clients include foreign dealers, interior decorators, and private collectors often with a taste for the dramatic. Whatever one's faith, religious objects can provide a fascinating area of collecting.

A silver devotional pendant, with the Virgin and Child, a crucifixion scene on the reverse, in red, green, blue and white watercolour on velum, possibly southern German, c1700, 3in (7.5cm) high.
£270–300 JSM

A Flemish brass ciborium or communion wafer container, 18thC, 13in (33cm) high.
£190–210 DHA

A Flemish oak tabernacle door, early 18thC, 11in (28cm) high.
£120–140 DHA

A parcel-gilt cross, moulded with religious scenes, in original blue-lined box, 1870, 6in (15cm) high.
£400–450 JSM

◀ A Belgian silver miniature holy water font, by Berthold Müller, c1840, 8in (20.5cm) high.
£350–400 EXC

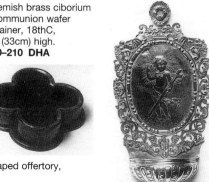

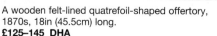

A wooden felt-lined quatrefoil-shaped offertory, 1870s, 18in (45.5cm) long.
£125–145 DHA

A parcel-gilt Normandy cross, with fish clasp, 19thC, 3in (7.5cm) high.
£120–140 JSM

A Bavarian carved black wood crucifix, with white and gilt ceramic figure of Christ, 1890, 18in (45.5cm) high.
£40–45 DP

A European church brass and red velvet collection box, with chain mail interior, c1900, 8in (20.5cm) high.
£50–55 DP

► A pair of brass church candlesticks, c1900, 13in (33cm) wide.
£260–300 RUL

A scarlet velvet gold braid-trimmed ecclesiastical hat, with leather and silk lining, c1900, 8in (20.5cm) diam.
£18–22 DP

A gilt-bronze figure of St Anthony, c1900, 4in (10cm) high.
£50–60 DP

A Mosanic Winchester Cathedral model, 1900–14, 5¾in (14.5cm) long.
£55–65 G&CC

A Czechoslovakian Meerschaum religious figure, in fitted red-lined case, c1910, 8in (20.5cm) high.
£30–35 DP

A spelter crucifix, c1910, 11in (28cm) high.
£20–25 DP

A shell-covered miniature shrine, with a porcelain figure of Virgin Mary in white, blue and gold, c1910, 8in (20.5cm) high.
£20–25 DP

A Czechoslovakian silver specimen stone-inlaid cross, c1910, 5in (12.5cm) high.
£20–25 DP

A Grafton St. Paul's Cathedral model, 1910–30, 5¾in (14.5cm) high.
£35–40 G&CC

A silver-plated religious souvenir from Lourdes, marked, c1920, 4in (10cm) high.
£15–18 DP

A silver-plated religious souvenir from Prague, 1920–30, 3in (7.5cm) high.
£12–15 DP

Two Czechoslovakian carved bone religious souvenirs, with painted inserts, c1920, 4½in (11.5cm) high.
£12–16 each DP

Two metal book-shaped boxes, containing miniature rosaries, with coloured religious pictures on the covers, c1920, 1½in (4cm) high.
£15–18 each DP

Two Osborne plaques, 'The Good Shepherd' and 'The Light of the World', in greens, blues, reds and gold, c1940, 10½in (26.5cm) high.
£45–55 each JMC

A Poole charger, commemorating the 800th anniversary of the martyrdom of St. Thomas à Becket, blue, green and white on a red ground, limited edition of 25, 1970, 16in (40.5cm) diam.
£1,000–1,200 HarC

BIBLES & RELIGIOUS BOOKS

An eastern European leather-bound bible, with gilt-brass mounts, bone cross and roundels, 1840, 6 x 4in (15 x 10cm) high.
£25–30 DP

◄ *Christian Year Thoughts & Verse*, by James Parker & Co, with black tooled cover and brass clasp, 1827, 6¾ x 5in (17 x 12.5cm).
£10–12 DHA

Common Prayer, leather-bound with brass clasp, 1862, 6 x 4in (15 x 10cm).
£35–40 DHA

An eastern European bible, the embossed celluloid cover with angels over Prague, engraved brass clasp, 1880, 5 x 3in (12.5 x 7.5cm).
£30–35 DP

An eastern European bible, with embossed leather cover, brass edges and ivory cross, 1880, 5 x 3in (12.5 x 7.5cm).
£25–30 DP

An eastern European bible, the white celluloid cover with brass edges and gothic brass cross, 1887, 4 x 3in (10 x 7.5cm).
£18–22 DP

An eastern European bible, the mother-of-pearl cover with engraved brass edging, 1890, 4 x 3in (10 x 7.5cm).
£28–32 DP

An eastern European bible, with leather cover and gilt-brass clasp and panel with ivory centre-piece, c1890, 6 x 4in (15 x 7.5cm).
£30–35 DP

A brass-bound bible, with leather and gilt scrollwork cover and etched brass fittings, 1890, 10 x 13in (25.5 x 33cm).
£140–160 DHA

An eastern European bible, with ivorine cover with gilt-metal mounts and mother-of-pearl inlay, 1897, 5 x 3in (12.5 x 7.5cm).
£35–40 DP

An eastern European bible, the black celluloid cover painted with flowers, brass clasp, 1920, 4 x 3in (10 x 7.5cm).
£15–20 DP

◀ An eastern European bible, the white celluloid cover with green and gilt decoration, gilt and mother-of-pearl clasp, 1936, 5 x 3in (12.5 x 7.5cm).
£20–25 DP

Church Services Hymns & Appendix, published by Eyre & Spottiswoode, leather-bound and with enamel and brass decoration, brass clasp, 1900, 5½ x 3½in (14 x 9cm).
£45–55 DHA

Rock & Pop

This section includes rock and pop memorabilia, instruments, videos, records and, for the first time in this guide, picture discs. The picture disc was a predominantly a 1980s phenomenon, one of vinyl's final decorative flourishes before the CD took over in the market place. Its main selling factor was visual appeal rather than listening quality, since the standard of the pressing was not as high as that of normal records. Although serious collectors will always go for the best example of any item, condition is not as important with these decorative records as in other areas of vinyl, where the slightest scratch will affect the price, and the ideal state for a collectable record is mint and unplayed.

Values of picture discs depend largely on image and artist, and examples that were issued as small-scale promotional items, ie not for general sale, or that were withdrawn from sale following some problem or complaint, are likely to be rarer and as such worth more than other more easily available items. Although the heyday of the picture disc was the extravagant, 'New Romantic' '80s, they are still produced to a limited extent today, and an independent label might issue a 7in vinyl picture disc as a publicity item for an act.

A 7in picture disc, The Associates, *Breakfast*, 1984.
£5–10 MVX

A compilation album, *The Best of The Beach Boys*, EMI Records special disc jockey producer copy, 1966.
£450–500 MVX

A 12in album picture disc, Marc Bolan and T. Rex, *Across The Airwaves*, 1982.
£10–15 MVX

A withdrawn promotional single CD, The Doors *Peace Frog*, produced by Elektra Records, 1997.
£75–100 MVX

◄ A Fender Stratocaster guitar, Eric Clapton 'Signature' model, in Torino red, signed and dated '90' in black marker on the body, with tremolo and Fender tweed case, with statements of provenance, c1990.
£5,000–5,500 S

This was used by Eric Clapton during the 'Journeyman' tour and donated to the Philadelphia Music Foundation for inclusion in a charity auction.

> Items in the Rock & Pop section have been arranged in alphabetical order by artist.

An American promotional album, Duran Duran, *Duran Goes Dutch Live in Rotterdam, May 1987*, produced by Capital Records.
£65–75 MVX

A Bob Dylan autograph, in blue ballpoint on a clipped album page, with inscription and signing as Bob Zimmerman, together with a photocopied page from his senior yearbook, Hibbing High School, Minnesota, c1958.
£500–600 S

An autograph by Debbie Harry on a Hot 100 Billboard Chart for the week ending April 19 1980, with Blondie's *Call Me* at No. 1, 14 x 10½in (35.5 x 26.5cm).
£130–150 FRa

A 7in single, King Crimson, *Epitaph 21st Century Schizoid Man*, produced by Island Records, 1976.
£25–35 MVX

▶ A 7in promotional only single, Kraftwerk *Pocket Calculator*, in dayglo yellow vinyl, produced by Warner Brothers Records, 1981.
£15–20 MVX

A 12in picture disc, Frankie Goes To Hollywood, produced by ZTT Records, c1984.
£5–10 MVX

Twenty-one colour slides of the Jimi Hendrix Experience at the Saville Theatre, Shaftesbury Avenue, London, good close-ups and stage shots taken during rehearsals, sold with copyright, 1967.
£11,000–12,000 S

These were taken by a university entertainments officer who regularly booked groups through NEMS and was permitted to attend rehearsals.

A wedding dress worn by Geri Halliwell for the Comic Relief video of *Who Do You Think You Are?*, with pearl-embroidered lace bodice and tulle skirt, altered to fit Geri, with letter of provenance, 1997.
£1,200–1,400 S

The owner of the dress worked as agent to the stylist on the video and lent it to Geri for the shoot.

A black Höhner Rockwood electric guitar, signed on the white scratch-plate 'Mark Knopfler', 1990s.
£450–500 Bon

A Welsh only album, Dafydd Iwan *Yma Mae 'Nghan*, includes Dave Edmunds, John Williams etc, produced by Sian Records, 1972.
£180–200 MVX

A shaped single picture disc, Madonna, *Angel*, with plinth, produced by Sire Records, 1985.
£35–40 MVX

A 7in picture disc, Nirvana and the Jesus Lizard, *Oh, The Guilt*, produced by Touch and Go Records, 1993.
£130–150 MVX

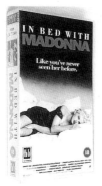

◄ A VHS music video, *In Bed With Madonna*, produced by Cinema Club Videos, 1995 Second Edition.
£20–25 MVX

An unreleased CD single, Nirvana, *Pennyroyal Tea*, produced by Geffen Records, 1994.
£650–750 MVX

A Pink Floyd concert poster advertising a barn dance, organized by Gwent Constabulary, printed in blue on pink paper, 1967, 19¾ x 14½in (50 x 37cm).
£700–800 S

A box of 32 cassettes, *Nurse with Wound* etc, with hand-painted brass plaque, produced by United Dairies Records, 1979–87.
£1,000–1,200 MVX

► An MGM publicity card, signed 'Elvis Presley' in blue ballpoint pen, mounted, framed and glazed, c1963, 13 x 10in (33 x 25.5cm).
£500–550 Bon

A Japanese Roy Orbison Gibson-style semi-acoustic guitar, in cherry sunburst finish with mother-of-pearl scratchplate, in shaped case, with statement of provenance, 1970s.
£3,500–3,750 S

An MGM publicity card, signed 'Elvis Presley' in blue ballpoint pen, framed, c1957, 13 x 10in (33 x 25.5cm).
£700–800 Bon

A shaped single disc, Orchestral Manoeuvres in the Dark *Locomotion*, produced by Virgin Records, 1984.
£5–10 MVX

A 7in extended play single disc, Elvis Presley, *Love Me Tender*, produced by HMV Records, 1957.
£50–75 MVX

A British promotional sampler CD, Elvis Presley, *Elvis Off-Camera*, produced by BMG Records, 1997.
£200–250 MVX

Prince's silk shirt, together with a colour picture showing him wearing it, c1980s.
£2,500–2,750 FRa

◀ A Cloud guitar, played by Prince, with blue metallic finish and gold-coloured hardware, frets with male/female symbol, in card box, 1993.
£2,500–2,750 S

A VHS video, Queen, *The Miracle EP*, produced by PMI Videos, 1989.
£20–25 MVX

Mirabelle magazine, featuring and autographed by Cliff Richard, 1960s, 11 x 8in (28 x 20.5cm).
£30–40 BTC

▶ A *Record Mirror* article, autographed by The Rolling Stones, in blue ballpoint pen, Brian Jones signing twice, some damage, February 29th 1964.
£575–625 S

A gilt-metal pendant, with a picture of Cliff Richard, 1950s, 1½in (4cm) diam.
£10–12 HUX

▶ A Rolling Stones presentation award with plaque inscribed 'Gold Record *Black & Blue* for sales of 25,000 units in the Netherlands', mounted, framed and glazed, 1976, 18 x 17in (45.5 x 43cm).
£500–600 Bon

A Rolling Stones *Original Steel Wheels* CD, in limited edition steel case, produced by Columbia Records, 1989.
£80–100 MVX

BEATLES & POP

MEMORABILIA WANTED!
WE PAY A FORTUNE FOR
THE RIGHT MATERIAL!

For further details contact
**TRACKS, PO Box 117
Chorley, Lancashire, PR7 2QZ**

TEL: 01257 269726

**FAX: 01257 231340
e-mail: sales@tracks.co.uk**

A 7in promotional single disc, The Scaffold, *Lily The Pink*, with demo copy picture sleeve, produced by Parlophone Records, 1968.
£80–100 MVX

A platinum sales award for the CD, *Dusty – The Silver Collection*, presented for sales of more than 300,000 copies in the UK, BPI certified, 1997.
£1,400–1,600 S

A 9ct gold and black *Top of the Pops* medallion, worn by Dave Lee Travis, made by The Jewellery Shop, London, 1970s.
£40–50 BND

A 10in mono album, 'Hank Williams Memorial Album', by MGM, 1955.
£65–80 MVX

A Sex Pistols *Suicide* T-shirt, signed in pink and black felt pens, together with a colour copy picture of the group's visit to the shop Suecide, Stockholm, framed and glazed, 18th July 1977, 16in (40.5cm) square.
£650–750 S

An LP, The Strawbs, *Strawberry Music Sampler No. 1*, from a limited edition of 100, produced by Strawberry Music Publishing, 1968.
£1,000–1,200 MVX

A promotional compilation CD, *U2, October 1991*, produced by Island Records.
£130–150 MVX

A promotional CD album, Paul Weller, *Kings Road*, produced by Island Records, 1997.
£80–100 MVX

◀ A 10in mono album, 'Hank Williams Memorial Album', by MGM, 1955.
£65–80 MVX

A 12in single disc, The Smiths, *Ask*, signed on the reverse of the sleeve in red by all 5 original members of the band, 1980s.
£170–200 FRa

A VHS music video, Throbbing Gristle, recording *Heathen Earth* live at Oundle School, produced by Doublevision Videos, 1983.
£20–25 MVX

A promotional LP picture disc, Wings, *Back to the Egg*, limited edition of 150, produced by EMI Records, 1979.
£1,300–1,500 MVX

THE BEATLES

The Beatles occupy number one position in the collectors' charts, and recently few items have created more interest than John Lennon's Gallotone acoustic guitar, which opens our section devoted to Beatles memorabilia. The photograph accompanying this very ordinary instrument shows Lennon playing the guitar with his band, the Quarry Men, at a church fête in Woolton on the 6th July 1957, the day of his historic first meeting with Paul McCartney. According to former band member, Rod David, Lennon had recently bought this guitar by mail-order for around £10. Sold by

Sotheby's over 40 years later, at the Hard Rock Cafe in London, part of a chain of restaurants famous for their collection of rock memorabilia, this guitar made a remarkable hammer price of £140,000.

While good quality items associated with other major artists can fetch high prices, the Beatles are consistently the best and most reliable sellers in the rock and pop market. Demand encompasses everything from unique pieces, such as this early Lennon guitar, to the cheap and cheerful ephemera mass-produced for the fans in the 1960s, when Beatlemania was at its height.

A Dutch acoustic guitar, John Lennon's Gallotone 'Champion', in cherry sunburst, lined finish with original 'Guaranteed Not To Split' label inside body, neck with 3 dot markers, headstock with logo and later brass plaque engraved 'Remember You'll Never Earn Your Living By It', restored, late 1950s; together with a letter from Aunt Mimi, undated but probably early 1980s, a guitar tutor *Play the Guitar*, *Radio Luxembourg Magazine*, a photograph of Lonnie Donegan, October 1956, and a series of clippings of John.
£140,000–180,000 S

A newspaper cutting signed by Paul McCartney, c1962, 4in (10cm) square.
£100–125 BTC

A Washington Pottery Beatles mug, 1964, 5in (12.5cm) high.
£35–40 BTC

THE BEATLES

A Beatles Fan Club black and white publicity photograph, signed in blue ballpoint pen 'To Dianne Love From George Harrison, John Lennon, Paul McCartney, Ringo Starr', c1963–64, 4½ x 5½in (11.5 x 14cm).
£2,000–2,200 Bon

A poster for The Beatles at the Music Hall, Shrewsbury, December 14th 1962, printed in red and black on yellow, some damage, 30 x 20in (76 x 51cm).
£3,700–4,000 S

A Paul McCartney Bendy Doll, with red coat and blue trousers, 1964, 9in (23cm) high.
£50–60 BTC

An American Beatles Pin-Up Screamers poster, in sealed packet, 1964, 11¾ x 9in (30 x 23cm).
£80–100 TBoy

A Beatles Fan Club cloth patch, with order form, 1960s, 4 x 2½in (10 x 6.5cm).
£15–20 BTC

A Beatles plastic flasher brooch, 1964, 3in (7.5cm) square.
£20–25 BTC

Cross Reference
See Colour Review

▶ A Beatles black and white cushion, 1960s, 9in (23cm) square.
£20–25 BTC

A collection of Beatles Fan membership cards, 1960s, 4in (10cm) square.
£5–10 each BTC

A mono LP album, The Beatles *Please Please Me*, 1963.
£200–250 MTM

This was the Beatles' first LP and the only one to be produced on the black and gold Parlophone label, which was superseded in summer 1963 by the yellow and black Parlophone label. This album was also produced in stereo, far rarer than this mono version, and today worth £1,200 upwards depending on condition.

▶ A Beatles *Hard Day's Night* film poster, for Hammersmith Odeon Sunday Aug 2nd, 1964, 30 x 40in (76 x 101.5cm).
£800–900 S

A pair of Beatles Carefree textured seamfree nylon stockings, with faces and guitars patterned into nylon, top garter with 'The Beatles' and head and signature of each, in original black, red and yellow packaging. 1960s, 9¼ x 7in (23.5 x 18cm).
£80–100 MTM

▶ An American complete ticket for The Beatles *Help!* premiere, on Wednesday Sept 1st, 1965, 4 x 9in (10 x 23cm).
£80–100 BTC

A roll of wallpaper, with pictures of The Beatles in repeating 21in (53.5cm) pattern, in blue, orange and black, made in Canada and UK, 1960s, 21in (53.5cm) wide.
£150–175 MTM

A set of 4 Beatles *Yellow Submarine* cardboard coat hangers, with plastic hooks, made by Henderson-Haggard, 1960s, 17in (44cm).
£475–525 S

A black Rickenbacker 330 guitar, autographed by George Harrison, with 'George' in black marker on the white scratchplate, in rigid case, with statement of provenance, 1990s.
£2,400–2,800 S

A mono LP album, The Beatles, *Yesterday and Today*, 1966.
£700–800 MTM

The Americans were so upset by the record sleeve with dolls that they withdrew it and replaced it with new 'paste over' artwork to cover the original.

A set of 4 Royal Doulton character jugs depicting the Beatles, in red, blue, yellow, green and orange, modelled by Stanley James Taylor, 1984, 5½in (14cm) high.
£650–750 MTM

JUKEBOXES

The Golden Age of the jukebox was the 1940s when it became the centrepiece of every American teenage hangout. The best known name in the field was Wurlitzer who produced their first jukebox in 1933. The model 1015 (pronounced Ten-Fifteen), illustrated below, was designed ten years later and once war was over the company retailed 56,000 of these 1015 jukeboxes, the largest production run of all time.

Whereas pre-war jukeboxes consisted predominantly of wood, the 1940s saw the introduction of bright plastics. The bubble light tubes framing the 1015 jukebox were designed by Paul Fuller and featured on many 1940s models. Other manufacturers include Rock-Ola, AMI and Seeberg. Up until the late 1940s jukeboxes played 78rpm records, but in the 1950s and '60s these were replaced by 45s, and jukeboxes became squarer and less opulent in design. With certain exceptions older jukeboxes tend to be worth more than the later models. Surface condition affects price ranges. On many models, the internal mechanism is likely to have been restored or replaced but if an old machine has been converted to play 45s rather than 78s it will be devalued. Modern reproductions of vintage classics such as the 1015 have been produced, and these will take 45s and even CDs.

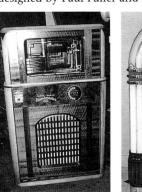

A Wurlitzer P10 Bandmaster, 1934.
£4,500–5,000 HALB

A Wurlitzer 1015, 1946, 60in (152.5cm) high.
£10,000–12,000 CJB

A Rock-Ola 1422, brown with red, yellow and white panels, 1948, 55in (139.5cm) high.
£4,500–5,000 HALB

A Rock-Ola 1455, with 200 selections, 1955, 57in (145cm) high.
£8,000–9,000 JU

A Seeburg V200, with 200 selections, 1955, 58in (147.5cm) high.
£9,000–10,000 JU

An AMI Model H, with 200 selections, nicknamed the Bumper, 1957.
£5,000–5,500 CJB

An AMI Continental 200, with 100 selections, 1962, 64in (162.5cm) high.
£6,500–7,500 JU

An AMI Continental 200, with 200 selections, 1961, 56in (142cm) high.
£7,500–8,500 JU

Scent Bottles

The past few years have seen growing interest in collecting scent bottles, and the flourishing of collectors' clubs, specialist dealers and dedicated auctions. Up until the turn of the 19th century, ladies and gentlemen would decant scents, oils and flower waters, bought from their perfumer or home-mixed, into their personal bottles. These came in every size, from large dressing table flacons, to small portable flasks, carried in a reticule or suspended from finger rings and chains.

The 20th century saw the development of the commercial industry as we know it today, with branded perfumes sold in specifically designed bottles and packaging. Chanel No. 5, created in 1921, was the first scent to bear a designer's name and, from the 1920s onward, the great fashion houses competed in the fragrance market with long-established specialist perfumeries such as Guerlain.

Both commercial and non-commercial bottles have their collectors and, with each, condition is crucial to value – check bottles for chips or damaged surfaces and ensure that stoppers are original. With commercial perfume bottles values are enhanced by the presence of the packaging and the original perfume.

A French perfume *étui*, with gold topped crystal bottles, in original Shagreen case lined with red velvet, 1770, 2¼in (5.5cm) high.
£550–650 CHAP

> **Cross Reference**
> See Colour Review

An earthenware scent bottle, carved as an acorn, with a silver top, c1850, 2in (5cm) high.
£300–350 LeB

A French silver and blue enamel scent bottle, decorated with figure of a child in pink, green and white, slight restoration, c1880, 2½in (6.5cm) high.
£1,200–1,400 THOM

◀ A cut-glass scent bottle, by T. Stockwell, with silver dog's-head lid, 1884, 4in (10cm) high.
£2,200–2,600 THOM

A silver-gilt and cut-glass scent bottle, in the form of a cross, c1880, 4½in (11.5cm) high.
£1,600–1,800 THOM

A green glass flute-cut double perfume bottle, with moulded silver tops, c1890, 4in (10cm) long.
£80–90 MED

A cut-glass scent bottle, by J. Gloster & Sons, Birmingham, the silver cover decorated with flutes, reeds and foliage, 1891, 6¼in (16.5cm) high.
£230–260 Bea(E)

A cranberry glass scent bottle, decorated with enamelled lacework, with glass stopper and gilt hinged lid, chain and finger ring, 1880–1900, 2¾in (7cm) high.
£70–85 MED

A hobnail cut-glass ovoid scent bottle, by Mappin Bros, with hinged heavily figured silver top inscribed 'Katherine 1900', hallmarked London 1899, 4in (10cm) high.
£90–100 MED

A blown-glass novelty scent bottle, in the form of a bird, with gilt beak, tail tip and feet, 1890s, 3in (7.5cm) high.
£40–45 LeB

An Italian Tabacco D'Harar scent bottle, with cameo moulded stopper, 1930s, 4in (10cm) high.
£120–150 LeB

A Potter & Moore Bonzo scent bottle, with red stopper and tongue, black nose and whiskers and yellow ribbon, 1930s, 3in (7.5cm) high.
£80–90 LeB

A Devon Violet black plastic scent bottle, in the form of a poodle, 1950s, 3¼in (8.5cm) high.
£40–45 LBe

▶ A Capucci Parce Que! eau de toilette display scent bottle, with black plastic top, c1980, 8¾in (22cm) high.
£20–25 BTB

A Givenchy Gentleman display scent bottle, c1980, 13½in (34.5cm) high.
£40–50 BTB

▶ An Yves Saint Laurent Champagne display scent bottle, with moulded gilt rim, c1980, 5in (12.5cm) high.
£25–30 BTB

Science & Technology

A Bleulur drawing set, in original sharkskin case, 1810, 5¾in (14.5cm) high.
£250–280 DHo

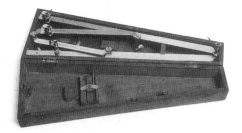

A Schmalcalder lacquered brass pantograph, in original fitted mahogany box, c1810, 15in (38cm) wide.
£350–400 TOM

A pantograph is an instrument for the mechanical copying of a plan on an enlarged, reduced or identical scale.

A thermometer, on a tortoiseshell obelisk-shaped stand, 1840, 9in (23cm) high.
£475–525 CHAP

◄ An engraved brass station pointer, by Thomas Jones, London, 1830, 27in (68.5cm) long, with box.
£400–450 DHo

An early brass mining dial, for surveying mines, replaced stand, 1820–30, 10in (25.5cm) high.
£250–300 DHo

A set of brass apothecary scales, with weights, 1830, 17in (43cm) high, in an inlaid mahogany box.
£200–235 DHo

◄ A mahogany medicine chest, the front opening to reveal a fitted interior with square clear glass bottles, 2 long and 4 small drawers with turned ivory handles, 19thC, 9in (23cm) wide.
£550–600 AH

A brass protractor, by Stanley, late 19thC, 8in (20.5cm) diam.
£120–150 ET

A Lownes patent anemometer, by Stanley, London, c1890, 7in (18cm) high, in original green felt-lined mahogany case.
£200–300 TOM

An anemometer is an instrument for measuring the force of the wind.

A Belgian brass level, 1900, 16in (40.5cm) wide, in a wooden box.
£370–400 DHo

A brass meridian instrument, on a folding tripod, 12¼in (32cm) high, in original mahogany box, inscribed on lid 'J. England, 1910'.
£350–400 DHo

A Dr Pachon's oscillometer, or blood pressure gauge, in original red-lined case, 1920s, 7in (18cm) wide.
£75–85 PC

A brass sextant, by Stanley London, 1911, 3¼in (8.5cm) diam.
£150–175 WO

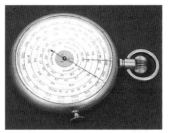

A pocket watch calculator, by Scientific Publishing Co, Manchester, 1920s, 3in (7.5cm) diam.
£30–50 TOM

▶ A grey plastic and Perspex thermograph, by Jules Richard, Paris, with cast aluminium base, c1955, 17in (43cm) wide.
£120–150 RTW

A Fuller calculator and circular slide-rule, by Stanley, London in original box with stand and instructions, 1930, box 18in (45.5cm) wide.
£130–150 TOM

A cream-painted metal dentist's stand, with mouthwash attachments, cut glass bowl and chrome fitments, 1920s, 49in (124.5cm) high.
£350–400 SPa

COMPASSES

An enamel-faced silver pocket compass, 1800, 2in (5cm) diam.
£350–400 TOM

A silver-plated sovereign case with compass, c1880, 1½in (4cm) diam.
£50–60 AOH

A painted metal compass, with cream face, c1920, 1½in (4cm) diam.
£20–25 AOH

A compass, by Benj. Dawson Wensley, in wooden case, 18thC, 6 x 4½in (15 x 11.5cm).
£250–280 DHo

A brass pocket sun dial and compass, by Watkins in original sharkskin case, 1880, 4in (10cm) diam.
£1,000–1,100 DHo

◄ A German brass compass, with a black face and side lock, c1920, 2in (5cm) diam.
£20–25 AOH

A spirit-filled compass, by Georg Hechelmann, 1940–70, 12in (30.5cm) diam.
£120–140 NC

ELECTRIC FANS

A Revo pizza-style stationary fan, with brass blades, guard and arms, on a black stand, 1912–18, 12in (30.5cm) high.
£100–120 MRO

A GEC four-blade fan, with cream-painted metal blades, on a black stand, 1930s, 17in (43cm) high.
£80–100 JUN

A chrome Limit electric fan, on a black base, c1940, 12in (30.5cm) high.
£90–100 HHa

► A Rallifan chrome and plastic extending fan, 1960s, 60in (152.5cm) high.
£120–150 ZOOM

MICROSCOPES

The microscope is an instrument for producing enlarged images of objects that are too small to be seen by the naked eye. One-lens microscopes were developed as early as the mid-15th century. By the 18th century affordable and portable screw barrel microscopes were being produced, using a screw thread to focus the lens. The turn of the 16th century saw the invention in the Netherlands of the compound microscope, in which two or more lenses are used to create an enlarged picture of the object.

Early lenses suffered from chromatic aberrations, so that objects viewed were surrounded by fringes of colour. As glass technology advanced, the principles applied to telescopes were used for microscopes, resulting in the development of the achromatic microscope lens, which freed images from colour distortion. English microscopist Joseph Lister (1786–1869) pioneered the application of achromatic, high-powered microscope lenses, and in the second half of the 19th century German physicist Ernst Abbe (1840–1905) made a range of contributions to microscope theory and design, introducing distortion-free lenses that unleashed the full viewing power of the instrument.

A lacquered brass improved compound microscope, by Carpenter, with all original accessories and hand-written list of objects, c1820, in original fitted mahogany case, 16in (40.6cm) wide.
£2,000–2,200 TOM

A brass microscope, by Gilbert, 1820, 16½in (42cm) high, in original fitted case.
£2,000–2,250 DHo

A Martin-type lacquered-brass microscope, with 6 numbered lenses and various ivory slides, c1820, 11in (28cm) wide, in original fitted mahogany case.
£250–300 TOM

A brass microscope, by Andrew Pritchard, 1835, 26in (66cm) high, in original wooden case.
£2,400–2,700 DHo

A microscope, by C. Reichert, No. 29025, with accessories, c1900, 14in (35.5cm) high, in original mahogany box.
£230–260 DHo

A brass microscope, by Baker, with black steel and Bakelite base, 1920s, 13½in (34.5cm) high, in original fitted box.
£100–125 DHo

OPTICAL EQUIPMENT

A pair of John Holmes blue tinted glass reading/sun spectacles, in silver frames, with tortoiseshell and silver case, 1825, 5½in (14cm) wide.
£1,000–1,150 CHAP

A pair of Chinese spectacles, with quartz lenses, c1860, 5½in (14cm) wide.
£120–150 HUM

A Victorian tortoiseshell and silver lorgnette, inlaid with a silver flower, 6in (15cm) wide.
£255–285 JACK

► An ophthalmoscope, 1900, 3¼in (8.5cm) wide, in original purple-lined leather case.
£90–110 DHo

A blue glass eyebath, 1900, 2½in (6.5cm) high.
£20–25 DHo

TELESCOPES & SPYGLASSES

A three-draw horn and vellum telescope, early 18thC, open 31in (78.5cm) long.
£500–600 TOM

◄ A stained ivory and silver-plated spyglass, 1840, 2¼in (5.5cm) high, in original case.
£250–275 CHAP

A Meade LX5 8in Schmidt-Cassegrain astronomical telescope, with field tripod, equatorial wedge and electric drive, c1985, 60in (152.5cm) high, with carrying case.
£650–750 DDM

◄ A brass and mahogany three-draw telescope, c1840, 25in (63.5cm) long.
£150–175 DHo

A leather-covered eight-draw brass telescope, by White, Glasgow, c1870, 29in (73.5cm) long.
£170–200 TOM

Scripophily

A Confederate States of America $500 bond, authorized by Act of Congress in 1861, with 'Montgomery' crossed out and 'Richmond' inserted.
£850–950 P

A Confederate States of America pink $1,000 bond, with portrait of General 'Stonewall' Jackson, 1861–65.
£55–65 SCR

A Standard Oil Company share certificate, signed by J. D. Rockefeller as President and H. M. Flagler as Secretary, with vignette of Capitol Buildings and grounds, Liberty, flag and sword, 1878.
£3,800–4,200 P

◀ A Republic of Bolivia green 1,000 peso note, never issued, 1870.
£15–20 SCR

Confederate Bonds

Once relatively easy to find, Confederate bonds have become increasingly scarce. Interest in these bonds was slow to develop but the realization that they represent a major historical event, other than merely economic progress, has finally pushed up demand and therefore prices. The bonds were issued during the American Civil War of 1861–65 to fund the Confederate army. As the South lost, the bonds were never repaid and many Europeans were left holding 'worthless' pieces of paper. Around $900m fell into default by the war's end.

◀ A Cheque Bank Ltd share certificate No. 1612, inscribed 'Economising Currency Increases National Wealth', on pink paper, dated '1898'.
£25–30 SCR

▶ A Paris-France 500 francs bond, with vignette of 5 ladies by A. Mucha, 1898.
£450–500 P

Alphonse Mucha (1860–1933) was a Czech Art Nouveau painter and poster designer who worked in Paris from 1887.

A Grand Casino Municipal de la Ville de Biarritz share certificate No. 03,424, with vignettes of the Casino and a lady in a swimming costume, 1900.
£130–150 P

An Automobile Charron Giradot & Voigt SA share certificate No. 14102, with several vignettes of cars and a stylized flying machine, green and yellow, dated '1902'.
£85–95 SCR

An Association Phonique des Grands Artistes share certificate, with vignettes of a lady, gramophone, records, violin and the Opera House, 1906.
£480–520 P

◄ A Hidroélectrica Española SA share certificate, with engraving of horses leaping over a waterfall held back by Hermes, yellow and black with red seal, issued in Madrid, 1964.
£16–18 SCR

► A Republic of China 6% Gold Loan Treasury Notes of 1919 $1,000 bond, with vignette of a pagoda, on orange paper.
£850–950 GKR

► A Compagnie des Claridges Hotels share certificate No. 05,177, with vignettes of a cruise ship and a train, orange, yellow and black, dated '1919'.
£75–85 SCR

A Planet Hollywood International Inc share certificate No. PH7240, with vignette of Planet Hollywood and fascimile signatures of Demi Moore, Arnold Schwarzenegger, Sylvester Stallone and Bruce Willis as Directors, blue, red and black on white paper, dated '1998'.
£55–65 GKR

Sewing

A base-metal pincushion, modelled as a shoe, 1840, 2¾in (7cm) long.
£45–50 VB

A carved wood knitting sheath, c1870, 11in (28cm) long.
£80–90 HUM

▶ A Tunbridge Ware needle holder, 1870, 3¾in (9.5cm) long.
£90–110 VB

A set of 3 brass linen weights, 19thC, largest 1½in (4cm) diam.
£35–40 DHA

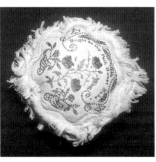

An Anglo-Indian sewing box, decorated with ivory, horn and quill, in the shape of a sarcophagus, with flowerhead feet and sandalwood interior with removable tray, mid-19thC, 14in (35cm) wide.
£2,000–2,200 P

A bog oak pincushion, modelled as a skillet, 19thC, 1½in (4cm) high.
£35–40 STA

◀ A white silk pincushion, celebrating a baby's birth, stitched in silver with 'Bright be thy Path Sweet Babe', c1880, 6in (15cm) diam.
£70–80 JPr

▶ A silver needle holder, 1870, 2½in (6.5cm) wide.
£30–35 VB

Four mother-of-pearl thread-winders and a waxer, 1840–80, largest 1½in (4cm) wide.
£10–35 each VB

Embroidery silks were wound on to thread winders to prevent the silk from tangling. These were made in a variety of shapes, often resembling stars or flowers, in mother-of-pearl, wood, ivory and other materials. The circular object is a thread waxer. To make cotton smoother and stronger it was drawn across candle wax or beeswax. The wax was bought in a small cake and, as shown here, sandwiched between two mother-of-pearl discs.

A wooden lucet, 1870, 4½in (11.5cm) wide.
£20–25 VB

Lucets were used for cord making.

A silver pincushion, modelled
as a jockey's cap, marked 'ES.FS.',
Birmingham 1891, 2½in (6.5cm) wide.
£200–225 GH

A Continental yellow metal
thimble, with blue enamelled
band and buckle mount,
late 19thC, 2mm high.
£180–200 GAK

A Ruskin beige linen pincushion,
with cut-work panel, c1900,
5½in (14cm) square.
£65–75 ChA

◄ A black
celluloid turtle
tape measure,
with red collar,
eyes and toes,
1920s, 2½in
(6.5cm) wide.
£70–80 VB

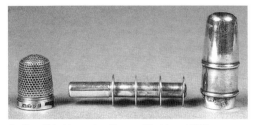

A silver thimble and cotton-reel holder, c1920,
2in (5cm) high.
£100–120 MRW

A pair of steel tailor's scissors, c1920, 12½in (32cm) long.
£30–35 WAB

Two Bakelite and metal tape measure clocks, 1920s,
largest 2in (5cm) high.
£70–85 each VB

► A Bakelite
darner, 1930s,
4½in (11.5cm) long.
£3–5 GIN

Shipping

A wooden half-block model of *Astarte*, mounted, 19thC, 66½in (169cm) wide.
£2,750–3,000 JBe

A full colour print of Lord Nelson No. 222, by George Baxter, 1830s, 4½ x 3in (11.5 x 7.5cm), mounted and framed.
£60–70 SAS

A brass sextant, by Imray, early 19thC, in a mahogany case, 10¾in (27.5cm) wide.
£650–750 DHo

A pair of Minton tureens, from the Royal Yacht *Osborne*, decorated and gilt with enamelled badges with an anchor and 'Royal Yacht *Osborne*', one cover missing, mauve mark for Minton and retailer T. Goode & Co, late 19thC, 4½in (11.5cm) diam.
£575–650 DN

A carved bone needle case, decorated with nautical scenes, made by a prisoner of war, c1850, 4¼in (11cm) high.
£550–600 DQ

A photograph of Edward J. Smith RNR Captain of the *Titanic*, and his Certificate of Discharge from the *Britannic*, framed and glazed, 1893, 23½ x 15½in (59.5 x 39.5cm).
£2,750–3,000 TBoy

Two sepia postcards, with pictures of shipwrecks, 1907.
£15–20 MRW

Disasters, including road and rail crashes, fires and floods or, as here, shipwrecks, were often featured on Victorian postcards.

◀ A brass pocket sextant, by Troughton & Simms, 1860, 3in (7.5cm) diam.
£400–450 REG

▶ A cast marine cable shackle, with brass eye pin, 1900, 5in (12.5cm) wide.
£80–100 REG

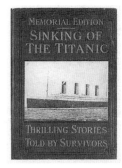

Memorial Edition Sinking of the Titanic Thrilling Stories told by Survivors, with illustrated cover and embossed gilt titles, published by The Minter Company, Harrisburg, Pa, 1912.
£300–350 VS

A copy of an original *Titanic* launch card, printed in black, 1990s, 4 x 6in (10 x 15cm).
£2–5 COB

A Sestral Sitall hand-held bearing compass, with wooden handle and black dial, 1920–40, 7in (18cm) long.
£110–130 REG

A wooden jewellery box, hand-painted in black with a WWI ship, inscribed 'Made by British sailor interned in Holland', c1914–18, 4in (10cm) wide.
£45–50 BAf

A Royal Doulton combined ashtray and matchbox holder, with mottled green and brown glaze, made for P& O shipping company, c1930, 6in (15cm) diam.
£70–80 BAf

A pair of Cunard Line Bakelite ashtrays, in black and white, 1930s, 4in (10cm) diam.
£20–25 each TIH

◄ A pocket sextant, in brown leather case, 1932, 3½in (9cm) diam.
£160–180 REG

A silver-plated Royal Navy teaspoon, with enamelled crest and HMS *Auckland*, late 1930s, 4½in (11.5cm) long.
£6–8 BAf

A collection of wooden mementos made from British ships broken up in the 1930s, HMS *Iron Duke*, *Ganges*, *Mauretania* etc, with inscribed brass plaques, largest 6in (15cm) high.
£10–25 each NC

A pair of full colour shipping postcards, SS *Chitral* and *United States*, 1930s.
£5–7 each MRW

A German cigarette lighter, modelled as a ship's wheel, with badge inscribed 'München', 1940, 5¼in (13.5cm) high.
£110–130 REG

A crested china ship, with Blackpool crest, c1950, 4in (10cm) high.
£10–15 CRN

A Sestrel Sitall brass compass, with brass-trimmed wooden box, 1940, box 9¾in (25cm) square.
£500–600 REG

A Siebe Gorman brass deep-sea diver's torch, 1949–65, 11¼in (28.5cm) long.
£220–250 REG

A full colour postcard, with the ship SS *Canberra*, 1961.
£2–4 COB

Silver

An Irish silver sauce boat with scroll handle, on 3 cabriole legs and hoof feet, Dublin 1792, 8in (20.5cm) wide.
£430–480 RTO

Silver Marks

Hallmarking was first instituted in Britain in 1300. On British silver there are usually 4 basic marks, read from left to right:
1 The 'Hall' or 'Town' mark, the stamp of the Assay office where the quality of the metal was tested.
2 The 'Standard' or 'Quality' mark, indicating the standard of the silver – Sterling silver bears the device of the lion passant.
3 The annual date letter, showing the year in which the object was hallmarked.
4 The maker's or sponsor's mark, consisting of the symbol or initials of the maker or retailer.
When assessing a piece of silver, the first mark that should be looked up is the hallmark since each Assay office used different date letters to indicate the year of production.

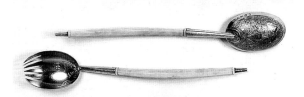

A pair of silver-gilt salad servers, by Fredk Elkington, engraved in the manner of Dr Christopher Dresser, with curved octagonal ivory handles, Birmingham 1873, 12¾in (32.5cm) long.
£330–360 Bri

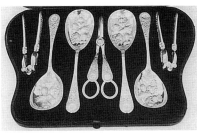

A set of 4 silver fruit serving spoons, 2 grape shears and 2 pairs of nutcrackers, all with matching ornate handles, the serving spoons with gilt bowls, c1880, in a case.
£200–240 GAK

An American silver paper knife and stamp container, c1880, 9½in (24cm) long.
£350–400 JBU

A silver-mounted magnifying glass, by William Comyns, 1887, 9in (23cm) long.
£140–160 HUM

Further Reading

Miller's Silver & Plate Antiques Checklist, Miller's Publications, 1994

A silver travelling photograph frame, London 1902, 3 x 2in (7.5 x 5cm).
£425–475 JBU

A set of 4 napkin holders, by John William Kirwan, with enamelled bands in red, blue and green, Birmingham 1896, 2in (5cm) high.
£750–825 JBU

A silver cigar cutter, Birmingham 1892, 1¼in (3cm) long.
£50–60 EMC

A silver photograph frame,
by Rogers & Whitehouse,
decorated with clover leaf pattern,
Birmingham 1903, 4¾in (12cm) diam.
£340–380 THOM

A Liberty & Co silver cream jug,
with plain looped handle and
3 ball feet, Birmingham 1904,
3in (7.5cm) high.
£240–280 GAK

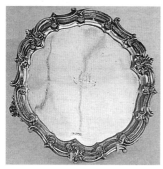

A George II-style silver salver,
with foliate and scrolled rim and
3 cast acanthus feet, Sheffield
1910, 10½in (26.5cm) diam.
£170–200 GAK

A silver vesta case and
candle-holder, London 1903,
1¾in (4.5cm) square.
£400–450 JBU

A silver pig bookmark,
by Samson Mordan,
Chester 1907,
3in (7.5cm) high.
£340–380 THOM

A set of 4 silver owl menu holders, with
amber-coloured eyes, damage to one eye,
Chester 1908, 1½in (4cm) high.
£650–750 JBU

◀ A silver teaset, by Cooper Bros & Sons,
comprising teapot with ebonized handle
and finial, milk jug and sugar bowl,
Sheffield 1917, teapot 7in (18cm) high.
£375–425 CGC

A set of 4 Art Nouveau silver salts,
by Elkington & Co, each with
3 scroll handles, fitted blue glass
liners, with case, 3 spoons missing,
Birmingham 1903, 2in (5cm) high.
£300–340 RTO

An Art Nouveau silver belt, by William Hutton
& Sons probably to a design by Kate Harris,
composed of 15 shaped round plaques and
a larger clasp, each depicting a young girl in
profile, Birmingham 1905, 30in (76cm) long.
£450–500 DN

A cut-glass dressing table box, with a floral
and foliate embossed silver lid, Birmingham
1907, 8½in (21.5cm) wide.
£120–140 GAK

Cross Reference
See Colour Review

A pair of silver toast
racks, in original case,
Sheffield 1911, each
2½in (6.5cm) long,
in original case.
£120–140 GAK

SILVER PLATE

A late George III Sheffield-plated argyle, with wood handle, 8½in (21.5cm) high.
£500–550 DN

A late George III Sheffield-plated tray, engraved with the arms of Pearce of Penzance, Cornwall, 24in (61cm) wide.
£375–425 DN

A silver-plated engraved coffee pot, c1870, 11in (28cm) high.
£300–350 DIC

Two silver-plated and crested game dish covers, engraved with crests, largest 21in (53.5cm) wide.
£270–320 MEA

A pair of Regency Sheffield-plated entrée dishes, 12¾in (32.5cm) wide.
£500–550 DN

A silver-plated silver spoon warmer, modelled as a lifebuoy on rocks, c1870, 8in (20.5cm) long.
£350–400 DIC

A pair of silver-plated candelabra, each adapting with 4 or 2 branches, 19thC, 19in (48.5cm) high.
£1,300–1,500 DN

▶ A pair of silver-plated coasters, with crested wood bases, 19thC, 6¾in (17cm) diam.
£300–330 DN

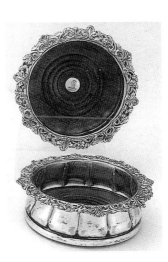

◀ A silver-plated jewellery casket, by Elkington & Co, decorated with relief panels of classical figures and on 4 swan and shell feet, with original velvet buttoned interior, stamped 'Philadelphia Exhibition 1876', 11in (28cm) wide.
£340–380 GAK

Following the invention of the electric battery in the early 19thC and the first attempts to coat base metals with silver in 1840, the Birmingham firm of Elkington & Co took out the first patent on the new process of electroplating. Elkington produced a huge range of items, both functional and decorative, in the Victorian period, contributing to all the major international exhibitions and world fairs.

An Aesthetic style silver-plated engraved biscuit barrel, c1880, 8in (20.5cm) high.
£250–300 DIC

A silver-plated engraved table lighter, modelled as a grenade and 2 cartridges, on oval base, c1880, 10in (25.5cm) wide.
£280–325 DIC

A pair of fruit dishes, by Elkington & Co, in the form of vine leaves with grapes, 1881, 13in (33cm) wide.
£350–400 DIC

A silver-plated embossed oval fruit dish, with grape scissors, in original burgundy silk-lined case, c1885, 12in (30.5cm) wide.
£250–275 DIC

A silver-plated table bell, the stand modelled as twigs, c1890, 8in (20.5cm) high.
£150–175 DIC

A glass biscuit box, with a silver-plated base and top, c1890, 7in (18cm) high.
£300–350 DIC

A mid-European silver-plated desk seal, late 19thC, 4in (10cm) high.
£245–285 ChA

▶ A silver-plated spirit kettle, with matching base and spirit burner, c1900, 12in (30.5cm) high.
£110–130 GAK

A Swedish silver-plated dish, 1930s, 9in (23cm) diam.
£50–60 MARK

A silver-plated miniature tea set, 20thC, largest 1in (2.5cm) high.
£40–45 TAC

Sixties & Seventies

The 1990s saw a revival of 1960s and '70s design, expressing itself in every form from the return of the platform boot (reborn as a platform trainer) to the resurgence of the lava lamp, perfect illumination for an Austin Powers-style groovy pad. At the same time, interest has flourished in the original artefacts of the period that saw the birth of the teenager and a style, as well as a social revolution.

This section is devoted to the sixties and seventies, looking at fashion, furnishings, film and TV-inspired collectables, ranging from works by the big names of the day, to disposable ephemera created for a new, throwaway society.

Increasingly, auction houses and dealers are concentrating on the 1960s and '70s, but while at the top end of the market fine designer pieces can already fetch high prices, there is much that can still be picked up very affordably from flea markets and car boot fairs, which is

one of the reasons why works from these decades are attracting many young collectors.

Britain, most notably London, set the world swinging when it came to sixties fashion, and of all the designer names to look out for none is more famous than Mary Quant, pioneer of mini skirts, high boots, tights and a host of other fashion statements. In furnishing and technology, plastic was a favourite modern medium, some of the best and most collectable of new space age furniture and technology coming from Italian and Scandinavian designers.

As the television consolidated its prime position in the family home, so children's toys and interests became increasingly influenced by TV programmes. As well as the collectables shown here, sixties and seventies items can be found throughout this book in sections such as Dolls (look out for Barbie and Action Man), Lighting and Toys.

FASHION

An Apple label olive green lady's jacket, 1960s.
£150–175 BTC

The Apple Boutique in London was opened by the Beatles in the 1960s.

LOCATE THE SOURCE

The source of each illustration in Miller's can be found by checking the code letters below each caption with the Key to Illustrations, pages 476–484.

A pair of Mary Quant ribbed tights, Wild Lilac colour, in original packaging, 1960s.
£5–8 HarC

► A Mary Quant black and white suspender belt, 1960s.
£18–20 HarC

A pair of German Beatles nylon stockings, by Vroom & Dreesmann in original packaging, 1960s.
£20–25 BTC

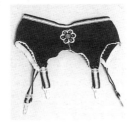

An Afghan coat, decorated with brown and gold embroidery, 1960–70s.
£50–60 HarC

The Afghan coat became a favourite hippy garment in the 1960s and '70s. Buyer beware, however, the sheep or goat skin was often imperfectly cured, and even after 20 to 30 years coats can still be smelly, especially in the rain!

A pair of black leather and snakeskin wedge shoes, 1970s.
£30–35 HarC

▶ A clear plastic clutch bag, designed as a copy of *Harper's & Queen* magazine, 1970s.
£25–35 HarC

A Jean Varon cotton print dress, black with red and yellow pattern, 1970s.
£12–14 HarC

A Miss Moneypenny psychedelic nylon top, in red, blue, yellow and green, 1970s.
£15–20 HarC

FURNISHING

A Charles Eames chrome chair, with black upholstery, 1960s, 36in (91.5cm) high.
£550–650 ZOOM

The Garden Egg Chair, by Reliter Products, designed by Peter Ghyczy, red fibreglass reinforced plastic with black upholstery, c1968, 39in (99cm) high.
£500–600 MARK

A clear Perspex stool, with leopard-skin covered sprung seat, 1960s, 25in (63.5cm) high.
£450–500 ZOOM

A Charles Eames white fibreglass shell chair, with Eiffel Tower chrome base, 1970s, 30in (76cm) high.
£200–230 PLB

An Arkana chair, with aluminium base and white plastic seat and cushion, 1960–70s, 32in (81.5cm) high.
£180–220 ZOOM

A brown glass table, with chrome base, 1970s, 28½in (72.5cm) high.
£220–250 ZOOM

A Joe Colombo red plastic Boby office trolley, designer's signature in relief on bottom shelf, 1970s, 29in (73.5cm) high.
£250–300 ZOOM

Italian-born Joe Colombo (1930–71) is one of the most celebrated designers of the sixties and the Boby trolley is one of his best-known designs. Manufactured by Bieffplast from 1970 and available in red, yellow, black and white, the wheeled plastic trolley was colourful and space-saving, epitomizing Colombo's desire to create multi-functional, moveable furniture that expressed the dynamism of the modern age.

An Italian white plastic magazine rack, by Giotto Stoppino for Kartell, 1971–72, 18in (45.5cm) high.
£125–140 MARK

A Giancarlo Piretti Castelli edition Plona chair, brown Perspex with aluminium base, 1970s, 30in (76cm) high.
£185–235 PLB

A Wall-All red plastic organizer, 1970s, 26½in (67.5cm) high.
£150–180 PLB

An Italian black plastic and aluminium chair, 1970s, 35in (89cm) high.
£280–300 ZOOM

GLASS & CERAMICS

A Portmerion black and white Totem coffee pot, 1960s, 13¾in (35cm) high.
£25–30 LEGE

An Arthur Wood utensil pot, with green, yellow, black and red pattern, 1960s, 7in (18cm) high.
£20–30 BTB

A green glass Flame vase, by Holmegaard, Denmark, designed by Per Lutkin, marked 'Holmegaard PL 1961' on base, 1961, 9½in (24cm) high.
£120–140 FF

A green cased glass bottle vase, by Holmegaard, Denmark, 1970s, 11¾in (30cm) high.
£65–85 PLB

A Murano glass red, yellow, blue and green, ashtray, 1960s, 6¼in (16cm) diam.
£80–100 ZOOM

> **Further Reading**
> *Miller's Collecting the 1960s*, Madeleine Marsh, Miller's Publications, 1999

◀ A Portmerion black and white Greek Key pattern coffee cup and saucer, 1960s, saucer 5in (12.5cm) diam.
£8–10 LEGE

TECHNOLOGY

A toilet paper holder, incorporated in a radio, 1960s, 8in (20.5cm) wide.
£15–20 ZOOM

An Olivetti Valentine red portable typewriter, designed by Ettore Sotsass and Perry King, 1969, 12in (30.5cm) wide.
£100–120 MARK

A pair of B & W speakers, each with teak case and black tripod stand, 1960s, 28in (71cm) high.
£150–175 ZOOM

▶ An American red and gold circular Hoover, 1970s, 18in (45.5cm) diam.
£35–55 ZOOM

A German spage-age alarm clock, white with a black face, 1960s, 8½in (21.5cm) high.
£35–40 MARK

An Italian red and white Eclisse lamp, designed by Vico Magstretti, 1966, 7in (18cm) high.
£55–65 PLB

Much 1960s design was inspired by space and the Eclisse (eclipse) light, designed in 1966, resembles an astronaut's helmet. Created by Italian designer Vico Magstretti (b1920), the aluminium light contains an inner shade that could be swivelled round to vary light levels and 'eclipse' the bulb. Sixties and seventies lighting, stylish and functional, is currently a very popular area with collectors.

TV, FILM & MUSIC

The Flintstones Big TV Bumper Book, the blue cover with yellow, mauve and green, 1962, 12 x 9in (30.5 x 23cm).
£5–7 YR

A set of Dutch Milk Premium plastic Beatles figures, in brown, pink and black, 1964, 4½in (11.5cm) high.
£85–100 TBoy

▶ A Bendy blue and yellow Smurf, 1960s, 8½in (21.5cm) high.
£8–10 CMF

A Monkees Creamy
Toffee Bar wrapper,
printed in black and
orange, 1967,
4in (10cm) square.
£7–10 YR

*Flowerpot Men and
Woodentops* annual,
with blue, red, yellow
and green cover, 1970,
10 x 8in (25.5 x 20.5cm).
£4–6 YR

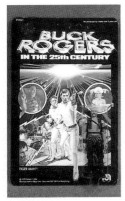

A *Buck Rogers in the
25th Century* action
figure, Tiger Man, 1979,
card 9 x 6in (23 x 15cm).
£30–35 OW

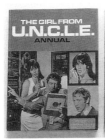

The Girl From U.N.C.L.E. Annuals,
with full colour covers, 1967 and 1968,
10 x 8in (25.5 x 20.5cm).
£5–8 each YR

A *Land of the Giants* Picture Card Bubble Gum,
with red, blue and yellow wrapper, 1968, 2 x 3in
(5 x 7.5cm).
£8–10 YR

A Corgi *Magic Roundabout* Playground, No. 853,
comprising an oval playground with hand-operated
roundabout and train track, a clockwork musical see-
saw, a train with carriage and truck, Mr Rusty and
various other figures in the locomotive, Brian, Dougal,
Dylan, Ermintrude and Zebedee, trees, shrubs and
flowers, in original box, inner packing missing, 1970s.
£320–360 DN

**Created by Frenchman Serge Danot and narrated
by Eric Thompson (father of actress Emma), the
Magic Roundabout first appeared on British TV in
1965. The Technicolour series became an instant
hit, with both children and adults, particularly
students, who appreciated the surreal and
occasionally spaced-out quality of the story and
characters. This playground set is among the most
collectable of all *Magic Roundabout* merchandise
and it is rare to find it complete.**

Lady Penelope annual,
the red leather-effect
cover embossed in gold,
with inset full-colour
picture of Lady Penelope,
1968, 11 x 9in (28 x 23cm).
£5–7 YR

A *Battlestar Galactica*
Imperious Leader action
figure, 1978, on original
card, card 9 x 6in
(23 x 15cm).
£12–15 OW

The Black Hole action
figure, Dr Kate McRae,
in brown and pink, 1979,
on original card,
9 x 6in (23 x 15cm).
£12–15 OW

Smoking

A silver parcel-shaped vesta box, Birmingham 1894, 2in (5cm) wide.
£300–350 THOM

A metal vesta case with a sepia picture of Llandudno Bay, a yellow metal vesta case with Vichy Casino, and a Mauchline ware vesta case, 1880–1916, largest 2¾in (7cm) long.
£30–55 each VB

A spelter vesta case, in the form of a skull, c1910, 1½in (4cm) high.
£100–110 CHe

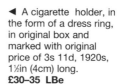

◀ A gold cigar cutter, engraved 'IV June 1916', 2in (5cm) high.
£235–265 EMC

A pewter match-striker, in the form of a bearded man smoking a pipe, 19thC, 3½in (9cm) high.
£75–90 COCO

A French silver-plated lift-arm lighter, c1930, 4in (10cm) high.
£50–55 HarC

A brass cigar cutter, in the form of a bottle, inscribed 'Veuve Cliquot', 1906, 2in (5cm) high.
£65–75 EMC

◀ A cigarette holder, in the form of a dress ring, in original box and marked with original price of 3s 11d, 1920s, 1½in (4cm) long.
£30–35 LBe

A Parker Roller Beacon silver-plated table lighter, 1930s, 5in (12.5cm) high.
£60–70 FAM

A Dunhill silver-plated leather-bound table lighter, 1930s, 4in (10cm) high.
£80–100 FAM

▶ A set of 6 simulated tortoiseshell cigarette holders, on original sales card, c1935, card 5in (12.5cm) wide.
£14–16 DAC

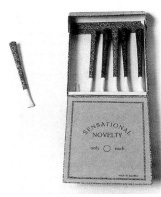

A brown Bakelite cigarette box, 1940s, 6in (15cm) wide.
£45–50 DHAR

An Austrian mock shagreen box of blue and brown cigarette holders, 1930s, 4in (10cm) long.
£85–95 LBe

A Swiss base metal combined cigarette lighter and ashtray, 1936, 5in (12.5cm) high.
£25–30 DAC

Two cigarette packets, Abdulla Number Seven, Player's Navy Cut 'Medium', 1930–40s, 2¼in (5.5cm) wide.
£3–4 each MRW

A cigarette lighter, in the form of a standing camel, 1950s, 5in (12.5cm) high.
£25–30 WAB

◀ A metal cigarette case, 1940s, 6in (15cm) wide, in original box,
£15–20 DAC

A chrome and black ashtray, with rotating top, 1950s, 21½in (54.5cm) high.
£75–100 ZOOM

An Italian orange and black ashtray, 1970s, 20½in (52cm) high.
£75–85 ZOOM

A chrome cigarette lighter, in the form of a jet aircraft, on a black octagonal base, 1950s, 4in (10cm) long.
£110–140 JUN

◀ A Dunhill petrol lighter, 1972, 3in (7.5cm) high.
£50–60 RAC

Sport

A Stevengraph, entitled 'Are You Ready?', No. 169, May 1880, 5 x 8in (12.5 x 20.5cm).
£240–280 VINE

Two leather-covered ping pong bats, c1900, 12in (30.5cm) long.
£30–35 WaR

A mahogany billiard scoreboard, c1900, 39in (99cm) wide.
£300–500 STS

A set of table bowls, by Jaques & Son, in original wooden case, c1900, 19in (48cm) long.
£140–160 ARo

◄ An American metal display unit, for Pabst Blue Ribbon Beer, with a boxer in blue and white striped trousers beside a bottle of beer, both standing in a boxing ring, rubbed and marked, early 1900s, 16½in (42cm) high.
£675–750 P(C)

> ### Cross Reference
> See Colour Review

Two lignum lawn bowls, by Jaques & Son, c1910.
£15–20 each AL

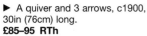

A rounders bat, c1900, 18in (45.5cm) long.
£10–12 AL

► A quiver and 3 arrows, c1900, 30in (76cm) long.
£85–95 RTh

A card game entitled New Base Ball, by Parker Brothers, USA, c1910, 6in (15cm) wide.
£140–155 HALL

A pair of hockey goal-keeper's leather kickers, c1920.
£25–30 WAB

A pair of brown leather skating boots, c1920.
£14–16 AL

A wooden hockey stick, c1930.
£15–20 AL

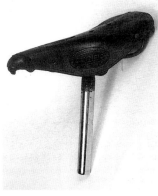

A Olympic brown leather bicycle saddle, c1930, 12in (30.5cm) long.
£12–15 AL

A Japanese leather Kendo mask, and 2 Kendo sticks, 1930s, sticks 36in (91.5cm) long.
£120–135 WAB

A brown leather cycling helmet, 1930s, 10½in (26.5cm) long.
£25–35 WAB

A brown leather volley ball, 1940, 9in (23cm) diam.
£16–18 DQ

A Harvard rowing jug, decorated in red, green and grey on cream and brown ground with a portrait of an oarsman, 1930s, 12in (30.5cm) high.
£280–310 SMAM

▶ A leather and wood lacrosse stick, 1950s, 42in (106.5cm) long.
£15–18 WAB

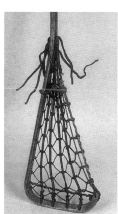

◀ A brown leather rugby helmet, 1950s,
£10–15 AL

A white leather fencing mask, c1950, 7in (18cm) wide.
£15–20 AL

A pair of brown leather boxing gloves, 1950s.
£45–55 JUN

A set of 19 British Lions in South Africa match programmes, 3rd Test Match programme missing, marked with score/scorers, 1968.
£300–350 P(C)

CRICKET

An original *carte de visite* photograph, depicting W. G. Grace holding a bat and James Southerton holding a ball, late 1800s, 4 x 2½in (10 x 6.5cm).
£380–420 KNI

William Gilbert Grace

William Gilbert Grace (1848–1915) was the most famous cricketer in Victorian England. In his career in first class cricket (1865–1908) he scored 54,896 runs, registered 126 centuries and as a bowler took 2,876 wickets. He evolved the modern principles of batting, achieved many notable performances on the roughest of grounds and in 1880 played in the first Test Match in England against Australia. His imposing physique, giant beard and huge energy made him a national hero, and over a century on, thanks to the wealth of photographs and memorabilia that he inspired, his face is still one of the best known in the history of British cricket. Objects connected with 'W. G.' are sought after by collectors today.

A Continental briar pipe, carved in the shape of W. G. Grace with cricket bat stem, stamped 'W. G. G. at 47 AD 1895', 5½in (14cm) high.
£130–150 MUL

▶ A cricket scorecard, England v. Australia at Lord's, signed in ink by 17 of the Australian team, June 1948.
£275–300 P(C)

A silver cricket bats and ball compass, Birmingham 1900, 1in (2.5cm) diam.
£200–225 BEX

A New Zealand black cloth Test cap, worn by Warren Lees Otago and New Zealand 1972–88, with embroidered silver fern leaf of New Zealand.
£375–425 KNI

Wisden Cricketer's Almanack, with original beige and black paper cover, 1945, 7 x 4in (18 x 10cm).
£95–110 KNI

FISHING

A leather stitched minnow lure,
early 19thC, 3¾in (9.5cm) long.
£400–450 MUL

A pair of fly tying scissors,
engraved 'C. Farlow and Co.',
c1890, 4in (10cm) long.
£5–10 OTB

A river keeper's fish spear,
with harpoon-style detachable
head and retrieving line, c1900,
7in (18cm) long.
£40–50 OTB

◀ A French
reed trout
fisher's creel,
early 20thC,
7in (18cm) high.
£65–80 OTB

A Hardy Phantom lure minnow, with nickel fins,
unused in original box, c1920, 4in (10cm) long.
£80–90 RTh

A Hardy Ward oak
line drier, c1915,
arms 12in (30.5cm) wide.
£140–160 OTB

A bamboo landing net,
with brass fittings, 1920,
62in (157.5cm) long.
£20–25 AL

A Hardy waistcoat pocket oil bottle for dry fly fishing,
with milled edge black stopper, c1920, 2in (5cm) high,
in original box.
£150–170 OTB

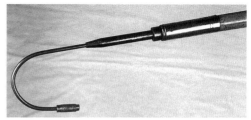

A Hardy travelling landing net, c1920, 37in (94cm) long.
£75–90 STS

A bamboo gaff, with brass fittings, 1920, 55in (139.5cm) long.
£15–20 AL

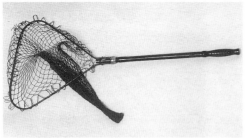

A wicker creel, with leather strap, c1920, 20in (51cm) wide.
£25–30 AL

A Hardy jointed green Wiggler and gold Jock Scott bait, late 1930s, 3in (7.5cm) long.
£8–12 each OTB

A green-enamelled metal live bait kettle, with hinged perforated lid, mid-20thC, 14in (35.5cm) wide.
£20–25 OTB

A Common Bream, mounted in a setting of fern and grasses against a green ground, with interior plaque "Bream. 5lbs. 3oz. 2drms. Caught by H. H. Warwick. Trout Inn Water. 4th December 1953', case 26in (66cm) wide.
£500–550 Bon(C)

A Hardy pocket gaff, with grey anodised sheath housing steel gaff head, 2oz, c1962, 5in (12.5cm) long.
£100–120 OTB

An Edward Paton of Perth 4½in brass and rosewood Perth-style reel, with rosewood back and faceplate rim and engraved brass face, c1870.
£160–190 OTB

A 1½in brass pole winch, with waisted ivory handle, curved crank, riveted foot and triple pollared cage, late 19thC.
£120–140 Bon(C)

A brass Jardine-style trout fly reel, with perforated face, ebonite back and drum, nickel-silver rims, c1880.
£60–75 OTB

► A 4in ebonite and brass centre pin reel, with perforated brass-backed ebonite drum and ebonite back with brass star and check button, c1900.
£90–110 OTB

◄ A 1¼in brass collar winch, with horn handle, curved crank, triple pillared cage and lyre screw to collar, late 19thC.
£220–250 Bon(C)

A Hardy Birmingham all-brass plate wind reel, with ebonite handle and enclosed oval Hardy Bros logo, c1900.
£140–160 DDO

An Illingworth No. 3 Threadline casting reel, with finger-style line pick up, c1920.
£70–90 OTB

▶ An Allcock Aeriel 3½in centrepin reel, with brass on/off rim check lever, spokes and ventilated drum with spoke balance, backplate with Stag Regd trademark 'Allcock Aerial', ' S. Allcock & Co.' and details and Regd. Design No, c1930s.
£300–350 Bon(C)

◀ A Helical Reel Co threadline casting reel, with half bale arm, in original box with tools and oil bottle, c1935.
£40–50 OTB

A 4in wooden Nottingham reel, with star back fitting and slater catch horn handle, c1930.
£40–45 WAB

A Hardy Eureka 3½in alloy trotting reel, with perforated alloy drum and grey enamelled backplate, in original box, c1950.
£100–120 OTB

A Hardy Conquest 4½in alloy trotting reel, with dark grey enamelled back plate and bright alloy drum, c1960.
£120–140 OTB

FOOTBALL

A shield-shaped trade card 'West Ham United', by J. Baines Ltd Bradford, printed in black and green, small tear and wear, 1897, 3in (7.5cm) high.
£50–55 KNI

A shield-shaped trade card 'Everton', by J. Baines Ltd Bradford, printed in blue, yellow, red, green and brown, 1897, 5in (12.5cm) high.
£60–65 KNI

A fine-paper napkin programme and souvenir of the English Cup Final 1906, with central black and white print of Everton and Newcastle United sides, surrounded by colour-printed floral border, 14in (35.5cm) square.
£500–600 S

The Villa News and Record, printed in red on grey, published by The Rover Co Ltd Birmingham, Aston Villa home programme season 1907–08, 9 x 7in (23 x 18cm).
£65–75 KNI

A Manchester United v. Blackburn Rovers match programme, 26 December 1927, slight damage.
£420–470 P(C)

A chrome-plated brass car mascot, in the form of a footballer, 1930s, 6in (15cm) high.
£145–165 JUN

A Huddersfield Town v. Preston North End match programme, Final Tie of the Football Association Challenge Cup Competition at the Empire Stadium, Wembley, April 30th 1938, 8°.
£120–140 DW

A West Bromwich Albion v. Birmingham programme, for a match played in season 1939–40, 9 x 7in (23 x 18cm).
£35–40 KNI

▶ A silver presentation cigar box, inscribed 'To Harry F. Homer "Marksman" from the Directors of the Arsenal Football Club...7th May 1949', with fitted interior, 9¼in (24cm) wide.
£475–525 S

Harry Homer was known to thousands of Arsenal fans as the organizer of the Arsenal Club Enclosure which he founded in 1936. It is said that he never missed an Arsenal match and as 'Marksman' he contributed famous articles in the club's match programmes. As an Oxford MA he was a senior English professor, and later taught English in Spain.

A coloured lithographic poster for the 1966 World Cup Finals, published by Sayles & Booth, Halifax, 29½ x 20in (75 x 51cm).
£475–525 S

GOLF

A silver-plate cruet set, with golf clubs surmounted by a golf ball, 1910, 4¾in (12cm) high.
£80–100 WaR

A Golfing Brownies cup, transfer-printed in brown, red and green, with gilt rim, c1910, 4in (10cm) high.
£65–75 WaR

A Penfold Patented Golf Balls cardboard box, printed in red on a blue ground, no contents, 1920s, 5in (12.5cm) wide.
£35–45 WaR

A ceramic figure of a golfer, painted in brown, blue, red, yellow and green, c1925, 7½in (19cm) high.
£250–300 HUX

◀ A Willow crested china golf ball, with of City & Royal Borough of Elgin crest, 1910–30, 1¾in (4.5cm) diam.
£22–26 G&CC

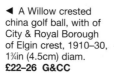

◀ A Silver King Golf Ball cardboard box, printed in black, no contents, c1920s, 7¼in (18.5cm) wide.
£30–35 WaR

A Dunlop silver Hole in One trophy, on black base, 1930, 3in (7.5cm) high.
£55–65 WaR

Cross Reference
See Colour Review

▶ An Arnold Palmer Pro Shot Golf, by Marx, 1960s, 36½in (92.5cm) high.
£15–25 WaR

HORSES & HUNTING

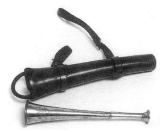

A Swaine & Adeney brass and copper hunting horn, 1905, and a solid hide case, c1860, case 11in (28cm) long.

Horn   **£100–120**

Case   **£50–60 STS**

A folding boxwood and brass horse measure, with level and tape, by Cooper W. Jones & Co, patent No. 13268, in original leather case, 9in (2cm) long.
£100–120 TOM

A wooden decoy duck, painted in green and red, c1890, 12½in (32cm) long.
£145–165 RTh

A pair of French tan leather cavalry boots, with wooden trees, c1900, 21in (53.5cm) high.
£120–150 STS

An Edwardian pigskin cartridge bag, embossed with 'V. A.', 11in (28cm) wide.
£60–80 STS

LOCATE THE SOURCE

The source of each illustration in Miller's can be found by checking the code letters below each caption with the Key to Illustrations, pages 476–484.

A shooting stick, with wooden shaft and brown leather seat, c1920, 36in (91.5cm) high.
£18–22 AL

A curry comb, with wooden handle and metal teeth, c1920, 6in (15cm) wide.
£6–8 AL

A leather case containing a metal sandwich tin for a side-saddle, by Champion & Wilson London, c1920, case 11in (28cm) wide overall.
£65–80 STS

A wooden game carrier, with brass fittings, c1930s, 19½in (49.5cm) long.
£50–60 WAB

▶ A lady's pigskin hunting whip and thong, with silver collar and bone handle, by Andrews, 1953, whip 21in (53.5cm) long.
£60–70 STS

TENNIS

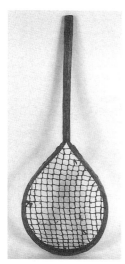

A French one-piece wooden garden racket, c1880, 19in (48.5cm) long.
£35–45 WaR

A silver trophy for Branksome Park Tennis Club Men's Singles, c1900, 9in (23cm) high.
£100–120 WaR

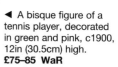

A Slazenger 'Flicker' book, featuring Miss Betty Nuthall, Forehand and Backhand Drives, 1920s, 2in (5cm) wide.
£50–60 WaR

◄ A bisque figure of a tennis player, decorated in green and pink, c1900, 12in (30.5cm) high.
£75–85 WaR

A mahogany and brass tennis racket press, c1905, 14in (35.5cm) long.
£130–150 STS

A photograph of Oxford & Cambridge Lawn Tennis Team, with crest in red and blue, signed by photographer, 1929, 15½in (39.5cm) wide.
£70–85 WAB

A ceramic racket, with crest of Southport in red, blue and yellow, 1920s, 5½in (14cm) high.
£20–25 WaR

A Lillywhite's tennis racket, c1950s, head 10in (25.5cm) wide.
£14–16 AL

A silver tennis trophy, from Palace Hotel Torquay, hallmarked, 1930s, 4in (10cm) high.
£50–60 WaR

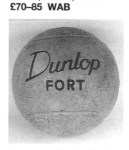

A ceramic Dunlop Fort tennis ball shop display, 1950s, 39in (99cm) circumference.
£130–150 WaR

Miller's is a price GUIDE not a price LIST

Stanhopes

Stanhopes are named after Charles, 3rd Earl of Stanhope (1753–1816), British nobleman, statesman and inventor of a range of scientific devices including the Stanhope microscope lens. It was not until the second half of the 19th century, however, and with the development of micro-photography, that the custom emerged of placing a tiny Stanhope lens over a miniature photograph, and containing it in a piece of jewellery or a small souvenir. The man credited with first producing these decorative 'Stanhopes' in 1864, was Victorian scientist Sir David Brewster, well known for his optical work.

Queen Victoria herself was an early fan of Stanhope jewellery, and these novelty items soon became a popular craze. Stanhopes appear in many materials, from ivory to wood to minerals, and in every form from needlework tools to writing implements to brooches and charms. The majority contain photographs of favourite tourist attractions, and other subjects include portraits, famous events (such as major exhibitions) and, occasionally, naughty pictures, generally found on smoking implements or other objects likely to appeal to a male rather than female user.

Although Stanhopes were produced well into the 20th century, the golden age was the late Victorian and Edwardian periods. Values depend on material and design.

Four Stanhope animals, an ivory dog's head, bog oak pig and cat, and a marble pig, 1880–1910, largest ¾in (20mm) high.
£35–90 each VB

A carved wood Stanhope, with the Exposition Nationale, Brussels, 1880, 2in (5cm) long.
£130–150 MLa

A horn Stanhope whistle, 1880, 2in (5cm) high.
£65–75 VB

A pair of bone Stanhope binoculars, and a Stanhope barrel, 1880–1900, largest ¾in (1.5cm) high.
£30–35 each VB

Two Stanhopes, a bog oak cross and an agate book, 1890, 1¼in (3cm) high.
£15–30 each VB

Four Stanhopes, pencil, manicure, and 2 needle cases, in bone, wood and silver, 1890–1910, largest 4in (10cm) wide.
£40–60 each VB

An Austrian carved wood paperknife Stanhope, 1900s, 2in (5cm) long.
£170–190 MLa

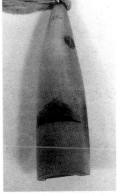

► An ivory Stanhope showing 'the biggest wheel made in France', from the Paris Exhibition, 1900, ¾in (20mm) high.
£25–30 WAB

Teddy Bears & Soft Toys

A French pull-along Boston Terrier, with rough-textured body, brown glass eyes, nodding head, red leather collar and wooden wheels, chain-pull to neck operating head and mechanism that opens jaw and growl, chain-pull to neck missing, worn, 1890s, 13in (33cm) long.
£140–160 Bon(C)

Two mohair teddy bears,
l. with stitched snout, amber glass eyes, large ears set on side of head and swivel-jointed body with excelsior filling, pads replaced, snout worn, head and limbs loose, c1930, 22in (56cm) high.
£450–500 S(S)
r. a Steiff bear, with button in ear, stitched snout, black button eyes, swivel-jointed body, side-press growler and excelsior filling, some wear, mouth stitiching missing, c1908, 13in (33cm) high.
£625–700 S(S)

A tiger cub automaton, with brown and beige fur, in need of some restoration, late 19thC, 20in (51cm) long.
£170–200 TMA

A plush mohair Steiff-style teddy bear, early 20thC, 15½in (39.5cm) high.
£350–400 WiLP

A Queens of Leicester Winnie the Pooh-style teddy bear, in brown corduroy with green waistcoat, 1920s, 13in (33cm) high.
£90–100 BLH

◀ A Merrythought blonde mohair bear cub, with large brown glass eyes, brown stitiched nose, mouth and claws, button to left ear, straw and kapok-filled body with swivel head and arms, tan felt paw pads, c1930, 17in (43cm) high.
£650–750 Bon(C)

A Steiff centre-seam teddy bear, with curly cinnamon mohair, black boot-button eyes, clipped snout, black stitched nose, mouth and claws, straw-filled jointed body, elongated arms and large feet with felt paw pads, hump to back, minor wear, some holes to paw pads, c1904, 19in (48.5cm) high.
£3,000–3,500 Bon(C)

A plush straw-filled toy chicken, yellow with red felt crest, 1920s, 6in (15cm) high.
£60–70 HUM

A black plush straw-filled terrier, with growl, 1930, 13in (33cm) long.
£50–60 HUM

A Mickey Mouse-type velveteen doll, with embroidered mouth and eyebrows, leatherette eyes, 1930s, 15in (38cm) high.
£250–300 SK(B)

A clockwork drummer bear, in beige plush, 1950s, 8½in (21.5cm) high.
£70–90 TED

A Pedigree Womble, Orinoco, with grey fur, 1970s, 11in (28cm) high.
£16–18 CMF

▶ A Gremlin, with brown and white body,1980s, 10½in (26.5cm) high.
£4–6 UNI

A Schuco beige mohair Yes/No bear, tail operating the head up and down and side to side, c1960, 8in (20.5cm) high.
£400–500 TED

▶ A Chad Valley Snow White and the Seven Dwarfs, with moulded painted faces, 5 with original card labels, Doc's glasses missing, c1936, largest 12½in (32cm) high.
£850–1,000 AH

A Chad Valley brown and beige bulldog, with glass eyes, sailor's cap with 'HMS *Vindictive*', collar with metal Chad Valley button and original paper label, 1930s, 8½in (21.5cm) wide.
£60–70 MED

l. A black and white plush Felix the Cat, c1930, 18in (46cm) high.
r. A Chad Valley Bonzo the Dog, with jointed arms, legs and neck, slight wear and tear, c1930, 16in (41cm) high.
£700–800 Bon(C)

BEANIE BABIES

The most significant event in soft toys of the 1990s was certainly the rise of the Beanie Baby. These bean-bag animals are the invention of American stuffed toy manufacturer, and famous recluse, H. Ty Warner who, in 1986, established Ty Inc in Chicago. The company began making cats, bears and other plush animals retailing for $10–20 (£6–12) each. However, Warner wanted to produce a pocket-sized toy that could sell for pocket money prices and 1993 saw the launch of the Beanie Baby and the beginning of a carefully orchestrated world-wide collectable craze – a lethal combination of cute, well-made toys and cynical marketing.

From the very start Beanie Babies were retailed through specially selected outlets and shops, with some 'must-have' examples only available with the purchase of a specified number of other Beanies. To stimulate demand Ty worked out a schedule of planned obsolescence, in which toys would be retired after a certain period, and limited availability in which some designs would only be distributed in certain countries. Britannia Bear (born 1997) was exclusively produced for the UK, inspiring some American collectors to pay up to $500 (£300) and more for a £4–6 bear.

The Internet played a huge part in promoting Beanie mania across the globe, and by 1997 when McDonalds in the USA launched their first Teenie Beanie promotion, it was adults as much as children who were fighting over the Happy Meal toys.

The 1990s have seen some astonishing prices paid for Beanie babies, most famously for Peanut the Royal Blue Elephant (1995), whose colour was a mistake and remained in production for only four months. Originally retailing for $5 (£3) Peanut, the most collectable of all Beanies, recently changed hands at auction for $5,200 (£3,200). Beanie prices have depended above all on rarity and condition.

The presence of the heart-shaped Ty ear tag is crucial both to value and dating since the cardboard hang tag has changed, albeit minutely, with new generations of Beanies.

Although at the end of the 1990s Beanie prices were beginning to fall when, in a final marketing coup, Ty announced that all Beanies would be retired on 31 December 1999 at 11.59pm, literally the last minute of the millennium, there was a sudden revival in interest. How this will be maintained in the 21st century time will tell, and Miller's will report.....

A Pelican Beanie Baby, with blue body, orange beak and feet, 1997, 8in (20.5cm) long.
£4–5 BeG

A Britannia Beanie Baby, with Union flag, 1997–8, 6in (15cm) high.
£4–6 BeG

A Tiger Beanie Baby, with beige and black fur, 1997, 8in (20.5cm) long.
£4–5 BeG

A Princess Diana Beanie Baby, with black fur, 1997–8, 6in (15cm) high.
£4–6 BeG

◀ A set of McDonalds Teenie Beanie Babies, 1999.
£20–30 the set PC

◀ A Meanie Toy Donkeyng, in a purple suit, 1998, 6½in (16.5cm) high.
£12–15 TBoy

Beanie Babies have inspired many immitators, such as these American toys – the 'Meanies'.

Telephones

A black candlestick telephone, No. 1, with walnut bellbox, mid-1920s, 13in (33cm) high.
£500–600 DOM

The phone itself contains no bell so a bellbox was used.

A pair of black candlestick telephones, No. 1 and No. 2, each with steel base and column, and brass collar, 1918, 13in (33cm) high.
£600–700 DOM

These telephones were used as demonstration phones by the GPO. They retain their original tulip mouthpieces, and bulbs on the base that light up when the telephone receives an incoming call. These phones often came in pairs, but it is unusual to find a true pair today.

A Farr Telephone Co Mae West-style tandem oak wall phone, the backboard converted for answering, 1896, 41in (104cm) high.
£1,800–2,00 EKK

▶ A black Skeleton telephone, No. 16, c1900, 11in (28cm) high.
£750–900 DHAR

A black Bakelite telephone, with original handset, cord, alphabet dial and drawer, with bellset with brass bells, 1930s, 6in (15cm) high.
£350–400 OTC

A micro-phone, with steel base and brass collar, black Bakelite transmitter, possibly used on transmitting radio set or switchboard, housing No. 22 PX/1, 1940–50, 12in (30.5cm) high.
£40–45 DOM

A Belgian black cast iron bell telephone, with brass dial and base trim, gold-coloured pattern to base, known as teapot phone, 1940s, 5½in (14cm) wide.
£85–95 DHAR

◀ A railway signal telephone with black Bakelite handset, with wooden base and metal bell, 1952, 17in (43cm) high.
£35–45 DOM

▶ A black Bakelite pyramid telephone, No. 232, with integrated bellbox, restored, 1945, 8in (20.5cm) high.
£300–350 DOM

A black Bakelite wall telephone, No. 311, c1955, 9in (23cm) high.
£180–220 DOM

These telephones were less common than table phones, and are now more collectable. This example came from Leeds, Yorkshire, and is in excellent condition.

A black Bakelite internal GPO telephone, No. 332L, with drawer and dial label, c1950, 9in (23cm) high.
£30–35 DOM

Cross Reference
See Colour Review

▶ A Siemens black Bakelite push-button intercom telephone, for table or wall, with special brackets on base, 1950s, 9in (23cm) wide.
£20–25 DOM

An ivory 300 series GPO telephone, with matching braided cord and drawer, 1950s, 9in (23cm) high.
£275–300 DAC

Coloured phones cost more to rent and so are rarer and more expensive today than the standard black version.

A yellow dial telephone, 1960s, 9in (23cm) wide.
£14–16 SAF

A two-tone beige and grey plastic Delta phone, with push buttons, 1981, 8in (20.5cm) wide.
£20–25 DOM

◀ A red telephone, No. 332, with bell on/off switch, c1955, 9in (23cm) long.
£300–350 CAB

A Trimphone, in two-tone beige, with luminous dial, 1960–70s, 7½in (19cm) wide.
£30–40 DHAR

Designed by Martyn Rowlands in 1966, the Trimphone was one of the first British phones to have a handset covering the dial. For bedside use, it was half the weight of a traditional phone and the dial was illuminated by radioactive Tritium gas. The two-tone colour schemes were chosen by Lord Snowdon. Health concerns about the radioactive dial caused many Trimphones to be discarded, and they were superseded by the Delta, one of the first popular push-button phones, again designed by Rowlands.

PHONECARDS

◀ Ireland's Europe, 50 units, issued for IMI Conference, Killarney, 1989.
£330–360 WA

A set of BT Disney special edition Hercules phonecards, c1997.
**Mint £40–45
Used £8–10 JCa**

A set of Greek phonecards, 1998.
£2–3 each TAC

Textiles

A composite cloth, with fillet squares linked by linen sections with a wide variety of cutwork decoration, within a scalloped border of Genoese plaited bobbin lace, early 17thC, 76½ x 49¼in (194 x 125cm).
£1,100–1,300 P

A Chinese dress length of sea-blue silk, painted with a design of meandering stems of berries, carnations, leaves and blossom, purple, red, white and green, c1770, 324 x 28¾in (823 x 73cm).
£5,600–6,200 P

A Continental foliate embroidered tapestry, with central cartouche of a fountain, in silver and silk threads, with silver fringing, 19thC, 36 x 82in (91.5 x 210cm).
£1,200–1,400 SR

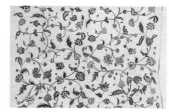

An undyed linen cover, with embroidered design of birds and exotic flowers, in chain stitch with coloured wools, c1700, 34 x 23½in (86 x 60cm).
£5,000–5,500 P

A needlework sampler, worked with a verse above foliate bands embroidered with animals and figures, and 'Ann Sarah Coleman Finished This Work in the Tenth Year of Her Age 1804', in a rosewood frame, 18 x 15¼in (46 x 39cms).
£500–600 S(S)

A Victorian woolwork sampler, with silk highlights, depicting a spaniel surrounded by foliage and stylized flowers, 2 birds and a pair of angels, and 'Sarah Bray's Work Aged 11 Year', 11½ x 11in (29 x 28cm), in a glazed giltwood frame.
£300–350 WW

A Italian plaited bobbin lace border, with alternating male and female figures separated by lattice design, the dentate edging displaying the same male figure, early 18thC, 5¾ x 30in (14.5 x 76cm).
£1,500–1,750 P

A pair of needlework pictures, depicting a cat and a dog seated upon cushions within floral borders, in rosewood frames, mid-19thC, 18in (46cms) square.
£800–1,000 Bon

A Victorian needlework sampler, worked in colours with a verse, floral swags, butterflies, animals, birds and a vase of flowers, and 'Lydia Briggs aged 16 years 1844', 15¼ x 12¼in (39 x 31cm), framed.
£425–475 Bea(E)

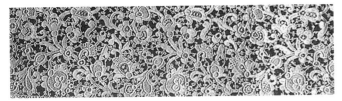

A length of Venetian lace, with foliate design, 19thC, 7 x 171in (17.8 x 434.5cm).
£110–130 FWec

From the Nour I Mah collection of lace formed between 1905 and 1909, the price includes the manuscript catalogue of the collection.

A Venetian raised point lace collar and yoke, purchased from the Scuola Neeletti, Burano in 1906 for £6, with original sealed tape label.
£325–375 FWec

A pair of woven wool double cloth, designed by William Morris, decorated with birds and flowers in blue, red, green and fawn wools, 1878, 54¼ x 43¼in (138 x 110cm).
£750–825 P

◀ A red cotton coverlet, printed with undulating stems and flowers in blue, yellow and green, padded and quilted, late 19thC, 82¾ x 78¾in (210 x 200cm).
£325–375 P

◀ A crocheted linen tray cloth, c1900, 19 x 26½in (48.5 x 67.5cm).
£25–30 Ech

An Irish linen tray cloth, with crocheted border, c1900, 30 x 21in (76 x 53.5cm).
£25–30 AIL

A linen cloth, with crocheted bird and flower border, 1900, 25½in (65cm) square.
£20–25 Ech

▶ A linen cloth, with cut-work pattern and crocheted border, 1940s, 35in (89cm) square.
£35–45 Ech

COSTUME

A young man's brown cotton velvet jacket, with standing collar and mother-of-pearl buttons to front and cuffs, c1790.
£425–475 P

A printed silk summer shawl, decorated with paisley design in green, brown, red and black, with fringed border, c1840, 132 x 66in (335 x 167.5cm).
£120–180 JPr

A quilted lilac silk bonnet, the brim decorated with white net and ribbon, later purple silk ribbon ties, c1850.
£240–270 P

An ivory silk pleated-waist petticoat, the border brocaded with coloured silk flowers and foliage, lined with ivory silk, c1780.
£3,500–4,000 P

A cream silk scarf, printed and hand-coloured with 'The Reformers attack on the old rotten tree or the foul nests of the cormorants in danger', the Anti-Reformers including Wellington leaning with palms against the falling trunk, Peel pushing with his back, within an enclosed border, 1831, 32in (82cm) square.
£300–350 P

A gentleman's waistcoat, the ivory silk fronts embroidered with rose and carnation sprigs in coloured silks, with linen back and lining, c1810, and 2 proclamations concerning the Brass Founders and Braziers.
£500–550 P

This waistcoat is understood to have been worn at the procession held in support of Queen Caroline on 6th November 1820. The wearer could have been a member of the Guild of Armourers and Braziers, since the family name Dudley appears under 'Apprenticies' in 1739 and 1777 in the company's record.

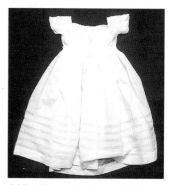

A Victorian cotton lawn child's dress, the bodice and sleeves decorated in Ayrshire work.
£50–55 CHU

> **Cross Reference**
> Weddings

◀ A printed fine wool double shawl, red, green, cream and brown, 1850s, 130 x 65in (279.5 x 165cm).
£200–220 L&L

An Irish cream cashmere blouse, with Victorian lace border and cuffs and open-work lace inserts, made up c1930s.
£600–675 JVa

An Irish hand-embroidered cream silk cape, with silk fringe, c1860, 40in (101.5cm) long.
£1,200–1,500 JVa

A green silk parasol, 1880, 26in (66cm) long.
£40–50 JPr

A pair of French black silk satin shoes, with slightly waisted heel, with label 'Henry Marshall, 74 Oxford Street, London', c1860.
£140–160 P

An Edwardian wide-brimmed black velvet hat, trimmed with black feathers and pink roses, 14in (35.5cm) diam.
£110–130 TT

▶ A pair of black leather north of England, children's clogs, late 19thC, 5in (12.5cm) long.
£60–70 SWN

A Edwardian black silk evening dress, with beadwork trimming.
£130–150 TT

An Irish Clones lace blouse, in shamrock and rose design, late 19thC.
£900–1,000 JVa

An Irish lady living in America made garments such as this one, often for Hollywood stars.

▶ A black velvet silk-lined coat, decorated with silk rosettes, 1900.
£110–120 HarC

An Edwardian plume hair decoration, 15in (38cm) long.
£60–70 L&L

A Edwardian cream lace skirt, bolero and modesty vest.
£340–380 L&L

A French lady's black silk riding hat, by Rousseau of Saumur, in original box, c1910, 12in (30.5cm) wide.
£100–120 L&L

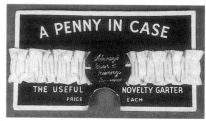

A pink novelty garter, inscribed 'Always keep a penny by you', on original card, 1920, 6¼in (16cm) wide.
£10–15 WAB

Three pairs of Dent's sports socks, with red, blue, orange and green borders, 1920s, 11½in (29cm) long.
£8–10 pair PC

A red umbrella, with composite duck's head handle, 1930, 27in (68.5cm) long.
£60–75 JPr

A black beaded dress, on cotton muslin, with dropped waist and scalloped hem, 1920.
£350–400 TT

A black silk devoré evening jacket, with deep cuffs, 1930s.
£100–135 TT

◄ A black and silver lamé tea gown, labelled 'Marshall & Snelgrove, The Teagown Department', 1923.
£140–160 TT

A red, yellow green and brown chiffon dress and jacket, 1930.
£80–100 TT

A purple and yellow silk chiffon dress and jacket, with scalloped hem, 1930s.
£100–130 L&L

◀ A pair of blue and white cloth gauntlets, 1930s, 13in (33cm) long.
£12–15 PC

A pair of Russell & Bromley green silk shoes, with silver leather decoration and ankle straps, 1930s, 10½in (26.5cm) long.
£60–70 PC

A pair of French lady's high-heeled shoes, by Raoul Shoe of Paris, with ankle strap, 1930s.
£20–25 Har

A black satin evening dress, with silk fringed skirt and cream lace modesty vest, 1930s.
£80–100 L&L

A black velvet hat, decorated with black feathers, 1930s.
£40–45 Ech

◀ A straw boater, with black ribbon band, 1930, size 6¾in.
£40–45 DQ

A green silk georgette evening dress, with cross-over bodice and cap sleeves, 1940s.
£100–125 BMo

A French light-green crepe dress, with red, blue, yellow and brown, 1940s.
£25–35 TT

A Hebe Sports tailored suit, grey with beige stripes, 1940s.
£35–45 TT

◄ A pair of Styleez navy blue suede shoes, with matching leather trim and bow, 1940s, size 5.
£35–40 TIN

A Cohama Casual gentleman's brown and beige tie, 1940s, 50in (127cm) long.
£10–12 RAD

A Forsyth Plumage Prints gentleman's tie, with orange and black birds on an orange and grey ground, 1940s, 50in (127cm) long.
£20–25 RAD

A red chiffon ball gown, with red silk underskirt, 1950s.
£40–50 HarC

A green silk evening coat, with roll collar and cuffs, made in Dublin by I. B. Jorgenson, 1950s.
£180–200 JVa

A pair of Simpson's green and gold brocade peep-toe evening shoes, with gold straps, 1950s.
£10–15 Ech

A pair of GWG Kings ringspun 16oz denim work jeans, 1960s, 34in (86.5cm) waist.
£40–50 ROK

◄ A Vivienne Westwood World's End label Pirate Collection three-piece striped Madras cotton unisex suit, with trousers and waistcoat, in grey, green and red, reversible to grey, 1981–82, jacket 38in (96.5cm) long.
£400–450 ID

◄ A Vivienne Westwood Savage Collection white cotton dress, with Andy Warhol soup can printed on the train, c1981, dress 44in (112cm) long.
£300–350 ID

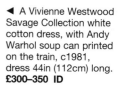

A Kellog tiger oak cathedral top picture frame wall telephone, 1901, 25in (63.5cm) high.
£500–550 EKK

A Bakelite telephone, with alphabet dial and drawer, c1920–30, 8½in (20.5cm) wide.
£450–500 DHAR

A Bakelite candlestick telephone, with alphabet dial, early 20thC, 8in (20.5cm) high.
£90–110 GAZE

A Coteg child's tinplate telephone exchange, 1940s, 11in (28cm) wide.
£30–35 BLH

A 332 acrylic telephone, with original handset, cord, alphabet dial and drawer, 1950s, 6in (15cm) high.
£320–350 OTC

An EricoFon 600 acrylic one-piece telephone, the dial contained in base, produced by L. M. Ericsson, 1960s, 9in (23cm) high.
£75–80 DOM

A Merlin S2616LS Series 3 multi-function telephone, with simulated stainless steel buttons, and medium wave radio, c1970, 8in (20.5cm) wide.
£15–20 DOM

A Compact plastic telephone, 1970, 5in (12.5cm) wide.
£70–80 DOM

This telephone came with an external bell-box as there was no bell within.

A BT £10 phonecard, produced for troops in Bosnia, 1994.
Used   £5–10
Mint   £35–40 JCa

◀ A BT Tiddywinkles trial phonecard, mint condition, early 1996.
£450–500 JCa

An American El Monte California Telecommunications Corporation plastic Mickey Mouse telephone, 1970s, 16in (40.5cm) high.
£175–195 DHAR

A double-sided wool and cotton fringed paisley shawl, c1870, 66in (167.5cm) square.
£4000–450 JPr

A Victorian black bonnet, with ostrich feathers and artificial flowers, in original box, box 10in (25.5cm) high.
£65–85 L&L

A Simpsons of Kendall oak firescreen, with original needlework panel, c1920, 28 x 20in (71 x 51cm).
£340–375 RUSK

A pair of quilted satin slippers, with brown fur trim, 1920s.
£35–45 L&L

A silk kimono jacket, 1920s.
£50–60 HarC

A Ridgemont straw hat, with ribbon bands and decoration, 1920s, 7in (18cm) high.
£80–90 PC

An Ethiopian wedding dress, decorated with beads, 1920s.
£200–250 TT

► A chiffon tabard, woven with lamé roses, 1920s.
£60–70 TT

► A printed cotton evening dress, decorated with sequins, labelled 'Saks, New York, Gallerie Moderne', 1930s.
£90–100 TT

A Vivienne Westwood Buffalo Collection sheepskin coat, 1982–83.
£1,400–1,600 ID

A set of milliners' moulds, c1900–10, largest 11in (28cm) long.
£75–150 each RUL

A craftsman-made gunmetal shoulder plane, with ebony wedge and infill, 19thC, 8in (20.5cm) long.
£160–200 WO

A set of 4 boxwood spokeshaves, c1900, largest 7½in (19cm) wide.
£40–50 MRT

A Deering cast-iron scythe blade grinder, restored, 1910, 15in (38cm) wide.
£55–65 JUN

► Two Swedish Sievert brass oil-burning soldering blow lamps, c1940–50, 7in (18cm) high.
£8–10 each DOM

A Norris 50G steel-soled gunmetal smoother, with original blade 1920, 9in (23cm) wide.
£300–350 TOM

A Farrbest steel and brass electric hat stretcher, c1920, 13in (33cm) high.
£220–250 RUL

A carved and painted wood peacock chariot fairground ride, 72in (183cm) long.
£1,000–1,200 JUN

An Orton & Spooner carved and painted wood cockerel carousel ride, c1900, 58in (147.5cm) long.
£1,200–1,500 JUN

A Stollwerk printed tin child's gramophone, playing chocolate records, in original boxes, c1903, 11in (28cm) high.
£1,500–2,000 HHO

A wooden pond yacht, 'Claughton', painted and varnished with lined decking, heavily weighted keel, mast and rigging, early 20thC, 27½in (70cm) long.
£220–240 AH

A painted wood gypsy caravan, 1905, 22in (56cm) long.
£400–450 JUN

A Lahman wind-up tin delivery truck, model AHA, c1920, 5in (12.5cm) long.
£450–500 HOB

A Bing 240 tinplate clockwork steam engine, 1912, 16in (40.5cm) long.
£850–950 JUN

The Hornby Clockwork Train, in Great Northern green livery, brass numberplate 2710, 1920, 14in (35.5cm) wide, in original box.
£1,100–1,300 S(S)

A Hornby No. O clockwork train set, in Great Northern livery, including an 0-4-0 locomotive and tender, 2 coaches and track, in original box, early 1920s, box 21in (53.5cm) wide.
£300–350 BKS

A Marx Merry-makers tinplate wind-up toy, by Louis Marx & Co, c1923, 10in (25.5cm) wide.
£1,700–2,000 HOB

▶ A wooden model of a gypsy caravan, 1920s, 11in (28cm) long.
£85–95 JUN

A Bassett-Lowke 0 gauge clockwork LMS locomotive and tender, restored, 1920s, 17in (43cm) long, in original box.
£230–270 BKS

Two Bing Pygmyphone children's tin gramophones, c1925, 6in (15cm) square.
£80–120 each HHO

A metal toy fort, on a wooden base, 1920–50, 18in (45.5cm) wide.
£45–55 UNI

▶ A Hornby railway wagon, inscribed with 'Crawford's Biscuits' and crest in gold, c1927, 7in (18cm) long.
£150–200 HOB

A Tipp & Co tinplate fire engine, with working bell under, manually controlled front wheels and tin tyres, 1927, 10in (25.5cm) long.
£150–180 BKS

A Hornby 0 gauge single wine wagon, c1928, 6in (15cm) long.
£250–300 HOB

A Hornby No. 2 electric LNER 201 Bramham Moor locomotive and tender, 1930, 16in (40.5cm) long.
£1,600–2,000 HOB

A Triang toy wheelbarrow, c1930, 22in (56cm) long.
£15–20 GAZE

A Hornby No. 2 Special Bramham Moor clockwork locomotive and tender, 1930s, 14in (35.5cm) long.
£700–800 BKS

◀ A Casio tinplate toy sewing machine, 1930s, 7in (18cm) wide.
£45–55 PC

▶ A Hornby Lord Nelson electric locomotive, with boxed tender, 1930s, 16in (40.5cm) long.
£280–300 BKS

A Hornby station, with note indicating its history and ownership, 1930s, 33in (84cm) long, in original box.
£110–130 BKS

An LMS 4–4–2 locomotive and tender, 3½in gauge engineered live steam model, in GNR, early 1930s, 45in (114.5cm) long.
£1,000–1,200 ROS

A Mettoy tinplate Rolls Royce, rusted condition, 1930s, 14in (35.5cm) long.
£50–60 DRJ

In good condition this toy could be worth £500–600.

A Triang Gyro Cycle, with original oil bottle, box and operating leaflets, 1930s, 8in (20.5cm) long.
£190–210 BKS

A Ubilda tinplate Tower Bridge, with approximately 92 screw-together parts, 1930s, 16in (40.6cm) wide, in original box.
£240–260 BKS

A Hornby snow plough railway wagon, 1936, 7in (18cm) long.
£70–85 HOB

A Meccano Elektron Electrical Experiments kit, 1935–36, in original box, 15in (38cm) wide.
£200–240 RAR

A Dinky Toys petrol truck, 1930–40s, 4in (10cm) long.
£250–300 MRW

A Hornby LNER 234 clockwork locomotive and tender, c1938, 15in (38cm) long.
£750–900 HOB

A Mar Pinocchio tinplate wind-up walking toy, c1939, 8in (20.5cm) high.
£800–900 HOB

◄ A Meccano No. 10 outfit, 1930s, 28in (71cm) wide, in original wooden box.
£1,200–1,400 BKS

Three Hornby 0 gauge railway wagons, c1940, 6in (15cm) long, in original boxes.
£30–40 each STK

A German Schuco
Varianto 3010H racing
set, comprising 2 tinplate
clockwork vehicles and
3 sections of tinplate track,
in original box, unused,
together with 2 unboxed
vehicles, some wear to
both, late 1930s.
£260–300 WAL

A Triang Spot-On
Arkitex Construction Kit,
c1950, in original box,
17in (43cm) wide.
£18–20 GAZE

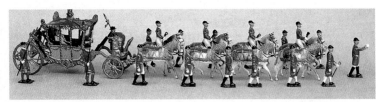

A Britains State Coach, set No. 1470, in original box, 1950s, 10in (25.5cm) long.
£140–160 WAL

A Triang tricycle, with original bell,
c1950, 19in (48.5cm) long.
£25–30 GAZE

A Marx plastic wind-up Mickey
the Musician xylophone player,
c1950, 12in (30.5cm) high,
in original box.
£180–200 HOB

A Dinky Toys 39 series Chrysler Royal
Sedan, late 1940s, 4in (10cm) long.
£110–130 WAL

A Japanese Return Top Deluxe yo-yo, 1940,
2in (5cm) diam.
£18–20 YO

A Dinky Supertoys dumper truck No. 562,
1948–54, 4in (10cm) long, in original box.
£35–40 DAC

A Basset-Lowke 0 gauge Queen Elizabeth electric
locomotive and tender, c1952, 20in (51cm) long.
£1,700–2,000 HOB

A Mettoy tinplate Cottage Hospital, with interior furniture
and figures, 1950–60s, 19½in (49.5cm) wide, in original box.
£60–70 BLH

An Elm Toys plastic Acrobat Friction Ice Cream
Peddler, 1950s, 5½in (14cm) high.
£40–45 UNI

A Dinky Toys 156 Rover 75 saloon car, 1954–56, 4in (10cm) long, in original box.
£150–170 Bon(C)

A Dinky Toys 108 MG Midget Sports No. 24, 1955–59, 3½in (9cm) long, in original box.
£100–120 Bon(C)

◄ A Dinky Gift Set Post Office Services No. 299, in original box, 1957, 10in (25.5cm) long.
£180–200 RAR

A tinplate Noddy's Jack in the Box, 1956, 6in (15cm) wide.
£50–60 GAZE

A Lumar 34 pressed metal yo-yo, 1950s, 2¼in (5.5cm) diam.
£18–20 YO

A tinplate Atomic Rocket, with lever action, 1950s, 7in (18cm) long, in original box.
£220–250 HUX

A Marx battery-operated tinplate and plastic Nutty Mad Indian with War Whoop, No. J-9619, 1950–60s, 14in (35.5cm) high, in original box.
£110–120 MED

A Britains Model Farm, set No. 152F, comprising 10 pieces, slight damage, 1950s, in original box.
£110–130 WAL

A Dinky Toys No. 771 International Road Signs, c1958, 7in (18cm) wide, in original box.
£90–95 DAC

A Dinky Toys Foden Flat Truck, No. 902, late 1950s, 7in (18cm) long, in original box.
£150–170 WAL

A Dinky Toys Racing Cars Gift Set No. 249, comprising 5 cars, minor damage, late 1950s, 12in (30.5cm) wide, in original display box.
£630–700 WAL

A Wells tinplate toy coach, 1950s, 7in (18cm) long.
£55–65 JUN

A Lumar pressed metal whistling yo-yo, 1950s, 2½in (6.5cm) diam.
£60–80 YO

A plastic horse on metal rockers, restored, 1960s, 36in (91.5cm) high.
£65–75 UNI

A plastic battery-operated Clown in Car, with control box, 1960s, 14in (35.5cm) long.
£100–120 UNI

A Marx battery-operated walking Batman, with inflatable body, in original box, 1966, 17in (43cm) high.
£280–300 GAZE

A Japanese Taiyo tinplate US Army tank, 1960s, 11in (28cm) long.
£80–90 JUN

A Britains Horseguard, 1960s, 3in (7.5cm) high.
£8–10 UNI

An Alps Japan tinplate battery-operated Mambo Jolly Drumming Elephant, in original box, some wear to box, 1960s, 10in (25.5cm) high.
£150–200 UNI

A Dinky Alfa Romeo O. S. I. Scarabeo, in original box, 1968, 3¾in (9.6cm) long.
£35–45 OTS

A tinplate Flying Saucer X–7, with mechanical bump-and-go mechanism and animated pilot, small dent to front, 1950–60s, 7¾in (19.5cm) diam.
£50–60 BLH

A Triang Blue Pullman electric train set, No. RS52, early 1960s, in original box, 15in (38cm) wide.
£60–70 GAZE

A Captain Scarlet Lone Star diecast cap gun, 1960s, 7in (18cm) long.
£40–45 GAZE

A Marx Speedmarx Over and Under Auto Racing Set, in original box, 1960s, 19in (48.5cm) wide.
£10–15 GAZE

A Japanese robot, 1960s,
16in (40.5cm) high.
£400–450 CW

This robot is unusually large, hence its high price range.

A Japanese Tomiyama tinplate Man Blowing Bubbles, 1960s,
10in (25.5cm) high.
£40–50 RAR

A Micronauts Biotron, 1976, in original packaging,
14in (35.5cm) high.
£45–50 OW

A *Star Wars* figure of Greedo, gun missing, 1978, 4in (10cm) high.
£5–6 UNI

A Wills Finecast 00 gauge LSWR class T9 kit-built locomotive and tender, 1975,
9in (23cm) long, in original box.
£140–160 RAR

► An MB Electronics Super Simon game, 1970s, 12in (30.5cm) wide.
£15–20 CGX

An Airfix Micronauts Microtron Motorized Mini-Robot, 1976, box 10 x 8in (25.5 x 20.5cm).
£25–30 OW

A Walt Disney Maximillian Action Figure, from *The Black Hole,* 1979,
3¾in (9.5cm) high, on original card.
£20–25 OW

A Space Hopper, 1970s, 21in (53.5cm) high.
£25–30 ZOOM

A foam rubber Noddy in his car, 1970s, 5in (12.5cm) long.
£25–30 GAZE

An American yo-yo instruction book, by Linda Sengpiel, 1972, 8in (20.5cm) diam.
£20–25 YO

A *Star Wars* Chewbacca, 1980, 3¾in (9.5cm) high.
£5–6 UNI

A Mattel figure of Mantenna from *The Masters of the Universe*, on original card, 1984, 11in (28cm) high.
£10–15 PC

A set of 4 ERTL *Star Trek III* figure of Captain Kirk, 1984, 6in (15cm) high, in original packaging.
£130–150 OW

A Mosaic Bookware The Adrian Mole Secret Diary Kit computer game and diary, 1986, 8½ x 6in (21.5 x 15cm).
£4–5 CGX

A Schleich French Fries Smurf, 1981, 2in (5cm) high.
£7–8 CMF

A Kenner *Star Wars Return of the Jedi* AST–5 Mini-Rig, unopened and in original packaging, 1980s, 6¼in (16cm) high.
£12–15 UNI

A Nintendo Game Boy game, 1980–90, 2½in (6.5cm) square.
£5–7 MEX

A Thunderbird rocket station and models, 1992, 20in (51cm) wide.
£14–18 GAZE

An SNK Neo-Geo Baseball Stars computer games, and 3 other computer games, 1990s.
Baseball Stars **£25–30**
Other games **£10–15 each CGX**

A Japanese Billiken National Kid tinplate wind-up robot, 1991, 9in (23cm) high.
£125–150 TOY

▶ A Team Losi Cherry Bomb yo-yo, 1998, 2in (5cm) diam.
£15–20 YO

An Ultimate Proyo II limited edition yo-yo, 1999, 2¼in (5.5cm) diam.
£12–15 YO

A Bakelite and chrome clock, by Japy, c1930, 14in (35.5cm) wide.
£170–200 BTB

An American rosewood-veneered clock, with white-painted dial and painting of rural scene beneath, open sprung 30-hour movement with alarm, original clock paper, c1850, 12½in (32cm) high.
£180–200 PC

A Swiss silver and enamel watch, by C. Bucherer, 1900, 2in (5cm) long.
£400–450 LBe

A Rotary Swiss Companion Set, 1950s, 8½in (21.5cm) wide.
£75–85 LBe

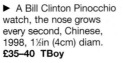

A Heuer Autavia GMT manual wind chronograph, with 12-hour indicator and second hand for reading different time zones, c1965.
£1,000–1,200 HARP

A Swiss Mr Peanut wristwatch, with leather strap, 1970s, 1¼in (3cm) diam.
£35–40 TBoy

A Heuer wrist mechanical stop watch, c1970.
£100–120 HARP

◀ A Zeon James Bond 007 alarm clock, 1980s, 7in (18cm) high.
£30–35 PLB

▶ A Bill Clinton Pinocchio watch, the nose grows every second, Chinese, 1998, 1½in (4cm) diam.
£35–40 TBoy

A POP Swatch Vivienne Westwood putti design wristwatch, in original packaging, 1992.
£130–150 ID

A carton of Monk & Glass Egg Substitute Powder, unopened, 1939–45, 3in (7.5cm) high.
£12–15 HUX

A cardboard packet of Rinso, stating 'Save this carton for wastepaper collection', 1939–45, 5in (12.5cm) high.
£9–11 HUX

A cardboard container of Mirro scourer, 1940, 10in (25.5cm) high.
£7–10 YR

A 1939–45 Star, Africa Star, Italy Star, War Medal, Territorial Efficiency Medal (Geo VI) awarded to Bdr. H. R. Osman, Royal Artillery.
£40–45 RMC

A pair of linen shoes, 1940s.
£30–35 HarC

Three officers' service dress caps, Gloucestershire Regiment, Green Howards and Hampshire Regiment, 1940s.
£35–40 each FAM

A homemade floral evening dress, 1940.
£45–50 TT

An American National Household Dried Machine Skimmed Milk, 1943–45, 4¾in (12cm) high.
£10–12 HUX

A British Civil Defence steel helmet, with Fire Guard arm band, 1941.
Helmet   **£10–15**
Arm band   **£5–6 FAM**

A pair of quilted shoes, with Utility mark, 1940s.
£30–35 TT

A carton of Orlox Beef Suet, 1939–45, 4in (10cm) wide.
£3–4 HUX

A Jacob Petit ceramic inkstand, c1830–62, 14in (35.5cm) wide.
£200–225 SER

A boulle inkstand, late 19thC, 13in (33cm) wide.
£800–900 TMi

An Edwardian post box, with lock and key, 34in (86.5cm) high.
£550–600 ACT

A silver and enamel half and one penny stamp envelope, Birmingham 1903, 1½in (4cm) wide.
£500–560 THOM

A papier mâché inkstand, with cinoiserie decoration, replacement inkwell, c1900, 8in (20.5cm) wide.
£80–100 MRW

◄ A De-La Rue Onoto mottled piston-filling fountain pen, 1919, 6in (15cm) long.
£150–170 RUS

A Waterman's Red Ripple piston-filling fountain pen, with nickel trim, 1920–30, 4in (10cm) long.
£145–165 AOH

A Swan Viso-Fill green basketweave fountain pen, with No. 3 nib, 1939, 5⅛in (14cm) long.
£180–200 RUS

A Dunhill Namiki lacquered desk base and pen, decorated with flowers and a butterfly, Dunhill Namiki No. 3 nib, 1930s, 6in (15cm) wide.
£500–600 RUS

A Simplex Special Demonstrated Model D tin Typewriter, c1940, 9in (23cm) wide.
£45–55 HarC

A Tom Thumb typewriter, by Western Stamping Co, Jackson, Michigan, c1950s, 9in (23cm) wide.
£25–35 SMAM

► A set of 6 Beatles pens, German, 1963, 6in (15cm) high.
£80–100 BTC

Two French cardboard cotton winders, 1900, 2¾in (7cm) diam.
£4–5 each VB

A Skyline wood and metal scoop and zester, 1950s, 8in (20.5cm) long.
£2–3 each AL

A pack of decimalisation playing cards, 1971, 4 x 2½in (10 x 6.5cm).
£1–2 CMF

Three Tomy automated toys, 1980s, largest 9in (23cm) high.
£3–5 each MED

Though individually these robotic toys could sell for higher prices from a dealer, the examples shown here were purchased as a group lot at a local auction, often a good venue for the bargain hunter.

◀ Four BT Radio Times phone-cards, early 1990s, 3½in (9cm) wide.
£1–2 CMF

A Reintal & Newman postcard, Nocturne by Philip Boileau, 1902, 5½ x 3½in (14 x 9cm).
£4–5 JMC

Sheet music, *When I Grow Too Old To Dream*, 1935, 12¾ x 9¾in (32.5 x 25cm).
£2–3 RAD

Two Eclipse Nursery Rhyme 6d records, in original sleeves, 1920s, 8in (20.5cm) diam.
£4–5 each GAZE

A metal milk crate, with 12 glass bottles, 1930s, 18in (45.5cm) wide.
£4–5 AL

An Early Bird matchbox, decorated with a sputnik, c1950s, 2in (5cm) wide.
£3–4 BTC

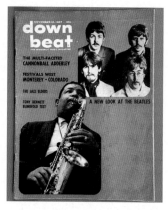

▶ A *Down Beat* magazine, featuring The Beatles, November 16, 1987, 11in (28cm) high.
£4–5 BTC

A set of Russian wooden babushka dolls, hand-painted as Bill Clinton, Monica Lewinsky, Paula Jones, Genifer Flowers and Hillary Clinton, 1999, Clinton 6in (15cm) high.
£40–50 PC

Bill Clinton's indiscretions have inspired a wealth of satirical memorabilia which is already being collected by political enthusiasts.

A Nintendo Game Boy Pokémon computer game, Blue Version, and promotional leaflet, 1999, 5in (12.5cm) square.
£24.99 PC

Created in Japan, Pokémon is one of the latest children's crazes. Tied in with the cartoon series, the range includes computer games, pocket monsters, trading cards, and a host of merchandise for the 'Pokémaniac'.

A Lulu Guiness hand-embroidered beaded black satin bag, with double handle, inside pocket and button-loop fastening, 1999, 8in (20.5cm) wide.
£249 Hds

Handbags have been a favourite accessory of the 1990s, and Lulu Guiness is one of the best known names in modern British handbag design.

▶ A German Vitra Design Museum Miniatures Collection chair, by Charles & Ray Eames, on a metal Eiffel Tower base, 1990s, 5¼in (13.5cm) high.
£75–90 PC

The Vitra Design Museum have produced a range of exact scale models of classic designer chairs from the 20thC, perfect collectables for the design enthusiast.

A wooden table lamp, by Anish Kapoor, from the At Home with Art range created for Homebase, 1999.
£56.99 Hmb

Homebase commissioned 9 leading British artists, including recent Turner Prize winners, to each create a domestic object for mass production. The aim of the project was to make the work of contemporary artists more accessible and more affordable.

An American Infamous Meanies Buddy the Dog, Clinton's dog, with Monica's knickers in his mouth, and a poem, c1997–98, 6in (15cm) high.
£15 TBoy

The Beanie Baby is dead, long live the Beanie Baby! Ty decided to retire its Beanie Babies on the last day of 1999. Shown here is 'The End', the last Ty bear to be produced. Ty's success has spawned a host of imitators, or 'wanna-beanies', including this Andrex bear and Buddy, Bill Clinton's dog, from the 'Infamous Meanie' range.

◀ A Rexel Staple Wizard electronic stapler, 1990s, 6in (15cm) wide.
£9.99 PC

Look out for new technology and interesting and decorative office equipment.

A Beanie Baby Ty bear 'The End', with no date of birth, he was the last to be produced, 1999, 8½in (21.5cm) high.
£4–6 BeG

An Andrex bean baby labrador puppy, complete with pouch and box, available for £2.50 plus tokens from Andrex as a special offer, made in 1999.
£2.50 PC

Tools

A sportsman's combination tool set, contained in turned horn handle, late 18thC, 6½in (16.5cm) long.
£200–225 WO

A brass and steel goneostat, for sharpening ornamental turning tools, c1840, 4in (10cm) wide.
£80–100 TOM

A pair of architect's brass trammels, c1870, 9¼in (23.5cm) long.
£70–80 WAB

A pair of blacksmith's shears, 19thC, 14in (35.5cm) long.
£35–45 AAN

A rosewood bow saw, probably made for exhibition, early 20thC, 20½in (52cm) wide.
£50–55 WO

l. A Sharratt & Newth glass cutter, with wheel and diamond, 3½in (9cm) long.
£16–20
r. An A. Shaw & Son diamond cutter for plate glass, c1900, 8in (20.5cm) long.
£7–9 MRT

A cobbler's cast-iron last, c1900, 23in (58.5cm) high.
£50–60 RUL

◀ A Norris London No. A3 parallel-sided wood and steel smoother, 20thC, 7½in (19cm) long.
£400–450 WO

A sailmaker's lignum vitae sewing mallet, 1930s, 13½in (34.5cm) long.
£25–30 WO

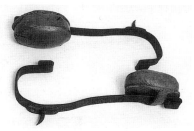

A pair of telegraph climbing hooks, with leather pads, 1950s, 12in (30.5cm) long.
£25–30 ET

Toys

A German Noah's Ark and animals, with Noah and his family, 38 paired animals, 7 paired birds and 13 odd animals and birds, painted in bold colours, some damage, mid-19thC, ark 19¼in (49cm) long.
£650–750 S(S)

A German pull-along toy, the composition-headed trainer with cloth clothing, the stick moving and the plush bear's head nodding when pulled along, c1900, 12¼in (31cm) long.
£650–750 Bri

Bill and Ben, The Flowerpot Men, and Weed, with painted faces, by Sacul Playthings Ltd, and 2 terra-cotta flowerpots, small chips, 1951, 3¼in (8.5cm) high, with original box.
£1,000–1,200 S(S)

Launched in 1952, Bill and Ben, The Flowerpot Men, accompanied by Weed, were among the earliest stars of British Children's TV. Parents complained that their speech, consisting almost entirely of the word 'Flobadob', would impair children's develop-ment, a charge that has more recently been levelled at the Teletubbies. This is an extremely rare toy, hence its value.

◄ A box of 3 Stinkbombes, with original label and packaging, 1950s, 1¾in (4.5cm) diam.
£15–20 HUX

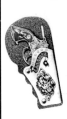  
BOATS

A Hobbies launch, entitled *Peggy*, mark one version, with steam engine and non-spill spirit burner, painted in yellow and green, 1923, 30in (76cm) long, with original box.
£475–525 BKS

A wooden Star pond yacht, with blue hull, c1950, on a new stand, 15in (38cm) high.
£30–35 AL

► A Gen Toy Sea Rover Catamaran, with red hull and white sails, 1960–70s, 24in (61cm) high, with original box.
£55–65 UNI

DIECAST VEHICLES

A Hornby Series Modelled Miniatures Set No. 22 Motor Vehicles, comprising red Open Sports Car No. 22a, yellow Sports Coupé No. 22b, blue Motor Truck No. 22c, orange Delivery Van No. 22d, yellow Tractor 22e, Tank No. 22f missing, some paint chips, c1933, in original box.
£5,000–5,500 S(S)

▶ A Dinky 39 series Studebaker State Commander coupé No. 39f, in dark green, late 1930s, 3½in (9cm) long.
£90–100 WAL

A Dinky 30 series Vauxhall No. 30d, in light brown with dark brown open base, black smooth hubs with original white rubber tyres, some chipping, late 1930s, 3½in (9cm) long.
£170–200 WAL

> **Cross Reference**
> See Colour Review

A Dinky Supertoy Continental Touring Coach No. 953, in light blue with white roof, with original box, 1950s, 5½in (14cm) long.
£170–200 DN

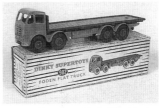

A Dinky Supertoys Foden Flat Truck No. 902, orange cab and chassis, green flatbed and wheel hubs, 1954–57, 7in (18cm) long, with box.
£150–180 Bon(C)

A Matchbox eight-wheeled turquoise and orange Crane No. 30c, 1960s, 1½in (4cm) long.
£2,700–3,000 VEC

Colour can be extremely important to the value of model vehicles. Because this crane is painted in turquoise and orange, which is a very rare colour combination, it surpassed its £100–150 estimate at auction.

A Dinky Captain Scarlet Maximum Security Vehicle No. 105, white with red interior, and a Spectrum Patrol Car No. 103, red with blue tinted windows, 1960s, 5in (12.5cm) long, with original boxes.
£140–160 GAZE

A Dinky Beats Morris Oxford No. 486, pink, turquoise and red, and 3 figures with black with red guitars, 1965–69, 3½in (9cm) long.
£35–40 MED

▶ A Corgi Junior Popeye Paddle Wagon, yellow, blue, red and black, 1969, 3in (7.5cm) long.
£30–35 GAZE

A Corgi Classics James Bond Aston Martin DB5 No. 04302, silver with red interior, 1998, 6in (15cm) wide, with original box.
£10–15 GRa

SOLDIERS

A Britains Scots Guards Set No. 130, and others, 237 figures, slight damage, 1930s, 2¼in (5.5cm) high, in original box.
£850–950 S(S)

A Britains Band of the Life Guards Set No. 101, comprising 12 pieces, director of music, drum horse and instrumentalists in state dress, with 2 spare drum horses, baton missing from director's hand, some damage, 1953, 2¼in (5.5cm) high.
£190–220 WAL

A Heyde Set No. 348 Dragoons Band, bandmaster conducting from fenced rostrum, Swiss clockwork musical mechanism within, 11 standing instrumentalists each at sheet music stand, in original red box with handwritten label, card insert and straw packing, one bugle detached, c1920, figures 2in (5cm) high.
£875–1,000 S(S)

A Britains Ski Troupers Set No. 2017, in white snow uniforms, with dark grey back packs and belts, 4 detachable rifles, skis and poles, minor wear, 1950s, 2¼in (5.5cm) high, in original box.
£240–280 WAL

A Britains Algerian Spahis Set No. 2172, comprising 4 troopers on white horses, and a standard-bearer on a brown horse, minor restoration, 1958–59, 2¼in (5.5cm) high, in reproduction box.
£360–420 Bon(C)

▶ A Britains Band of the 1st Life Guards Set No. 9406, comprising 12 band members on horseback, 1960–65, 14in (35.5cm) high, in original box.
£140–170 Bon(C)

◀ A Britains set of 3 models, a Guardsman, a Beefeater, and a Horseguard, c1974, 3½in (9cm) high, in original box.
£35–45 UNI

PEDAL & PUSH-ALONG TOYS

A French Déposé red scooter, with chain-driven rear wheel driven when the treadle on the platform is foot-depressed, 1920–30s, 33in (84cm) long.
£80–100 CARS

A Triangtois Dairy cart, the wooden body painted in green and yellow, 1920s, 18in (45cm) high.
£200–240 JUN

◄ An American Ertle cast-aluminium tractor, model No. D–65, 1950s, 38½in (98cm) long.
£100–120 JUN

A Lines Bros pressed aluminium pedal aeroplane, with wooden frame and pedals, working ailerons, rudder and propeller, 2 propellor blades missing, early 1920s, 46in (117cm) long.
£850–1,000 CARS

Lines Bros Ltd later formed Triang Toys Ltd. This aeroplane has original balloon-style wheels, solid rubber tyres and rubber drive-belt, complete with its contemporary half-circle steering wheel. The transfers/decals were applied at a later date.

► A Mobo yellow, red and green metal walking snail, 1954–55, 22in (56cm) wide.
£55–65 PC

A Mobo Joy Rider yellow, black and red metal go-cart, 1960s, 27in (68.5cm) long.
£14–18 GAZE

A carved wood rocking horse, dappled brown with grey mane and tail, with black and red saddle, mane and tail replaced, saddle restored, 1860, 73in (185.5cm) wide.
£2,400–2,650 RdeR

An F. H. Ayres carved wood rocking horse, with dappled finish, some damage, tail, stirrups, reins and part of saddle missing, c1900, 56in (142cm) high.
£3,400–3,800 S(S)

A carved wood rocking horse, with dappled body, leather harness, amber glass eyes, horsehair mane and tail, wrought-iron and painted wood stand with turned supports, early 20thC, 54in (137cm) long.
£380–430 AH

◀ A Triang carved wood rocking horse, painted white, with red saddle, the base with turned supports, c1920, 36in (91.5cm) long.
£500–600 CRU

A Lines Bros rocking horse, with Thistle badge on front, overpainted, c1920, 44in (112cm) long.
£500–600 STE

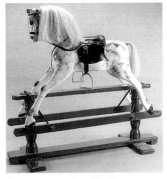

A carved wood rocking horse, with dappled grey body, horsehair mane and tail, black leather saddle and bridle, the painted pine base with turned supports, early 20thC, 44in (112cm) long.
£500–600 DN

◄ A platform carved wood rocking horse, in dappled grey, with hair mane and tail, leather saddle and red platform, one eye missing, early 20thC, 40in (101.5cm) long.
£480–500 SK(B)

A Triang wooden rocking horse, with white head and red seat, c1920s, 48in (123cm) long.
£30–35 GAZE

A Lines Bros rocking horse, requires restoration, c1920, 44in (112cm) long.
£1,800–2,000 STE

A white and brown plastic rocking horse on blue metal rockers, with red handles, 1960s, 23in (58.5cm) high.
£20–25 UNI

A Leeway rocking horse, c1970, 52in (132cm) long.
£300–350 STE

A carved wood rocking horse, with dappled grey body, horsehair mane and tail, stud eyes, with red velvet saddle cloth, probably by J. Collinson & Sons, Liverpool, 1960–70s, 54in (137cm) long.
£450–550 DN

▶ An F. H. Ayres rocking horse, retailed by Gamages, London, 1910, 54in (137cm) long.
£2,000–2,200 STE

A rocking horse, possibly by Frew, Ireland, tail and mane missing, c1900–10, 33in (84cm) long.
£700–800 STE

STAR WARS

A *Star Wars* Millennium Falcon ship, fawn with grey, blue and orange, 1978, 21in (53.5cm) long.
£30–35 UNI

In its original box, this item would be worth between £65–75.

A *Star Wars* Ree Yees figure, from *Return of the Jedi*, brown and beige, 1983, 4in (10cm) high.
£5–6 UNI

◄ A *Star Wars* Logray figure, from *Return of the Jedi*, in beige, brown and black, 1983, 3¾in (9.5cm) high.
£6–7 UNI

A *Star Wars* Darth Vader figure, cape and light sabre missing, 1980s, 16½in (42cm) high.
£20–25 UNI

Complete and in its original box this item would be worth between £110–125.

A *Star Wars* Han Solo figure, carbonite chamber missing, 1983, 4in (10cm) high.
£15–20 UNI

This was one of the 'last 15', the final set of *Star Wars* figures produced in the 1980s. Fewer were made, and these are therefore rarer than models from earlier *Star Wars* series.

Twelve Topps Star Wars Candy Containers, Yoda, Chewbacca, C3PO and Darth Vader, in original packaging, 1997, 7in (18cm) high.
£12–14 MED

◄ A *Stars Wars* Speeder Bike Vehicle, from *Return of the Jedi*, 1983, 8in (20.5cm) high, in original box.
£12–15 UNI

TINPLATE

A Lehmann clockwork tinplate crawling beetle, c1895, 2½in (6.5cm) long, with original cardboard box.
£190–220 DN

An American tinplate horse and cart, 'Best Coal Co', decorated in blue, yellow and brown, c1900, 25in (63.5cm) long.
£140–160 GAZE

A Lehmann 'Paddy and the Pig', No. EPL 500, hand-enamelled and with red and white saddle cloth, Paddy in cloth garments, printed label, pig's ears missing, c1910, 4in (10cm) high.
£360–400 S(S)

A Lehmann tinplate clockwork walking coolie, 'Nu-Nu' EPL 733 lithographed with blue smock, red trousers, pulling a tea chest printed in blue and fawn, printed marks, 1920s, coolie 5½in (14cm) high.
£400–450 S(S)

A SIJIM tinplate and composition organ grinder, with cloth jacket and trousers, the clockwork mechanism concealed in the barrel organ, c1915, 8¼in (21cm) high.
£230–260 Bri

A Brepsomy Toys tinplate Citroen B-14 four-door saloon, painted in yellow and brown, French, 1927, 21in (53.5cm) long.
£250–280 RAR

> **Cross Reference**
> See Colour Review

A Lawley tinplate Crazy Jeep 'Home James', painted in red, blue, yellow and fawn, c1930s, 6½in (16.5cm) long, with original box.
£50–60 RAR

A tinplate frog clacker, painted in red, green, white and black, 1920–30, 3½in (9cm) high.
£16–18 UNI

A Macfarlane Lang lithographed biscuit tin, in the form of a working water mill, painted in yellow, red, blue and green, 1930s, 7in (18cm) high.
£30–35 GAZE

Biscuit tins were often designed to be used as toys once the contents had been eaten.

A Tomiyama tinplate battery-powered remote-control 'Donny' smiling bulldog, with red mouth and studded leather collar, 1930–40, 8in (20.5cm) long.
£30–35 BLH

A Happy Nak toy tin drum, decorated with clowns in red, blue and yellow, c1950, 5½in (14cm) diam.
£15–18 OD

A Joustra tinplate electric key-wind Paris bus, painted in green and cream with red stripe, 1950s, 15in (38cm) long.
£150–170 DRJ

A battery-operated Space Patrol Car, lithographed in blue, cream and silver with red astronaut, 1950s, 9½in (24cm) long, in original box.
£750–850 SK(B)

Miller's is a price GUIDE not a price LIST

A Cragstan battery-operated tinplate robot, with silver-grey body, red arms and chest, clear plastic domed head, with visible mechanism, c1960, 10½in (26.5cm) high, in original box.
£1,000–1,100 SK(B)

A Wells Brimtoy tinplate and plastic friction drive Breakdown Truck, and a Cement Mixer, painted in red and yellow, 1950–60s, 4in (10cm) long.
£15–20 each UNI

► A Russian Aemompacca tinplate track and 4 buses, painted green, red, yellow and white, 1960s, 10in (25.5cm) wide, in original box.
£12–15 GAZE

◄ A Japanese Billiken tinplate wind-up Frankenstein robot, beige, brown, black and blue, in original brown and yellow box, 1991, 9in (23cm) high.
£125–150 TOY

TRAINS

A Hornby Pullman Dining Saloon car, green, gold and white, 1923, 13in (33cm) long.
£220–250 HOB

A Bowman Models LMS live steam 0 gauge 4-4-0 maroon and black locomotive and tender, late 1920s, 14in (35.5cm) long, in original wooden boxes.
£120–140 BKS

A Bassett-Lowke 0 gauge United Dairies Milk Tank, white and grey with red lettering, 1930s, 6in (15cm) long.
£220–250 WaH

Five Hornby 0 gauge petrol tank cars, green Pratts, blue Redline, grey Mobiloil, red Shell and cream British Petroleum, c1920–30, 6in (15cm) long.
£40–100 each HOB

Two Hornby 0 gauge double arm signals, bulb series, cream, black and red, 1930s, 14in (35.5cm) high.
£160–180 GAZE

Two Hornby junction points, in original green box, 1930s, 14in (35.5cm) long.
£25–30 HOB

A selection of coach destination name boards, 1935, 5in (12.5cm) long.
£25–30 each HOB

A Hornby Dublo Rail Cleaning Wagon, 1964, 3in (7.5cm) long, in original red and white box.
£260–300 RAR

A Hornby 'Princess Elizabeth' locomotive with tender, in maroon and black, complete with a 20v electric motor, 1937–39, 23in (58.5cm) long, in original blue presentation box.
£650–750 BKS

A Delton Locomotive Works '6' scale Mack Rail Bus, in red with black roof and snow plough, 1970–80, 16in (40.5cm) long.
£120–140 RAR

YO-YOS

Yo-yos have existed since ancient times and in many different cultures but, as yo-yo historian Martin Burton explains, the first documented yo-yo craze happened in France at the end of the 18thC. French Foreign Minister and chinoiseries collector Jean Baptiste Berlin imported the new toy from China and it became an instant hit with the upper classes. As the Terror spread, the aristocrats fled France to escape the guillotine and took their yo-yos with them.

According to Burton, the word itself is probably a corruption of the French term joujou (toy). The yo-yo became popular on the Continent and in Great Britain, where it was also known as the 'emigrette' and the 'quiz' and notable enthusiasts included the Prince of Wales (later George IV) and the Duke of Wellington.

By the end of 1820s, the yo-yo had waned in popularity and the next major craze was not until 100 years later in Los Angeles. Filipino émigré Pedro Flores was amazed that Americans did not play with yo-yos, hugely popular in his native country, where according to legend, they were derived from a traditional Philippine hunting weapon. Flores set about manufacturing yo-yos and also invented the two-stranded slip string, which enables yo-yos to do tricks. Chicago businessman Donald F. Duncan recognized the potential of this new toy, setting up his own business in 1927, and eventually buying out the Flores trademark. Duncan yo-yos came to dominate the market, thanks to aggressive publicity.

Duncan collaborated with newspaper magnate, William Randolph Hearst, launching major advertising campaigns, competitions, and professional displays, creating millions of sales and a national yo-yo passion that lasted up to World War II. From the 1950s onwards there have been various yo-yo crazes across the world, most recently in the UK in 1998 and yo-yos have developed hugely in technology and price.

Values of vintage yo-yos depend on age, rarity, material, decoration and performance, since most collectors are enthusiasts of the sport itself and like yo-yos that they can play with.

A rosewood yo-yo, c1880,
2½in (6.5cm) diam.
£80–100 HUM

A Victorian turned wood yo-yo,
2½in (6.5cm) diam.
£4–6 YO

The Art of Yo-Yo Playing book of tricks, orange and brown, 1950s,
5 x 4in (12.5 x 10cm).
£20–25 YO

A Lumar 99 yo-yo, red with black lettering, 1966,
2¼in (5.5cm) diam.
£8–10 YO

A Toberlone promotional yo-yo, yellow, green and blue with red lettering, late 1960s,
3in (7.5cm) diam.
£3–5 YO

A Lumar Wombles pressed metal yo-yo, green and purple on a blue ground, 1973, 2½in (6.5cm) diam.
£8–10 YO

A Lumar pressed metal promotional yo-yo, with yellow lettering *The Black Hole in Space* on a grey and purple, 1980s, 2¼in (5.5cm) diam.
£15–18 YO

A Tiffany & Co, New York, sterling silver and wood yo-yo, the top left blank for engraving, 1987, 2¼in (5.5cm) diam, in original box.
£120–130 YO

A Trag.E Toys Inc special edition reproduction of 1963 Pro-Yo, only sold in Arizona, green, yellow and red, 1983, 2¼in (5.5cm) diam, on original red and yellow card.
£12–14 YO

An American Spectra Star blue plastic yo-yo, *Star Trek Deep Space Nine*, with silver moulded spaceship, 1993, 2¼in (5.5cm) diam.
£10–12 YO

A MAG Predator custom yo-yo, with precision-engineered aluminium cut-out pattern in purple and silver, the pattern changed every 3 months, 1990s, 2¼in (5.5cm) diam.
£55–65 YO

▶ Two Playmaxx ProYo turquoise and green yo-yos, 1995–96, 2¼in (5.5cm) diam.
£8–10 YO

A German Moonstar Came-yo 1997, 2in (5cm) diam, in original box.
£100–125 ROU

A Yomega Metallic Missile aluminium yo-yo, purple with silver lettering, 1998, 2in (5cm) diam, on original blue and red stand.
£70–90 ROU

A German Mondial Injection Came-yo, in metallic blue with aluminium roller bearings, serial numbered, 1998, 2in (5cm) diam, in original box.
£100–125 ROU

A Revolution Enterprises Inc carbon fibre and aluminium yo-yo, purple and silver, 1999, 4in (10cm) square, in original box.
£80–100 YO

Treen

A Welsh sycamore love spoon, the carved handle decorated with hearts, 19thC, 8in (20.5cm) long.
£600–680 CoA

A lidded wooden barrel, late 18thC, 4¾in (12cm) high.
£70–80 OD

A rosewood Tunbridge Ware sovereign case, 1840, 1¼in (3cm) diam.
£65–75 MB

◀ Three Tunbridge Ware boxes, decorated with rabbit, stag and windmill designs, 1870–80, largest 2½in (6.5cm) wide.
£150–200 each VB

A pair of miniature mahogany shoes, with brass studs, 1860, 4½in (11.5cm) long.
£650–750 CHAP

A Tunbridge Ware kettle stand, with chequered pattern, c1880, 4½in (11.5cm) long.
£130–160 AMH

A Tartan ware egg-timer, replaced glass, c1900, 3in (7.5cm) high.
£80–100 MRW

An ivory and hardwood gavel, c1910, 8½in (21.5cm) long.
£400–450 ARE

Watches & Clocks

An Edward Hemmen, London, silver pair-cased verge pocket watch, with fusee movement, finely pierced and engraved balance cock, Tompion-type regulation and square pillars, marked H. M. London 1791, 50mm diam.
£300–350 PC

Cross Reference
See Colour Review

A silver full hunter verge watch, with fusee movement and enamel face, silver hands, key-wind and set, c1842, 50mm diam.
£400–450 DQ

A transitional half-hunter wristwatch, in silver case, 1920s, 35mm diam.
£150–180 BWC

A Hamilton 14ct gold manual wind wristwatch, the white gold case with hinged lugs and black enamelled bezel, c1925, 20mm diam.
£1,300–1,500 HARP

◀ An H. Samuel, London, gold wristwatch, with rolled-gold strap, 1913, 25mm diam.
£100–120 AOH

A Swiss Record rolled-gold wristwatch, with 15 jewel lever movement, c1933, 25mm high.
£150–170 DQ

An Omega 9ct gold wristwatch, with 15 jewel 265 calibre movement, c1937, 32mm diam.
£260–300 DQ

A Rotary 9ct gold lady's wristwatch, with subsidiary seconds, c1940, 20mm diam.
£100–125 BWC

A Swiss Universal manual wind steel-cased wristwatch, showing day, date, moonphases and month, with subsidiary seconds, c1948, 30mm diam.
£750–900 HARP

A French Favre-Leuba silver watch, the leather strap with silver adornment, c1960, 19mm wide.
£200–250 DID

A Samy Lay French silver wristwatch, c1960, 17mm diam.
£250–300 DID

A Rolex Oyster Perpetual 'Bubble-Back' automatic wristwatch, with steel case and blue sweep second hand, c1948, 28mm diam.
£1,000–1,200 HARP

A Tudor Royal shock-resisting mechanical wristwatch, with champagne dial and stainless steel case, with subsidiary seconds, 1950, 38mm diam.
£220–250 TIH

A Heuer Monaco manual-wind wristwatch, with 12-hour counter, c1969, 38mm diam.
£2,000–2,500 HARP

Heuer Monaco was made famous as the watch chosen by Steven McQueen in the 1973 film *Le Mans*.

A Rolex Oyster 18ct gold Calendar Chronograph, with silvered dial, telephone recording dial, day/month apertures, c1951, 40mm diam.
£20,000–25,000 Bns

An Old England chrome and Perspex wind-up wristwatch, with 17 jewel movement, 1970s, 38mm diam.
£65–75 LBe

A Heuer Carrera automatic chronograph, with blue face, 30-minute marker and date indicator, and blue leather strap, c1974, 32mm diam.
£850–1,000 HARP

A Heuer Skipper yachting wristwatch, the blue dial with 15-minute register and 5-minute markings, marked 'Valjoux Cal. 7734', c1975, 43mm diam.
£700–800 HARP

A Heuer Monte Carlo RAF aircraft mechanical stopwatch, c1980, 51mm diam.
£200–250 HARP

A Heuer manual wind chronograph, with 30-minute marker and date, c1980, 33mm diam.
£500–600 HARP

▶ A Zeon E.T. official quartz watch, in original red, black, blue and white packaging, 1980s, 10in (25.5cm) high.
£12–15 MED

◀ A Fossil Gold Limited Edition '007' Watch, No. 0874 of 1,000, in original gold case and black and gold box, 1997, 6in (15cm) wide.
£120–135 GRa

A French carriage clock, with gilt mask dial and subsidiary alarm, original platform cylinder escapement, c1880, 4½in (11.5cm) high.
£200–220 PC

A carved mahogany wall clock, by Wales & McCulloch, Ludgate Hill, London, with brass numerals and hands, c1880, 17in (43cm) diam.
£650–750 BYG

▶ A Welsh slate clock, 19thC, 14in (35.5cm) high.
£240–270 CoA

A French 8-day mahogany balloon clock, with inlay and boxwood stringing, brass ball feet, the movement by Marti striking to a gong, c1900, 12¼in (31cm) high.
£600–700 PC

A spelter novelty clock, the marble base with a figure standing on one leg, holding the clock on one raised hand, 1930s, 18in (45.5cm) high.
£400–450 BTB

▶ An Ingram red and green plastic Apple clock, in the shape of an apple, with black and white paper dial, one leaf broken, some staining to dial, 1960s, 11in (28cm) high.
£290–320 S

A Peter Pan combined alarm clock and gramophone, 1926, 7in (18cm) wide.
£700–800 HHO

A cream marble clock garniture, with winged sphinx, 1930s, clock 16in (40.5cm) wide.
£750–850 NET

A black and white Bakelite and chrome clock, 1940, 10in (25.5cm) wide.
£28–32 UTP

Miller's is a price GUIDE not a price LIST

A Westclox 'Big Ben' repeater clock, with purple face and chrome stand, 1970s, 7½in (19cm) high.
£35–40 ZOOM

A National Time Recorder Co wooden-cased factory time recorder, c1930, 34in (86.5cm) high.
£250–280 JUN

Weddings

Although traditionally women have always worn their best dress to get married in, the custom of a white wedding is a comparatively recent one, popularized in Britain by Queen Victoria, who married in a white dress. Blue was another 19th-century favourite, symbolic of the virgin and thought to be a lucky colour.

Many wedding customs derive from age-old superstitions. Bridesmaids dressed in a similar fashion to the bride and entered the church before her so as to confuse the devil and ward off any bad luck. In order to protect them in their turn from ill fortune, any pins used in fixing the wedding outfit had to be thrown away. Confetti is the modern equivalent of rice and wheat, thrown at the couple to ensure fertility, and a bride would save a length of her wedding dress fabric to make a christening gown, and the top tier of her wedding cake for the christening celebration.

The most decorative centrepiece of any wedding, however, is always the bride's outfit. Unless this was subsequently altered to serve as an evening gown, dresses would only be worn once and then carefully packed away. As such, vintage wedding gowns surface quite frequently, everywhere from auction houses to dealers to charity shops. Values depend on age, quality and condition – handmade lace veils and trimmings can be the most valuable part of the outfit; silks are often fragile and should be carefully examined for deterioration. Also, if you are buying to wear, remember that women have grown over the decades and have abandoned the corset – vintage wedding dresses are often small in size, with diminutive waists and armholes.

A Limerick lace bonnet veil, 1840–50, 40in (101.5cm) square.
£140–160 TT

A pair of cream silk satin wedding boots, 1870s, narrow size 4.
£140–160 CCO

A top hat, 1900.
£80–100 CCO

A cream satin wedding dress, decorated with lace, with diamanté trim, blue sash and pink rose, 1900, size 10.
£180–200 CCO

A Brussels bobbin and needlepoint appliqué bridal veil, with flowers and ferns, late 19thC, 88in (220cm) long.
£3,600–4,000 P

▶ A silk damask wedding dress, with cross-over bodice, sash and bow, 1912.
£200–225 TT

A silk and lace wedding dress, the sash with tassels, 1918.
£130–150 TT

An ivory silk satin and Chantilly lace wedding dress, with dropped waist skirt and diamanté clasp on a matching belt, 1920s, size 12–14.
£225–250 TIN

A bias-cut silk satin wedding dress, by Capt. E. Molyneux, the neck, sleeves and train heavily beaded with glass bugles, sequins and claw-set paste, 1930s, size 8–10.
£1,250–1,450 TIN

A Kewpie celluloid bride and groom wedding cake decoration, 1930s, 4in (10cm) high.
£130–150 SMAM

An ivory ostrich plume wedding cape, lined with silk georgette, and a matching wrist bag, 1930.
Cape   **£150–175**
Bag   **£65–75 TIN**

► A pearl-beaded silk tulle bridal headdress, with georgette lining, trimmed with wax flowers and leaves, 1930.
£55–65 TIN

◄ A bridal headdress, with waxed flowers and pink silk net petals, 1930, 13in (33cm) long.
£25–30 CCO

A box of Lucky Man wedding confetti, decorated in red and blue, late 1940s, 6in (15cm) high.
£7–10 YR

A silk wedding gown, 1940s.
£60–75 CCO

A plaster bride and groom wedding cake decoration, 1940s, 6in (15cm) high.
£55–60 SMAM

◄ An ivory feather bridal headdress, with matching wax flowers, with 2 bridesmaids' headdresses in pale blue, and a wedding photograph dated 1947.
£75–85 TIN

A morning suit, 1958, 40in (101.5cm) chest.
£40–50 CCO

World War II

World War II and post-war shortages stimulated a new breed of emergency decorative arts. The Utility Scheme was launched by the Government in the UK in the early 1940s to provide essential clothing and furnishings 'of good, sound construction, in simple but agreeable designs, for sale at reasonable prices, and ensuring the maximum economy of raw materials and labour'.

Goods were marked with the famous trademark CC 41, (see p429), standing for Civilian Clothing 1941, though the letters were deliberately abstracted so that the public would not recognize their specific meaning.

With people being bombed out of their homes, and the proliferation of marriages during and after the war, there was a huge need for domestic items. The Utility Scheme, which was not abolished until January 1953, was one way to beat the shortages; another was to 'make do and mend'. The second-hand market flourished and considerable ingenuity was shown in home dressmaking, transforming men's suits into women's clothing and exploiting every available resource from blackout material (one of the few unrationed fabrics) to parachute silk, used for wartime wedding dresses and underwear.

Along with food rationing came a range of products (dried egg, powdered milk) which provided a substitute for fresh produce. Manufacturers adapted their packaging to meet austerity restrictions. Containers were simplified, colours reduced and packages carried stern instructions about saving paper for salvage collection. Graphic creativity flourished, however, in the creation of propaganda posters, which spread wartime messages, often with great imagination. This section looks at World War II collectables, from military items to home front ephemera.

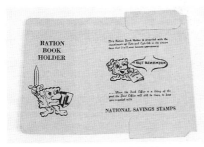

A Tate & Lyle Ltd Ration Book Holder, 1940s, 6¼ x 8in (16 x 20.5cm).
£3–5 HUX

A Sylvan Flakes washing powder box, 1939–45, 10 x 7½in (25.5 x 19cm).
£15–18 HUX

A Vim packet, printed in black on yellow and white with 'Save this carton for waste paper collection', 1939–45, 4in (10cm) high.
£12–15 HUX

An American Pure Dried Whole Eggs tin, packed for the Ministry of Food, with black lettering on white paper label, 1943–45, 3¼in (8.5cm) diam.
£14–16 HUX

A 4lb bag of sugar, 1940s, 7in (18cm) high.
£1–3 YR

◄ An American National Household Dried Machine Skimmed Milk tin, with red, blue and white label, 1940, 5in (12.5cm) high.
£3–5 YR

A tea packet, printed in green with 'Without coupon purchase cannot be admitted', 1940s, 7in (18cm) long.
£5–7 YR

A Horlicks Tablets tin, with cream, blue and red lid, as supplied to the Air Ministry, 1939–45, 4¼in (11cm) wide.
£6–8 HUX

An Austin's Wash Easy packet, printed in red and blue, sealed and unused, 1939–45, 5 x 3in (12.5 x 7.5cm).
£8–10 HUX

An American Dietaids Kup Kafay Instant Powdered Coffee tin, 1943–45, 2in (5cm) diam.
£8–10 HUX

A Rinso soap powder packet, printed in red and blue, 1940, 5 x 3in (12.5 x 7.5cm).
£5–7 YR

An Air Raid Precaution Sealing Tape tin, with brown lid, for sealing windows and doors during blackout restrictions, 1939–45, 5½in (14cm) diam.
£8–10 PC

A set of 7 Fougasse colour lithographs, 'Careless Talk Costs Lives', printed by the Ministry of Information in red, mauve, yellow and black, 1940, 12½ x 8in (32 x 20.5cm).
£675–750 S

Fougasse (1887–1965), whose real name was Cyril Kenneth Bird, was the son of England cricketer Arthur Bird. An engineer, he was badly wounded at Gallipoli in 1915 during WWI and, unable to work at his chosen profession, he turned to illustration. He chose as his pseudonym Fougasse, a French word for an unpredictable mine, a reference both to his own battlefield experiences and the fact that his drawings were full of surprises. As Art Editor for Punch, Fougasse produced his most famous work during World War II, when he created posters for the Ministry of Information, including the celebrated series 'Careless Talk Costs Lives'.

A chalk-stripe wool worsted suit, originally a gentleman, recut and styled to produce a lady's suit in an attempt to overcome the clothing coupon shortage, 1940, size 10–12.
£85–95 TIN

An American poster, 'Where Shall I Work Today?', printed on linen in yellow, black and orange, 1940, 28 x 24in (71 x 61cm).
£125–145 Do

458　**WORLD WAR II**

A pair of Air Raid Warden's battery-powered metal lamps, in khaki and green, 1940s, 4in (10cm) high.
£15–20 each DOM

The amount of light could be varied by lowering or lifting the obscurer hood especially useful for blackouts during wartime.

An chrome nameplate, 'Air Raid Warden', 1940s, 8¾in (22cm) long.
£25–30 HUX

► A J. Hudson & Co A.R.P. whistle, with chain and hook, early 1940s, 4in (10cm) long.
£16–18 AOH

An door nameplate 'A.R.P. Warden', brown with white lettering, early 1940s, 3 x 4½in (7.5 x 11.5cm).
£25–30 HUX

A British Home Comforts scarf and gloves set, in khaki wool, 1940s.
£10–15 FAM

A pair of maroon suede shoes, with utility mark impressed on sole, 1940s, 10in (25.5cm) long.
£45–55 PC

◄ Three pairs of Warnorm British Army grey, brown and khaki wool socks, 1940s.
£4–6 each FAM

A pair of British Army wool mixture underpants, 1940s.
£5–6 FAM

A Hampshire Regiment cap badge, pattern No. 12229, on card, dated '21.9.42'.
£90–100 WAL

During wartime restrictions, metal badges were replaced by plastic.

An other ranks' service dress cap, Dorsetshire Regiment, in khaki serge material, 1930s.
£35–40 FAM

A British MkI helmet, 1940s.
£10–15 FAM

A German flying cap, in blue-grey serge, with embroidered insignia, 1941.
£45–50 FAM

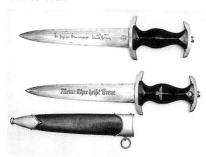

A Nazi M1933 SS dagger, by Carl Eickhorn, the blade with an un-erased Rohm inscription, the crosspiece stamped '16999', in its mounted metal sheath with dark blued finish, with single hanging strap, minor damage, 1940s.
£4,000–4,500 WAL

This rare dagger was captured in Heidl, Schleswig Holstein a few days after the end of WWII.

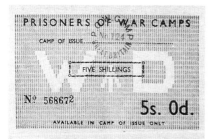

A set of Prisoners of War Camp notes, 3d, 6d, 1s, 2s 6d, 5s and 10s, printed 'Available in Camp of Issue Only', with various date stamps between October 1944 and November 1945.
£1,400–1,600 P

The notes, issued by the War Department are stamped 'P.O.W. Camp 124 Great Britain'. Records indicate that Camp 124 was Wapley Camp, Yate, near Bristol. The higher values in this series are quite scarce and a full set like this is rarely available.

A stainless steel and enamel surgeon's field washbasin, 59½in (151cm) high.
£475–525 ZOOM

A signed photograph of Winston Churchill, by Stoneman, slight damage, 6½ x 4½in (16.5 x 11.5cm).
£550–600 VS

A German Luftwaffe other ranks' blue-grey serge M43 cap, with embroidered insignia, 1940s.
£100–120 FAM

An aluminium 'V For Victory' Winston Churchill ashtray, 1940s, 5¾in (14.5cm) high.
£28–32 MED

A 'States of Guernsey' German occupation £1 note, printed in green on white, No. ZI 2279, dated '1st January 1943', 5¾in (14.5cm) long.
£220–240 WP

◄ A typewritten document entitled 'The Instrument of Surrender of all German Armed Forces in Holland, in north west Germany including all Islands and in Denmark', believed to be one of 6 made at the time of surrender at Luneburg Heath, signed by Field Marshall Bernard Law Montgomery and the 5 German representatives, dated '4th May 1945', 13 x 8in (33 x 20.5cm), framed.
£10,000–12,000 DDM

Writing

A Rogers ebony and brass quill cutter, 1840s,
4in (10cm) long.
£120–150 AnS

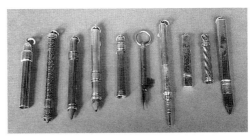

A collection of silver pencils, 1870–1910,
longest 4½in (11.5cm) long.
£18–35 each VB

Three travelling inkwells, in leather and brass
cases, 1880s, largest 3in (7.5cm) wide.
£40–80 each VB

A collection of novelty pencils, in metal,
wood and carved nuts, 1880–1910,
largest 3in (7.5cm) long.
£10–45 each VB

◀ A horn
paper knife,
with inlaid
flowers and
leaves, minor
damage,
late 19thC,
9in (23cm) long.
£35–40 MRW

A sheet-brass letter clip,
commemorating Queen
Victoria's Golden Jubilee,
1887, 4½in (11.5cm) high.
£70–80 CHe

A collection of bookmarks and letter-
openers, in mother-of-pearl, silver, wood,
jet, bloodstone, and brass-handled,
1880–1900 largest 3½in (9cm) long.
£15–44 each VB

Three stamp boxes, the lids
painted with Swiss scenes in blue,
green, brown and red, 1900–15,
largest 4in (10cm) wide.
£20–25 each VB

▶ An oak stationery cabinet with
inkstand, with fretworked and
studded brass hinges and decoration,
the base with a small drawer,
pen recess and 2 glass inkwells,
the sloping stationery cupboard
opening to reveal a fitted interior,
late 19thC, 11¾in (30cm) high.
£200–220 DDM

A bone-handled Sheffield steel ink eraser, 1890s, 5in (12.5cm) long.
£15–20 AnS

Three carved wood stamp boxes,
1910–15, largest 6¼in (16cm) wide.
£15–30 each VB

<table>
<tr><td>Cross Reference</td></tr>
<tr><td>See Colour Review</td></tr>
</table>

An 18ct gold-plated Zenith 'Safety' fountain pen, 1920, 4¾in (12cm) long.
£120–140 RUS

A Waterman's green marbled fountain pen No. 32½, with gold-plated
fittings, 1936, 5in (12.5cm) long.
£60–70 RUS

A mahogany desk calendar, 1920s,
11in (28cm) high.
£250–275 GeM

A De La Rue red and black mottled lever-filled
fountain pen, 1936, 4¾in (12cm) long.
£40–50 RUS

A National Security grey snakeskin lever-filled fountain
pen, 1940s, 4¾in (12cm) long.
£75–85 AOH

A rolled-gold 'Yard-o-Led' pencil, 1950,
5in (12.5cm) long.
38–42 ABr

A Mont Blanc green striated fountain pen, No. 644,
with gold-plated cap, 1950, 5½in (13.5cm) long.
£400–450 RUS

A Conway Stewart blue marbled fountain pen, No. 58,
with Duro nib, 1950, 5in (12.5cm) long
£60–70 RUS

A Conway Stewart red herringbone fountain pen,
No. 93, 1955, 5in (12.5cm) long.
£60–70 RUS

A Conway Stewart black fountain pen, No. 100,
with gold fittings, c1960, 5in (12.5cm) long.
£110–130 AOH

A Parker 45 Harlequin Shield fountain pen, 1980,
5½in (13.5cm) long.
£40–50 RUS

Directory of Specialists

If you require a valuation for an item it is advisable to check whether the dealer or specialist will carry out this service, and whether there is a charge. Please mention Miller's when making an enquiry. Having found a specialist who will carry out your valuation, it is best to send a description and photograph of the item to them, together with a stamped addressed envelope for the reply. A valuation by telephone is not possible. Most dealers are only too happy to help you with your enquiry, however, they are very busy people and consideration of the above points would be welcomed.

London

20th Century Glass, Kensington Ch St Antique Centre, 58–60 Kensington Ch St W8 4DB
Tel: 020 7938 1137
Tel/Fax 020 7729 9875
Mobile 07971 859848
Glass. Open Thurs, Fri & Sat 12–6pm or appt

Angling Auctions, PO Box 2095 W12 8RU
Tel: 020 8749 4175
Angling auctions

A. H. Baldwin & Sons Ltd Numismatists, 11 Adelphi Terr WC2N 6BJ
Tel: 020 7930 6879
Coins & commemorative medals

Barclay Samson Ltd, 65 Finlay St SW6 6HF
Tel: 020 7731 8012

Linda Bee Art Deco, Stand 18–21, Grays Antique Mkt, 1–7 Davies Mews W1Y 1AR
Tel: 020 7629 5921
Costume, perfume bottles & handbags

Beverley, 30 Church St, Marylebone NW8 8EP
Tel: 020 7262 1576
Art Deco furniture, glass, figures, metalware and pottery

Christie's South Kensington Ltd, 85 Old Brompton Road SW7 3LD
Tel: 020 7581 7611
Auctioneers

Comic Book Postal Auctions Ltd, 40–42 Osnaburgh St NW1 3ND
Tel: 020 7424 0007
Comic book auctions

Dix-Noonan-Webb, 1 Old Bond St W1X 3TD
Tel: 020 7499 5022
Auctioneers & valuers of historical & military medals

Liz Farrow t/a Dodo, Admiral Vernon Mkt, Portobello Rd W11
Sats only 9am–4pm. Posters & old advertising

Liz Farrow t/a Dodo, Stand F073/83, Alfie's Antique Mkt, 13–25 Church St NW8 8DT
Tel: 020 7706 1545
Tues–Sats only 10.30am–5.30pm. Posters & old advertising

Francis Joseph Publications, 5 Southbrook Mews SE12 8LG
Tel: 020 8318 9580

Michael C. German, 38B Kensington Ch St W8 4BX
Tel: 020 7937 2771
Walking canes

Brenda Gerwat-Clark, Granny's Goodies, G3/4 Alfie's Antique Mkt, 13–25 Church St NW8 8DT
Tel: 020 7706 4699
Dolls & teddy bears

Richard Gibbon G067 Alfie's Antique Mkt, 13–25 Church St NW8 8DT
Tel: 020 7723 0449
Costume jewellery

Harlequin House, Puppets & Masks, 3 Kensington Mall W8 4EB
Tel: 020 7221 8629

Best collection of Pelham puppets, also antique rod puppets from Polka Theatre, Wimbledon, old ventriloquist dummies, Czech puppets, Punch & Judy. Open Tues, Fri & Sat 11.00am–5.30pm. Top of Kensington Ch St, nearest tube Notting Hill Gate.

Adrian Harrington, 64a Kensington Ch St W8 4DB
Tel: 020 7937 1465
Antiquarian books, prints & maps

Peter Harrington, 100 Fulham Road SW3 6HS
Tel: 020 7591 0220/0330
Antiquarian books

Herzog, Hollender Phillips & Co, The Scripophily Shop, PO Box 14376 NW6 1ZD
Tel & Fax: 020 7433 3577
email:hollender@dial.pipe x.com website:
www.Currency.dealeronline.com/ScripophilyShop
Scripophily

David Huxtable, Stand S03/05 (Top Floor), Alfie's Antique Market, 13–25 Church St, Marylebone NW8 8DT
Tel: 020 7724 2200
Old advertising collectables

Murray Cards (International) Ltd, 51 Watford Way, Hendon Central NW4 3JH
Tel: 020 8202 5688
Cigarette & trade cards

Stevie Pearce, G144 Ground Floor, Alfie's Antique Market, 13–25 Church St NW8 8DT
Tel: 020 7723 2526
Costume jewellery & fashion accessories1900–70

Phillips, Blenstock House, 101 New Bond St W1Y 0AS
Tel: 020 7629 6602/ 7468 8233
Auctioneer

Geoffrey Robinson, GO77–78 (Grnd floor), Alfie's Antique Mkt, 13–25 Church St, Marylebone NW8 8DT
Tel: 020 7723 0449
Art Deco & post-war lighting, glass & chrome, small furniture etc

Rumours, 10 The Mall, Upper St, Camden Passage, Islington N1 0PD
Tel: 01582 873561
Moorcroft pottery

Vintage Cameras Ltd, 256 Kirkdale, Sydenham SE26 4NL
Tel: 020 8778 5416
Antique & classic cameras

Nigel Williams Rare Books, 22 & 25 Cecil Court WC2N 4HE
Tel: 020 7836 7757
Books – first editions, illustrated, children's & detective

Yesterday Child, Angel Arcade, 118 Islington High St N1 8EG
Tel: 020 7354 1601
Antique dolls & dolls' house miniatures

Zoom, 312 Lillie Rd Fulham SW6 7PS
Tel: 07000 ZOOM 2000 or 020 7386 9522
Mobile 0958 372975
'50s, '60s, '70s furniture, lighting & unusual retro objects

Bedfordshire

Paperchase,
77 Wingfield Rd,
Bromham, Bedford
MK43 8JY
Tel: 01234 825942
*The bi-monthly magazine
for all printed transport
collectables*

Christopher Sykes,
The Old Parsonage,
Woburn, Milton Keynes
MK17 9QM
Tel: 01525 290259
*Corkscrews & wine-
related items*

Berkshire

Collect It!, Unit 11,
Weller Drive, Hogwood
Ind Est, Finchampstead
RG40 4QZ
Tel: 0118 973 7888
Magazine for collectors

Mostly Boxes,
93 High St, Eton,
Windsor SL4 6AF
Tel: 01753 858470
Antique wooden boxes

Special Auction Services,
The Coach Hse,
Midgham Pk,
Reading RG7 5UG
Tel: 0118 971 2949
*Commemoratives, pot
lids & Prattware, fairings,
Goss & Crested, Baxter
& Le Blond prints*

Cambridgeshire

Antique Amusement Co,
Mill Lane, Swaffham
Bulbeck CB5 0NF
Tel: 01223 813041
*Vintage amusement
machines also auctions
of amusement machines,
fairground art & other
related collectables*

Cloister Antiques,
1a Lynn Road, Ely
CB7 4EG
Tel: 01353 668558
*Sewing, writing, heavy
horse, smoking*

James Fuller & Son,
51 Huntingdon Rd,
Chatteris P16 6JE
Tel: 01354 692740
Architectural antiques

Warboys Antiques,
Old Church School,
High St, Warboys,
Huntingdon PE17 2SX
Tel: 01487 823686
Sporting antiques & tins

Cheshire

Collectors' Corner,
PO Box 8, Congleton
CW12 4GD
Tel: 01260 270429
*Rock & Pop, Sci-Fi, TV
and Beatles memorabilia*

Dollectable, 53 Lower
Bridge St, Chester CH1 1RS
Tel: 01244 344888/679195
Antique dolls

Glass Collectors' Fair,
155 St John's Rd,
Congleton CW12 2EH
Tel: 01260 271975
Glass Collectors' Fairs

On The Air, 42 Bridge Str
Row, Chester CH1 1NN
Tel: 01244 348468
Vintage radios

Sweetbriar Gallery,
Robin Hood Lane,
Helsby WA6 9NH
Tel: 01928 723851
Paperweights

Charles Tomlinson, Chester
Tel & Fax: 01244 318395
email:charles.tomlinson
@lineone.net
*Antique scientific
instruments*

Treasures in Textiles,
Chester
Tel: 01244 328968
*Antique textiles & vintage
clothing*

County Durham

Michael's Antiques,
1 Friar Street,
Shotten Colliery,
Durham D86 2PA
Tel: 0191 517 0098
*Gold jewellery & watches,
collectors' items,
bric-a-brac, gold & silver,
repairs*

Derbyshire

Goss Collectors' Club,
Mrs Schofield
Tel: 0115 930 0441

Chuck Overs
Tel: 01298 83806
Transistor radios

Devon

Torquay Pottery Collectors'
Socy, Torre Abbey, Avenue
Rd, Torquay TQ2 5JX
email:tpcs@btinternet.com

Dorset

Ancient & Gothic,
PO Box 356,
Christchurch BH23 1XQ
Tel: 01202 478592
Antiquities

Books Afloat, 66 Park St,
Weymouth DT4 7DE
Tel: 01305 779774
*Books, shipping
memorabilia, models,
old postcards, paintings*

The Crow's Nest,
3 Hope Sq, opp. Brewers
Quay, Weymouth DT4 8TR
Tel: 01305 786930
*Curios, bygones, nautical
items, china etc*

Dalkeith Auctions,
Dalkeith Hall, Dalkeith
Steps, Rear of 81 Old
Christchurch Rd,
Bournemouth BH1 1YL
Tel: 01202 292905
*Auctions of postcards,
cigarette cards, ephemera
& collectors' items*

Hardy's Collectables,
862 Christchurch Rd,
Boscombe BH7 6DQ
Tel: 01202 422407/473744
Mobile 07970 613077
Poole Pottery

Old Button Shop Antiques,
Lytchett Minster BH16 6JF
Tel: 01202 622169
Buttons & collectables

Paddy Cliff's Clarice,
77 Coombe Valley Rd,
Preston, Weymouth
DT3 6NL
Tel: 01305 834945 email:
bizarre@uk.packardbell.or
website: paddycliff.com
Clarice Cliff

Poole Pottery, The Quay,
Poole BH15 1RF
Tel: 01202 666200
Poole Pottery

Michael Steen, 15 Bury
Rd, Poole BH13 7BE
Tel: 01202 700140
Wristwatches, glass fishes

Essex

GKR Bonds Ltd, PO Box 1,
Kelvedon CO5 9EH
Tel: 01376 571711
*Old bonds & share
certificates*

Haddon Rocking Horses
Ltd, 5 Telford Rd,
Clacton-on-Sea CO15 4LP
Tel: 01255 424745
website: www.haddon
horse.u-net.com
Rocking horses

Megarry's & Forever
Summer, Jericho Cottage,
The Duckpond Green,
Blackmore CM4 0RR
Tel: 01277 821031
& 01277 822170
*Antiques, Arts & Crafts.
Teashop & garden.
Summer opening:
10am–6pm daily except
Mon & Tues. Winter
opening: 11am–5pm
every day except Mon
& Tues. Member Essex
Antiques Dealers
Association. Car Parking*

The Old Telephone Co,
The Old Granary,
Battlesbridge Antiques
Ctr, Nr Wickford SS11 7RF
Tel: 01245 400601
Period telephones

Saffron Walden Saleroom,
1 Market St, Saffron
Walden CB10 1JB
Tel: 01799 513281
Auctioneer

Gloucestershire

Bread & Roses, Durham
House Antique Centre,
Sheep Street, Stow-on-
the-Wold GL54 1AA
Tel: 01451 870404 or
01926 817342
*Kitchen, laundry & dairy
antiques. Rural &
domestic bygones*

Grimes House Antiques,
High Street, Moreton-in-
Marsh GL56 0AT
Tel/Fax: 01608 651029
Glass

J Cards, PO Box 12,
Tetbury GL8 8WB
Tel: 01454 238600
Telephone cards

Park Hse Antiques & Toy
Museum, Park St, Stow-
on-the-Wold GL54 1AQ
Tel: 01451 830159
*Come & see one of the
best private collections
of old toys in the country.
Admission £1.50 OAPs
£1. Summer 10am–1pm,
2–5pm. Winter 11am–1pm,
2–4pm. Closed Tues and
all May. We buy old toys
and teddy bears*

Q&C Militaria, 22 Suffolk
Rd, Cheltenham GL50 2AQ
Tel: 01242 519815
Mobile 0378 613977
*Orders, decorations,
medals, uniforms,
militaria, Trench Art*

Specialised Postcard
Auctions,
25 Gloucester Street,
Cirencester GL7 2DJ
Tel: 01285 659057

Telephone Lines Ltd,
304 High Street,
Cheltenham GL50 3JF
Tel: 01242 583699
Antique Bakelite telephones

Greater Manchester

Acorn Auctions, PO Box
152, Salford M17 1BP
Tel: 0161 877 8818
*Postcard & ephemera
auctions*

Hampshire

Bona Arts Decorative Ltd,
The Hart Shopping
Centre, Fleet GU13 8AZ
Tel: 01252 372188/616666
website: www.bona.co.uk
*Art Deco, glass, lighting,
furniture, ceramics,
Clarice Cliff*

Classic Amusements
Tel: 01425 472164
Vintage slot machines

Cobwebs,
78 Northam Rd,
Southampton SO14 0PB
Tel: 023 8022 7458
*Ocean liner memorabilia.
Naval & aviation items*

Goss & Crested China
Club & Museum, inc
Milestone Publications,
Pat Welbourne,
62 Murray Rd,
Horndean PO8 9JL
Tel: 023 9259 7440

The Old Toy Shop,
Tel & Fax 01425 476899
*Clockwork, steam &
electric vintage toys,
memorabilia, figures*

Romsey Auction Rooms,
86 The Hundred,
Romsey SO51 8BX
Tel: 01794 513331
Toys, auctions

Romsey Medal Centre,
PO Box 169,
Romsey SO51 6XU
Tel: 01794 324488
*Orders, decorations
& medals*

Solent Railwayana
Auctions, 31 Newtown
Road, Warsash SO31 9FY
Tel: 01489 578093/584633
*Railway relics & model
railway items. Also
railwayana auctions*

Herefordshire

Unicorn Fairs,
PO Box 30,
Hereford HR2 8SW
Tel: 01989 730339
Antiques & collectors' fairs

Hertfordshire

Forget Me Knot Antiques,
Over the Moon,
27 High St,
St Albans AL3 4EH
Tel: 01727 848907
Jewellery

Isle of Wight

Nostalgia Toy Museum,
High St, Godshill,
Ventnor PO38 3HZ
Tel: 01983 730055
Die-cast toys

Kent

20th Century Marks,
12 Market Square,
Westerham TN16 1AW
Tel: 01959 562221
*20th century designs &
works of art, specializing
in British 'Pop'*

Amherst Antiques,
23 London Rd, Riverhead,
Sevenoaks TN13 2BU
Tel: 01732 455047
Mobile: 0850 350212
Tunbridge Ware

Beatcity, 56 High St,
Chatham ME4 4DS
Tel: 01634 844525/
077 70 65 08 90
*Beatles & Rock & Roll
memorabilia*

Candlestick & Bakelite,
PO Box 308,
Orpington BR5 1TB
Tel: 020 8467 3743/3799
Telephones

Carlton Ware Collectors
International,
Helen Martin, PO Box 161,
Sevenoaks TN15 6GA
Tel: 01474 853630

Claris's Tearooms,
1–3 High Street,
Biddenden TN27 8AL
Tel: 01580 291025
*Moorcroft, Dennis China,
Kingsley Enamels,
Okra Glass, TY Beanie
BabiesTM, Merrythought
Bears, Boyd's Bears,
Hantel miniatures*

Corridors of Time
(Historical Presentations)
Ltd, 22 Palace Street,
Canterbury CT1 2DZ
Tel: 01227 478990
*Arms, armour, artefacts,
militaria*

Delf Stream Gallery,
14 New Street,
Sandwich CT13 9AB
Tel: 01304 617684

Dragonlee Collectables
Tel: 01622 729502
Noritake

Paul Haskell
Tel: 01634 669362
Mobile 0374 781160
*Old mechanical slot
machines, Alwins, bandits,
fortune tellers, Mutoscopes*

Stuart Heggie,
14 The Borough, Northgate,
Canterbury CT1 2DR
Tel: 01227 470422
*Vintage cameras, optical
toys & photographic images*

J & M Collectables
Tel: 01580 891657
*Postcards, Crested china,
Osborne plaques, Ivorex
& small collectables*

Barbara Ann Newman,
London House Antiques,
4 Market Square,
Westerham TN16 1AW
Tel: 01959 564479
Mobile 0850 016729
*Antique dolls, teddy
bears and collectables*

Old Tackle Box,
PO Box 55, High St,
Cranbrook TN17 3ZU
Tel & Fax: 01580 713979
Old fishing tackle

Pretty Bizarre, 170 High
St, Deal CT14 6BQ
Tel: 0973 794537
*1920s–70s ceramics &
collectables*

Neville Pundole,
8A & 9 The Friars,
Canterbury CT1 2AS
Tel: 01227 453471
*Moorcroft, contemporary
pottery & glass*

St Clere – Carlton Ware,
PO Box 161,
Sevenoaks TN15 6GA
Tel: 01474 853630
*St Clere – Carlton Ware,
the UK's leading specialists
in Carlton Ware. Selling
& buying Carlton 1890-
1992. Mail orders taken.
Visa & Mastercard
accepted. Contact Helen
& Keith Martin*

Stevenson Brothers,
The Workshop, Ashford
Road, Bethersden,
Ashford TN26 3AP
Tel: 01233 820363
Rocking horses

Variety Box,
16 Chapel Place,
Tunbridge Wells TN1 1YQ
Tel: 01892 531868
*Tunbridge Ware, silver,
glass, fans, hat pins,
writing, sewing and other
collectors' items*

Wenderton Antiques
Tel: 01227 720295
(by appt only)
Kitchenware

Woodville Antiques,
The Street, Hamstreet,
Ashford TN26 2HG
Tel: 01233 732981
Tools

Wot a Racket,
250 Shepherds Lane,
Dartford DA1 2PN
Tel/Fax: 01322 220619
email: wot-a-
racket@talk21.com
Sporting

Lancashire

Brittons Jewellers,
34 Scotland Rd,
Nelson BB9 7UU
Tel: 01282 697659
Watches and jewellery

Farmhouse Antiques,
Corner Shop, 23 Main
St, Bolton-by-Bowland,
Clitheroe BB7 4NW
Tel: 01200 447294/441457
*Good selection of antique
textiles, linen, lace,
samplers, baby gowns -
no costume. Open Sat,
Sun & Bank Hols 12.00-
4.30pm. Winter Sun only
or by appt 01200 441457.
Trade welcome*

Pendelfin Studio Ltd,
Cameron Mill,
Housin St,
Burnley BB10 1PP
Tel: 01282 432301

Tracks, PO Box 117,
Chorley PR7 2QZ
Tel: 01257 269726
*Beatles & rare pop
memorabilia*

Leicestershire

House of Burleigh
Tel: 01664 454570
Burleigh Ware

Pooks Motor Bookshop,
Fowke St, Rothley
LE7 7PJ
Tel: 0116 237 6222
*Motoring books &
automobilia*

Lincolnshire

20th Century Frocks,
65 Steep Hill (opp Jews
Hse), Lincoln N1 1YN
Tel: 01522 545916
Vintage clothing &

*accessories bought
& sold. Costume - all
periods, handbags,
compacts, accessories.
Open Tues, Thurs, Fri &
Sat 11am-5pm*

Anthony Jackson,
Rocking Horse Maker
and Restorer,
20 Westry Corner,
Barrowby,
Grantham NG32 1DF
Tel: 01476 567477
Rocking horses

Junktion, The Old
Railway Stn, New
Bolingbroke, Boston
PE22 7LB Tel: 01205
480068/480087
*Advertising & packaging,
automobilia*

Frank Munford, Brooke
Bond Cereal & Trade
Dealer, Brooke House,
108 West Parade,
Lincoln LN1 1LA
Tel: 01522 878362
Email:frank.munford@virgin.
net
*Collector/dealer of
Brooke Bond Tea Cards,
ephemera & memorabilia
& other cereal/trade cards.
Buy-Sell-Exchange
Tel: 01522 878362
anytime after 9am &
before 8pm please*

Skip & Janie Smithson
Tel & Fax: 01754 810265
Kitchenware

Middlesex

Hobday Toys
Tel: 01895 636737
*Tinplate toys, trains &
dolls' houses*

John Ives,
5 Normanhurst Drive,
Twickenham TW1 1NA
Tel: 020 8892 6265
*Reference books on
antiques & collecting*

When We were Young,
The Old Forge, High
Street Harmondsworth
Village, UB7 0AQ
Tel: 020 8897 3583
*Collectable items related
to British childhood
characters & illustrators*

Norfolk

Roger Bradbury Antiques,
Church St, Coltishall NR12
7DJ Tel: 01603 737444
Oriental pottery

Cat Pottery, 1 Grammar
School Rd, North
Walsham NR28 9JH
Tel: 01692 402962
Animal pottery

Church Street Antiques,
2 Church Street, Wells-
Next-the-Sea NR23 1JA
Tel: 01328 711698
*Open Tues-Sun incl
10am-4pm. Hat pins,
linen & lace, textiles,
kitchenware,
collectables, jewellery*

Northamptonshire

The Old Brigade,
10A Harborough Road,
Kingsthorpe NN2 7AZ
Tel: 01604 719389
Militaria

Nottinghamshire

T. Vennett-Smith,
11 Nottingham Rd,
Gotham NG11 0HE
Tel: 0115 983 0541
*Ephemera & sporting
auctions*

Oxfordshire

Dauphin Display Cabinet
Co, PO Box 602,
Oxford OX44 9LU
Tel: 01865 343542
Display stands

Michael Jackson
Antiques, The Quiet
Woman Antiques
Centre, Southcombe,
Chipping Norton
OX7 5QH
Tel: 01608 646262
Cigarette cards

Alvin Ross,
Tel: 01865 772409
Pelham puppets

Stone Gallery,
93 The High St,
Burford OX18 4QA
Tel/Fax: 01993 823302
*Specialist dealer in
antique & modern*

*paperweights, gold &
silver designer jewellery
& enamel boxes*

Teddy Bears of Witney,
99 High St, Witney
OX8 6LY
Tel: 01993 702616
Teddy bears

Pembrokeshire

Pendelfin, Arch Hse,
St George St, Tenby
SA70 7JB
Tel: 01834 843246

Republic of Ireland

Michelina & George
Stacpoole, Main Street,
Adare, Co Limerick
Tel: 00 353 6139 6409
*Pottery, ceramics, silver,
prints*

Whyte's Auctioneers,
30 Marlborough St,
Dublin 1
Tel: 00 353 1 874 6161
*Specialist auctioneer &
valuer of books, autographs,
maps, photographs,
posters, toys, ephemera,
stamps, coins, militaria,
memorabilia*

Scotland

Edinburgh Coin Shop,
11 West Crosscauseway,
Edinburgh EH8 9JW
Tel: 0131 668 2928/0131
667 9095
*Coins, medals, militaria,
stamps*

Rhod McEwan Golf Books,
Glengarden, Ballater,
Aberdeenshire AB35 5UB
Tel: 013397 55429
*Rare & out-of-print
golfing books*

Shropshire

Apple Tree House
Tel: 01694 722953
*Hummel figures and
collectables*

Decorative Antiques,
47 Church Street,
Bishop's Castle
SY9 5AD
Tel: 01588 638851
*Decorative objects of the
19th & 20th century*

Mullock & Madeley,
The Old Shippon,
Wall-under-Heywood,
Nr Church Stretton
SY6 7DS
Tel: 01694 771771
Sporting auctions

Somerset

Bath Dolls' Hospital,
2 Grosvenor Place,
London Rd, Bath BA1 6PT
Tel: 01225 319668
Doll restoration

Bonapartes, 1 Queen
Street, Bath BA1 1HE
Tel: 01225 423873
Military figures

Lynda Brine, Assembly
Antique Ctre, 5-8 Saville
Row, Bath BA1 2QP
Tel: 01225 448488
Perfume bottles

Philip Knighton, 11 North
St, Wellington TA21 8LX
Tel: 01823 661618
*Wireless, gramophones,
all valve equipment*

T. J. Millard Antiques,
Assembly Antiques,
5–8 Saville Row,
Bath BA1 2QP
Tel: 01225 448488
Boxes & games

Richard Twort
Tel & Fax: 01934 641900
Mobile 077 11 939789
*Barographs & all types of
meteorological instruments*

Staffordshire

Keystones, PO Box 387,
Stafford ST16 3FG
Tel: 01785 256648
Denby Pottery

Gordon Litherland,
25 Stapenhill Rd, Burton
upon Trent DE15 9AE
Tel: 01283 567213
*Bottles, breweriana, pub
jugs, commemoratives*

Peggy Davies Ceramics,
28 Liverpool Road,
Stoke-on-Trent ST4 1VJ
Tel: 01782 848002
*Ceramics. limited
edition Toby jugs and
figures*

The Potteries Antique
Centre, 271 Waterloo
Road, Cobridge, Stoke-
on-Trent ST6 3HR
Tel: 01782 201455
*Royal Doulton, Beswick
and Wade*

Trevor Russell, PO Box
1258, Uttoxeter ST14 8XL
Fountain pens & repairs

The Tackle Exchange,
95B Trentham Rd, Dresden,
Stoke-on-Trent ST3 4EG
Tel: 01782 599858
Old fishing tackle

Suffolk

Jamie Cross, PO Box 73,
Newmarket CB8 8RY
Tel: 01638 750132
*We buy & sell German,
Italian and British WWI
and WWII medals,
badges and decorations*

W. L. Hoad,
9 St. Peter's Rd, Kirkley,
Lowestoft NR33 0LH
Tel: 01502 587758
Cigarette cards

John Ramsay,
Swapmeet Publications,
22 Foxgrove Lane,
Felixstowe IP11 7JO
Tel: 01394 670700
*Publishers of books on
collectable toys & models*

Surrey

David Aldous-Cook, PO
Box 413, Sutton SM3 8SZ
Tel: 020 8642 4842
*Reference books on
antiques & collectables*

British Notes, PO Box 257,
Sutton SM3 9WW
Tel: 020 8641 3224
Banking collectables

Childhood Memories,
The Farnham Antique
Centre, 27 South Street,
Farnham GU9 7QU Tel:
01252 724475/793704
*Antique teddies, dolls
and miniatures*

Church Street Antiques,
10 Church Street,
Godalming GU7 1EH
Tel: 01483 860894

*Art Deco ceramics.
antique silverware, glass
& ceramics*

Gooday Gallery,
14 Richmond Hill,
Richmond TW10 6QX
Tel: 020 8940 8652
Mobile 0410 124540
*Art Deco, Art Nouveau,
tribal*

Howard Hope,
21 Bridge Rd,
East Molesey KT8 9EU
Tel: 0181 941 2472/
0181 398 7130
Mob 0585 543267
*Phonographs,
gramophones*

Julian Eade
Tel: 020 8394 1515
Mobile 0973 542971
*Doulton Lambeth
stoneware and signed
Burslem wares*

East Sussex

Tony Horsley
Tel: 01273 550770
*Candle extinguishers,
Royal Worcester and
other porcelain*

Ann Lingard,
Ropewalk Antiques,
Rye TN31 7NA
Tel: 01797 223486
Pine and kitchenware

Mint Arcade, 71 The
Mint, Rye TN31 7EW
Tel: 01797 225952
Cigarette cards

Wallis & Wallis, West
Street Auction Galleries,
Lewes BN7 2NJ
Tel: 01273 480208
Email: auctions@wallis
andwallis.co.uk Website:
www.wallisandwallis.co.uk

West Sussex

Limited Editions,
2 Tarrant Street,
Arundel BN18 9DG
01903 883950
*Ceramics incl Kevin
Francis, David Winter,
Lilliput Lane, J. P.
Editions, Moorcroft,
Royal Doulton, Pendelfin,
Belleek, Lladro etc*

Tyne & Wear

Antiques at H & S
Collectables, No1
Ashburton Rd, Cnr Salters
Rd, Gosforth NE3 4XN
Tel: 0191 284 6626
*Curios, Victoriana,
Maling specialist*

Wales

A.P.E.S. Rocking Horses,
20 Tan-y-Bwlch, Mynydd
Llandanygai, Bangor,
Gwynned LL57 4DX
Tel: 01745 540365
Rocking horses

Corgi Collector Club,
Dept MP00, PO Box
323, Swansea SA1 1BJ
Tel/Fax: 0870 607 1204

The Emporium, 112 St
Teilo St, Pontarddulais,
Nr Swansea SA4 1QH
Tel: 01792 885185
Brass & cast iron

Islwyn Watkins, Offa's
Dyke Antique Centre,
4 High Street, Knighton,
Powys LD7 1AT
Tel: 01547 528635
*18th/19thC Pottery, 20thC
country & Studio pottery.
small country furniture,
treen & bygones*

Warwickshire

The Antique Shop,
30 Henley St, Stratford-
upon-Avon CV37 6QW
Tel: 01789 292485
*Dolls, teddy bears,
fishing tackle, glass,
porcelain, jewellery,
Oriental, silver, collectables*

Chinasearch,
9 Princes Drive,
Kenilworth CV8 2FD
Tel: 01926 512402
*Discontinued dinner, tea
and collectable ware*

Chris James Medals
& Militaria, Warwick
Antiques Ctre,
22-24 High St,
Warwick CV34 4AP
Tel: 01926 495704
*Specialists in antique arms,
edged weapons, medals,
militaria & aviation items.
For sale & purchased*

Jolly Good Fun Co Ltd,
The Old Elephant House,
38–42 Morton Street,
Leamington Spa CV32 5SY
Tel: 01223 812570
Vintage slot machines

West Midlands

Antiques Magazine,
HP Publishing,
2 Hampton Court Road,
Harborne,
Birmingham B17 9AE
Tel: 0121 681 8000

Birmingham Railway
Auctions & Publications,
7 Ascot Road,
Moseley,
Birmingham B13 9EN
Tel: 0121 449 9707
*Railway auctions and
publications*

Mr P. Cane,
Tel: 0121 427 5991
*Toy Cowboy Cap Guns,
Hats, holsters, rifles
& playsuits from 1950s,
'60s & early '70s*

Tango Art Deco,
22 Kenilworth Rd,
Knowle,
Solihull B93 0JA
Jenny & Martin Wills
Tel: 01564 776669
*Art Deco. Open Fri, Sat
9-6pm*

Wiltshire

Robert Mullis,
55 Berkeley Rd,
Wroughton,
Swindon SN4 9BN
Tel: 01793 813583
Rocking horses

Dominic Winter
Book Auctions,
The Old School,
Swindon SN1 5DR
Tel: 01793 611340
*Auctions of antiquarian
and general printed
books & maps, sports
books and memorabilia,
art reference & pictures,
photography &
ephemera (including
toys, games and other
collectables)*

Worcestershire

BBM Jewellery & Coins
(W. V. Crook),
8–9 Lion Street,
Kidderminster
DY10 1PT
Tel: 01562 744118
Antique jewellery, coins

John Edwards Antiques,
Worcester Antiques
Centre, 15 Reindeer
Court, Mealcheapen St,
Worcester WR1 4DF
Tel: 01905 353840 email:
john@royalworcester.free
serve.co.uk website:
www.royalworcester.free
serve.co.uk
Royal Worcester

John Neale, Platform 6,
11A Davenport Drive,
The Willows,
Bromsgrove B60 2DW
Tel: 01527 871000
*Vintage train & toy
auctions*

Yorkshire

Antique & Collectors'
Centre, 35 St Nicholas
Cliff, Scarborough
YO11 2ES
Tel: 01723 365221
website: collectors.
demon.co.uk email: sales
@collectors.demon.co.uk
*International dealers in
stamps, postcards, silver,
gold, medals, cigarette
cards and many more
collectables*

BBR, Elsecar Heritage
Centre, Wath Rd, Elsecar,
Barnsley S74 8HJ
Tel: 01226 745156
*Advertising, breweriana,
pot lids, bottles,
Doulton and Beswick*

Briar's 20thC Decorative
Arts, Skipton Antiques
& Collectors Centre,
The Old Foundry,
Cavendish St,
Skipton BD23 2AB
Tel: 01756 798641
*Art Deco ceramics and
furniture, specialising
in Charlotte Rhead
pottery*

The Camera House,
Oakworth Hall,
Colne Road (B6143),
Oakworth, Keighley
BD22 7HZ
Tel: 01535 642333
website: www.the-camera-
house.co.uk email: colin
@the-camera-house.co.uk
*Cameras & photographic
equipment from 1850.
Purchases, sales, part
exchange, repairs.
Valuations for probate
& insurance. Open
Thurs, Fri 10am–5pm
Sat 10am–3pm
Prop. C Cox*

Country Collector,
11–12 Birdgate,
Pickering YO18 7AL
Tel: 01751 477481
*Art Deco ceramics,
blue & white, pottery
& porcelain*

Crested China Co,
The Station House,
Driffield YO25 7PY
Tel: 01377 257042
Goss & Crested China

Echoes,
650a Halifax Road,
Eastwood,
Todmorden
OL14 6DW
Tel: 01706 817505
*Antique costume,
textiles including linen,
lace and jewellery*

Gerard Haley,
Hippins Farm,
Black Shawhead,
Nr Hebden Bridge
HX7 7JG
Tel: 01422 842484
Old military toys

John & Simon Haley,
89 Northgate,
Halifax HX6 4NG
Tel: 01422 822148/
360434
*Old toys & money
boxes*

Harpers Jewellers Ltd,
2–6 Minster Gates,
York YO7 2HL
Tel: 01904 632634
*Vintage & modern wrist
& pocket watches*

Linen & Lace, Shirley
Tomlinson, Halifax
Antiques Centre,
Queens Road/
Gibbet Street,
Halifax HX1 4LR
Tel: 01422 366657
Mobile 077 11 763454
*Antique linen, textiles,
period costume and
accessories*

Old Copper Shop &
Posthouse Antiques,
69 & 75 Market Place,
South Cave
HU15 2AS
Tel: 01430 423988
General stock

Sheffield Railwayana
Auctions,
43 Little Norton Lane,
Sheffield S8 8GA
Tel: 0114 274 5085
*Railwayana, posters
and models auctions*

Yorkshire Relics
of Haworth,
16 River Street,
Haworth BD22 8NE
Tel: 01535 642218
Mobile 07971 701278
*Advertising and
packaging*

Directory of Collectors' Clubs

This directory is in no way complete. If you wish to be included in next year's directory or if you have a change of address or telephone number, please inform us by 1 November 2000. Entries will be repeated in subsequent editions unless we are requested otherwise.

American Business Card Club Robin Cleeter, 38 Abbotsbury Road, Morden, Surrey SM4 5LQ

The Antiquarian Horological Society
New House, High Street, Ticehurst, E Sussex TN5 7AL Tel: 01580 200155 Fax: 01580 201323 email: secretary@ahsoc.demon.co.uk Internet:http://ourworld.compuserve.com/home pages/ahsoc/

Antique Collectors' Club 5 Church Street, Woodbridge, Suffolk IP12 1DS
Tel: 01394 385501

The Arms and Armour Society
Hon Sec Anthony Dove FRSA,
PO Box 10232, London SW19 2ZD

Association of Bottled Beer Collectors
127 Victoria Park Road, Tunstall, Stoke-on-Trent, Staffs ST6 6DY Tel: 01782 821459

Association of Comic Enthusiasts (ACE)
17 Hill Street, Colne, Lancashire BB8 0DH
Tel: 01282 865468

Avon Magpies Club Mrs W. A. Fowler, 36 Castle View Road, Portchester, Fareham, Hampshire PO16 9LA Tel 023 9264 2393

Badge Collectors' Circle c/o Mary Setchfield, 3 Ellis Close, Quorn, Nr Loughborough, Leicestershire LE12 8SH Tel: 01509 412094

British Association of Sound Collections
c/o Alan Ward, National Sound Archive, The British Library, 96 Euston Road, London NW1 2DB

British Compact Collectors' Society
SAE to: PO Box 131, Woking, Surrey GU21 9YR Tel: 01483 828081

British Matchbox Label and Booklet Society
Hon Sec Arthur Alderton, 122 High Street, Melbourn, Cambridgeshire SG8 6AL
Tel: 01763 260399

British Numismatic Society c/o Warburg Institute, Woburn Square, London WC1H 0AB

British Teddy Bear Association
PO Box 290, Brighton, East Sussex BN2 1DR

British Watch & Clock Collectors Association Tony Woolven, 5 Cathedral Lane, Truro, Cornwall TR1 2QS Tel: 01872 264010 Fax: 01872 241953 email: tonybwcca@cs.com URL: http://timecap.co.uk

Bunnykins News 7 Spout Copse, Sheffield S6 6FB Tel: 0114 2340199 email: bunnykinsnews@talk21.com

The Burleigh Ware International Collectors' Circle The Old Shop Cottage, 2 Braunston Road, Knossington, Oakham, Rutland LE15 8LN

The Buttonhook Society
c/o Paul Moorehead, 2 Romney Place, Maidstone, Kent ME15 6LE

The Buttonhook Society (US contact)
c/o Priscilla Stoffel, White Marsh, Box 287, MD 21162-0287, USA

Carlton Ware Collectors International
Helen Martin, PO Box 161, Sevenoaks, Kent TN15 6GA Tel: 01474 853630 Fax: 01474 854480 email: cwciclub@aol.com website: www.stclere.co.uk

The Carnival Glass Society (UK) Limited
PO Box 14, Hayes, Middlesex UB3 5NU

The Cartophilic Society of Great Britain
Mr A. W. Stevens, 63 Ferndale Road, Church Crookham, Fleet, Hampshire GU13 0LN Tel: 01252 621586

Chintzworld International
Dancers End, Northall, Bedfordshire LU6 2EU Tel: 01525 220272

Cigarette Case Collectors' Club
Mr C. F. Grey, 19 Woodhurst North, Raymead Road, Maidenhead, Berkshire SL6 8PH

The City of London Photograph and Gramophone Society Ltd
Suzanne Lewis Membership Secretary, 51 Brockhurst Road, Chesham, Buckinghamshire HP5 3JB

Clarice Cliff Collectors' Club
Fantasque House, Tennis Drive, The Park, Nottingham NG7 1AE website: www.claricecliff.com

Collectors' Penpal Club
SAE to: Joan Charles, 15 Thetford Road, Great Sankey, Warrington WA5 3EQ

The Comics Journal
c/o Bryon Whitworth, 17 Hill Street, Colne, Lancashire BB8 0DH
Tel: 01282 865468

Corgi Collector Club Dept MP00, PO Box 323, Swansea, Wales SA1 1BJ Tel/Fax 0870 607 1204

Cornish Collectors' Club PO Box 18, Glossop, Derbyshire SK13 8FA Tel: 01457 864833

The Costume Society Moore Stephens,
St Paul's House, Warwick Lane,
London EC4P 4BN

Crunch Club (Breakfast Cereal Collectables)
John Cahill, 9 Weald Rise, Tilehurst, Reading,
Berkshire RG30 6XB Tel: 0118 942 7291
email: crunch@jcahill99.freeserve.co.uk

Egg Cup Collectors' Club of Great Britain
Sue Wright Tel: 01494 485 406
email: suewright@sue.coll.freeserve.co.uk

The English Playing Card Society
c/o Major Donald Welsh, 11 Pierrepont Street,
Bath, Somerset BA1 1LA Tel: 01225 465218
Fax: 01225 424993

The European Honeypot Collectors' Society
John Doyle, The Honeypot, 18 Victoria Road,
Chislehurst, Kent BR7 6DF
Tel/Fax 020 8467 2053
email: John@thehoneypot10.freeserve.co.uk

Fashion Doll Collectors' Club of Great Britain
PO Box 228, Brentford, Middlesex TW8 0UU

Festival of Britain Society c/o Martin Packer,
41 Lyall Gardens, Birmingham, West Midlands
B45 9YW Tel: 0121 453 8245
email: martin@packer34.freeserve.co.uk

Fieldings Crown Devon Collectors' Club
PO Box 74, Corbridge, Northumberland
NE45 5YP Tel: 0802 513784

Friends of Blue c/o Terry Sheppard,
45a Church Road, Bexley Heath,
Kent DA7 4DD

Friends of Fred Homepride Flour Men
Jennifer Woodward Tel: 01925 826158

The Furniture History Society
c/o Dr. Brian Austen, 1 Mercedes Cottages,
St. John's Road, Haywards Heath, West
Sussex RH16 4EH Tel: 01444 413845

Goss Collectors' Club Mrs Schofield,
Derbyshire Tel: 0115 930 0441

**Goss & Crested China Club & Museum
incorporating Milestone Publications**
Pat Welbourne, 62 Murray Road, Horndean,
Hampshire PO8 9JL Tel: 023 9259 7440
Fax: 023 9259 1975
email: info@gosschinaclub.demon.co.uk
website: www.gosschinaclub.demon.co.uk

The Hat Pin Society of Great Britain
PO Box 74, Bozent, Wellingborough,
Northamptonshire NN29 7JH

The Hornby Railway Collectors' Association
2 Ravensmore Road, Sherwood,
Nottingham NG5 2AH

**King George VI Collectors' Society
(Philately)** 98 Albany, Manor Road,
Bournemouth, Dorset BH1 3EW
Tel: 01202 551515

Knife Rest Collectors' Club Doreen
Hornsblow, Braughingbury, Braughing,
Hertfordshire SG11 2RD Tel: 01920 822654

Lock Collectors' Club Mr Richard Phillips
'Merlewood', The Loan, West Linton,
Peebleshire EH4 7HE Tel: 01968 661039

The Maling Collectors' Society
PO Box 1762, North Shields NE30 4YJ

Mauchline Ware Collectors' Club Unit 37
Romsey Industrial Estate, Greatbridge Road,
Romsey, Hampshire SO51 0HR

Memories UK Mabel Lucie Attwell Club
Abbey Antiques, 63 Great Whyte, Ramsey,
Nr Huntingdon, Cambridgeshire PE17 1HL
Tel: 01487 814753

The Model Railway Club The Hon Sec,
Keen House, 4 Calshot Street, London N1 9DA
website: www.themodelrailwayclub.org

Moorcroft Collectors' Club W. Moorcroft PLC,
Sandbach Road, Burslem, Stoke-on-Trent,
Staffordshire ST6 2DQ
Tel: 01782 214345 Fax: 01782 283455

Muffin the Mule Collectors' Club
12 Woodland Close, Woodford Green,
Essex IG8 0QH Tel/Fax: 020 8504 4943

Musical Box Society of Great Britain
PO Box 299, Waterbeach,
Cambridgeshire CB4 8DT

New Baxter Society Membership Secretary,
205 Marshalswick Lane, St Albans,
Hertfordshire AL1 4XA

**Observers Pocket Series Collectors' Society
(OPSCS)** Alan Sledger, Secretary, 10 Villiers
Road, Kenilworth, Warwickshire CV8 2JB
Tel: 01926 857047

**The Official International Wade Collectors'
Club** Royal Works, Westport Road, Burslem,
Stoke on Trent, Staffordshire ST6 4AP
Tel: 01782 255255 Fax: 01782 575195
email: club@wade.co.uk

Old Bottle Club of Great Britain
Alan Blakeman, c/o BBR, Elsecar Heritage
Centre, Nr Barnsley, Yorkshire S74 8HJ
Tel: 01226 745156

The Old Hall Club
Nigel Wiggin, Sandford House, Levedale,
Stafford ST18 9AH Tel: 01785 780376
email: oht@gnwiggin.freeserve.co.uk

**Ophthalmic Antiques International
Collectors' Club** 3 Moor Park Road,
Northwood, Middlesex HA6 2DL

Orders and Medals Research Society
123 Turnpike Link, Croydon, Surrey CR0 5NU

The Oriental Ceramic Society The Secretary,
30b Torrington Square, London WC1E 7JL
Tel: 020 7636 7985 Fax: 020 7580 6749

Pen Delfin Family Circle Matthew Baldock, Shop 28, Grove Plaza, Stirling Highway, Peppermint Grove, Australia 6011 Tel: 09 384 9999

Pen Delfin Family Circle Ronnie Marnef, Fazantenlaan 29, 2610 Antwerp, Belgium Tel: 03 440 5668

Pen Delfin Family Circle Nancy Falkenham, 1250 Terwillegar Avenue, Oshawa, Ontario, Canada L1J 7A5 Tel: 0101 416 723 9940

Pen Delfin Family Circle Irene Svensson, Svebi AB, Box 143, S-562 02 Taberg, Sweden Tel: 036 656 90

Pen Delfin 'Family Circle' Collectors' Club Cameron Mill, Howsin Street, Burnley, Lancashire BB10 1PP Tel: 01282 432301

Pen Delfin, The Family Circle of Susan Beard, 230 Spring Street NW, Suite 1238, Atlanta, Georgia 30303, USA Tel: Freephone US only 1-800 872 4876

Pewter Society Llananant Farm, Penallt, Monmouth NP25 4AP email: hayw@clara.net

Photographic Collectors' Club of Great Britain Membership Office P.C.C.G.B., 1B Church Street Industrial Estate, Haydon Bridge, Hexham, Northumberland NE47 6JG Ansaphone/Fax: 01434 688129

Poole Pottery Collectors' Club Clive Bailey, The Quay, Poole, Dorset BH15 1RF Tel: 01202 666200 Fax: 01202 682894 website: www.poolepottery.co.uk

The Postcard Club of Great Britain c/o Mrs D. Brennan, 34 Harper House, St James's Crescent, London SW9 7LW Tel: 020 7771 9404

E. Radford Collectors' Club Michael and Delyse Rodwell, St Claver, Victoria Avenue, Kirby-le-Soken, Essex CO13 0DJ

Railwayana Collectors' Journal 7 Ascot Rd, Moseley, Birmingham, West Midlands B13 9EN

Royal Doulton International Collectors' Club Minton House, London Road, Stoke-on-Trent, Staffordshire ST4 7QD Tel: 01782 292127 Fax: 01782 292099

Scientific Instrument Society Wg Cdr G. Bennett (Executive Officer), 31 High Street, Stanford in the Vale, Faringdon, Oxfordshire SN7 8LH Tel: 01367 710223 email sis@hidex.demon.co.uk

Scottish Exhibitions Study Group S. K. Hunter, 34 Gray Street, Glasgow G3 7TY

The Shelley Group 4 Fawley Road, Regents Park, Southampton, Hampshire SO2 1LL

Silhouette Collectors' Club c/o Diana Joll, Flat 5, 13 Brunswick Square, Hove, East Sussex BN3 1EH Tel: 01273 735760

The Silver Spoon Club of Great Britain c/o Terry & Mary Haines, Glenleigh Park, Sticker, St Austell, Cornwall PL26 7JD Tel/Fax 01726 65269

Snuff Bottle Society Michael Kaynes, 1 Tollard Court, West Hill Road, Bournemouth, Dorset BH2 5EH Tel/Fax: 01202 292867

The SylvaC Collectors' Circle 174 Portsmouth Road, Horndean, Waterlooville, Hampshire PO8 9HP Tel: 02392 591725 Fax: 02392 788494 email: sylvac.club@mcmail.com website: www.sylvac.mcmail.com

Telecommunications Heritage Group PO Box 561, South Croydon, Surrey CR2 6YL Tel: 020 8407 2129 Fax: 020 8407 0808 email: membership@thg.org.uk

The Thimble Society of London c/o Bridget McConnel, The Portobello Studios, 101 Portobello Road, London W11 2OB Tel: 020 7727 4295 Sat only

To-Ken Society of Great Britain Clive Sinclair, 340 Hurst Road, Bexley, Kent DA5 3LA Tel: 01322 523832

Torquay Pottery Collectors' Society Torre Abbey, Avenue Road, Torquay, Devon TQ2 5JX email: tpcs@btinternet.com

Totally Teapots The Novelty Teapot Collectors' Club Vince McDonald, Euxton, Chorley, Lancashire PR7 6EY Tel/Fax 01257 450366

The Transport Ticket Society c/o Courtney Haydon, 4 Gladridge Close, Earley, Reading, Berkshire RG6 7DL Tel: 0118 9264109 email: courtney@gladridgecl.demon.co.uk

Trix Twin Railway Collectors' Association c/o Mr C B Arnold, 6 Ribble Avenue, Oadby, Leicester LE2 4NZ Tel: 0116 271 5943

UK Perfume Bottles Collectors Club Lynda Brine, Assembly Antique Centre, 5–8 Saville Row, Bath, Somerset BA1 2QP Tel: 01225 448488

The Victorian Military Society 20 Priory Road, Newbury, Berkshire RG14 7QN Tel: 01635 48628

The Vintage Model Yacht Group c/o Russel Potts, 8 Sherard Road, London SE9 6EP Tel: 020 8850 6805

Kathie Winkle Collectors Club SAE to Mrs Nadin-Leath, Greenacres, Calbourne Road, Carisbrooke, Isle of Wight PO30 5AP Tel: 01983 525981

The Writing Equipment Society c/o Dr M. L. Greenland, Cartledge Cottage, Cartledge Lane, Holmesfield, Dronfield, Derbyshire S18 7SB Tel: 0114 289 0669

Directory of Markets & Centres

Berkshire

Stables Antiques Centre,
1a Merchant Place
(off Friar Street),
Reading RG1 1DT
Tel: 0118 959 0290
Open 10am–5pm.
Over 30 dealers.

Buckinghamshire

Jackdaw Antiques
Centres Ltd,
25 West Street,
Marlow SL7 2LS
Tel: 01628 898285

Marlow Antique Centre,
35 Station Road,
Marlow SL7 1NW
Tel: 01628 473223
*Wide range of antique
and collectable items
from over 30 dealers.
Georgian, Victorian and
Edwardian furniture,
country pine, decorative
furniture, silverware, glass,
china, Art Deco,
bedsteads, cameras,
old tools, garden items,
jewellery, pens, cufflinks,*

*vintage toys. Second-
hand book section.
Open 7 days
Mon–Sat 10am–5.30pm,
Sun 11am–4.30pm.*

Cambridgeshire

Fitzwilliam Antiques Centre,
Fitzwilliam Street,
Peterborough PE1 2RX
Tel: 01733 565415

Cheshire

Davenham Antique Centre
and Tea Room,
461 London Rd,
Davenham,
Northwich CW9 8NA
Tel Shop: 01606 44350
Office: 0161 973 3385

Derbyshire

Alfreton Antique Centre,
11 King Street,
Alfreton DE55 7AF
Tel: 01773 520781

*40 dealers on 2 floors.
Antiques, collectables,
furniture, books,
postcards, etc.
Open 7 days
Mon–Sat 10am–4.30pm,*

Sundays, Bank Holidays
11am–3pm.

Bakewell Antiques
& Collectors' Centre,
King Street,
Bakewell DE45 1DZ
Tel: 01629 812496
email: bacc@chappells-
antiques.co.uk
website: www.Chappells
antiques.co.uk
*30 established dealers
inc. BADA & LAPADA
members. Quality period
furniture, ceramics, silver,
plate, metals, treen,
clocks, barometers,
books, pictures, maps,
prints, textiles, kitchenalia,
lighting and furnishing
accessories 17th–20thC,
scientific, pharmaceutical
and sporting antiques.
Open Mon–Sat 10–5pm,
Sun 11–5pm. Closed
Christmas Day, Boxing
Day & New Year's Day.*

Duesbury's Antiques
Centre, 220 Siddals Road,
Derby DE1 2QE
Tel: 01332 370151
website:
www.antiquesplus.co.uk
*Open Mon–Sat 10am–5pm,
Sun 11am–4pm.*

Heanor Antiques Centre,
Ilkeston Road,
Heanor DE75
Tel: 01773 531181
*Open 7 days
10.30am–4.30pm.
70+ dealers.*

Matlock Antiques
Collectables & Crafts,
7 Dale Road,
Matlock DE4 3LT
Tel: 01629 760808

Devon

Quay Centre, Topsham,
Nr Exeter EX3 0JA
Tel: 01392 874006
*80 dealers on 3 floors.
Antiques, collectables
and traditional furnishings.
Ample parking.
Open 7 days, 10am–5pm.
All major cards accepted.*

Dorset

Castle Antiques &
Collectors Centre,
12a Castle Street,
Christchurch BH23 1DT
Tel: 01202 875167/486439
Open Mon–Sat 10am–5pm.

Essex

Gallerie Antiques,
62–70 Fowler Road,
Hainault, Essex IG6 3XE
Tel: 020 8501 2229

Flintshire

Afonwen Craft & Antique
Centre, Afonwen Caerwys,
Nr Mold CH7 5UB
Tel: 01352 720965
*Open all year Tues–Sun
9.30am–5.30pm, closed
Mondays, open Bank
Holiday Mondays.
The largest Antique &
Craft Centre in North
Wales. 14,000 sq.ft. of
showrooms, antiques,
collectables from fine
jewellery to furniture.
Restaurant.*

Gloucestershire

Cirencester Arcade
& Ann's Pantry,
25 Market Place,
Cirencester GL7 2NX
Tel: 01285 644214
*Antiques, gifts, furnishings
etc. Restaurant/tea rooms,
private room for hire.*

Durham House Antiques
Centre, Sheep Street,
Stow-on-the-Wold
GL54 1AA
Tel: 01451 870404
*30+ dealers.
Extensive range of town
and country furniture,
metalware, books, pottery,
porcelain, kitchenalia,
silver, jewellery and art.
Mon–Sat 10am–5pm,
Sunday 11am–5pm.
Stow-on-the-Wold,
Cotswold home to over
40 antique shops,
galleries and bookshops.*

Hampshire

Dolphin Quay Antique
Centre, Queen Street,
Emsworth PO10 7BU
Tel: 01243 379994
www.antiquesbulletin.com
/dolphinquay
*Open 7 days a week
(including Bank Holidays)
Mon–Sat 10am–5pm,
Sunday 10am–4pm.
Marine, naval antiques,
paintings, watercolours,
prints, antique clocks,
decorative arts, furniture,
sporting apparel, luggage,
specialist period lighting,*

conservatory, garden antiques, fine antique/country furniture, French/antique beds.

Lymington Antiques Centre, 76 High Street, Lymington SO41 9AL Tel: 01590 670934

Secondhand Rose, 20 Stakes Road, Purbrook PO7 5LX Tel: 02392 241152

Open Mon–Sat 9am–6pm.

Southampton Antiques Centre, Britannia Road, Northam, Southampton SO14 0QL Tel: 01703 221 022

Herefordshire

The Hay Antique Market, 6 Market Street, Hay-on-Wye HR3 5AF Tel: 01497 820175

Open 6 days 10am–5pm, Sundays 11am–5pm.
Central location with large car park nearby. 17 separate units on 2 floors selling pine, country and period furniture. Rural and rustic items. China, glass, jewellery, linen and period clothes. Pictures, lighting, brass and collectables.

Mulberry's Antiques & Collectables, 30/32 St Owen St, Hereford HR1 2PR Tel: 01432 269925

On display throughout 2 floors is a wide range of antiques and collectables – furniture, fine china, porcelain, silver, jewellery, textiles, pre-1930s clothing and accessories, objets d'art, prints, oils and watercolours. Trade welcome.

The Old Merchant's House Antique Centre & Victorian Tearooms, 10 Corn Square, Leominster HR6 8LR Tel: 01568 616141 Mobile: 077 21 433171

Dealers in a wide variety of antiques, collectables and memorabilia. Licensed tearooms open daily, except Sunday, from 10am–5pm.

Hertfordshire

Herts & Essex Antiques Centre, The Maltings, Station Road, Sawbridgeworth CM21 9JX Tel: 01279 722044

30 Antique Shops and 90 showcases. Open everyday (except Monday), Tues–Fri 10am–5pm, Sat–Sun 10.30am–6pm (including most Bank Holidays). Over 10,000 items of antiques, furniture, jewellery, porcelain, collectables, stamps, coins, postcards, costume, paintings, glass, ceramics and ephemera. All in pleasant, well lit showrooms serviced by friendly staff.

Riverside Antiques Centre, The Maltings, Station Road, Sawbridgeworth CM21 9JX Tel: 01279 600985 or 0956 844792

Kent

Castle Antiques,
1 London Road,
(next to Post Office),
Westerham TN16 1BB
Tel: 01959 562492

*Open 10am–5pm
Mon–Sat. Phone for
Sunday times. 4 rooms of
antiques, small furniture,
collectables, rural
bygones, costume, tools,
glass, books, linens,
jewellery, kitsch, retro-
clothing. Services: advice,
valuations, theatre props,
house clearance, talks
on antiques.*

The Chapel Antiques
Centre, The Chapel,
Chapel Place,
Tunbridge Wells TN1 1YR
Tel: 01892 619921

Copperfields Antique &
Craft Centre,
3c/4 Copperfields, Spital
Street, Dartford DA9 2DE
Tel: 01322 281445

*Open Mon–Sat 10am–5pm.
Antiques, bygones,
collectables, stamps,
Wade, Sylvac, Beswick,
Royal Doulton, clocks,
Victoriana, 1930s–60s,*

*Art Deco, craft, hand-
made toys, dolls' houses
& miniatures, jewellery,
glass, china, furniture,
Kevin Francis character
jugs, silk, lace and lots
more. American-style bistro.*

Malthouse Arcade,
Malthouse Hill,
Hythe CT21 5BW
Tel: 01303 260103

Sidcup Antique & Craft
Centre, Elm Parade,
Main Road, Sidcup
DA14 6NF
Tel: 020 8300 7387

*Over 100 dealers and
crafts people in one
unique setting. Coffee
Shop. Open 7 days
10am–5pm.
Easy parking nearby.*

Unicorn Antique Centre,
2 Romney Enterprise
Centre, North Street,
New Romney TN28 8DW
Tel: 01797 361940

Lancashire

The Antique Centre,
56 Garstang Road,
Preston PR1 1NA
Tel: 01772 882078
Open 7 days a week.

GB Antiques Centre
Lancaster Leisure Park,
(the former Hornsea
Pottery), Wyresdale Road,
Lancaster LA1 3LA
Tel: 01524 844734

*Over 140 dealers in
40,000 sq. ft. of space.
Showing porcelain,
pottery, Art Deco, glass,
books and linen. Also a
large selection of
mahogany, oak and pine
furniture. Open 7 days
10am–5pm.*

Kingsmill Antique Centre,
Queen Street, Harle Syke,
Burnley BB10 2HX
Tel: 01282 431953

Leicestershire

Oxford Street Antiques
Centre, 16–26 Oxford
Street, Leicester LE1 5XU
Tel: 0116 255 3006

*30,000 sq.ft. of showrooms
on 4 floors. Extensive range
of Victorian, Edwardian
and later furniture etc. On
site parking. Open Mon–Fri
10am–5.30pm,
Sat 10am–5pm,
Sun 2pm–5pm.*

Lincolnshire

St Martins Antiques
Centre, 23a High Street,
St Martins, Stamford
PE9 2LF
Tel/Fax: 01780 481158
Day 01780 751446
Evening email:
stmartinsantiquecentre
@hotmail.com

London

Alfie's Antique Market,
13–25 Church Street
NW8 8DT
Tel: 020 7723 6066

Antiquarius Antique
Market, 131/141 King's
Road, Chelsea SW3 5ST
Tel: 020 7351 5353

Bermondsey Antiques
Market, Corner of Long
Lane & Bermondsey
Street SE1 5QH
Tel: 020 7351 5353

Bond Street Antiques
Centre, 124 New Bond
Street W1Y 9AE
Tel: 020 7351 5353

Grays Antique Market,
1–7 Davies Mews W1Y 2LP
Tel: 020 7629 7034

The Mall Antiques Arcade,
Camden Passage,
359 Upper Street N1 8DU
Tel: 020 7351 5353

Northcote Road Antique
Market, 155a Northcote
Road, Battersea SW11 6QB
Tel: 020 7228 6850

Palmers Green Antiques
Centre, 472 Green Lanes,
Palmers Green N13 5PA
Tel: 020 8350 0878
020 8886 9552
Mobile: 0961 342 528

*Over 40 dealers selling
antiques and collectables.
Specializing in furniture,
jewellery, clocks, pictures,
porcelain, china, glass,
silver & plate, metalware,
kitchenalia and lighting,
etc. Open 6 days a week,
closed Tuesdays.
Weekdays & Sats
10am–5.30pm,
Sun 11am–5pm, open
Bank Holidays. Removals
& house clearances,
probate valuations
undertaken, quality
antiques and collectables
sold on commission basis.*

Roger's Antiques Gallery,
65 Portobello Road W11
Tel: 020 7969 1500

St James's Antiques
Market, 197 Piccadilly
W1V 0LL
Tel: 020 7734 4511

Nottinghamshire

Newark Antiques Centre,
Regent House, Lombard
Street, Newark NG24 1XP
Tel: 01636 605504

Top Hat Antiques Centre,
70–72 Derby Road,
Nottingham NG1 5FD
Tel: 0115 941 9143

Oxfordshire

Antiques on High,
85 High Street,
Oxford OX1 4BG
Tel: 01865 251075

*Open 7 days a week
10am–5pm. Sun & Bank
Holidays 11am–5pm. 35
friendly dealers with wide
range of quality stock.*

Deddington Antiques
Centre, Laurel House,
Market Place, Bull Ring,
Deddington, Nr Banbury
OX15 0TW
Tel: 01869 338968

Didcot Antiques Centre,
220 Broadway,
Didcot OX11 8RS
Tel: 01235 510819
*Tues–Sat 10am–5pm,
Sunday 11am–4pm,
Closed Monday.
25 Friendly Dealers for*

ceramics, glass, silver,
jewellery, furniture,
pictures, Art Deco, wind-
up gramophones, Dinky &
Corgi, Steiff & collectable
toys, railwayana,
metalware, textiles,
smoking accessories and
more. Bookshop, tea
room & parking.

Jackdaw Antiques
Centres Ltd, 5 Reading
Road, Henley-on-Thames
RG9 0AS
Tel: 01491 572289

Lamb Arcade Antiques
Centre, 83 High Street,
Wallingford OX10 0BS
Tel: 01491 835166

*Open 10am–5pm daily,
Sat till 5.30pm, Bank
Holidays 11am–5pm.
Furniture, silver, porcelain,
glass, books, boxes,
crafts, rugs, jewellery,
brass bedsteads and
linens, pictures, antique
stringed instruments,
sports & fishing items,
decorative & ornamental
items. Coffee shop and
wine bar.*

Shropshire

Stretton Antiques Market,
Sandford Avenue,
Church Stretton
SY6 6BH
Tel: 01694 723718

Somerset

Bartlett Street Antiques,
7 Princes Buildings,
George Street,
Bath BA1 2QX
Tel: 01225 401717

Bath Antiques Market,
Guinea Lane,
(off Landsdown Rd),
Bath BA1 5NB
Tel: 01225 337638

Bath Antiquities Centre,
4 Bladud Buildings,
Bath BA1 5LS
Tel: 01225 460408

Fountain Antiques Centre,
3 Fountain Buildings,
Lansdown Road,
Bath BA1 5DU
Tel: 01225
428731/471133

Fountain Antiques Market,
6 Bladud Buildings
The Paragon,
Bath BA1 5LS
Tel: 01225 339104

Taunton Antiques Centre,
27–29 Silver Street,
Taunton TA1 3DH
Tel: 01823 289327

Staffordshire

Rugeley Antique Centre,
161 Main Road, Brereton,
Nr Rugeley WS15 1DX
Tel/Fax: 01889 577166

*Open Mon–Sat 9am–5pm,
Sun/Bank Holidays
12noon–4.30pm.
Find us: A51,
1 mile south Rugeley.*

Tutbury Mill Antiques
Centre, Tutbury Mill
Mews, Tutbury DE13 9LU
Tel: 01283 520074
Website:
www.antiquesplus.co.uk

*Open Mon–Sat
10.30am–5.30pm,
Sun 12noon–5pm.*

Surrey

The Antiques Centre,
22 Haydon Place,
Corner of Martyr Road,
Guildford GU1 4LL
Tel: 01483 567817

Esher Antiques Centre,
128 High Street,
Esher KT10 9QJ
Tel: 01372 471166

Fern Cottage Antique
Centre, 28/30 High Street,
Thames Ditton
KT7 0RY
Tel: 020 8398 2281

Maltings Monthly Market,
Bridge Square,
Farnham GU9 7QR
Tel: 01252 726234

West Sussex

Antiques & Collectors
Market, Old Orchard
Building, Old House,
Adversane,
Nr Billingshurst
RH14 9JJ
Tel: 01403 783594

Roundabout Antiques
Centre,
7 Commercial Square,
Haywards Heath
RH16 7DW
Tel: 01273 835926

*Several specialist dealers
with good quality
extensive stock, including
musical instruments.
Open Mon–Sat
9.30am–5.30pm.*

Tyne & Wear

The Antique Centre,
2nd floor,
142 Northumberland St,
Newcastle-upon-Tyne
NE1 7DQ
Tel: 0191 232 9832

Mon–Sat 10am–5pm.

Wales

Offa's Dyke Antique
Centre, 4 High Street,
Knighton, Powys
LD7 1AT
Tel: 01547 528635

Romantiques Antique
Centre, Bryn Seion
Chapel, Station Road,
Trevor, Nr Llangollen
LL20 7PF
Tel: Day 077 78 279614
Eve 01978 752140

*Open 7 days 10am–5pm.
2,500 sq ft displaying
a wide range of
antiques/collectables.
Parking – Trade welcome.
Services – furniture
restoration, upholstery,
clock repairs and
valuations.*

Warwickshire

Barn Antiques Centre,
Station Road,
Long Marston,
Nr Stratford-upon-Avon
CV37 8RB
Tel: 01789 721399

*Open 7 days 10am–5pm.
Large selection of antique
furniture, antique pine,
linen and lace, old
fireplaces and surrounds,
collectables, pictures and
prints, silver, china,
ceramics and objets d'art,
antique-style reproduction
furniture, clocks –
including longcase clocks,
country kitchens.*

Dunchurch Antiques
Centre, 16a Daventry
Road, Dunchurch
(Nr Rugby)
Tel: 01788 522450

Under new management.

Malthouse Antiques
Centre, 4 Market Place,
Alcester B49 5AE
Tel: 01789 764032

*Open 7 days.
Good selection of
furniture, ceramics,
pictures & collectables.*

The Stables Antique
Centre, Hatton Country
World, Dark Lane,
Hatton, Warwick
CV35 7LD
Tel: 01926 842405

*25 Independent dealers.
Come & browse in friendly
surroundings. Home
baked refreshments. Free
parking. Farm Park and
adventure playground
for children.*

Stratford Antiques Centre,
59–60 Ely Street,
Stratford-upon-Avon
CV37 6LN
Tel: 01789 204180

West Midlands

Birmingham Antique
Centre, 1407 Pershore
Road, Stirchley,
Birmingham
B30 2JR
Tel: 0121 459 4587

Yorkshire

Cavendish Antique
& Collectors Centre,
44 Stonegate,
York
YO1 8AS
Tel: 01904 621666

*Open 7 days 9am–6pm.
Over 50 dealers on
3 floors.*

Halifax Antiques Centre,
Queens Road,
Halifax
HX1 4LR
Tel: 01422 366657

Sheffield Antiques
Emporium & The Chapel,
15–19 Clyde Road,
(off Broadfield Road),
Sheffield S8 0YD
Tel: 0114 258 4863

*Open 7 days.
Over 70 dealers displaying
a wide range of antiques
and collectables including
specialists in clocks, Art
Deco, French furniture,
books, pine, fabrics,
porcelain and much more.
Services: Upholstery,
furniture restoration,
re-caning, pottery
restoration, French
polishing, delivery,
refreshments.
Suitable for trade & retail.*

Stonegate Antiques
Centre, 41 Stonegate,
York YO1 8AW
Tel: 01904 613888

*Open 9am–6pm 7 days a
week. Over 110 dealers
on 2 floors.*

East Yorkshire

The Mall Antique Centre,
400 Wincolmlee,
Hull HU2 0QL
Tel: 01482 327858

*60 local antique dealers.
12,500 sq ft of Georgian,
Victorian, Edwardian,
reproduction,1930s
furniture, silver, china,
clocks, hardware, etc.
Open 7 days 9am–5pm,
10am–4pm Sat–Sun.*

Key to Illustrations

Each illustration and descriptive caption is accompanied by a letter code. By referring to the following list of Auctioneers (denoted by *) and Dealers (•), the source of any item may be immediately determined. Inclusion in this edition in no way constitutes or implies a contract or binding offer on the part of any of our contributor to supply or sell the goods illustrated, or similar articles, at the prices stated. Advertisers in this year's directory are denoted by (†).

If you require a valuation for an item, it is advisable to check whether the dealer or specialist will carry out this service and if there is a charge. Please mention Miller's when making an enquiry. Having found a specialist who will carry out your valuation it is best to send a photograph and description of the item to the specialist together with a stamped addressed envelope for the reply. A valuation by telephone is not possible. Most dealers are only too happy to help you with your enquiry; however, they are very busy people and consideration of the above points would be welcomed.

A&H • Architectural & Historical Salvage, Spa Street, Ossett, Wakefield, Yorkshire WF5 0HJ Tel: 01924 262831

AAN • Appledore Antiques. Tel: 01233 758272

AAV * Academy Auctioneers & Valuers, Northcote House, Northcote Avenue, Ealing, London W5 3UR Tel: 020 8579 7466

ABr • Avril Brown, Bartlett Street, Bath, Somerset BA1 2QZ Tel: 01225 310457/446322

ACT • Alscot Bathroom Co, The Stable Yard, Alscot Park, Stratford-upon-Avon, Warwickshire CV37 8BL Tel: 01789 450861

ADE •† Art Deco Etc, 73 Upper Gloucester Road, Brighton, East Sussex BN1 3LQ Tel: 01273 329268

AH * Andrew Hartley, Victoria Hall Salerooms, Little Lane, Ilkley, Yorkshire LS29 8EA Tel: 01943 816363

AHa •† Adrian Harrington, 64a Kensington Church Street, London W8 4DB Tel: 020 7937 1465

AIL • Antique Irish Linen, Dublin, Republic of Ireland Tel: 00 353 1 451 2775

AL •† Ann Lingard, Ropewalk Antiques, Rye, E Sussex TN31 7NA Tel: 01797 223486

ALiN • Andrew Lineham Fine Glass, The Mall, Camden Passage, London N1 8ED Tel: 020 7704 0195 Wed & Sat 01243 576241

AMc •† Antique Amusement Co, Mill Lane, Swaffham, Bulbeck, Cambs CB5 0NF Tel: 01223 813041

AMH •† Amherst Antiques, 23 London Road, Riverhead, Sevenoaks, Kent TN13 2BU Tel: 01732 455047 Mobile 0850 350212

AND • Joan & Bob Anderson, Middlesex Tel: 020 8572 4328

ANG •† Ancient & Gothic, PO Box 356, Christchurch, Dorset BH23 1XQ Tel: 01202 478592

ANO • Art Nouveau Originals, Stamford Antiques Centre, The Exchange Hall, Broad Street, Stamford, Lincolnshire, PE9 1PX. Tel: 01780 762605

AnS •† The Antique Shop, 30 Henley Street, Stratford-upon-Avon, Warwickshire CV37 6QW Tel: 01789 292485

AnSh • Antique Shop, 136A High Street, Tenterden, Kent TN30 6HT Tel: 01580 764323

ANT • Anthemion, Bridge Street, Cartmel, Grange Over Sands, Cumbria LA11 7SH Tel: 015395 36295

AOH • Antiques on High, 85 High Street, Oxford OX1 4BG Tel: 01865 251075

AOS • Antiques on the Square, c/o Gray's Market, London W1Y 2LP

AOT •† Annie's Old Things, PO Box 6, Camphill, Queensland 4152, Australia. Tel: 0061412353099

ArD • Art Deco Vintage Designer, Warwickshire. Tel: 01926 854745

ARE • Arenski, 185 Westbourne Grove, London W11 2SB Tel: 020 7727 8599

ARo •† Alvin Ross, Oxfordshire. Tel: 01865 772409

ARP • Arundel Photographica, The Arundel Antiques Centre, 51 High Street, Arundel, W Sussex BN18 9AJ Tel: 01903 882749

ART • Artemis Decorative Arts Ltd, 36 Kensington Church St, London W8 4BX Tel: 020 7376 0377/020 7937 9900

ASA • A. S. Antiques, 26 Broad Street, Pendleton, Salford, Gt. Manchester M6 5BY Tel: 0161 737 5938

ASB • Andrew Spencer Bottomley, The Coach House, Thongs Bridge, Holmfirth, Yorkshire HD7 2TT Tel: 01484 685234

ASe • Alan Sedgwick. Tel: 01452 521337

ATH •† Apple Tree House, Shropshire Tel: 01694 722953

B&R •† Bread & Roses, Durham House Antique Centre, Sheep Street, Stow on the Wold, Glos GL54 1AA Tel: 01451 870404 or 01926 817342

BAB • The Barn at Bilsington, Ashford, Kent TN25 7JR Tel: 01233 720917

BAC • Bath Antiquities Centre, 4 Bladud Buildings, Bath, Somerset, BA1 5LS Tel: 01225 460408

BAf • Books Afloat, 66 Park Street, Weymouth, Dorset DT4 7DE Tel: 01305 779774

BAL •† A.H. Baldwin & Sons Ltd, Numismatists, 11 Adelphi Terrace, London WC2N 6BJ Tel: 020 7930 6879

BAS • Brighton Architectural Salvage, 33 Gloucester Road, Brighton, East Sussex BN1 4AQ Tel: 01273 681656

BB • Brian Bates, Newcastle, Staffs. Tel: 01782 680667

BBR *† BBR, Elsecar Heritage Centre, Wath Road, Elsecar, Barnsley, Yorkshire S74 8HJ Tel: 01226 745156

BCA • Bealieu Cars Automobilia, Beaulieu Garage, Brockenhurst, Hampshire SO42 7YE Tel: 01590 612999

BDA • Briar's C20th Decorative Arts, Skipton Antiques & Collectors Centre, The Old Foundry, Cavendish Street, Skipton, Yorkshire BD23 2AB Tel: 01756 798641

Bea(E)* Bearnes, St Edmund's Court, Okehampton Street, Exeter, Devon EX4 1DU Tel: 01392 422800

BeG • Bears Galore, 8 The Fairings, High Street, Tenterden, Kent TN30 6QX Tel: 01580 765233

BELL • Bell Antiques, Glos. Tel: 0121 745 9034

BEV •† Beverley, 30 Church Street, Marylebone, London NW8 8EP Tel: 020 7262 1576

BEX • Daniel Bexfield Antiques, 26 Burlington Arcade, London W1V 9AD Tel: 020 7491 1720

BGC •† Brenda Gerwat-Clark, Granny's Goodies, G3/4 Alfie's Antique Market, 13–25 Church Street, London NW8 8DT Tel: 020 7706 4699

BHA • Bourbon Hanby Antiques & Jewellery, 151 Sydney Street, Chelsea, London SW3 6NT Tel: 020 7352 2106

BKK •† Bona Art Deco Store, The Hart Shopping Centre, Fleet, Hampshire GU13 8AZ Tel: 01252 616666

BKS * Brooks (Auctioneers) Ltd, 81 Westside, London SW4 9AY Tel: 020 7228 8000

BLH * BBG Ambrose, Ambrose House, Old Station Road, Loughton, Essex IG10 4PE Tel: 020 8502 3951

BMo • Beau Mo'nde Costume, By George Antique Centre, 23 George Street, St Albans, Hertfordshire AL3 4ES Tel: 01727 853032/855572

BND • Brian Barnfield, Bourbon Hanby Antiques Centre, 151 Sydney Street, Chelsea, London SW3 6NT Tel: 020 7565 0002

Bns •† Brittons Jewellers, 34 Scotland Road, Nelson, Lancashire BB9 7UU Tel: 01282 697659

BOH • Bohemia, 11 Warner Street, Accrington, Lancashire Tel: 01254 231119

Bon * Bonhams, Montpelier Street, Knightsbridge, London SW7 1HH Tel: 020 7393 3900

Bon(C)* Bonhams, 65-69 Lots Road, Chelsea, London SW10 0RN Tel: 020 7393 3900

BOS * Bosley's, 42 West Street, Marlow, Bucks. SL7 2NB Tel: 01628 488188

BQ • The Button Queen, 19 Marylebone Lane, London W1M 5FE Tel: 020 7935 1505

Bri * Bristol Auction Rooms, St John's Place, Apsley Road, Clifton, Bristol, Glos BS8 2ST Tel: 0117 973 7201

BRU • Brunel Antiques, Bartlett Street Antiques Centre, Bath, Somerset BA1 2QZ Tel: 0117 968 1734

BSL •† Barclay Samson Ltd, 65 Finlay Street, London SW6 6HF Tel: 020 7731 8012

BTB/• Behind the Boxes, 98 Kirkdale,
BtB Sydenham, London SE26 4BG Tel: 020 8291 6116

BTC •† Beatcity, 56 High Street, Chatham, Kent ME4 4DS Tel: 01634 844525/077 70 65 08 90

BUR •† House of Burleigh, Leicestershire. Tel: 01664 454570

BWA • Bow-Well Antiques, 103 West Bow, Edinburgh, Scotland EH1 2JP Tel: 0131 225 3335

BWC • British Watch & Clock Collectors Association, 5 Cathedral Lane, Truro, Cornwall TR1 2QS Tel: 01872 264010 email: tonybwcca@cs.com URL: http://www.timecap.co.uk

BYG • Bygones Reclamation (Canterbury), Nackington Road, Canterbury, Kent Tel: 01227 767453

Byl • Bygones of Ireland Ltd, Lodge Road, Westport, County Mayo, Republic of Ireland Tel: 00 353 98 26132/25701

CAB •† Candlestick & Bakelite, PO Box 308, Orpington, Kent BR5 1TB Tel: 020 8467 3743/3799

CAG * The Canterbury Auction Galleries, 40 Station Road West, Canterbury, Kent CT2 8AN Tel: 01227 763337

CaH • The Camera House, Oakworth Hall, Colne Road (B6143), Oakworth, Keighley, Yorkshire BD22 7HZ Tel: 01535 642333

CAm •† Classic Amusements, Hampshire. Tel: 01425 472164

CARS • C.A.R.S. (Classic Automobilia & Regalia Specialists), 4–4a Chapel Terrace Mews, Kemp Town, Brighton, East Sussex BN2 1HU Tel: 01273 60 1960

CB • Christine Bridge Antiques, 78 Castelnau, London SW13 9EX Tel: 07000 445277

CBP *† Comic Book Postal Auctions Ltd, 40–42 Osnaburgh Street, London NW1 3ND Tel: 020 7424 0007

CCC •† Crested China Co, The Station House, Driffield, Yorkshire YO25 7PY Tel: 01377 257042

CCO • Collectable Costume, Fountain Antique Centre, 3 Fountain Buildings, Lansdowne Road, Bath, Somerset BA1 5DU Tel: 01225 428731

CGC * Cheffins Grain & Comins, 2 Clifton Road, Cambridge, Cambs CB2 4BW Tel: 01223 358731

CGX • Computer & Games Exchange, 65 Notting Hill Gate Road, London W11 3JS Tel: 020 7221 1123

ChA • The Chapel Antiques, The Chapel, Chapel Place, Tunbridge Wells, Kent TN1 1YR Tel: 01892 619921

CHAP• Bill Chapman, Stand 11, Bourbon Hanby
Antiques Centre, 151 Sydney Street,
Chelsea, London SW3 6NT
Tel: 020 7352 2106

CHe • Chelsea Clocks & Antiques, Antiquarius,
Stand H3–4, 135 Kings Road, London
SW3 4PW Tel: 020 7352 8646

CHU • Church Street Antiques, 2 Church Street,
Wells Next the Sea, Norfolk NR23 1JA
Tel: 01328 711698

CJB • Classic Juke Boxes, London N1
Tel: 020 7493 1849

CMF •† Childhood Memories, The Farnham
Antique Centre, 27 South Street,
Farnham, Surrey GU9 7QU
Tel: 01252 724475/793704

CoA • Country Antiques (Wales), Castle Mill,
Kidwelly, Carms, Wales SA17 4UU
Tel: 01554 890534

COB •† Cobwebs, 78 Northam Road,
Southampton, Hampshire SO14 0PB
Tel: 023 8022 7458

COCO• Country Collector, 11–12 Birdgate,
Pickering, Yorkshire YO18 7AL
Tel: 01751 477481

CoHA• Corner House Antiques, High Street,
Lechlade, Glos GL7 3AE
Tel: 01367 252007

COHU• Stephen Cohu Antiques, The Village
Gallery, Ville de l'Eglise, St Ouen, Jersey,
Channel Islands JE3 2LR
Tel: 01534 485177/630845

COLL• Collinge Antiques, Old Fyffes Warehouse,
Cowry Road, Llandudno Junction, Wales
LL31 9LU Tel: 01492 580022

CP •† Cat Pottery, 1 Grammar School Road,
North Walsham, Norfolk NR28 9JH
Tel: 01692 402962

CPA • Cottage Pine Antiques, 19 Broad Street,
Brinklow, Nr Rugby, Warwickshire
CV23 0LS Tel: 01788 832673

CRIS • Cristobal, Unit G125–127, Alfies Antique
Market, 13-15 Church Street, London
NW8 8DT Tel: 020 7724 7789

CRN •† The Crow's Nest, 3 Hope Square, opp.
Brewers Quay, Weymouth, Dorset
DT4 8TR Tel: 01305 786930

CRU • Mary Cruz Antiques, 5 Broad Street,
Bath, Somerset BA1 5LJ
Tel: 01225 334174

CS •† Christopher Sykes, The Old Parsonage,
Woburn, Milton Keynes, Bedfordshire
MK17 9QM Tel: 01525 290259

CSA •† Church Street Antiques, 10 Church
Street, Godalming, Surrey GU7 1EH
Tel: 01483 860894

CSAC• Church Street Antiques Centre, 3–4
Church Street, Stow 0n the Wold, Glos
GL54 1BB Tel: 01451 870186

CWo/ Collectors World, Stand G101, G130/143
CWO• Alfies Antique Market, 13–25 Church
Street, Marylebone, London NW8 8DT
Tel: 020 7723 0564 Mobile 078 60 791588

CY • Carl & Yvonne, Grays in the Mews, South
Molton Lane, London W1Y 2LP
Tel: 020 7629 7034/01785 606487

DA * Dee, Atkinson & Harrison, The Exchange
Saleroom, Driffield, Yorkshire YO25 7LD
Tel: 01377 253151

DAC • Didcot Antiques Centre, 220 Broadway,
Didcot, Oxfordshire OX11 8RS
Tel: 01235 510819

DBr • David Brown, 23 Claude Street, Larkhall,
Lanarkshire, Scotland ML9 2BU
Tel: 01555 880333

DDM * Dickinson Davy & Markham, Wrawby
Street, Brigg, Humberside DN20 8JJ
Tel: 01652 653666

DeA • Delphi Antiques, Powerscourt
Townhouse Centre, South William Street,
Dublin 2, Republic of Ireland
Tel: 00 353 1 679 0331

DEC •† Decorative Antiques, 47 Church Street,
Bishop's Castle, Shropshire SY9 5AD
Tel: 01588 638851

DgC • Dragonlee Collectables, Kent.
Tel: 01622 729502

DHA • Durham House Antiques Centre, Sheep
Street, Stow-on-the-Wold, Glos
GL54 1AA Tel: 01451 870404

DHAR• Dave Hardman Antiques, The George
Arcade, Broad Street, South Molton,
Devon EX36 3AB
Tel: 01769 574066/07979 737126

DHo/ Derek Howard, Chelsea Antique Market,
DHO• 245-253 King's Road, London SW3 5EL
Tel: 020 7352 4113

DIC • D & B Dickinson, The Antique Shop,
22 & 22a New Bond St, Bath, Somerset
BA1 1BA Tel: 01225 466502

DID • Didier Antiques, 58-60 Kensington
Church Street, London W8 4DB
Tel: 020 7938 2537/078 36 232634

DKH • David K. Hakeney, 400 Wincolmlee, Hull,
Humberside HU2 0QL Tel: 01482 228190

DMa • David March, Abbots Leigh, Bristol, Glos
Tel: 0117 937 2422

DN * Dreweatt Neate, Donnington Priory,
Donnington, Newbury, Berkshire
RG13 2JE Tel: 01635 553553

DNW *† Dix-Noonan-Webb, 1 Old Bond Street,
London W1X 3TD Tel: 020 7499 5022

Do • Liz Farrow t/as Dodo, Stand F073/83,
Alfies Antique Market, 13–25 Church St,
London NW8 8DT Tel: 020 7706 1545

DOL •† Dollectable, 53 Lower Bridge Street,
Chester, Cheshire CH1 1RS
Tel: 01244 344888/679195

DOM • Peter Dome, Sheffield.

DP • David Payne, Paragon Antiques &
Collectors Market, 3 Bladud Buildings,
The Paragon, Bath, Somerset BA1 5LS
Tel: 01225 463715

DPO • Doug Poultney, 219 Lynmouth Ave,
Morden, Surrey SM4 4RX
Tel: 020 8330 3472

DQ • Dolphin Quay Antique Centre, Queen
Street, Emsworth, Hampshire PO10 7BU
Tel: 01243 379994

DRJ • The Motorhouse, DS & RG Johnson,
Thorton Hall, Thorton, Bucks MK17 0HB.
Tel: 01280 812280

DSG •† Delf Stream Gallery, 14 New Street,
Sandwich, Kent CT13 9AB
Tel: 01304 617684

DuM * Du Mouchelles, 409 East Jefferson,
Detroit, Michigan 48226, USA
Tel: 001 313 963 0248

DW *† Dominic Winter Book Auctions, The Old School, Maxwell Street, Swindon, Wiltshire SN1 5DR Tel: 01793 611340

E * Ewbank, Burnt Common Auction Room, London Road, Send, Woking, Surrey GU23 7LN Tel: 01483 223101

EAS • Eastgate Antiques, Stand 7/9 Alfies Antique Market, 13–25 Church Street, London NW8 8DT Tel: 077 74 206289

EBB • Ella's Button Box, South View, Twyford, Bucks MK18 4EG Tel: 01296 730910

Ec/ Ech•† Echoes, 650a Halifax Road, Eastwood, Todmorden, Yorkshire OL14 6DW Tel: 01706 817505

EKK • Ekkehart, USA Tel: 001 415 571 9070

ELe • Elizabeth Lee

ELI • Eli Antiques, Stand Q5 Antiquarius, 135 King's Road, London SW3 4PW Tel: 020 7351 7038

EMC • Sue Emerson & Bill Chapman, Bourbon Hanby Antiques Centre, Shop No 18, 151 Sydney Street, Chelsea, London SW3 6NT Tel: 020 7351 1807

EON • Eugene O'Neill Antique Gallery, Echo Bridge Mall, 381 Elliot Street, Newtown Upper Falls, MA 02164, USA Tel: (617) 965 5965

ERC • Zenith Antiques (Elizabeth Coupe), Hemswell Antiques Centre, Caenby Corner Estate, Hemswell Cliff, Gainsborough, Lincolnshire DN21 5TJ Tel: 01427 668389

ET • Early Technology, 84 West Bow, Edinburgh, Scotland EH1 2HH Tel: 0131 226 1132

EXC • Excalibur Antiques, Taunton Antique Centre, 27–29 Silver Street, Taunton, Somerset TA13DH Tel: 01823 289327/0374 627409

F&C * Finan & Co, The Square, Mere, Wiltshire BA12 6DJ Tel: 01747 861411

FAM • Fountain Antiques Centre, 3 Fountain Buildings, Lansdown Road, Bath, Somerset BA1 5DU Tel: 01225 428731/471133

FD • Frank Dux Antiques, 33 Belvedere, Bath, Somerset BA1 5HR Tel: 01225 312367

FF • Freeforms, Unit 6 The Antique Centre, 58–60 Kensington Church Street, London W8 4DB Tel: 020 7937 9447

FHF * Frank H. Fellows & Sons, Augusta House, 19 Augusta Street, Hockley, Birmingham, West Midlands B18 6JA Tel: 0121 212 2131

FMu • Frank Munford, Brooke Bond Cereal & Trade Dealer, Brooke House, 108 West Parade, Lincoln, Lincolnshire LN1 1LA Tel: 01522 878362

FRa • Frasers, 399 The Strand, London WC2 Tel: 020 7836 9325

FrG • The French Glasshouse, P14/16 Antiquarius, 135 King's Road, Chelsea, London SW3 4PW Tel: 020 7376 5394

G&CC•† Goss & Crested China Centre & Museum incorporating Milestone Publications, 62 Murray Road, Horndean, Hampshire PO8 9JL Tel: (023) 9259 7440

GaB • Garden Brocante. Tel: 0118 9461905

GAK * G A Key, 8 Market Place, Aylsham, Norfolk NR11 6EH Tel: 01263 733195

GAZE * Thomas Wm Gaze & Son, Diss Auction Rooms, Roydon Road, Diss, Norfolk IP22 3LN Tel: 01379 650306

GeM • Gerald Mathias, R5/6 Antiquarius, 135 King's Road, Chelsea, London SW3 4PW Tel: 020 7351 0484

GeW • Geoffrey Waters Ltd, F1 to F6 Antiquarius Antiques Centre, 135–141 King's Road, London SW3 4PW Tel: 020 7376 5467

GH * Gardiner Houlgate, The Old Malthouse, Comfortable Place, Upper Bristol Road, Bath, Somerset BA1 3AJ Tel: 01225 447933

GHC • Great Haul of China, PO Box 233, Sevenoaks, Kent TN13 3ZN Tel: 01732 741484

GIN • The Ginnell Gallery Antique Centre, 18–22 Lloyd Street, Gt. Manchester M2 5WA Tel: 0161 833 9037

GKR •† GKR Bonds Ltd, PO Box 1, Kelvedon, Essex CO5 9EH Tel: 01376 571711

GLA • Glasform Ltd, 123 Talbot Road, Blackpool, Lancashire FY1 3QY Tel: 01253 626410

Gle * Glendinings & Co, 101 New Bond Street, London W1Y 9LG Tel: 020 7493 2445

GLT • Glitterati, Assembly Antique Centre, 6–8 Saville Row, Bath, Somerset BA1 2QP Tel: 01225 333294

GN • Gillian Neale Antiques, PO Box 247, Aylesbury, Bucks HP20 1JZ Tel: 01296 423754

GOR * Gorringes Auction Galleries, Terminus Road, Bexhill-on-Sea, East Sussex TN39 3LR Tel: 01424 212994

GR • Geoff Read, 176 Brown Edge Road, Buxton, Derbyshire SK17 7AA Tel: 01298 71234

GRa •† Gray's Antique Market, 1–7 Davies Mews, London W1Y 2LP Tel: 020 7629 7034

GrD • Gray's Dolls, Gray's in the Mews, 1–7 Davies Street, London W1Y 2LP Tel: 020 8367 2441/020 7629 7034

GRI •† Grimes House Antiques, High Street, Moreton-in-Marsh, Glos GL56 0AT Tel: 01608 651029

GS • Ged Selby Antique Glass, by appointment, Yorkshire Tel: 01756 799673

GSW • Georg S. Wissinger Antiques, 21 & 44 West Street, Chipping Norton, Oxfordshire Tel: 01608 641369

GV • Garth Vincent, The Old Manor House, Allington, Nr Grantham, Lincolnshire NG32 2DH Tel: 01400 281358

GWR/ GwR • Gwen Riley, Stand 12, Bourbon Hanby Antique Centre, 151 Sydney Street, Chelsea, London SW3 6NT Tel: 020 7352 2106

HAK •† Paul Haskell, Kent. Tel: 01634 669362 Mobile: 0374 781160

HALB • Halbzwolf, Eschstrabe 21b, 32257 Bunde, Germany Tel: 00 49 05223 52 58

HALL• Hall's Nostalgia, 21 Mystic Street, Arlington, USA, MA 02474 Tel: 001 781 646 7757

Har • Patricia Harbottle, Geoffrey Vann Arcade, 107 Portobello Road, London W11 2QB Tel: 020 7731 1972 Saturdays

HaR • Mr A. Harris, Middlesex. Tel: 020 8931 6591 or Mobile: 079 56 146083

HarC •† Hardy's Collectables, 862 Christchurch Road, Boscombe, Bournemouth, Dorset BH7 6DQ Tel: 01202 422407/473744 Mobile: 07970 613077

HARP•† Harpers Jewellers Ltd, 2/6 Minster Gates, York, Yorkshire YO7 2HL Tel: 01904 632634

Hds • Harrods, Knightsbridge, London Tel: 020 7730 1234

HEI • Heirloom Antiques, 68 High Street, Tenterden, Kent TN30 6AU Tel: 01580 765535

HEL • Helios Gallery, 292 Westbourne Grove, London W11 2PS Tel: 077 11 955 997

HEM • Hemswell Antique Centre, Caenby Corner Estate, Hemswell Cliff, Gainsborough, Lincolnshire DN21 5TJ Tel: 01427 668389

HEW •† Muir Hewitt, Halifax Antiques Centre, Queens Road Mills, Queen's Road/Gibbet Street, Halifax, Yorkshire HX1 4LR Tel: 01422 347377

HGh • Hungry Ghost, 1 Brewery Yard, Sheep Street, Stow on the Wold, Glos GL54 1AA Tel: 01451 870101

HHa • Henry Hay, Alfies Antique Market, Stand S54, 13–25 Church Street, Marylebone, London NW8 8DT Tel: 020 7723 6105

HHO • Howard Hope, 21 Bridge Road, East Molesey, Surrey KT8 9EU Tel: 0181 941 2472 0181 398 7130 Mobile: 0585 543267

HIG • Highcroft Antiques, Red Lion, 165 Portobello Road, London W11 2DY

Hmb • Homebase

HOB •† Hobday Toys, Middlesex Tel: 01895 636737

HofB • Howards of Broadway, 27A High Street, Broadway, Worcestershire WR12 7DP Tel: 01386 858924

HOK * Hamilton Osborne King, 4 Main Street, Blackrock, Co. Dublin, Republic of Ireland Tel: 353 1 288 5011

HT • Heather's Treasures. Tel: 01202 624018

HUM • Humbleyard Fine Art, Unit 32 Admiral Vernon Arcade, Portobello Road, London W11 2DY Tel: 01787 379287

HUM • Humbleyard Fine Art, Chapel Maltings, Long Melford, Suffolk CO10 9HX Tel: 01787 379287

HUR • Hurst Gallery, 53 Mt. Auburn Street, Cambridge, MA 02138, USA Tel: 617 491 6888 www.hurstgallery.com

HUX •† David Huxtable, Stand S03/05 (Top Floor) Alfies Antique Market, 13–25 Church Street, Marylebone, London NW8 8DT Tel: 020 7724 2200

ID • Identity, Portobello Green Mkt, Under the Canopy, London W11 Tel: 020 7792 4604

INC • The Incurable Collector, Surrey Tel: 01932 860800

IS • Ian Sharp Antiques, 23 Front Street, Tynemouth, Tyne & Wear NE30 4DX Tel: 0191 296 0656

IW •† Islwyn Watkins, Offa's Dyke Antique Centre, 4 High Street, Knighton, Powys, Wales LD7 1AT Tel: 01547 528635

J&J • J & J's, Paragon Antiques & Collectors Market, 3 Bladud Buildings, The Paragon, Bath, Somerset BA1 5LS Tel: 01225 313176

JAC • John & Anne Clegg, 12 Old Street, Ludlow, Shropshire SY8 1NP Tel: 01584 873176

JACK •† Michael Jackson Antiques, The Quiet Woman Antiques Centre, Southcombe, Chipping Norton, Oxfordshire OX7 5QH Tel: 01608 646262

JaG • Japanese Gallery, 66d Kensington Church Street, London W8 4BY Tel: 020 7229 2034/020 7226 3347

JAK • Clive & Lynne Jackson, Glos. Tel: 01242 254375 Mobile 078 89 715275

JAS • Jasmin Cameron, M16 Antiquarius, 131–141 King's Road, London SW3 5ST Tel Shop 020 7351 4154 Mobile: 077 74 871257 Home: 01494 774276

JBe * John Bellman Auctioneers, New Pound Business Park, Wisborough Green, Billingshurst, Sussex RH14 0AZ Tel: 01403 700858

JBU • John Bull (Antiques) Ltd, JB Silverware, 139a New Bond Street, London W1Y 9FB Tel: 020 7629 1251 Mobile: 0850 221 468

JCa • J Cards, PO Box 12, Tetbury, Glos GL8 8WB Tel: 01454 238600

JE •† Julian Eade, Surrey. Tel: 020 8394 1515 Mobile: 0973 542971

JEA/ CAW•† John Edwards Antiques, Worcester Antiques Centre, 15 Reindeer Court, Mealcheapen Street, Worcester WR1 4DF Tel: 01905 353840

JHa • Jeanette Hayhurst Fine Glass, 32a Kensington Church St, London W8 4HA Tel: 020 7938 1539

JHo/ JHO • Jonathan Horne, 66B&C Kensington Church Street, London W8 4BY Tel: 020 7221 5658

JMC • J & M Collectables, Kent. Tel: 01580 891657

JO • Jacqueline Oosthuizen, 23 Cale Street, Chelsea, London SW3 3QR Tel: 020 7352 6071

JP • Janice Paull, Beehive House, 125 Warwick Road, Kenilworth, Warwickshire CV8 1HY Tel: 01926 855253/851311

JPr • Joanna Proops Antique Textiles, 34 Belvedere, Lansdown Hill, Bath, Somerset BA1 5HR Tel: 01225 310795

JSM • J & S. Millard Antiques, Assembly Antiques, 5-8 Saville Row, Bath, Somerset BA1 2QP Tel: 01225 469785

JU • Jukebox Showroom, 9 Park Parade Gunnersbury Avenue, London W3 9BD Tel: 020 8992 8482/3

JUN •† Junktion, The Old Railway Station, New Bolingbroke, Boston, Lincolnshire PE22 7LB Tel: 01205 480068/480087

JUP • Jupiter Antiques, PO Box 609, Rottingdean, East Sussex BN2 7FW Tel: 01273 302865

JVa • Jenny Vander, 20-22 Market Arcade, George Street, Dublin 2, Republic of Ireland Tel: 00 353 1 677 0406

K • Kite, 15 Langton Street, Chelsea, London SW10 0JL Tel: 020 7351 2108 Mobile 077 11 887120

KEN • Alan Kenyon, PO Box 33, Port Talbot Tel: 01639 895359

KES •† Keystones, PO Box 387, Stafford, Staffordshire ST16 3FG Tel: 01785 256648

KNI * Knight's, Cuckoo Cottage, Town Green, Alby, Norwich, Norfolk NR11 7HE Tel: 01263 768488

KWCC§ Kathie Winkle Collectors Club, SAE to Mrs Nadin-Leath, Greenacres, Calbourne Road, Carisbrooke, Isle of Wight PO30 5AP Tel: 01983 525981

L&L •† Linen & Lace, Shirley Tomlinson, Halifax Antiques Centre, Queens Road/Gibbet Street, Halifax, Yorkshire HX1 4LR Tel: 01422 366657 Mobile: 077 11 763454

Law • Malcolm Law Collectables, Toren's Garden Centre, Bethersden, Kent Tel: Mobile: 077 11 015610

LBe • Linda Bee Art Deco, Stand L18-21, Gray's Antique Market, 1–7 Davies Mews, London W1Y 1AR Tel: 020 7629 5921

LBr • Lynda Brine, Assembly Antique Centre, 5–8 Saville Row, Bath, Somerset BA1 2QP Tel: 01225 448488

LCC • London Cigarette Card Co Ltd, Sutton Road, Somerton, Somerset TA11 6QP Tel: 01458 273452

LeB • Le Boudoir Collectables, Bartlett Street Antique Centre, Bath, Somerset BA1 2QZ Tel: 01225 311061

LEGE • Legend, Bristol. Tel: 0117 9264637

LF * Lambert & Foster, 77 Commercial Road, Paddock Wood, Kent TN12 6DR Tel: 01892 832325

LIB • Libra Antiques, 81 London Road, Hurst Green, Etchingham, E Sussex TN19 7PN Tel: 01580 860569

MAC • The Mall Antique Centre, 400 Wincolmlee, Hull, E. Yorks HU2 0QL Tel: 01482 327858

MAr •† Mint Arcade, 71 The Mint, Rye, East Sussex TN31 7EW Tel: 01797 225952

MARK•† 20th Century Marks, 12 Market Square, Westerham, Kent TN16 1AW Tel: 01959 562221

MAU • Sue Mautner, Stand P13, Antiquarius, 135 Kings Road, London SW3 4PW Tel: 020 7376 4419

MB •† Mostly Boxes, 93 High Street, Eton, Windsor, Berkshire SL4 6AF Tel: 01753 858470

MCA * Mervyn Carey, Twysden Cottage, Benenden, Cranbrook, Kent TN17 4LD Tel: 01580 240283

McG • Andy McGregor, East Sussex.

MCN • MCN Antiques, 183 Westbourne Grove, London W11 2SB Tel: 020 7727 3796

MEA * Mealy's, Chatsworth Street, Castle Comer, Co Kilkenny, Republic of Ireland Tel: 00 353 56 41229

MED * Medway Auctions, Fagins, 23 High Street, Rochester, Kent ME1 1LN Tel: 01634 847444

MEx/ Music Exchange, 21 Broad Street, Bath,
MEX• Somerset BA1 5LN Tel: Music 01225 333963 Records 01225 339789

MGC • Midlands Goss & Commemoratives, The Old Cornmarket Antiques Centre, 70 Market Place, Warwick, CV34 4SO Tel: 01926 419119

Mit * Mitchells, Fairfield House, Station Road, Cockermouth, Cumbria CA13 9PY Tel: 01900 827800

MLa • Marion Langham, London. Tel: 020 7730 1002

MLL • Millers Antiques Ltd, Netherbrook House, 86 Christchurch Road, Ringwood, Hampshire BH24 1DR Tel: 01425 472062

MoS • Morgan Stobbs, by appointment. Tel: Mobile 077 02 206817

MRo/ Mike Roberts, 4416 Foxfire Way, Fort
MRO • Worth, Texas 76133, USA Tel: 001 817 294 2133

MRT • Mark Rees Tools Tel: 01225 837031

MRW • Malcolm Welch Antiques, Warwickshire Tel: 01788 810 616

MSB • Marilynn and Sheila Brass, PO Box 380503, Cambridge, USA, MA 02238-0503 Tel: 617 491 6064

MTM • More than Music, PO Box 68, Westerham, Kent TN16 1ZF Tel: +44 (0) 1959 56 55 14

MUL •† Mullock & Madeley, The Old Shippon, Wall-under-Heywood, Nr Church Stretton, Shropshire SY6 7DS Tel: 01694 771771

MUR •† Murray Cards (International) Ltd, 51 Watford Way, Hendon Central, London NW4 3JH Tel: 020 8202 5688

MVX • Music & Video Exchange, 1st Floor, 38 Notting Hill Gate, London W11 3HX Tel: 020 7243 8574

NAR • Colin Narbeth & Son Ltd, 20 Cecil Court, Leicester Square, London WC2N 4HE Tel: 020 7379 6975

NC • The Nautical Centre, Harbour Passage, Hope Square, Weymouth, Dorset DT4 8TR Tel: Day 01305 777838

NCA • New Century, 69 Kensington Church St, London W8 4DB Tel: 020 7937 2410

NET • Nettlebed Antique Merchants, 1 High Street, Nettlebed, Henley-on-Thames, Oxfordshire RG9 5DA Tel: 0370 554559/01491 642062

No7 • No 7 Antiques, Newcastle-under-Lyme, Staffordshire. Tel: 01630 639613 Fax: 01630 647118

NP • Neville Pundole, 8A & 9 The Friars, Canterbury, Kent CT1 2AS Tel: 01227 453471

OCAC• Old Cornmarket Antiques Centre, 70 Market Place, Warwick, Warwickshire CV34 4SO Tel: 01926 419119

OD • Offa's Dyke Antique Centre, 4 High Street, Knighton, Powys, Wales LD7 1AT Tel: 01547 528635

OLM • The Old Mill, High Street, Lamberhurst, Kent TN3 8EQ Tel: 01892 891196

OO • Pieter Oosthuizen, Unit 4, Bourbon Hanby Antique Centre, 151 Sydney Street, London SW3 6NT Tel: 020 7460 3078

OOLA• Oola Boola, 166 Tower Bridge Road, London SE1 3LS Tel: 020 7403 0794/020 8693 5050

OTB •† Old Tackle Box, PO Box 55, High Street, Cranbrook, Kent TN17 3ZU Tel: 01580 713979

OTC •† The Old Telephone Company, The Old Granary, Battlebridge Antiques Centre, Nr Wickford, Essex SS11 7RF Tel: 01245 400601

OTS •† The Old Toy Shop, Hampshire Tel: 01425 476899

OTT • Otter Antiques, 20 High Street, Wallingford, Oxfordshire OX10 0BP Tel: 01491 825544

OW • Off World, Unit 20, Romford Shopping Halls, Market Place, Romford, Essex RM1 3AT Tel: 01708 765633

P *† Phillips, Blenstock House, 101 New Bond Street, London W1Y 0AS Tel: 020 7629 6602/7468 8233

P(B) * Phillips, 1 Old King Street, Bath, Somerset BA1 2JT Tel: 01225 310609

P(Ba) * Phillips Bayswater, 10 Salem Road, Bayswater, London W2 4DL Tel: 020 7229 9090

P(C) * Phillips Cardiff, 9–10 Westgate Street, Cardiff, Wales CF1 1DA Tel: 029 2039 6453

PAC •† The Potteries Antique Centre, 271 Waterloo Road, Cobridge, Stoke-on-Trent, Staffordshire ST6 3HR Tel: 01782 201455

PARS• Pars Antiques, Stand A14–15, Gray's in the Mews, 1–7 Davies Street, London W1Y 1AR Tel: 020 7491 9889

PBr • Pamela Brooks, Leicestershire Tel: 0116 230 2625

PC Private Collection

PCh * Peter Cheney, Western Road Auction Rooms, Western Road, Littlehampton, Sussex BN17 5NP Tel: 01903 722264/713418

PGA • Paul Gibbs Antiques, 25 Castle Street, Conway, Gwynedd, Wales LL32 8AY Tel: 01492 593429/596533

PHa •† Peter Harrington, 100 Fulham Road, London SW3 6HS Tel: 020 7591 0220/0330

PIC • David & Susan Pickles Tel: 01282 707673/0976 236983

PJa • P. Jacques, SO59/60, Alfies Antique Market, 13–25 Church Street, London NW8 8DT Tel: 020 7723 6066

PKT • Glitter & Dazzle, Pat & Ken Thompson Tel: 01329 288678

PLB • Planet Bazaar, 151 Drummond Street, London NW1

POSH• Posh Tubs, Moriati's Workshop, High Halden, Ashford, Kent TN26 3LZ Tel: 01233 850155

PPe • Past Perfect, 31 Catherine Hill, Frome, Somerset BA11 1BY Tel: 01373 453342

PPH • Period Picnic Hampers Tel: 0115 937 2934

PSA • Pantiles Spa Antiques, 4, 5, 6 Union House, The Pantiles, Tunbridge Wells, Kent TN4 8HE Tel: 01892 541377

PT • Pieces of Time, (1–7 Davies Mews), 26 South Molton Lane, London W1Y 2LP Tel: 020 7629 2422

Q&C • Q&C Militaria, 22 Suffolk Road, Cheltenham, Glos GL50 2AQ. Tel: 01242 519815 Mobile: 0378 613977

Rac/ Rochester Antiques Centre, 93 High
RAC • Street, Rochester, Kent ME1 1LX Tel: 01634 846144

RAD • Radio Days, 87 Lower Marsh, Waterloo, London SE1 7AB Tel: 020 7928 0800

RAR * Romsey Auction Rooms, 86 The Hundred, Romsey, Hampshire SO51 8BX Tel: 01794 513331

RAT • Room at the Topp, 1st Floor, Antiques Warehouse, Glass Street, Hanley, Stoke-on-Trent, Staffordshire ST1 2ET Tel: 01782 271070

RAW • The Original Reclamation Trading Co, 22 Elliot Road, Love Lane Estate, Cirencester, Glos GL7 1YS Tel: 01285 653532

RBA •† Roger Bradbury Antiques, Church Street, Coltishall, Norfolk NR12 7DJ Tel: 01603 737444

RBB * Russell, Baldwin & Bright, Fine Art Salerooms, Ryelands Road, Leominster, Herefordshire HR6 8NZ Tel: 01568 611122

RdeR • Rogers de Rin, 76 Royal Hospital Road, London SW3 4HN Tel: 020 7352 9007

RDG • Richard Dennis Gallery, 144 Kensington Church Street, London W8 4BN Tel: 020 7727 2061

REEL • The Reel Poster Gallery, 72 Westbourne Grove, London W2 5SH Tel: 020 7727 4488

REG • Regatta Antiques, Antiques Centre, 151 Sydney Street, Chelsea, London SW3 6NT Tel: 020 7460 0054

RMC •† Romsey Medal Centre, PO Box 169, Romsey, Hampshire SO51 6XU Tel: 01794 324488

ROK • Rokit Ltd, 225 Camden High Street, London NW1 7BU Tel: 020 7267 3046

ROS * Rosebery's, The Old Railway Booking Hall, Crystal Palace Station Road, London SE19 2AZ Tel: 020 8761 2522

ROU • Route One, Broad Street, Bath, Somerset BA1 5L2

RTh • The Reel Thing, 17 Royal Opera Arcade, Pall Mall, London SW1Y 4UY Tel: 020 7976 1840

RTo/ Rupert Toovey & Co Ltd, Star Road,
RTO * Partridge Green, West Sussex RH13 8RJ
Tel: 01403 711744
RTw/ Richard Twort, Somerset.
RTW • Tel: 01934 641900 Mobile: 077 11 939789
RUL • Rules Antiques, 62 St Leonards Road,
Windsor, Berkshire SL4 3BY
Tel: 01753 833210/01491 642062
RUM •† Rumours, 10 The Mall, Upper Street,
Camden Passage, Islington,
London N1 0PD Tel: 01582 873561
RUS • Trevor Russell, PO Box 1258, Uttoxeter,
Staffordshire ST14 8XL
RUSK• Ruskin Antiques, Ruskin Decorative Arts,
5 Talbot Court, Stow-on-the-Wold,
Cheltenham, Glos GL54 1DP
Tel: 01451 832254
S * Sotheby's, 34–35 New Bond Street,
London W1A 2AA Tel: 020 7293 5000
S(S) * Sotheby's Sussex, Summers Place,
Billingshurst, West Sussex RH14 9AD
Tel: 01403 833500
SAF *† Saffron Walden Saleroom, 1 Market
Street, Saffron Walden, Essex CB10 1JB
Tel: 01799 513281
SAS *† Special Auction Services, The Coach
House, Midgham Park, Reading,
Berkshire RG7 5UG Tel: 0118 971 2949
SCO • Peter Scott, Stand 39, Bartlett Street
Antiques Centre, Bath, Som BA1 2QZ
Tel: 01225 310457 or 0117 986 8468
Mobile: 078 50 639770
SCR •† Herzog, Hollender Phillips & Company,
The Scripophily Shop, PO Box 14376,
London NW6 1ZD Tel: 020 7433 3577
SER • Serendipity, 125 High Street, Deal, Kent
CT14 6BQ Tel: 01304 369165/366536
SFL • The Silver Fund, 40 Bury Street,
St James's, London SW1Y 6AU
Tel: 020 7839 7664
SHa • Shapiro & Co, Stand 380, Gray's Antique
Market, 58 Davies Street,
London W1Y 1LB Tel: 020 7491 2710
SK * Skinner Inc, The Heritage On The
Garden, 63 Park Plaza, Boston,
USA, MA 02116 Tel: 001 617 350 5400
SK(B)* Skinner Inc, 357 Main Street, Bolton,
USA, MA 01740 Tel: 001 978 779 6241
SLL • Sylvanna LLewelyn Antiques, Unit 5,
Bourbon-Hanby Antiques Centre,
151 Sydney Street, Chelsea, London
SW3 6NT Tel: 020 7351 4981
SMAM• Santa Monica Antique Market, 1607
Lincoln Boulevard, Santa Monica,
California 90404 USA
Tel: 310 314 4899
SMI •† Skip & Janie Smithson, Lincolnshire
Tel: 01754 810265
Som/ , Somervale Antiques, 6 Radstock Road,
SOM • Midsomer Norton, Bath, Somerset
BA3 2AJ Tel: 01761 412686
SOO • Soo San, 117 Stephendale Road,
London SW6 2PS
Tel: 020 7731 8989
Mobile: 077 70 874 557
SPa • Sparks Antiques, 4 Manor Row,
High Street, Tenterden, Kent TN30 6HP
Tel: 01580 766696

SpM • Sparkle Moore, The Girl Can't Help It!,
G100 & G116 Ground Floor, Alfies
Antique Market, 13–25 Church Street,
Marylebone, London NW8 8DT
Tel: 020 7724 8984
SpP *† Specialised Postcard Auctions,
25 Gloucester Street, Cirencester,
Glos GL7 2DJ Tel: 01285 659057
SPU • Spurrier-Smith Antiques,
28, 30, 39 Church Street, Ashbourne,
Derbyshire DE6 1AJ
Tel: 01335 343669/342198
SRA *† Sheffield Railwayana Auctions,
43 Little Norton Lane, Sheffield,
Yorkshire S8 8GA Tel: 0114 274 5085
STA • Michelina & George Stacpoole, Main
Street, Adare, Co Limerick,
Republic of Ireland
Tel: 00 353 6139 6409
StC •† St Clere – Carlton Ware, PO Box 161,
Sevenoaks, Kent TN15 6GA
Tel: 01474 853630
STE •† Stevenson Brothers, The Workshop,
Ashford Road, Bethersden, Ashford,
Kent TN26 3AP Tel: 01233 820363
STG • Stone Gallery, 93 The High Street,
Burford, Oxfordshire OX18 4QA
Tel: 01993 823302
STK • Stockbridge Antiques, 8 Deanhaugh
Street, Edinburgh, Scotland EH4 1LY
Tel: 0131 332 1366
STS • Shaw to Shore, Church Street Antiques
Centre, Stow on the Wold,
Glos GL54 1BB Tel: 01451 870186
SUC • Succession, 18 Richmond Hill,
Richmond, Surrey TW10 6QX
Tel: 020 8940 6774
SUS • Susannah, 142/144 Walcot Street,
Bath, Somerset BA1 5BL
Tel: 01225 445069
SVB • Steve Vee Bransgrove, 6 Catherine Hill,
Frome, Somerset BA11 1BY
Tel: 01373 453225
SWB •† Sweetbriar Gallery, Robin Hood Lane,
Helsby, Cheshire WA6 9NH
Tel: 01928 723851
SWN • Swan Antiques, Stone Street, Cranbrook,
Kent TN17 3HF Tel: 01580 712720
TAC • Tenterden Antiques Centre,
66–66A High Street, Tenterden, Kent
TN30 6AU Tel: 01580 765655/765885
TB • Millicent Safro, Tender Buttons,
143 E.62nd Street, New York NY10021,
USA Tel: (212) 758 7004
TBCC§ Fashion Doll Collectors' Club of Great
Britain, PO Box 228, Brentford,
Middlesex TW8 0UU
TBoy • Toy Boy, G64-65 Alfies Antique Market,
13–25 Church Street, Marylebone,
London NW8 8DT Tel: 020 7723 6066
TCG • 20th Century Glass, Kensington Church
Street Antique Centre, 58-60 Kensington
Church Street, London W8 4DB
Tel: 020 7938 1137/7729 9875
Mobile: 07971 859848
TED •† Teddy Bears of Witney, 99 High Street,
Witney, Oxfordshire OX8 6LY
Tel: 01993 702616

TEN * Tennants, The Auction Centre, Harmby Road, Leyburn, Yorkshire DL8 5SG Tel: 01969 623780

TH •† Tony Horsley, East Sussex Tel: 01273 550770

THOM• S & A Thompson Tel: 01306 711970 Mobile: 0370 882746

TIH • Time In Our Hands, The Platt, Wadebridge, Cornwall PL27 7AD Tel: 01208 815210

TIN • Tin Tin Collectables, G38-42 Alfies's Antique Market, 13–25 Church Street, London NW8 8DT Tel: 020 7258 1305

TMA * Brown & Merry, Tring Market Auctions, Brook Street, Tring, Hertfordshire HP23 5EF Tel: 01442 826446

TMi •† T. J. Millard Antiques, Assembly Antiques, 5-8 Saville Row, Bath, Somerset BA1 2QP Tel: 01225 448488

TOM •† Charles Tomlinson, Chester Tel: 01244 318395 email: charles.tomlinson@lineone.net

TOY • The Toy Store, 7 Thomas Street, Manchester City Centre, Gt. Manchester M4 IEU Tel: 0161 839 6882

TPCS §† Torquay Pottery Collectors' Society, Torre Abbey, Avenue Road, Torquay, Devon TQ2 5JX

TRE • No longer trading

TT •† Treasures in Textiles, Cheshire Tel: 01244 328968

TWa • Time Warp, c/o Curiouser & Curiouser, Sydney Street, Brighton, East Sussex Tel: 01273 821243

UNI • Unicorn Antique Centre, 2 Romney Enterprise Centre, North Street, New Romney, Kent TN28 8DW Tel: 01797 361940

UTP • Utility Plus, 66 High Street, West Ham, Pevensey, East Sussex BN24 5LP Tel: 01323 762316/078 50 130723

VB •† Variety Box, 16 Chapel Place, Tunbridge Wells, Kent TN1 1YQ Tel: 01892 531868

VCL •† Vintage Cameras Ltd, 256 Kirkdale, Sydenham, London SE26 4NL Tel: 020 8778 5416

VGC • Vintage Gas Cooker Collection, 4 Church Street, Cirencester, Glos GL7 1LE Tel: 01285 654351

VH • Valerie Howard, 4 Campden Street, Off Kensington Church Street, London W8 7EP Tel: 020 7792 9702

VINE • Vine Antiques, Oxfordshire Tel: 01235 812708

VS *† T. Vennett-Smith, 11 Nottingham Road, Gotham, Notts NG11 0HE Tel: 0115 983 0541

VSP * Van Sabben Poster Auctions, Oosteinde 30, 1678 HS Oostwoud, Holland Tel: 00 31 229 20 25 89

WA *† Whyte's Auctioneers, 30 Marlborough St, Dublin 1, Republic of Ireland Tel: 00 353 1 874 6161

WAB •† Warboys Antiques, Old Church School, High Street, Warboys, Huntingdon, Cambs PE17 2SX Tel: 01487 823686

WAC • Worcester Antiques Centre, Reindeer Court, Mealcheapen Street, Worcester, Worcestershire WR1 4DF Tel: 01905 610680

WaH • The Warehouse, 29–30 Queens Gardens, Worthington Street, Dover, Kent CT17 9AH Tel: 01304 242006

Wai • Peter Wain, Glynde Cottage, Longford, Market Drayton, Shropshire TF9 3PW Tel: 01630 639613

WAL *† Wallis & Wallis, West Street Auction Galleries, Lewes, East Sussex BN7 2NJ Tel: 01273 480208

WaR • Wot a Racket, 250 Shepherds Lane, Dartford, Kent DA1 2PN Tel: 01322 220619

WEE • Weedon Bec Antiques, 66 High Street, Weedon, Northants NN7 4QD Tel: 01327 349910

WELD• J. W. Weldon, 55 Clarendon Street, Dublin 2, Republic of Ireland Tel: 00 353 1 677 1638

WilP * BBG Wilson Peacock, 26 Newnham Street, Bedford, Bedfordshire MK40 3JR Tel: 01234 266366

WIM • Wimpole Antiques, Stand 349, Gray's Antique Market, South Molton Lane, London W1Y 2LP Tel: 020 7499 2889

WO • Woodville Antiques, The Street, Hamstreet, Ashford, Kent TN26 2HG Tel: 01233 732981

WP •† British Notes, PO Box 257, Sutton, Surrey SM3 9WW Tel: 020 8641 3224

WRe • Walcot Reclamations, 108 Walcot Street, Bath, Somerset BA1 5BG Tel: 01225 444404

WSA • West Street Antiques, 63 West Street, Dorking, Surrey RH4 1BS Tel: 01306 883487

WW * Woolley & Wallis, 51–61 Castle Street, Salisbury, Wiltshire SP1 3SU Tel: 01722 424500

WWY •† When We were Young, The Old Forge, High Street, Harmondsworth Village, Middlesex UB7 0AQ Tel: 020 8897 3583

YAN • Yanni's Antiques, 538 San Anselmo Avenue, San Anselmo, USA CA 94960. Tel: 001 415 459 2996

YC •† Yesterday Child, Angel Arcade, 118 Islington High Street, London N1 8EG Tel: 020 7354 1601

YO • Martin Burton, 201 Hull Road, York, Yorkshire YO10 3JY Tel: 01904 415347

YR •† Yorkshire Relics of Haworth, 16 River Street, Haworth, Yorkshire BD22 8NE Tel: 01535 642218 Mobile: 07971 701278

ZOOM•† Zoom, 312 Lillie Road Fulham, London SW6 7PS Tel: 07000 ZOOM 2000 or 020 7386 9522 Mobile: 0958 372975

Index to Advertisers

Index

Italic page numbers denote colour pages; **bold** numbers refer to information and pointer boxes

MYSTERY OBJECTS

A brass-bound mahogany letter duplicator, by James Watt, with original ivory handle, c1790, 17in (43cm) wide.
£850–1,000 TOM

A pair of tin scythe shields, or ankle shoes, late 19thC, 7in (18cm) wide.
£75–85 AAN

A Chinese rice funnel, early 20thC, 29in (74cm) high.
£170–200 K

A lacquered leather pillow box, northern China, 25in (63.5cm) wide.
£200–250 K

Two Chinese officer's hats, 19thC, 11½in (29cm) diam.
£50–60 each K

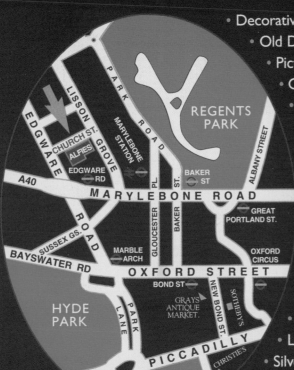